D1205674

War In Peace

Volume 9

War In Peace

The Marshall Cavendish Illustrated Encyclopedia of Postwar Conflict

MARSHALL CAVENDISH
NEW YORK, LONDON, TORONTO

Reference Edition Published 1985

Published by Marshall Cavendish Corporation
147 West Merrick Road
Freeport, Long Island
N.Y. 11520

Printed and Bound in Italy by L.E.G.O. S.p.a. Vicenza.

British Library Cataloguing in Publication Data

Brown, Ashley
War in peace : the Marshall Cavendish
illustrated encyclopaedia of post-war conflict.
1. History, Modern—1945- 2. War—History
—20th century
I. Title II. Dartford, Mark
909.82 D842

ISBN 0-86307-293-3
0 86307 302 6 vol. 9

Library of Congress Cataloging in Publication Data

Main entry under title:

War in peace.

Includes bibliographies and index.
1. Military history, Modern—20th century. 2. Military
art and science—History—20th century. 3. World politics—1945-
I. Marshall Cavendish Corporation.
U42.W373 1984 355'.009'04 84-19386
ISBN 0-86307-293-3
0 86307 302 6 vol. 9

Editorial Board

Contributors

David Blue served with the CIA in various countries of Southeast Asia, including Laos, and is a writer on and a student of small wars.

Gordon Brook-Shepherd spent 15 years in Vienna, first as lieutenant-colonel on the staff of the British High Commission and then as a foreign correspondent for the *Daily Telegraph.* A graduate in history from Cambridge, he is currently Chief Assistant Editor of the *Sunday Telegraph.*

Jeffrey J. Clarke is an expert on recent military history, particularly the Vietnam War, and has written for the American Center of Military History.

Major-General Richard Clutterbuck OBE has been Senior Lecturer in politics at Exeter University since his retirement from the army in 1972. His works include *Protest and the Urban Guerrilla, Guerrillas and Terrorists* and *Kidnap and Ransom.*

Alexander S. Cochran Jr is a historian whose area of research is modern Indochinese affairs with particular reference to the war in Vietnam since 1945. He is at present working in the Southeast Asia Branch of the Center of Military History, Department of the Army.

Colonel Peter M. Dunn is a serving officer in the USAF. His doctoral thesis is on the history of Indochina during the mid-1940s.

John B. Dwyer served both with the infantry and with armoured units in Vietnam. He was editor and publisher of the Vietnam veteran's newsletter *Perimeter* and has been a writer and correspondent for *National Vietnam Veteran's Review* for the past few years. His particular interest are Special Forces and Special Operations.

Brenda Ralph Lewis has specialised in political and military history since 1964. She s a regular contributor to military and historical magazines in both Britain and the United States.

Hugh Lunghi served in Moscow in the British Military Mission and the British Embassy for six years during and after World War II. He was interpreter for the British Chiefs of Staff at the Teheran, Yalta and Potsdam conferences, and also interpreted for Churchill and Anthony Eden. He subsequently worked in the BBC External Services and is a former editor of *Index on Censorship.*

Charles Messenger retired from the army in 1980 to become a fulltime military writer after 21 years service in the Royal Tank Regiment. Over the past 10 years he has written several books on 20th century warfare, as well as contributing articles to a number of defence and historical journals. He is currently a Research Associate at the Royal United Services Institute for Defence Studies in London.

Billy C. Mossman is a well-known American writer and historian. He is currently working on a volume on the Korean War for the US Army Center of Military History.

Bryan Perrett served in the Royal Armoured Corps from 1952 to 1971. He contributes regularly to a number of established military journals and acted as Defence Correspondent to the *Liverpool Echo* during the Falklands War. His recent books include *Weapons of the Falklands Conflict* and *A History of Blitzkrieg.*

Chapman Pincher is one of England's leading authorities on international espionage and counter-intelligence. He is the author of political novels and books on spying, the most recent of which is *Their Trade is Treachery*, which deals with the penetration of Britain's secret services by the Russian secret police.

Yehoshua Porath is a noted scholar at the Hebrew University in Jerusalem. He has made a special study of the Palestinian problem and is the author of two books on the subject, the most recent of which is *The Palestinian Arab National Movement 1929–39*, which was published in Britain in 1977.

Contributors

Antony Preston is Naval Editor of the military magazine *Defence* and author of numerous publications including *Battleships, Aircraft Carriers* and *Submarines.*

Brigadier-General Edwin H. Simmons, US Marine Corps, Retired, is the Director of Marine Corps History and Museums. At the time of the Inchon operation and the Chosin Reservoir campaign, he, as a major, commanded Weapons Company, 3rd Battalion, 1st Marines. Widely published, he is the author of *The United States Marines.*

Ronald Spector is an expert on Vietnam and has recently completed a book on that subject for the Center of Military History in the United States.

Andres Suarez served in the Cuban ministry of education from 1948–1951, took part in the Cuban revolution, and served in the ministry of housing from 1959. From 1965, he has been Professor of Latin American Studies at the University of Florida. Other publications include *Cuba and the Sino–Soviet Rift.*

Sir Robert Thompson KBE, CMG, DSO, MC is a world authority on guerrilla warfare, on which he has written extensively. He was directly involved in the Emergency in Malaya in the 1950s and rose to become permanent Secretary for Defence. From 1961 to 1965 he headed the British Advisory Mission to Vietnam and since then he has advised several governments, including the United States, on counter-insurgency operations Sir Robert Thompson is a Council member of the Institute for the Study of Conflict, London. His books include *Defeating Communist Insurgency* and *Revolutionary War in World Strategy, 1945–69.*

Patrick Turnbull commanded 'D' Force, Burma during World War II. His 29 published works include a history of the Foreign Legion.

Contents of Volume

Operation Motorman

The British Army enters the No-Go areas

For almost a year, from August 1971 to July 1972, some Catholic districts of Belfast and Londonderry effectively came under the control of the Provisional IRA in direct defiance of the British Army and the police. This situation could not have come about without the constraints on army action which political considerations imposed. Even without using any heavy equipment (it was always felt that putting tanks on the streets of Ulster would have such an emotive effect internationally as to be counter-productive) there were tens of thousands of lightly-armed infantry who could have been deployed to wrest control from the IRA's gunmen. What worried Westminster was the scale of the fighting that might be involved. There was no doubt that the army would win any clash, but a violent gun-battle involving heavy civilian casualties would have been regarded as a political defeat.

Even though political considerations allowed the IRA to establish the 'No-Go' areas, there is no doubt that their heavy military pressure also helped. In effect, the army did actually lose the battle to dominate the Creggan and the Bogside in Londonderry and Andersonstown in Belfast during 1971. The pressure on the soldiers in those areas was intense. The population was violently hostile so that the security forces were met with constant stoning and physical attack from unarmed civilians which was very difficult to counter. Behind this constant turbulence and disorder was the deadly threat of an increasingly armed and assertive IRA which was causing numerous casualties. As the Catholic population repeatedly threw up barricades around its areas and as their removal became a major and dangerous operation, the tendency to allow the barricades to remain grew. Not all local army commanders were happy about this and a number of efforts were made to change the situation.

When the barricades had first gone up in response to internment in August 1971, the army had responded immediately. In Londonderry the copybook Operation Huntsman was mounted in brigade strength at dawn on 18 August. The inhabitants of the Bogside and Creggan were taken by surprise and the barricades were quickly dismantled. In the gun-battles that took place, one gunman was killed and his body and weapon recovered; another two were almost certainly killed, while two more were arrested. There were no serious army casualties and the whole operation might have been accounted a resounding success had the army been able to consolidate its position. However, this was impossible and as soon as the army withdrew from the Bogside and Creggan, the barriers promptly went up again. To achieve a more permanent presence on the streets of Ulster's Catholic ghettos there would have to be a different approach.

At first it was hoped that a political solution could be found and that the Catholics could be talked into taking the barricades down as they had been in the autumn of 1969. While negotiations went on, the army was restricted to a containment policy which made the barricaded districts into official No-Go areas. This was a decided step backwards for the Province's security, and the level of shootings and bombings rose dramatically. The IRA was able to operate from within secure bases and plan raids and ambushes with impunity. Army commanders became restive under the absolute restrictions imposed on them so, in December 1971, the conditions of containment were slightly relaxed: the army could once more enter the No-Go areas but was not allowed to maintain a permanent presence in them.

The operations which the army undertook under these new rules gave some cause for alarm. No longer

Above: A corporal of the King's Own Royal Border Regiment, his face liberally smeared with cam cream, uses heavy steel fencing to give himself protection while he covers a patrol moving into a scrapyard in pursuit of terrorists. The strict rules governing use of weapons forced the army to adopt a largely defensive role even under fire.

could the population of the No-Go areas be taken by surprise as they had been in Operation Huntsman. Any army incursion was greeted by the banging of dustbin lids on the ground to summon the rapid assembly of hostile crowds backed by snipers. The level of resistance was so great that the army made no attempt to enter the rebel enclaves in less than battalion strength and always at night. The expenditure of CS gas and rubber bullets was inevitably high, while any barricades that might be removed were replaced within hours. It was an uncomfortable fact that the army was hard pressed to control even a corner of the enclaves for a comparatively short time when it entered them in considerable force.

Softly softly

To some extent the difficulties of the security forces in the No-Go areas were the result of restrictions on the level of violence they were allowed to employ. There is no doubt that it was not so much the gunmen who kept them out of the hostile enclaves as the angry response of the unarmed population. At the time comparisons began to be drawn between the conduct of General Jacques Massu's French paras during the Battle of Algiers (1957) and the British Army in Ulster. It was generally agreed that any open attack on the French soldiers by unarmed men would have been suicidal, for the French paras would simply have opened fire. As a result Massu did not have to worry about rioting crowds interfering with his operations –

The hostile reaction of the Catholic population to the army's presence on the streets of Belfast and Londonderry increasingly forced the army to adopt a low profile. Street patrols (left, armed with both standard and riot equipment, a patrol leader moves cautiously through a Londonderry street) became less frequent, while overt demonstrations of IRA control (below, a 'Free Derry' checkpoint manned by well armed gunmen) reflected the terrorists' domination of the No-Go areas.

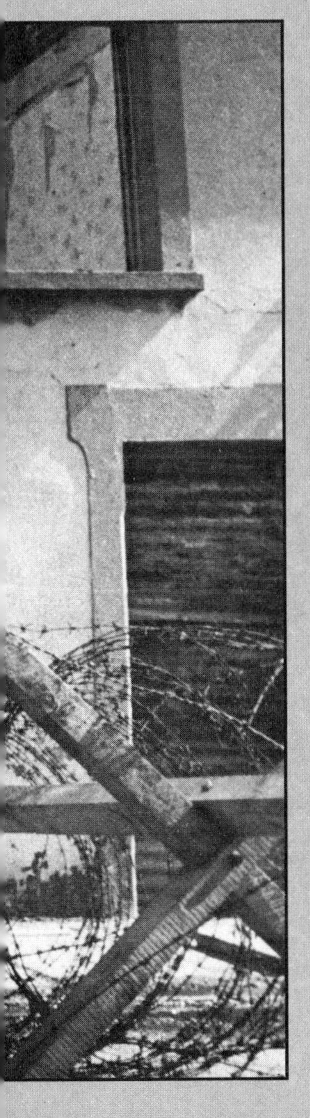

no Algerian would have been mad enough to riot. However, it was soon apparent that these fiercer tactics would not do for the British. On 30 January 1972 the so-called 'Bloody Sunday' action left 13 civilians dead in the only British response that in any way resembled the sort of methods used by the French in Algeria. It was a political disaster: the British embassy in Dublin was burned and there were widespread expressions of outrage both at home and abroad.

The security situation in Ulster worsened but it was obviously politically impossible for the army to end the No-Go areas while feelings were running so high. Comparisons were again made with the Battle of Algiers: it was recalled that the French Army had broken the terrorist movement in the city and established its grip on the Arab quarter but its ruthless methods had led to international condemnation. It was realised in Westminster that a method would have to be found of ending the No-Go areas without provoking a major battle and this would, in any case, have to wait until the time was more politically opportune.

Meanwhile the No-Go areas presented an extraordinary and embarrassing sight to the security forces. Services such as rubbish collection had been virtually abandoned in the littered streets and barricades were often openly manned by armed IRA men. The population barricaded within the enclaves, in common with Catholics throughout Ulster, generally refused to pay rent or rates, although they confidently left their IRA-controlled areas to draw their social security payments from the obliging British-controlled areas before returning behind the barricades. Within the No-Go areas the power of the Provisional IRA was virtually absolute and leaders such as Martin McGuinness in the Bogside became extremely well-known locally as they adopted a high profile. At the same time the campaign of violence mounted from behind the security of the barricades became ever more effective: vehicles were commandeered for car bombs that left the centres of Belfast and Londonderry looking as if they had suffered aerial bombardment. Nor did their low profile save British soldiers from attack: by 20 March 1972, 56 of them had been killed since the beginning of the current troubles.

During this agonising and humiliating time of waiting and watching while their enemy's credibility seemed to grow every day, there was a marked difference in the aggression shown by the various local British commanders. Many non-infantry units had been pressed into the infantry role to cope with the demands of Northern Ireland and, although they usually managed remarkably well at unfamiliar tasks, they did not normally tempt fate by stirring up the No-Go areas. On the other hand, regular infantry formations found such inactivity intolerable and contrived to menace their enemy's feeling of security at every opportunity. On 14 March a patrol of Royal Green Jackets entered the Londonderry No-Go area and sparked off an intense eight-minute gun-battle in which 600 rounds were exchanged. The result was two dead IRA men but a disquieting foretaste of the scale of battle that might occur during a full and final assault on the No-Go areas.

On 24 March, however, a major political development began a shift in the security situation: Westminster suspended Stormont and took over Direct Rule of Ulster. The British government hoped that this step might provide an opportunity to win back the allegiance of the Catholic minority. Internment was scaled down – by 8 June 520 internees had been released – and the army adopted a low-profile approach towards the Catholics. On the Protestant side, there was deep resentment at these developments. Vigilantes of the Protestant Ulster Defence Association (UDA) adopted a policy of erecting and manning barricades in Protestant areas, threatening to maintain them until the barricades in Catholic areas were taken down. A campaign of assassination by Protestant paramilitaries against the Catholic population was also initiated.

Luckily for the security forces, who were menaced with attack from both sides, the IRA's position was weakening. The imposition of Direct Rule by the Westminster government had been cautiously welcomed by the Catholic population. Then on 19 May the Official IRA caused revulsion among its host community in the Bogside by murdering a 19-year old Catholic British soldier, William Best of the Royal Irish Rangers, who was paying an off-duty visit to his Bogside home. On 29 May the Officials declared a truce. The Provisionals were under considerable pressure to do likewise. Tempted by the offer of negotiations with the British government, on 26 June the Provisionals did institute a ceasefire but this broke down on 9 July.

Bloody Friday

Shortly afterwards, on 21 July, occurred the intensive bombing of Belfast, known as 'Bloody Friday', which reduced the Provisionals' international and domestic reputation to an all-time low and decisively weakened their support in the Catholic neighbourhoods. Within little over an hour, between 2 and 3pm, 19 bombs exploded in the busy centre of the city, creating panic and terror. Although warnings were given for all the bombs, the scale of the attack overwhelmed the security forces' efforts to protect lives; the explosions at Oxford Street bus station and Cavehill Road shopping centre occurred before the areas had been cleared, killing nine people and injuring 130, many seriously. The British government felt free to act at last.

Military preference was for action that was drastic and permanent. Overwhelming force widely advertised in advance might convince the IRA that discretion was the better part of valour and persuade them to sneak out of the No-Go areas to avoid death or capture rather than fight it out. In hope of this the army began airlifting formidable reinforcements of 4000 men and some armoured vehicles (but no gun-armed tanks) into the Province on 27 July. There was no effort to conceal the scale of these preparations or to deny that they were being made for the purpose of ending the No-Go areas.

The army had learnt from the aftermath of Operation Huntsman that a successful invasion of the No-Go areas would not be enough in itself. Once the barricades were down, the troops would have to make their reconstruction pointless by maintaining a permanent presence in the heart of the Catholic enclaves. The plan was that certain suitably large buildings would be seized and converted into forts with permanent garrisons. The most likely buildings both in Londonderry and Belfast were Catholic schools; this was fair enough as long as the school holidays

lasted but alternative accommodation would have to be built before the autumn term began. So, in addition to the infantry, there were engineer battalions in the forces allocated to Operation Motorman, as it was code-named.

At 0430 hours on 31 July the long columns of armoured vehicles poured into the No-Go areas – both Catholic and Protestant. The Protestant No-Go areas had been formed simply to provoke such a military reaction and so no resistance was offered there. Although the army's soldiers and junior commanders confidently expected resistance in Andersonstown, the Bogside and the Creggan, particularly as the IRA had often claimed to be defending the Catholic population against the British Army, senior British officers had, in fact, taken action to minimise the prospects of battle. The road from the Bogside across the Foyle River and into the Republic of Ireland, for instance, had been left free of roadblocks so that wanted IRA men could make good their escape. Operation Motorman was simply undertaken to reoccupy the No-Go areas, not to force a battle of extermination upon the IRA.

In the event little resistance was experienced in Andersonstown. In Londonderry a gunman and a petrol bomber were shot dead. Elsewhere the operation proceeded extremely smoothly. The use of Centurion bulldozers made the clearing of barricades quick and easy. To some extent the Provisionals helped things along by engineering another massive blow to their popularity that very day by killing nine civilians in the village of Claudy through three callously-planted car bombs (it was widely rumoured that the bombers had tried to telephone a warning but

Above: From an observation point high above the streets of Belfast, a Marine covers possible terrorist movements while an officer uses high-powered binoculars to locate troublespots.

Below left: Baton-carrying troops manning a checkpoint on the perimeter of the Creggan search civilians coming into the area. Constant monitoring of local movements is an effective, though tedious, means of gathering good local intelligence.

Above: A Royal Engineers Centurion, fitted with a bulldozer blade, leads the way into the Bogside, pushing aside a barrier built of concrete and steel girders at the start of Operation Motorman on 31 July 1972.

Below: Operation Motorman. A Ferret armoured car leads a Saracen into the Bogside as bemused civilians look on. Although the army had expected resistance, the IRA were hardly in evidence.

had found the local phone box out of order). By the end of the day the army had established its presence in all the hardline areas of the Province, not only in Belfast and Londonderry but also in such country towns as Lurgan, Armagh, Newry and Coalisland. In Andersonstown they established no less than 16 defended strongpoints.

In order to achieve the desired result, very large numbers of soldiers had been used. In Londonderry alone there were nine battalions involved in Motorman, backed up by a host of supporting units including a 50-bed field hospital. Among the 11 battalions used in Belfast were the Prince of Wales Own Regiment of Yorkshire which, together with 2nd Battalion, the Royal Regiment of Fusiliers, went into the sensitive Andersonstown district. Although some of these units could be withdrawn once the No-Go areas had been secured, the remainder had to endure very cramped and uncomfortable accommodation while the engineers toiled at producing more permanent quarters. Eventually they were able to move into a number of heavily defended forts – four in the greater Andersonstown area alone. Meanwhile they asserted the army presence on the streets of the Catholic enclaves with patrols and house searches. They made considerable finds of explosives and weapons and, for a short while, IRA activity tailed off. In the event the Provisionals were able to reorganise from new havens in the Republic of Ireland and the campaign proved to be far from over. However, Operation Motorman had succeeded in eliminating the No-Go areas, whose existence had marked the lowest point in the security forces' control over Northern Ireland.

P. J. Banyard

Bombs and ballots

The search for a political solution in Northern Ireland

Left: Loyalist Protestants march on Stormont, demonstrating their opposition to any changes in the status of Northern Ireland. The ability of Protestant leaders to mobilise mass opposition to any moves that they felt might jeopardise the place that Northern Ireland had within the United Kingdom, was a critical factor in the search for a political solution during the mid-1970s.

The establishment of Direct Rule in the spring of 1972 meant that thenceforward London took primary responsibility for Northern Ireland policy-making. The political life of the Province since that time has been marked by a series of 'initiatives' put forward by the British government in order to set up some broadly-based local administration. A consistent feature of British policy has been the requirement that any devolved government should incorporate a high degree of active political cooperation between the two warring communities. But, with the exception of the short-lived 'power-sharing' Executive of 1974, every initiative so far has failed. Summed up by the traditional Unionist slogan 'Not an inch', Protestant politicians have adamantly refused to relinquish any of the 'Britishness' they treasure. For their part, Catholic leaders have been equally reluctant to abandon their own vision of a 're-united' Ireland.

In 1972 and 1973 William Whitelaw, the first Secretary of State for Northern Ireland, devoted much time and his considerable skills of conciliation towards bringing the Ulster politicians together. In the autumn of 1972, after a conference in Darlington, the government published a Green Paper which suggested the establishment of a power-sharing administration. The discussion document also tried to satisfy both sides by confirming that Northern Ireland would remain part of the United Kingdom while the majority of the population so wished – this was to reassure the Protestants – and, in order to meet Catholic aspirations, it also argued that there was an 'Irish dimension' to the situation.

In mid-1973 Whitelaw guided legislation through the Westminster parliament to provide for a Northern Ireland Assembly elected by proportional representation. The Assembly would have broadly the same powers as the suspended Stormont parliament, with one crucial exception – security. Instead of a Cabinet there would be a twelve-member Executive, appointed by the secretary of state. The Assembly elections were held at the end of June, and, following nearly five months of negotiations, sufficient agreement was reached between a group of Unionists led by the ex-Prime Minister Brian Faulkner, the constitutional nationalist Social Democratic and Labour Party (SDLP), and the moderate, centrist Alliance Party to form an Executive. In December 1973 at the Sunningdale conference between the Executive-designate and the British and Irish governments, the 'Irish dimension' was specifically recognised with an agreement to establish a 'Council of Ireland', comprising representatives from both parts of the island, which would oversee economic, social and political matters of common interest. On 1 January 1974, with Brian Faulkner at its head, the power-sharing Executive formally took office.

The search for some sort of political accommodation to supersede Direct Rule was given special urgency by the continuing high level of disorder. Operation Motorman in July 1972 hit hard at the terrorists' urban heartland and made it easier for the security forces to control all parts of the Province, but with much of Belfast sealed off officially with barbed wire and wooden barricades, and with bombings and shootings still a daily occurrence, there was no hope of a swift return to normality.

Security force successes were largely a result of improved intelligence-gathering, which was put on a more systematic and centralised basis. Some spectacular undercover operations were mounted to assemble information. One covert intelligence operation had the Four Square Laundry as a front. Offering cut-price dry cleaning, a van drove round Catholic West Belfast picking up laundry and local gossip. All the clothing was sent to a special unit where it was analysed for traces of explosives and gunpowder. The operation produced a great deal of information, but in October 1972 its cover was blown and the Provisionals attacked the van, killing its driver. Nevertheless, there were some notable successes. In June 1973 a number of senior Provisionals were arrested, including Gerry Adams, then Belfast commander of the organisation. His successor, Ivor Bell, was picked up in February 1974. In response to army and police successes the Provisionals began to abandon their old military structure of battalions and companies for a classic urban guerrilla structure of smaller, more secure 'Active Service Units', consisting of five to eight men each.

The total number of deaths in the Ulster conflict was almost 50 per cent lower in 1973 than in the previous year – 250 as against 468. Shooting incidents declined sharply as the Provisionals shifted a greater proportion of their efforts to the more cost-effective tactic (in terrorist terms) of bomb attacks. In June 1973 alone there were over 100 explosions. The Provisionals also spread their bombing campaign to England. In March 1973 two car bombs exploded in London, killing one person and injuring 180. Further attacks were launched in the summer of 1973 and the trend continued during the following year. On 4 February 1974 an army coach on the M62 in Yorkshire was blown up, killing 11 people. In October the Guildford pub bombings claimed five deaths. The next month 19 people were killed and 182 injured when bombs exploded in Birmingham.

In 1974, however, although security trends in Ulster showed a further slight improvement on the year before, with 3200 shooting incidents and 216 deaths, 50 of which were army and police, attention was focussed primarily on political events. All eyes were on the new power-sharing Executive. But the venture lasted less than six months.

Who rules in Ulster?

The 'beginning of the end' for the Executive was caused by events in Britain. In February 1974, faced with a national coal strike and having introduced a three-day week for industry, Prime Minister Edward Heath called a general election. In Northern Ireland, where the issue of 'Who rules in Britain?' was largely irrelevant, 11 out of the 12 Westminster seats were won by anti-power-sharing Unionists. For them the issue was 'Who rules in Northern Ireland?' and the Sunningdale proposal for a Council of Ireland seemed to favour the hated cause of Irish unification and the destruction of the union with Great Britain. Their success in the general election markedly boosted the opposition to Faulkner's fledgling administration. The return of Harold Wilson to power in London also brought in new men to manage Northern Ireland affairs at a particularly critical time.

The Executive was consistently opposed by the more extreme Loyalists. Before it had taken power the Reverend Ian Paisley had promised 'blood, sweat and tears'. On three occasions during the life of the Assembly the anti-Faulkner Unionists were so obstructive that the police had to be called. Despite all this, the Executive did demonstrate, albeit briefly, that power-sharing was feasible and that Protestant and Catholic leaders could cooperate at the highest level.

In the end the Executive was brought down by the

Above: William Whitelaw, Conservative Party Secretary of State for Northern Ireland, who devoted his conciliatory skills to achieving some agreement among Ulster politicians and in mid-1973 guided legislation through Parliament which would provide for a Northern Ireland Assembly. Above right: Merlyn Rees, who succeeded Whitelaw in February 1974 when a Labour Party administration came to power.

Right: Armed with a Lee Enfield rifle, converted to the Nato 7.62mm cartridge, a soldier uses sandbags and a corner wall to provide protection as he covers his colleagues. Below: Paras, armed with standard SLRs, move through Belfast streets.

Ulster Workers' Council (UWC) strike in May 1974. The strike dramatically illustrated the power which the Protestant population could exert. The impetus for action came from rank-and-file Loyalists upset by the liberal power-sharing line being taken by Unionist leaders such as Faulkner, and particularly to their support for the Council of Ireland idea. The strike was run by a 15-man Co-ordinating Committee which included UWC members, representatives of paramilitary groups and some politicians, notably Ian Paisley. The strike leaders used two main weapons to make the stoppage effective: intimidation and the control of electricity power workers. Forceful 'persuasion' and strict picketing ensured that public transport, commerce and industry were brought to a halt. The Co-ordinating Committee organised the rationing of food and essential supplies. But the key to success lay in cutting electric power supplies. All the manual workers in Northern Ireland's power stations walked out and a partial supply – down to 10 per cent of normal at the end – was kept going only with a skeleton staff of white-collar workers. These men refused to cooperate with military technicians, the army was incapable of running the power stations alone, and so the government could do nothing to boost power supplies. In the end, after the strike had been going for a fortnight and with the imminent breakdown of sewage services, the water system and fuel oil supplies, the Unionist members of the Executive resigned and the victorious UWC called off the action.

Hitting back

Another reason for the success of the strike lay in the response of the British government. It is clear that London completely misjudged the situation and underestimated the strength of Protestant feeling. This was partly because the new Labour administration had evidently not thought very deeply about Northern Ireland, and in any case the new secretary of state, Merlyn Rees, could not be expected immediately to be as knowledgeable about the Province as William Whitelaw. Yet, for all the intimidation, the strike undoubtedly provided ordinary Protestants with a welcome chance to 'hit back' at the defeats of the previous five years, to relieve their accumulated frustrations and to demonstrate their deep-seated unease with any political arrangement which seemed to compromise their cherished constitutional status within the United Kingdom. During the stoppage it also seemed that Loyalists had struck directly in the Irish Republic. On 17 May 31 people were killed by car bombs which exploded without warning in Dublin and Monaghan.

During the spring and early summer of 1974 the Provisional IRA, no doubt delighted to see the British government's discomfiture at the hands of extremist Protestants, kept a relatively low profile. But they were by no means entirely inactive during the year. In January one of the most imaginative actions took place when four terrorists hijacked a helicopter in the Irish Republic and forced the pilot to fly over Strabane where they dropped two milk churns full of explosive on the RUC station. The churns, however, failed to explode. The Provisionals' strategy of hitting at the Province's commercial life was illustrated in March and April when car-bomb attacks were aimed at shopping centres throughout Northern Ireland. Another line of attack was demonstrated in

The installation of the power-sharing Executive (left top, the tripartite Sunningdale talks with representatives from Great Britain, Ireland and the Executive-designate) which took place in January 1974 was met with furious antagonism by Loyalist Ulstermen (left centre, the Reverend Ian Paisley addresses his supporters). The ensuing strike by the Ulster Workers' Council (left below, strikers form a picket across a road in Belfast) crippled the infant Executive and inevitably brought it down, much to the joy of the Protestant community (left bottom, headlines held aloft as jubilant Loyalists celebrate their victory).

September when two leading members of the judiciary were murdered in their Belfast homes.

At the end of 1974 a group of Protestant churchmen made an effort to negotiate with the Provisionals, and met a number of them secretly at Feakle in County Clare. Although the Provisionals' demands included the withdrawal of all troops to barracks and the release of 'political prisoners' in Britain and Ireland, they agreed to a temporary ceasefire from 22 December in order to give the British government time to respond. The Wilson government officially took the line that the ceasefire was simply a unilateral action by the Provisionals which required no reciprocal action from the security forces, but in practice the army and police were ordered to respond by a new attempt at a low-profile approach. After initial difficulties, the truce got properly under way in February 1975. Incident centres were set up in West Belfast by the Provisionals and also by British civil servants. At the former, Catholics reported alleged harassment by the security forces as well as more general law and order problems; at the British centres the general public were invited to report any incidents that might threaten the truce. Direct attacks on the army and police virtually ceased, as did the bombing campaign against commercial targets. On its side, the British government stepped up its policy of running down internment – all internees had been released by the end of 1975. Since October 1973 the so-called Diplock courts had been in operation, trying terrorist cases without a jury. All arrests now had to be designed to achieve convictions in the courts, and such notable IRA figures as Seamus Twomey were able to walk the streets freely since it was apparently believed sufficient evidence would not be available to convict them.

The falling-off of encounters between the Provisionals and the security forces did not, however, mean an end to violence. The campaign of sectarian 'tit-for-tat' killings actually increased in ferocity as Protestant paramilitaries stepped up their attacks and the Provisionals responded brutally. Civilian deaths rose to the highest level since 1972, although security force deaths fell. There was also a bloody feud within the Republican movement after a group calling itself the Irish Republican Socialist Party (IRSP) broke away from the Official IRA. The IRSP demanded action in Northern Ireland and was soon to carry it out through the Irish National Liberation Army (INLA). In February 1975 the Officials and the IRSP fought a brief battle of assassination and counter-assassination, in which the Provisionals became involved. A straight confrontation between the Officials and the Provisionals was to follow later on in the year.

No end in sight

Against the background of this precarious truce – opposed both by many nationalists and by the heads of the security forces – the search for a political settlement continued. In the summer of 1974 Merlyn Rees had published proposals for setting up a Constitutional Convention in which, he believed, the Northern Irish political parties could meet to work out their own salvation, or, in his White Paper's words, 'consider what provisions for the government of Northern Ireland would be most likely to command the most widespread acceptance throughout the community'. Rees also reaffirmed London's faith in power-sharing and its belief in an 'Irish dimension'.

On 1 May 1975 elections were held for the Convention. Here, perhaps, was a renewed opportunity for Ulster politicians to establish the framework for a settled and generally-accepted local administration. But with Loyalists winning 47 out of the 78 seats (Faulkner and his moderate Unionist supporters took only five seats between them), the likelihood of the British government's basic requirement being met – full power-sharing including the SDLP – seemed remote. This, then, left a gloomy prospect in store for the decision-makers in London, for if the politicians could not agree, much of the initiative in Northern Ireland would inevitably remain in the hands of the gunmen.

Keith Jeffery

Below: Schoolboys look at the aftermath of a bomb blast. By the time that the power-sharing Executive collapsed, violence had become commonplace in the Province, with no sign of coming to an end.

Chronology 1971-75

EUROPE AND NORTH AMERICA

1971

February
6 Northern Ireland First British soldier, Gunner Robert Curtis, killed in Ulster.
May
3 East Germany Erich Honecker replaces Walter Ulbricht as leader of ruling Communist Party.
August
9 Northern Ireland Internment introduced with initial arrest of 342 people in the face of fierce Catholic resistance.

1972

January
30 Northern Ireland 13 civilians shot dead by British paratroopers after rioting on 'Bloody Sunday' in Londonderry.
February
22 Britain Official IRA bomb attack against paratroopers' base in Aldershot kills nine.
March
24 Northern Ireland British government takes over Direct Rule of Ulster.
May
22 Soviet Union Summit meeting in Moscow between Leonid Brezhnev and US President Richard Nixon results in arms limitation agreements under rubric of SALT I.
June
1 West Germany Andreas Baader, leader of Baader-Meinhof terrorist group, arrested after firefight with police; his colleague Ulrike Meinhof arrested two weeks later.
July
7 Northern Ireland Negotiations between Provisional IRA and British government during temporary ceasefire fail to reach agreement.
21 Northern Ireland 'Bloody Friday' in Belfast: nine people killed in 19 Provisional IRA bomb explosions.
31 Northern Ireland British Army occupies Catholic No-Go areas throughout Ulster in Operation Motorman.
September
5 West Germany Palestinian Black September terrorists kill 11 Israeli athletes at Olympic Games in Munich.
24 Britain expels 105 Soviet diplomats for spying.
December
8 France PLO representative murdered in Paris by Israeli agents: start of Israeli 'Wrath of God' assassination campaign.
21 Germany Governments of East and West Germany conclude treaty recognising full sovereignty of each.

1973

January
27 United States End of conscription announced.
June
1 Greece declared a republic under Colonel George Papadopoulos.
22 United States Brezhnev meets Nixon to discuss SALT II.
28 France Mohammed Boudia, leading Arab terrorist in Europe, killed by Israeli bomb.
July
21 Norway Israeli Wrath of God team mistakenly kills innocent Moroccan waiter; assassination campaign abandoned.
September
28 Austria Palestinian terrorists hijack train and demand closure of transit camp for Soviet Jews: Austria complies.
November
25 Greece Former head of military junta, George Papadopoulos, ousted in a new military coup.
December
17 Italy Terrorists of National Arab Youth kill 32 people in attack on Rome airport.
20 Spain Premier Luis Carrero Blanco killed by Basque terrorists

1974

January
1 Northern Ireland Power-sharing Executive takes office under Brian Faulkner.
February
4 Britain Start of Provisional IRA bombing campaign in England.
April
25 Portugal Armed Forces Movement (MFA) overthrows government of Marcello Caetano and establishes General Antonio de Spínola as head of government.
May
15-29 Northern Ireland Protestant Ulster Workers Council strike brings down the power-sharing Executive.
July
15 Cyprus Greek officers of Cypriot National Guard, with encouragement from Athens, carry out coup d'etat against President Makarios.
20 Cyprus Turkish Army invades the island and seizes northern coastal area.
24 Greece Military rule collapses
27-July 3 Soviet Union Nixon-Brezhnev summit in Moscow.
August
8 United States Nixon resigns as a result of Watergate scandal.
15 Cyprus Turkish Army enters Famagusta; island divided along Attila Line.
September
30 Portugal Spínola resigns the presidency under left-wing pressure; General Francisco da Costa Gomes becomes president.
November
23 Soviet Union President Ford meets Brezhnev in Vladivostok and agrees arms limitation figures intended to form the basis of a SALT II treaty.
December
14 United States Senate ratifies Geneva protocol on prohibition of chemical and biological warfare.

1975

February
9 Northern Ireland Provisional IRA announces indefinite suspension of hostilities.
27 West Germany Politician Peter Lorenz kidnapped and ransomed for the release of five Baader-Meinhof terrorists.
March
11 Portugal Attempted coup involving, among others, General Spínola, is defeated; the regime shifts to the left.
May
1 Northern Ireland Elections held for a Constitutional Convention.
November
12 Northern Ireland Provisional IRA ceasefire, repeatedly broken since April, is declared at an end by security forces.
25 Portugal Left-wing military coup foiled; many left-wingers removed from key positions, effectively ending the revolutionary process begun in April 1974.
December
21 Austria Six terrorists, including Carlos, seize 11 leading representatives of OPEC countries meeting ir Vienna; a ransom is paid and the hostages are release in Algeria.
22 Netherlands South Moluccans seeking the independence of their homeland from Indonesia hija a train and take over the Indonesian embassy.

MIDDLE EAST

1971

July
13-18 Jordan Jordanian Army carries out final offensive against Palestinian guerrilla contingents around Ras el Agra; Palestinians defeated and move t Lebanon.
November
28 Jordan Prime Minister Wafsi Tell assassinated Cairo by Palestinian Black September terrorists.
30 Iran Iranian troops seize Tanb Islands and Abu Musa in the Gulf, disputed by Arab states.

1972

May
8 Israel Israeli security forces successfully storm airliner hijacked by Palestinians.
30 Israel Three Japanese Red Army terrorists linke with the PFLP open fire indiscriminately at Lod airpo killing 26.
July
18 Egypt President Sadat orders withdrawal of all Soviet military personnel.

1973

February
21 Israel Israelis shoot down Libyan airliner which had strayed over Sinai, killing all passengers and crev
March
1 Sudan Black September terrorists murder three Western diplomats after seizing the Saudi Arabian embassy in Khartoum.
April
10 Lebanon Israeli commandos attack Palestinian guerrillas' homes in Beirut, killing 17 people.
October
6 Israel Egyptian air strike on Sinai front marks beginning of Yom Kippur War. Egyptian commando cross Suez Canal; simultaneous attack by Syrian forc on Golan front.
8 Israel Israeli counter-attacks in Sinai repulsed by Egyptian defenses.
9 Israel Syrian offensive in Golan halts after heavy losses.
13 Israel Advancing into Syria, the IDF encounter Iraqi armoured formations.
14 Israel Egyptian attack in Sinai thrown back in largest tank battle since 1943.
15-16 Israel Israeli paratroopers establish bridgehead across the Canal.
20-22 Israel Israeli forces break out of bridgehead and cut Suez-Cairo road; UN Security Council calls f ceasefire, and fighting on Syrian front stops.
24 Israel Israeli forces complete encirclement of Egyptian Third Army and ceasefire is instituted. End Yom Kippur War.

1974

January
18 Israel and Egypt agree on disengagement.
April
18 Egypt Sadat announces that Egypt will no longe rely on the Soviet Union for arms supplies.
May
15 Israel Palestinian guerrillas kill 25 Israelis, mostly children, in attack on Maalot near Lebanon border.

31 **Israel** agrees to give up territory captured from Syria in October 1973 and to respect a buffer zone.
June
13 **Yemen** Colonel Ibrahim al-Hamidi takes power in military coup.
July
8 **Lebanon** Israeli commandos attack Lebanese ports in retaliation for guerrilla raids.
November
13 **Palestine** Yassir Arafat, head of the PLO, addresses the UN General Assembly.
22 **Palestine** The UN grants the PLO observer status.

1975
April
1 **Iran** withdraws support from Kurdish rebels in Iraq, in return for Iraqi concessions over border disputes.
13 **Lebanon** Clashes between Palestinians and Christian militias mark beginning of Lebanese civil war.
August
5 **Lebanon** Israeli forces carry out air and amphibious attacks on port of Tyre.
September
4 **Israel and Egypt** sign accord on Sinai troop withdrawals.
December
Oman Sultan announces defeat of Dhofar rebellion.

SOUTH EAST ASIA
1971
February
8 **Vietnam** South Vietnamese forces enter Laos in Operation Lam Son 719; operation continues until 25 March.
August
18 **Vietnam** Australia and New Zealand announce withdrawal of troops.
November
17 **Thailand** Prime Minister General Thanom Kittikachorn seizes power and declares martial law.
December
31 **Vietnam** Total US strength in South Vietnam now 156,800.

1972
February
Laos Battle in the Plain of Jars, lasting until 6 March.
March
10 **Cambodia** Lon Nol confirms his power by taking post of head of state.
30 **Vietnam** North Vietnamese forces invade the South in strength: beginning of Spring offensive.
April
6 **Vietnam** US bombing and naval bombardment of the North resumed.
7 **Vietnam** Communists begin siege of An Loc.
May
1 **Vietnam** Quang Tri City falls to communist forces.
8 **Vietnam** President Nixon announces mining of Haiphong and other Northern harbours.
June
12 **Vietnam** Siege of An Loc lifted.
August
12 **Vietnam** Last US ground combat troops leave; 43,500 airmen and support personnel remain.
September
16 **Vietnam** Quang Tri City retaken by South Vietnamese troops.
23 **Philippines** President Marcos proclaims martial law to fight insurgency.
October
8 **Vietnam** North Vietnamese proposals break deadlock in peace talks.
December
18-30 **Vietnam** Massive US air attacks on Hanoi and Haiphong by B-52 bombers in Linebacker II.

1973
January
15 **Vietnam** US orders halt to offensive military action.
23 **Vietnam** Ceasefire agreement announced, signed formally in Paris on 27 January.
February
21 **Laos** Ceasefire announced.
March
1 **Cambodia** Phnom Penh under siege.
29 **Vietnam** Last US military personnel leave.
June
29 **Cambodia** US Congress bans bombing of Cambodia from 15 August.

1974
August
5 **Vietnam** US Congress cuts military aid to South Vietnam.

1975
March
5 **Vietnam** North Vietnamese offensive in Central Highlands.
18-25 **Vietnam** South Vietnamese Army collapses in face of Northern offensive; Hue falls.
April
16 **Cambodia** Lon Nol government surrenders to Khmer Rouge who occupy Phnom Penh.
21 **Vietnam** President Thieu resigns.
30 **Vietnam** North Vietnamese troops enter Saigon as remaining Americans flee; South Vietnam surrenders.
May
15 **Cambodia** US Marines free US freighter *Mayaguez* held by Khmer Rouge.
December
3 **Laos** becomes a communist state with Souphanouvong as president.

SOUTH ASIA
1971
March
25 **Pakistan** President Yahya Khan orders suppression of autonomy movement in East Pakistan.
December
3 Pakistan carries out pre-emptive air strike against the Indian Air Force as India prepares an offensive in East Pakistan in support of the Bangladesh independence movement.
4-17 **Pakistan and India** fight war on two fronts, in the East and the West; in the West there is virtual stalemate but in the East the Pakistanis are routed and East Pakistan becomes Bangladesh.

1973
July
17 **Afghanistan** General Mohammed Daoud Khan seizes power in king's absence and declares country a republic.

1974
May
18 **India** explodes first nuclear device.

1975
August
15 **Bangladesh** Military coup overthrows government of Sheikh Mujib, who is killed.

EAST ASIA
1972
February
China US President Nixon visits Peking.

SOUTH AMERICA
1971
January
8 **Uruguay** British ambassador Geoffrey Jackson kidnapped and held prisoner for eight months by Tupamaros guerrillas.
March
23 **Argentina** General Lanusse takes power.
July
1 **Argentina** Agreement with Britain to settle claim to sovereignty over Falkland Islands by negotiations.
August
22 **Bolivia** Military coup brings Colonel Hugo Banzer to power.

1972
April
14 **Uruguay** Government declares state of 'internal war' after Tupamaros kill members of death squads.

1973
February
Uruguay Military take over leading role in government.
July
13 **Argentina** Exiled leader Juan Perón returns to country, becomes president in September.
September
11 **Chile** Military coup against democratically-elected government of communist President Salvador Allende Gossens. Allende dies in fighting for presidential palace and is replaced by General Augusto Pinochet Ugarte.

1974
July
Argentina Perón dies and is succeeded by his wife Isabel.

AFRICA
1971
January
25 **Uganda** Group of army officers, led by General Idi Amin, seizes power from President Milton Obote.

1972
April
29 **Burundi** President Micombero foils attempted rebellion by members of minority Hutu tribe and initiates widespread massacres.
October
26 **Dahomey** Military coup brings Major Mathieu Kerekou to power.
December
Rhodesia ZANU and FRELIMO guerrillas launch raids into the north of Rhodesia from Mozambique.

1974
February
26-28 **Ethiopia** Army mutinies against rule of Emperor Haile Selassie.
June
28 **Ethiopia** Army seizes control, reducing Emperor to figurehead.
September
10 **Guinea-Bissau** Portugal recognises independence under PAIGC.
12 **Ethiopia** Haile Selassie deposed; General Anam Amdom becomes head of state.
October
15 **Angola** Ceasefire agreed after grant of autonomy under a transitional government that includes members of all guerrilla groups.
November
22-24 **Ethiopia** General Anam Amdom and 60 other leading military and civilian figures killed; Brigadier-General Teferi Bante becomes head of state.
25 **South Africa** suspended from UN.

1975
June
25 **Mozambique** gains independence under FRELIMO government.
October
Angola Civil war between MPLA, based in Luanda, and UNITA and the FNLA.
November
7 **Angola** Cuban troops arrive to support the MPLA.
11 **Angola** Independence granted by Portugal.

Backlash

The Protestant paramilitary organisations

Above: Members of the Ulster Defence Association (UDA) parading in Ulster. The UDA has never been illegal, unlike the Ulster Volunteer Force (UVF) (below: UVF recruits are addressed by a Protestant clergyman) which was first banned in 1966.

The Protestant population of Northern Ireland has a long tradition of armed action in defence of its interests against, or in assertion of its dominance over, the Catholic population. In the pre-1916 period Protestants created the formidable Ulster Volunteer Force (UVF) which threatened armed revolt if the British government tried to impose the rule of an independent Dublin over Ulster. Then, after the creation of Northern Ireland, the formation of police auxiliaries such as the B-Specials gave enthusiastic Loyalists a chance to participate as a legal force in operations against the IRA and, at times, in sectarian attacks against the Catholics.

Fear of Catholic republicanism and simple hatred of Catholics as such was widespread, especially among working-class Protestants, and these attitudes were sustained by many virulent propagandists in the Orange Lodges, the Protestant press and the Protestant churches. A widening divide opened up in the 1960s between the feelings of Protestants at this grass-roots level and the top Unionist political leaders, who were drawn almost exclusively from the higher levels of Ulster society and were alert to the advantages of breaking down prejudices and normalising social relations in the Province. Ulster prime ministers from Terence O'Neill to Brian Faulkner repeatedly found themselves deserted and politically undermined by their own constituency, who rejected their supposedly weak policies towards the Catholics. There were always Protestant hardliners ready to organise direct action against Catholics if the government was taking a conciliatory line.

The first rioting of the 1960s occurred in September 1964 when the Reverend Ian Paisley led protests against the display of a nationalist flag at the election headquarters of a Republican candidate in West Belfast. The riots were the worst seen in 25 years and lasted for four nights. Springboarded to notoriety, Paisley was henceforth never far from the limelight.

In 1966, moved to violence by the Republican commemoration ceremonies for the anniversary of the Easter rising of 1916, a small working-class group naming itself after the once-great UVF murdered a Catholic barman, John Scullion. After another killing later in the year the UVF was banned, but it was almost certainly responsible for bomb attacks on public utilities in early 1969. Gusty Spence, the UVF leader imprisoned for the 1966 killings, was at the time widely regarded as a lunatic extremist even by Protestants hostile to Prime Minister O'Neill's reform policies, but by 1970 he had been adopted as a Protestant hero.

The rising tide of violence which culminated in the riots and burnings of the summer of 1969 gave ample evidence of the depth of fear and prejudice in the Protestant community, but after the intervention of the British Army the wave of Protestant activism was soon subdued. The disbandment of the B-Specials left the Protestants without an irregular armed force for the first time since before World War I. Although there was sporadic Protestant rioting and much inflammatory rhetoric, until the autumn of 1971 the IRA had a virtual monopoly of shooting and bombing.

With the formation in August 1971 of the Ulster Defence Association (UDA), calling on Protestants

to organise themselves into 'platoons', sectarianism and would-be militarism began to come together. In December Protestants carried out their first bombing attack on Catholics when McGurk's bar in Belfast was destroyed and 15 people killed. On 12 February 1972 William Craig, a former Stormont minister, announced the formation of the Ulster Vanguard Movement with a parade of uniformed members at Lisburn, warning: 'God help those who get in our way for we mean business.' In the wake of Direct Rule in March 1972 UDA vigilantes organised No-Go areas in Protestant districts and a murder campaign against Catholics was launched – some 40 Catholics had been victims of these 'motiveless' killings by July.

The campaign of sectarian killings inevitably brought the Protestant paramilitaries into conflict with the security forces, and the first Loyalist was interned in February 1973. Perhaps understandably, however, the army and the police concentrated their intelligence and security operations against the side which threatened them directly – the IRA – and did not succeed in breaking the power of the Protestant paramilitaries.

Following the Provos

The sectarian murder campaign grew out of a widespread feeling among Protestants that they should themselves adopt the 'tactics of the minority', imitating the Provisional IRA. Unlike the Provisionals, however, Protestants could not generally take the security forces or the business life of Ulster as their targets, since it was the Ulster state and its economic life which they wished to uphold. There was only one possible target for their armed action, and that was the Catholic population itself.

Another main function of the Protestant paramilitaries was to impress on political leaders in Westminster, Stormont and Dublin that any attempt to unite Ireland against their wishes would be followed by civil war. Displays of armed men were carefully staged for the benefit of journalists, who were suitably impressed by the Protestants' readiness and ability to defend their interests if called upon to do so.

They also provided a vigilante force, notionally for the defence of Protestant areas against attack, but in fact more to impose discipline on their own neighbourhoods. This role came to the fore during the Ulster workers' strike of May 1974, when the organised intimidation exercised by the paramilitaries was crucial to the solidarity and hence the effectiveness of the strike action. The UDA, the UVF and other smaller groups formed themselves into an Ulster Army Council to back up the strike, but in general the various paramilitary bodies preferred to keep their distance from one another, at least in public.

Craig's Vanguard Movement, having held some military-style rallies and parades, soon retreated from violence, and the UDA was left as by far the largest Protestant armed organisation. In May 1972 its members were first seen on the streets of Belfast in military uniforms, but in subsequent years it tried to distance itself somewhat from the paramilitary image, cultivating an involvement in local politics and benevolent activities – although the organisation is thought to have had links with bombing attacks on Dublin and

Above: William Craig who, in 1972, founded the Ulster Vanguard Movement. Below: Both Protestant and Catholic youngsters have got involved in the atmosphere of violence.

other parts of the Irish Republic as late as 1974; attacks in which 31 people died. The UDA has never been banned, and in keeping with its legal status it has avoided implication in the terrorist activities of smaller groups with which its links are imprecise. Still, a large number of UDA members have found themselves interned or imprisoned because of their involvement in violence.

Apart from the UVF, which continued its activities into the 1970s, a number of small Protestant terror groups sprang to notoriety at different times. In 1973 both the Red Hand Commandos, led by John McKeague, and the Ulster Freedom Fighters (UFF) often regarded as a front for UDA assassination operations, were outlawed after admitting responsibility for a series of bombings and shootings of Catholics. Other shadowy groups formed and dissolved, like the Ulster Citizens Army which in October 1973 declared war on the army because of the conditions under which Protestants were being kept in the Maze prison, but came to little in practice. By the early 1980s it was the Protestant Action Force which was hitting the headlines through its sectarian murders.

Links and divisions

The links between the various Protestant paramilitary groups have remained obscure, as has the degree of influence of the UDA within the Royal Ulster Constabulary (RUC) and the British Army's Ulster Defence Regiment (UDR). Although police action against Protestant paramilitaries since 1973 has been extensive, there is no doubt that some sympathisers with Protestant extremism have found a chance to express their support for the state through membership of the RUC and, more especially, the part-time UDR, a number of whose members have been charged with the murder of Catholics. It seems that elements of the UDA have sought to use the UDR as a sort of training ground in which the employment of firearms and other skills could be learnt. Some UDA members even owe their ability in this area to a previous spell of enlistment in the regular British Army.

The fact that the paramilitaries have their roots in the Protestant working class and are generally hostile to the Ulster Unionist establishment, made them accessible at times to left-wing attitudes which would place the struggle against unemployment, poor housing and other social disadvantages above the sectarian conflict with the Catholics. This line of thinking, similar to that followed by the Official IRA and by the more politicised Provisionals of the later 1970s, gained support in 1973 from prominent UDA men who found themselves in conflict with the British Army and the police and began to think they might have more in common with their Catholic enemies than with the established order. Two early leaders of the UDA, Tommy Heron and Ernie Elliott, were assassinated by their colleagues for 'going soft on Republicanism' in this way, as was Red Hand leader John McKeague. On the whole, despite some rhetoric aimed at social reform, sectarianism remained uppermost.

It is, of course, the Catholic population who have borne the brunt of the paramilitaries' activities. By the early 1980s the number of Catholics assassinated by Protestants had reached around 500 – a high proportion of the total civilian deaths in the present Ulster conflict. Some of the killings have included the use of torture to increase the element of terror – the 'Shankhill Butchers' gang murdered and tortured at least a dozen Catholics before being apprehended. Like all paramilitary organisations, the Protestant groups have shown a tendency to tip over into gangsterism. Their finances have depended on protection rackets in Protestant areas – pubs and businesses yielded handsome pickings – as well as the running of drinking clubs and dances. The various groupings have at times indulged in brutal internecine conflict.

Calculations of the armed force of the Protestant paramilitaries are totally speculative. The decline in sectarian killings in the late 1970s did not, for example, necessarily reflect any drop in the number of armed men that the UDA leaders, or even such politicians as Ian Paisley, had at their disposal to call into action if they felt the occasion demanded. Their real power might be seen if an agreement was ever reached for a united Ireland.

Brian Markworthy

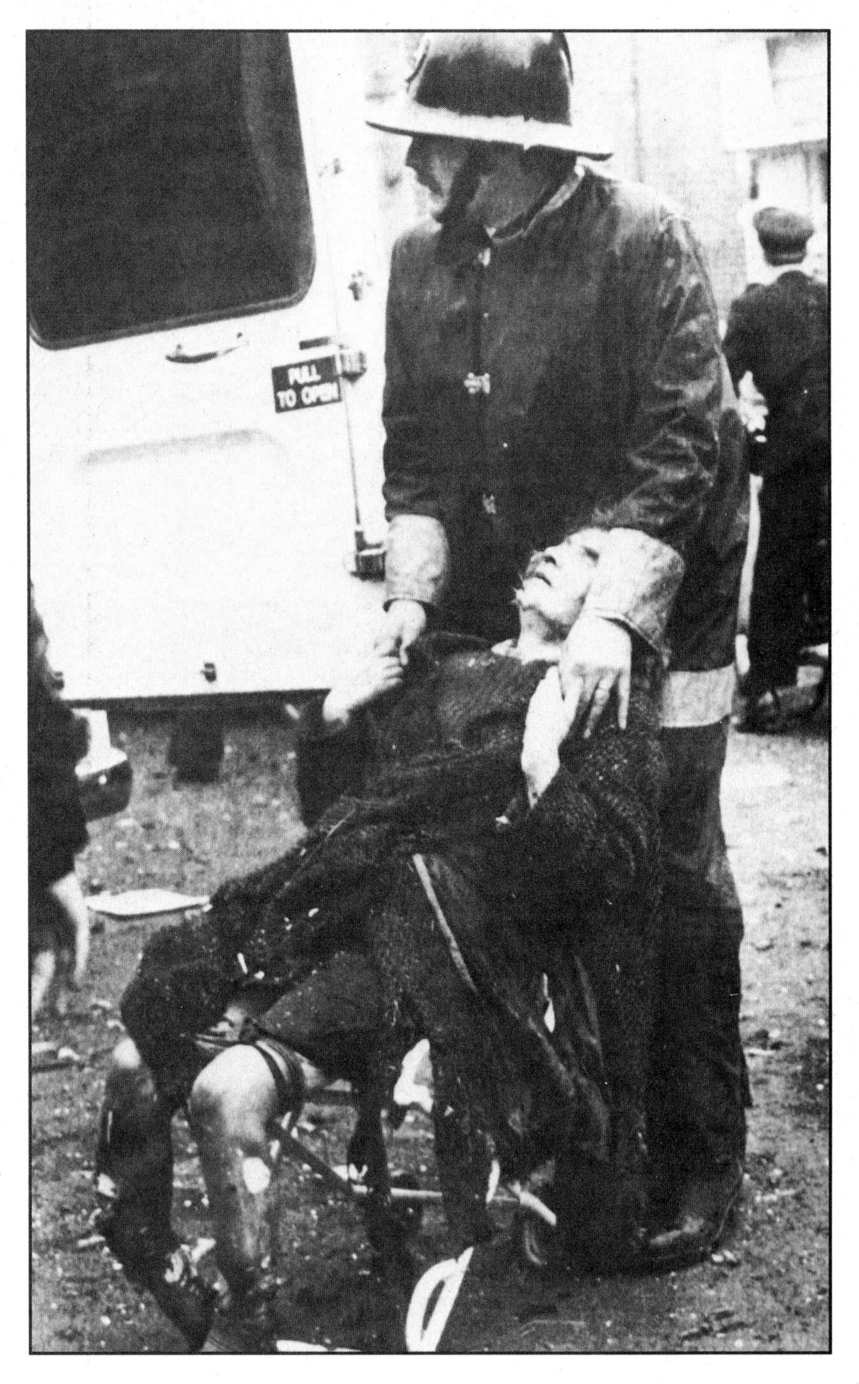

Above: An old woman, her shin split wide open, desperately clings to the hands of a rescuing fireman as she is loaded into an ambulance after a bomb attack in Dublin. The extension of violence to the Republic of Ireland, in a series of incidents in 1974, was widely believed to be the work of Protestant groups linked to the UDA.

Key Weapons

WESTERN SAMs

The ever increasing capabilities and numbers of Soviet attack aircraft has necessitated the provision of adequate AA (anti-aircraft) defences for Nato's land forces and strategically important installations in western Europe. The performance of the latest ground-attack aircraft is such that the traditional AA gun has, for the most part, become inadequate to counter the threat. Increasingly, therefore, reliance is being placed on the SAM (surface-to-air missile) to provide the necessary cover for effective operations in the face of the Warsaw Pact's numerically superior air forces.

The need for a flexible AA response has given rise to three distinct families of SAMs; man-portable, mobile (either towed or vehicle-mounted) and static systems. The first of these is intended to provide the humble infantryman with his own AA cover and, as such, uses simple aiming systems and (with some exceptions) infra-red guidance. The mobile systems usually comprise a launch unit and separate guidance and control equipment. They are used to provide cover for army formations, the defence of important strategic locations, and, on fully mobile mountings, they act as an integral part of armoured formations. The last category, the static system, is a permanent installation sited to provide cover for airfields, production centres and urban areas. Such systems, together with those which are mobile, usually rely on radar as the guidance and control medium.

Currently, France, West Germany, Italy, Sweden, the UK and the USA are producing SAMs. Taking these in turn, the major French system is the Thomson-CSF/Matra Crotale. Developed originally for a South African requirement, the R440 missile is an all-weather weapon optimised for use against low-flying aircraft. The system as a whole is made up of a launcher vehicle and a target AC (acquisition and coordination) unit, both mounted on a four-wheeled armoured chassis. The launch vehicle carries four missiles and is equipped with a J-band tracking and guidance radar. The AC unit has an E-band radar for target surveillance, identification and designation and carries a data-link system to pass information to the launcher. Maximum detection range is in the region of 18km (11 miles) and up to 12 targets can be handled by the AC unit at any one time. Currently, Crotale is in service with the French Air Force who use it for airfield defence, and the system has been widely exported, especially in the Middle East.

France, in collaboration with West Germany, also produces the Roland system. Like Crotale, Roland is optimised for use against low-flying aircraft and is mainly carried on fully-mobile tracked launchers based on the French AMX chassis or that of the German Marder. To date, there have been three variants of the basic weapon, Roland I and II and US Roland. Roland I is a clear-weather system which uses a launcher-mounted Siemens/Thomson-CSF surveillance radar for target acquisition and an optical sight for aiming. Roland II is an all-weather system which uses a Thomson-CSF tracking radar in addition to the Siemens/Thomson-CSF surveillance unit. As a back-up to the radar system, the optical sight is retained in this second model. US Roland is generally similar to Roland II and is mounted on a launch

Previous page: A British Bloodhound Mk2 long-range SAM blasts skywards. The Bloodhound has a maximum range of 80km (50 miles). Above: A French Crotale area-defence SAM is fired from its launcher. The missile's radar dish is visible, centred in the quad launcher.

Below: Mounted on a modified M109 tracked chassis a US Roland missile is fired on a test range. Despite the fact that the Roland is a highly effective short-range missile, it was abandoned by the US armed forces for cost reasons.

vehicle based on the American M109 chassis. In all cases, guidance commands are transmitted via a radio link and in the case of Roland II /US Roland, initial acquisition of the missile in the sighting system after launch is by means of infra-red. Once acquired, tracking is passed to the radar which simultaneously follows both the target and the missile.

Currently, the French armed forces operate both Roland I and II whilst those of Germany use only the second model. US Roland was intended to be the US Army's major SAM for the 1980s but cost overruns led to the whole programme being scrapped with only 27 launchers and 595 missiles delivered.

Italy's Spada system is based around the air-launched Aspide missile and is intended as an all-weather, point/area defence weapon for small strategic areas such as harbours and airfields. A Spada battery comprises between two and four static, six-round launchers, a search and IFF (identification-friend or foe) interrogation unit using an E/F-band radar, a tracking unit using a G/H-band radar and a control unit using an I-band radar for missile guidance. Operationally, these elements are grouped into two sections known as the detection centre (an overall command post and the search unit) and the firing section (the tracking unit, the control unit and the launchers). The detection centre handles target identification and allocation whilst the firing section performs target acquisition, tracking and missile guidance. Currently, this rather complicated system is only in service with the Italian Air Force.

Although outside Nato, Sweden's RBS-70 SAM is operated by Norway within the alliance in addition to Sweden itself and the Irish Republic. Developed by Bofors, the RBS-70 is a man-portable system comprising a launch tube, sighting unit and firing stand, each element constituting an individual man-load. The complete weapon can be assembled in roughly 30 seconds and guidance is provided by laser designation. Operation is simplicity itself, it only being necessary to keep the sighting unit aligned with the target during the engagement. A laser designator is slaved to the sight and the missile homes in on the target by 'riding' the beam of laser light.

The UK is a major producer in the SAM field and currently has operational the Blowpipe man-portable weapon, the Rapier mobile system and the static Bloodhound. Developed by Shorts, Blowpipe comprises a launch tube containing the missile and a clip-on aiming unit containing a command radio transmitter, an 'auto-gathering' unit and a monocular sight. To fire the missile, the operator acquires the target in the sight's cross wires, releases a safety catch and fires. Once in flight, the missile is automatically 'gathered' so that it remains centred on the sight and the operator guides the weapon by the movement of a thumb-operated joystick. To engage another target, he simply unclips the empty launch tube and replaces it with a fresh unit. In addition to the UK, Blowpipe is used by eight other countries including Argentina. This led to the bizarre situation of both sides in the Falklands War using the weapon against each other, with the British claiming nine and the Argentinians one Blowpipe 'kill'.

The Rapier system was designed originally as a missile replacement for the British Army's faithful 40mm Bofors anti-aircraft gun. In its basic form, Rapier comprises a four-round launcher with a built-in surveillance radar, a generator unit and an optical

Above: Perched on a Land Rover two Swedish soldiers fire a Bofors RBS-70 SAM. The weapon has a range of 5km (3 miles) and utilises a laser-designation system to guide the missile onto the target. Right: The multiple Blowpipe system in operation; the soldier on the right is guiding the missile onto its target while his companion is overseeing the operation through binoculars.

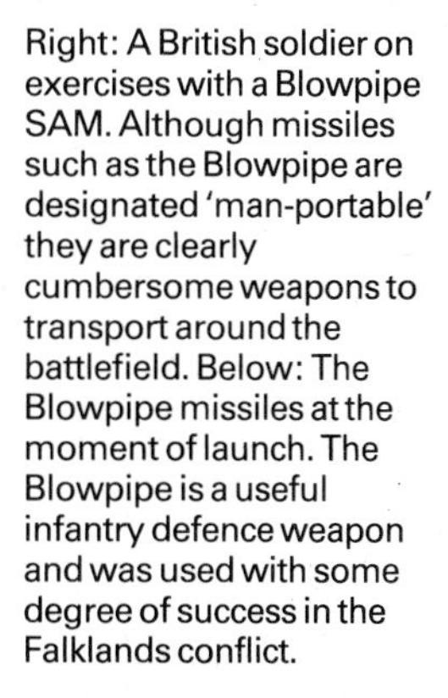

Right: A British soldier on exercises with a Blowpipe SAM. Although missiles such as the Blowpipe are designated 'man-portable' they are clearly cumbersome weapons to transport around the battlefield. Below: The Blowpipe missiles at the moment of launch. The Blowpipe is a useful infantry defence weapon and was used with some degree of success in the Falklands conflict.

tracker. Operationally, a target is acquired by the radar set and if deemed hostile, passed to the tracker operator. He then follows it through his optical sight and when it comes within range, a missile is automatically fired. The operator then continues to track the target and an in-built computer processes the missile's deviation from the 'line of sight' and generates guidance commands accordingly.

This basic Rapier has been combined with a fully-mobile tracked launcher based on the M548 cargo chassis. The towed system has been further developed into an all-weather weapon by the addition of a trailer-mounted DN181 Blindfire radar set which provides for a fully automatic engagement sequence. In addition to the British services, Rapier is in service with or ordered for 11 other countries including Switzerland and the USA. Rapier has been used in action on the Falklands (claiming 20 'kills') and by Iran in the Gulf War.

The remaining British SAM is the venerable Bloodhound Mk2 which is now used solely for airfield defence in the UK. Typically, a Bloodhound battery comprises of four missiles and static launchers, a target illuminating radar and a launch control post.

America has developed a wide range of SAMs which currently comprise the man-portable Redeye

Right: Men of the Royal Artillery prepare the tracker element of a Rapier SAM for operation. The launch system can be seen in the background with its four Rapier missiles ready for firing. The Rapier is a far more complex SAM than the simple infantry Blowpipe and is accordingly able to engage aerial targets in a wide variety of tactical situations.

Left: The Rapier SAM in action. Below: The Rapier system installed on the M548 cargo chassis, which extends tactical mobility and provides ground troops with improved air defence.

Left: A line of RAF Bloodhound Mk2 SAMs of No. 85 Squadron, defending a British airfield. Although its great range is a useful asset, the Bloodhound's ability to deal with the latest combat aircraft remains in question.

and Stinger weapons, the mobile HAWK, Chaparral and Patriot systems and the static Nike Hercules. The FIM-43A Redeye was the world's first infantry SAM when it entered service in 1964. Using infra-red homing, the weapon comprises a simple launching tube, containing a pre-packed missile and with a built-in optical sight. In combat, the operator aims at a target which has passed over him, waits for an audio tone, indicating that the infra-red seeker has 'locked-on' and fires. The shortcomings of this first generation weapon were numerous, not the least of which was that being a 'pursuit-course' missile it could only engage an aircraft after it had made its attack. Redeye has been exported to Denmark (where it is known as the Hamlet), Greece, West Germany and Sweden (known as the RBS-69).

Developed as a more effective replacement for Redeye, the FIM-92A Stinger has had a protracted development (stretching back to the mid-1960s). Again an infra-red homing missile, FIM-92A uses a similar launch tube/optical sight configuration as its predecessor but has the advantages of an 'all-aspect' infra-red seeker, allowing it to engage targets from any angle, and a built-in IFF capability for speedy identification of hostile aircraft.

Oldest of the American mobile SAMs is the Raytheon MIM-23 HAWK (homing all the way killer). Entering service in August 1960, the HAWK is by today's standards a very cumbersome system and only remains in service with the French. In 1972, an advanced model, the MIM-23B, was introduced which featured an improved guidance system, warhead and motor, combined with a digital fire control system. This version, known universally as Improved HAWK, also featured a 'load and forget' capability, the missiles requiring no further servicing once installed on the launcher. Currently, Improved HAWK remains in service with the US Army and those of Belgium, Denmark, West Germany, Greece, Italy, the Netherlands, Spain and Sweden (where it is known as the RB-77).

The MIM-72 Chaparral was developed to a US Army requirement for a low-altitude SAM some 20 years ago. Essentially a modified infra-red homing Sidewinder air-to-air missile, the Chaparral system uses a fully-tracked M730 launch vehicle carrying four missiles and eight re-loads, backed-up by a truck-mounted AN/MPQ-49 surveillance radar. The actual launch unit takes the form of a rotating turret mounted on the rear of the M730 which also houses the operator. In a typical engagement, a target is acquired visually or by the radar if available and passed to the operator who tracks it optically. Still tracking the target, he waits for an audio 'tone' to indicate that the seeker has 'locked on' and on receiving this, fires.

Chaparral should have been replaced by US Roland but the failure of this programme has meant that the system will continue in service until the mid-1990s. The current production model, the MIM-72C/F or 'Improved Chaparral', features an enlarged warhead and the DAW-1 'all aspect' infra-red seeker.

America's latest mobile SAM is the MIM-104 Patriot which originated in a 1965 specification for a replacement for both the HAWK and the Nike Hercules. Built by a consortium headed by Raytheon, MIM-104 entered service with the US Army during 1983 and has been evaluated by Denmark, France, West Germany, Greece and the Netherlands. A

Top: US MIM-72C Chaparral missiles and their launchers, ready to fire (left) and in transit (right). Above centre: Technicians work on the US Army's long-range SAM, the HAWK, at Key West, Florida. Above: A US soldier prepares to fire an FIM-92A Stinger SAM. Right: The Redeye SAM, being fired by soldiers of the Australian Army. This missile is now being replaced in US Army service by the more advanced Stinger.

Patriot battery comprises an AN/MPQ-53 multi-purpose radar, an AN/MSQ-104 control unit, five four-round trailer-mounted launchers, a powerplant and various support vehicles. The missile itself uses semi-active radar guidance combined with a command terminal mode.

The remaining operational SAM produced by the USA is the semi-static MIM-14B Nike Hercules. Introduced in 1958, the weapon remains in wide-scale service within Nato, being deployed by Belgium, West Germany, Greece, Italy, the Netherlands, Norway, Spain and Turkey. Intended for use against high-flying strategic bombers, Nike Hercules has proved capable of intercepting short-range ballistic missiles and the Nato rounds have been the subject of a major up-dating programme begun in 1981. A complete system comprises a low and high-powered acquisition radar, a target tracking radar, data processing equipment, remote-control launchers and a firing centre. Working independently or as part of an overall defence system, the Nike battery is cued by the surveillance radars and uses the tracking radar to provide the launch parameters. Once airborne, the MIM-14B's guidance system is activated, programming the missile to roll towards the target (from the vertical) and to dive onto it from above.

Given the Warsaw Pact's aerial supremacy Nato SAMs have an essential role to play in the defence of the West.

Left: A test launch of a Patriot SAM at the White Sands missile range in New Mexico. The Patriot and the older Nike Hercules (below) have very high interception speeds which provide them with an anti-missile capability. Although the Nike Hercules came into service in 1958 it remains an important SAM as the result of a major up-dating in 1981.

Western Surface-to-Air Missiles

Missile	Length	Launch Weight	Range	Speed	Ceiling	Warhead
Crotale	2.89m (9ft 5in)	85kg (187lb)	12km (6.8 miles)	Mach 2.3	3000m (9845ft)	HE
Roland II	2.4m (7ft 10in)	63kg (139lb)	6km (3.73 miles)	Mach 1.5	Not Known	HE
Aspide	3.7m (12ft 1in)	220kg (485lb)	Not Known	Mach 4.0	Not Known	HE
RBS-70	1.32m (4ft 4in)	24kg (53lb)	5km (3.1 miles)	Not Known	3000m (9845ft)	Fragmentation
Blowpipe	1.39m (4ft 5in)	11kg (25lb)	3-4km (1.86-2 miles)	Not Known	2000m (6560ft)	HE
Rapier	2.24m (7ft 4in)	42.6kg (94lb)	6.5km (4 miles)	Mach 2.0	3000m (9845ft)	HE
Bloodhound Mk2	7.75m (25ft 5in)	2300kg (5070lb)	80km (50 miles)	Mach 1.5+	23,010m (75,500ft)	HE
Redeye	1.22m (4ft)	8.2kg (18lb)	3.3km (2 miles)	Mach 2.5	Not Known	Fragmentation
Stinger	1.52m (5ft)	10.9kg (24lb)	5km (3.1 miles)	Mach 2.0	4800m (15,750ft)	Fragmentation
HAWK	5.03m (16ft 6in)	627.3kg (1383lb)	40km (25 miles)	Mach 2.5	11,580m (38,000ft)	HE
Chaparral	2.91m (9ft 6in)	84kg (185.18lb)	6km (3.72 miles)	Mach 2.5	3050m (10,000ft)	HE
Patriot	5.18m (17ft 0in)	998kg (2200lb)	60km (37.3 miles)	Mach 3.0	24,000m (78,750ft)	HE/Nuclear
Nike Hercules	12.70m (41ft 8in)	4858kg (10,712lb)	150km (93 miles)	Mach 3.5	Not Known	HE/Nuclear

Meeting fire

with fire

Western Europe's response to terrorism

In the 1970s the states of Western Europe were reluctantly forced to confront a widespread outbreak of terrorist attacks, connected with the aspirations of minorities like the Republicans in Northern Ireland or the Basques in Spain, or with the disaffection of middle-class intellectuals such as the Baader-Meinhof group in West Germany or the Angry Brigade in Britain, or with conflicts far from Europe as in the case of the Palestinians or the South Moluccans. The initial reluctance of the West European governments to respond vigorously to these developments was connected to their liberal democratic beliefs. Liberal democracies seek to govern by consensus, encouraging the largest possible proportion of the population to acquiesce in the form of government. They are unwilling to display the power of their armies and police forces in the domestic arena, calculating that a hardline response to opposition will tend to generate more discontent. Their instinct is to defuse hostility by tolerating it.

The urban guerrillas of the Western world were well aware of the nature of their opponent: their chief working principle was that by provoking ever greater violence by the state they would undermine tolerance and polarise society, creating the conditions for revolutionary action. The rules of a very subtle game were therefore laid down: the terrorists sought to stimulate an over-reaction from the authorities from which they might benefit, while the governments attempted to crack down on terrorist attacks without alienating the population in which the terrorists were embedded. The rulers of the less stable among the liberal democracies – such as Italy, and Spain after 1975 – were acutely aware of a further problem, the threat to their authority from the security forces themselves, who might have links with right-wing political groups equally hostile to liberal democracy. The solution pursued by the Western European states, when the problem refused to go away, was to attempt to establish specialist anti-terrorist forces which would be hand-picked and trained to carry out the necessary repressive operations with a precision that would avoid damage to the innocent, and would be free of any suspect ideology or links with right-wing groups.

Britain first faced terrorist activity on a significant scale when the Provisional IRA began its campaign in Northern Ireland in 1970. The British had an elite group ready to hand that could be used for special operations in Northern Ireland, the Special Air Service Regiment (SAS). But the brunt of anti-terrorist operations was borne by ordinary units of the British Army and by Northern Ireland's armed police force, the Royal Ulster Constabulary (RUC), with the part-time army reservists of the Ulster Defence Regiment (UDR). Although in many ways untypical of the terrorist problem in Europe – with its sectarian conflict, the lack of involvement of intellectuals, and the ambiguous position of the Irish Republic – Northern Ireland did offer the British a chance to make some classic mistakes and evolve improved techniques. The early operations improvised against IRA gunmen were of the indiscriminate 'blanket' variety that alienates local people from the authorities, and the introduction of internment in August 1971 gave a clear demonstration of how tough measures and the departure from the usual rule of law can make a security situation worse rather than better. Yet improved techniques were evolved which vastly improved intelligence gathering – especially through the filing of

Above: An SAS trooper in drab clothing prepares to burst into the Iranian embassy after throwing stun grenades through the window. A rescued hostage looks on from the safety of an adjacent balcony. The 1980 siege provided the public with a rare insight into the advances made in anti-terrorist techniques and weaponry and the whole operation was an outstanding success for the SAS.

material in a central computer – and enhanced the forces' ability to handle such standard terrorist situations as bombings, kidnappings and sieges. By 1975 the programme of 'criminalisation' had returned terrorist cases to the courts, ending arrest without trial, although the norms applying in the so-called Diplock courts were well below those usual in a liberal democracy. Nor had the British been able to stop contacts between the RUC and UDR security forces and Protestant extremists – a threat to the credibility of the law and to the state's ability to pursue a policy of moderation in search of consensus.

On the British mainland, the authorities were far better placed to maintain liberal principles while fighting terrorism. From the start of the Provisional IRA campaign in Britain in 1972, the task of repelling it fell to units of the police. Chiefly responsible was the Special Branch, in control of intelligence-gathering, and the bomb squad – formed in 1971 in response to the brief Angry Brigade bombing campaign and from 1976 expanded into the anti-terrorist squad C13. When facing gunmen, as in the Balcombe Street siege of December 1975, the 'blue berets' of Scotland Yard's firearms department could be called on for assistance. In general the police were able to operate without extra legal powers, but in 1974 a Prevention of Terrorism Act was passed, allowing suspected terrorists to be excluded from the United Kingdom without any right of appeal in court, and increasing police detention powers. The strength of popular hostility to terrorism and the stability of Britain's political system meant that the highly effective anti-terrorist operations were not felt to infringe civil liberties except by a small minority.

The SAS were on the whole kept in the background, since it was felt that the use of an army unit on the British mainland should be avoided. They did, of course, hit the headlines through the storming of the Iranian embassy in 1980, an event which brought to public attention the new devices that had been developed for the anti-terrorist armoury – such as the listening devices which tracked the movements of the hostage-takers within the embassy – and the high level of training for such contingencies that the SAS had achieved.

In fact, the SAS had long been playing a vital international role in helping other liberal democracies to develop their own elite forces. The most notable example was their contribution to West Germany. After the experience of the Nazi regime, the Germans had rebuilt their police on a principle of decentralisation, with each state of the Federal Republic having its own force. The only federal police organisation was the Federal Border Guard. There was also a deep suspicion of elite police units in a country that had produced the notorious SS. Yet after the shock of the Munich Olympics massacre in September 1972 it was clear that something had to be done. The marksmen from the Bavarian state police assigned to pick off the Palestinian hostage-takers had not been up to the job.

It was decided to develop an elite force with SAS-style training out of the Border Guard, the result being Grenzschutzgruppen 9 (GSG9). It was put under the command of Colonel Ulrich Wegener and its headquarters were established just outside Bonn. The formation consisted of a headquarters unit, a communications unit, a documentation unit, and three fighting units of 30 men each – comprising a five-man command section and four special tactical sections each composed of one officer and four men. Although officially a police group, its training was similar to that of elite army units. Favoured weapons of the group included the Mauser sniper's rifle and the Heckler and Koch MP5 sub-machine gun.

Such was the suspicion of an elite group under central government control in West Germany that until 1977 GSG9 were heavily trained but had been given nothing to do. The states of the Federal Republic had set up their own anti-terrorist forces and wanted no help from outsiders who were regarded as

Below: Dutch Marines on night exercises. The Royal Marine Corps provided units for special training in anti-terrorist techniques. These troops first saw action against South Moluccan terrorists in December 1975.

Despite the fact that terrorism had existed in Europe for some years, the creation of elite police forces was a particular problem in West Germany, because of worries about the re-creation of units similar to those of Nazi Germany. After the Munich massacres in September 1972, however, the GSG9 (left, members of the GSG9 armed with the Heckler and Koch MP5 sub-machine gun; far left, practising rapid deployment by helicopter) was formed and proved its worth in the Mogadishu raid of October 1977.

'trigger-happy'. This situation was transformed, however, by the events of October 1977 when, with a little help from the SAS, a GSG9 attack successfully freed a planeload of hostages at Mogadishu in Somalia. From that point they were confirmed as heroes.

GSG9 has not, in fact, posed any threat to liberal democratic principles, but other changes in West Germany under the impact of urban guerrillas like the Baader-Meinhof Red Army Fraction were more problematic. The small Federal Criminal Investigation Department (BKA) based in Wiesbaden grew to an organisation over 3000-strong during the 1970s, running a computer which carried more extensive records of personal details than any other such data bank in Europe. Many have argued that such an accumulation of information can effectively convict people without process of law or right of appeal and in itself constitutes a major loss of freedom. New laws were also passed which extended police powers of arrest and search. The ostentatious deployment of state power in the fortress of the Stammheim prison and court complex where the Baader-Meinhof trial was conducted, and the deaths of some of the terrorists in custody, awoke concern among many liberals. Yet if these developments showed the power of urban guerrillas to change a liberal state in an authoritarian direction – however mildly – the public response showed that where a solid consensus of support for the government existed, tough measures would be widely welcomed and social cohesion if anything strengthened.

In countries less directly menaced by terrorist activity, existing security forces and legislation provided an adequate framework. In the Netherlands it was the Royal Marine Corps which provided units for special training as an anti-terrorist shock force. Their moment for action came in December 1975 when it was deemed necessary to storm a train that had been hijacked by exiles from the former Dutch colony of the South Moluccas. This action, in which two hostages and six South Moluccans were killed, was widely felt to be contrary to Dutch traditions of peaceful negotiation, but it has left little trace on Dutch public life.

Counter-espionage and surveillance

In France, a proliferation of police forces and bureaux were available to carry out anti-terrorist activities, including the DST – chiefly concerned with counter-espionage – and the RG, who resembled the British Special Branch in their task of surveillance over potentially subversive political groups. The first attempt to form an anti-terrorist shock force came in 1972 with the announcement, in a fanfare of publicity, of the creation of 'anti-commando brigades'. Over-equipped and under-trained, these soon faded into obscurity, but in 1974 the paramilitary Gendarmerie Nationale was ordered to form a crack unit, the Intervention Group (GIGN). Each of the hand-picked 54 men in the group is a trained marksman with a range of other skills from parachuting to the martial arts. They have seen plenty of action – against Corsican nationalists in 1980, for example – but more against non-political criminals than terrorists. However, the regime established by General de Gaulle in 1958 was already more authoritarian than its neighbours in Britain or West Germany, and it cannot be said that the 'terror decade', as the 1970s have been nicknamed, had any effect on its nature.

In Italy, by contrast, the political system was profoundly shaken by the terrorist actions of such left-wing groups as the Red Brigades and Prima Linea, and of neo-fascist groups like Ordine Nuovo and the Armed Revolutionary Nuclei. This was partly

Below right: Members of the crack French anti-terrorist squad, GIGN, use hand pistols during target practice. With only 54 members the GIGN is a truly elite force whose members are trained marksmen and specialise in a variety of field skills.

because the Italian system had failed to produce the sort of consensus found further north; with about half the population supporting either the Communist Party or the right-wing Movimento Sociale Italiano (MSI), terrorists could expect some sympathy for their efforts to disrupt society. Racked by corruption and scandals, the ruling group centred on the Christian Democrat Party commanded little moral authority. What is more, the Italian intelligence services were heavily compromised by right-wing terrorism; undercover intelligence officers were implicated in a bomb attack that killed 14 people in Milan in December 1969, for example, and the lax treatment of right-wing militants eventually convicted for the attack was a scandal. The leader of the internal security service at that time, General Vito Miceli, later became a right-wing member of parliament. By 1976 considerable evidence had emerged that leading members of the intelligence services had conspired with right-wing elements in the armed forces with a view to attempting a coup, and as a consequence the services were totally reorganised, many senior figures being forced to resign. The new structure of intelligence, with a Democratic Security Information Service (SISDE) to deal with internal security, was at first hopelessly inefficient; there were insufficient staff and an atmosphere of total public distrust of secrecy made operations more difficult. To supplement SISDE, which came under the ministry of defence, the Italian police set up their own intelligence unit (UCIGOS) under the ministry of the interior, but this further anti-terrorist group only added to the confusion. Undoubtedly, the disorganisation of the Italian security services helped permit the rise of terrorism in Italy to the heights it reached in 1978, when there were on average more than seven terrorist acts a day.

It was the kidnapping of Christian Democrat leader Aldo Moro in March 1978 that finally pushed the Italian government into a more adequate response. Using the public sympathy generated by the cold-blooded murder of Moro, and supported by the Communist Party which had set its face against terrorism, legislation was passed between 1978 and 1980 which increased police powers at the expense of some civil liberties, especially in the field of personal privacy. An effective anti-terrorist team of 150 men was set up under General Dalla Chiesa, an officer in the Carabinieri, Italy's paramilitary police force. Given plenty of money and the increased police powers, the new team was able to arrest an impressive number of terrorists from the left and right by 1980, simply by applying traditional police detection techniques. As in other liberal democracies, successful police action against terrorism proved popular, despite a number of cases of the abuse of police powers during these operations. Bombings and kidnappings continued into the 1980s, and the Italian political establishment remained shaky, but an improved anti-terrorist effort had certainly been achieved without increasing opposition to the system.

Meeting force with force

All the countries so far discussed have been liberal democracies since World War II, but Spain presents a different picture. When Basque separatists began a terrorist campaign in the 1960s Spain was still under the dictatorship of General Franco, victor in the civil war of 1936-39. The internal security and intelligence forces deployed against the terrorists – such as the paramilitary Guardia Civil, the army with its own intelligence services, and the security police – were the main pillars of the Franco regime, hated and feared by a large section of the population. An authoritarian legal system, with military courts for special cases and harsh punishments, was immediately turned against the violent militants. The emphasis on meeting force with force contrasted strongly with the approach elsewhere in Europe.

When Spain became a liberal democratic monarchy in 1975, the country's past made it especially

Below: Members of the Spanish anti-terrorist unit GEO conceal themselves in a doorway prior to moving in against a group of terrorists holding over 100 hostages in the Central Barcelona Bank in May 1981. Terrified civilians throw themselves to the ground. Below right: Hostages flee the bank and are helped to cover by GEO troops. The unit successfully stormed the bank. They now provide a bodyguard for the Spanish King.

vulnerable. The highly politicised nature of the police and armed forces, led by devoted Franco supporters, made them an extremely unreliable arm of the fledgling democracy. At the same time, the liberalisation which swept the country made it far easier for terrorists to operate, whether Basques of ETA-Militar, left-wingers in GRAPO, or fascists of such groups as Warriors of Christ the King. The new regime sought, in true liberal democratic manner, to undermine opposition by tolerance and moderation, granting a large degree of autonomy to the Basques, leaving pro-Franco military and police leaders in their posts, and so on. But the violent efforts of left and right to destabilise the new democracy raged unchecked in the early years of the regime.

The total identification of the security forces with the right in politics was the crucial weakness in the government's position. It might be official policy, for example, to defend the proper rule of law in the face of terrorism, but on their own initiative the security forces would engage in torture or the summary killing of suspects. In the Basque country, the government was unable to benefit fully from popular revulsion at continuing terrorism because local hostility to the Guardia Civil remained deeply engrained. Matters came to a head in February 1981 when Colonel Tejero de Molino led a force of the Guardia Civil in an assault on the Spanish parliament, and army officers, including General Milans del Busch, brought their tanks onto the street. The resolute opposition of King Juan Carlos led the coup attempt to collapse, but the government still did not dare carry out a major purge of the armed forces. Instead, resolute measures against terrorism were promised to placate the army.

But the Spanish government had already acted to provide itself with a non-politicised elite security force. Had the coup attempt not collapsed of itself, the Spanish parliament building would have been stormed by the Special Operations Group (GEO), a newly-formed crack force, comprising recruits from the security police and the Guardia Civil hand-picked for their independence from links with the fascist groups. Foreign instructors, including a contingent from the SAS, helped provide an apolitical training in anti-terrorist operations. The GEO's first practical experience came when a group of fascist gunmen took hostages in a Barcelona bank in May 1981. The GEO troops stormed the bank very successfully, and now provide the king with a bodyguard.

Despite moments of crisis, liberal democracies in Europe have in fact proved well able to cope with terrorism while maintaining their basic attitudes towards civil liberties and the rule of law. Terrorist efforts to break down the consensus of support for authority have consistently failed. The most dangerous potential flaw in the democratic system was revealed as being the possibility of links between right-wing terrorism and security forces. An upsurge of right-wing terror in the 1980s – for example, there were murderous right-wing bomb attacks on Bologna station, the Munich beer festival and Jewish targets in Paris in 1980 – meant that this was a problem that had to be carefully watched for the future.

Brian Markworthy

Below: Beams and masonry scattered over a wide area after the right-wing terrorist bombing of the railway station at Bologna in Italy. The attack was one of the worst acts of European terrorism witnessed in the 1980s. In spite of mounting problems, it was not until after the killing of Aldo Moro in the late 1970s that Italy finally organised an effective anti-terrorist squad of some 150 men drawn from the Carabinieri.

ETA

The Basque guerrilla movement

One of the most persistent and violent of European terrorist movements is Euskadi Ta Askatasun (ETA) – translated as Basque Homeland and Liberty. From the 1960s through to the 1980s these Basque terrorists, never numbering many more than a thousand, have been a major influence on the political life of Spain.

The area inhabited by about one million Basques covers seven provinces of northern Spain and a part of southwest France. Distinct in language and race from other Europeans, the Basques have a distinguished history, although they have never had their own state. A modern Basque nationalist movement grew up in the late 19th century, and a desire for autonomy led the Basques to fight against General Franco's Nationalists in the Spanish Civil War. Franco's victory in 1939 was followed by the rigorous repression of Basque culture and political life through 36 years of dictatorship, although this did not prevent the Basque country from becoming one of the most economically advanced areas of Spain, with most businesses in Basque hands.

In 1959 radicals in the national movement who were keen for action broke away from the Basque Nationalist Party to form ETA. They adopted armed struggle as a tactic and divided their organisation into a political and a military wing, the latter known as ETA-Militar. A major terrorist campaign began in 1967, involving attacks against police and army officers, government officials and public installations. The Franco regime responded with the declaration of a state of emergency and brutal repression. The death penalty was freely used against ETA members after summary trials before military tribunals (the garotte was employed as a method of execution, although in practice many of these sentences were commuted), but support for the terrorists in the Basque country and abroad was reinforced by these tough measures.

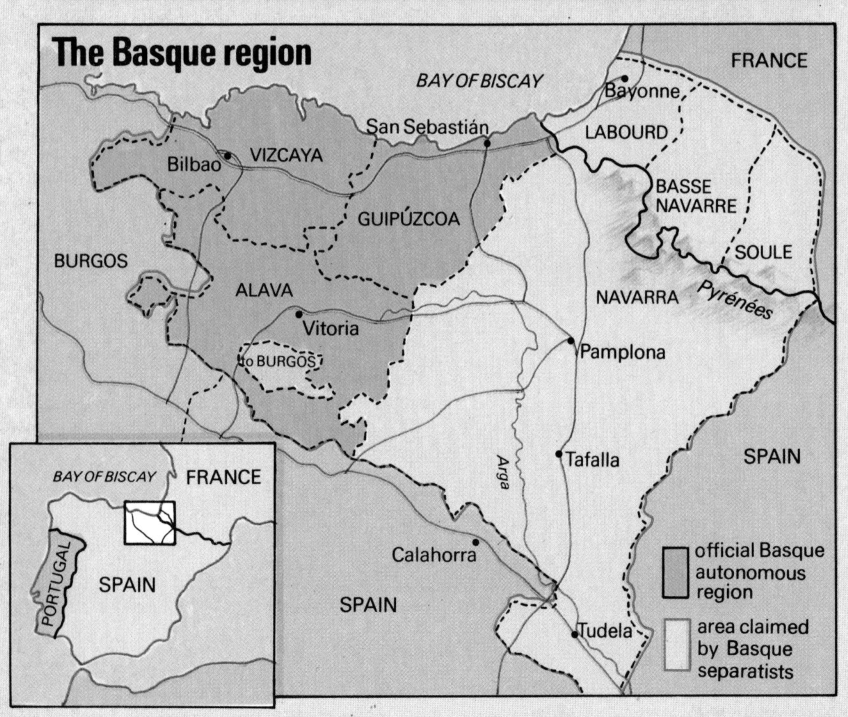

The desire for revolution

As their campaign advanced, ETA moved politically to the left. The old Basque goal of an independent state was joined to a Marxist ideology. The desired Basque state was now to be a socialist republic, but ETA's objectives also spread to embrace a wider perspective. From 1970 onwards they were in contact with terrorist groups from other countries, including the Palestinians, and they soon developed especially close links with the Provisional IRA. Their Basque nationalism became secondary to their desire for revolution, and their goal was set as a revolution in Spain.

The great problem in Spanish politics in the late 1960s and early 1970s was the succession to the ageing General Franco. The system he had established was clearly in need of major overhaul, and in Spain there was a clear desire for wide-ranging reform, but the ruling groups in Spanish society, particularly the army and the police, would be unlikely to tolerate radical change. The intended heir to Franco as head of state was Prince Juan Carlos, the grandson of the last King of Spain (who had left the country in

1931); under the succession law of 1969, Juan Carlos would become king on Franco's death. It was assumed, however, that the authoritarian Francoist regime would carry on, with the new strong man being Franco's prime minister, Admiral Luis Carrero Blanco.

On 20 December 1973, ETA made a decisive contribution to the future of Spanish politics by assassinating Carrero Blanco, in an action notable for the amount of explosive used. About 100 kilos (220lbs) of dynamite were set off under the Admiral's car, the remains of which ended up on the second-storey balcony of an inner courtyard, having been projected over a four-storey building by the force of the blast. It appears that the explosives had been obtained from the Provisional IRA.

Franco died on 19 November 1975, and the immediate result of the installation of the new head of state was a profound liberalisation of Spanish society; Juan Carlos (who had maintained a strictly non-committal political attitude before his accession) showed himself a firm believer in democratic institutions, determined to reinstate Spain within the mainstream of Western European political developments, including membership of Nato and the EEC.

The revolutionary tax

These developments were extremely popular in Spain, except with the main pillars of the Franco regime in the army and the police. ETA, however, set out to wreck the chances of a liberal democracy. Their strategy was to raise the level of terrorist activity to such a point that the army and police would revolt and install an authoritarian regime, theoretically stimulating a revolutionary uprising by the Spanish people. ETA also strove to prevent a solution to the Basque problem. A series of measures lifted the repression from which the Basques suffered, ending with the granting of a large measure of autonomy to the Basque region in 1979. This was acceptable to the moderate Basque nationalists and, as elections showed, to the majority of the Basque people, but this only caused ETA to redirect some of its attacks against moderate Basque leaders.

As democracy was installed and concessions were made, the level of ETA terrorism rose – they were responsible for 19 deaths in 1976, 30 deaths in 1977, 66 deaths in 1978, and 130 deaths in 1979. The army and the police remained the main targets, although Basque businessmen suffered severely as the terrorists attempted to impose a 'revolutionary tax' on local commerce – those who did not pay up were threatened with death. Among their most spectacular operations was the bombing of a Spanish destroyer in a northern port in 1981, causing great damage. The attempt to run a nuclear power station in the Basque country was held back by the assassination of two successive directors of the plant.

The terrorist campaign – in which ETA's efforts were augmented by the smaller-scale activities of the Spanish Grupo da Resistencia Antifascista Primo Octobre (GRAPO) – almost bore its perverse fruit when elements of the army and police attempted a coup in February 1981. If the coup had succeeded, the subsequent repression would have given ETA a chance to test its theory that this would present a favourable revolutionary situation. As it was the coup failed, and despite frequent excesses and abuses by the old Franco-style security forces, the Spanish government has resolutely stuck to its liberal line. A Basque security force is being established to take over control of security in the region from the hated Spanish Guardia Civil, and the political wing of ETA remains legal.

Although support for terrorism among Basques was low in the 1980s, the now-traditional terrorist cell structure adopted by ETA gave it high powers of survival. France provided a relatively safe base from which many of the terrorists could operate – in 1980 a Spanish anti-terrorist force created a diplomatic incident by killing two suspected terrorists in a bar on the French side of the border. The improvement in the quality of Spanish anti-terrorist operations led to numerous arrests and some killings of ETA-Militar members. In the 1980s the security forces were supported by the activities of a shadowy group known as the Anti-Terrorist Liberation Group (GAL) which murdered at least seven ETA gunmen in the frontier region. GAL was believed to consist largely of off-duty police officers hired by Basque industrialists to hit back at ETA.

Since no political concession could satisfy ETA's extremists and since a guerrilla cell structure is so hard to break down, ETA could be expected to continue its activities at some level more or less indefinitely.

Graham Brewer

The aspirations of Basque nationalists towards some form of autonomy were always ruthlessly stifled under General Franco (above left). Franco's authoritarian regime acted in ways that gave the Basque terrorists of ETA a certain amount of international sympathy. Franco's successor, King Juan Carlos (above) instituted a more liberal government, and began a movement towards more autonomy for the Basque country, although this did not satisfy ETA militants, who continued their campaign.

Far left: An ETA member poses with his M16. Below: Members of the ETA Vth Military Group at a bomb-making factory in the Pyrenees.

Death of a democrat

The Italian Red Brigades and the Moro kidnapping

Terrorist activity was a major feature of Italian life in the 1970s. In that decade it is officially estimated there were 9361 terrorist attacks, leading to the deaths of 116 people. And this time span narrowly excludes two major bomb atrocities that would almost double that death toll – one in Milan in December 1969 that killed 14 and the notorious Bologna railway station explosion in August 1980 which massacred 84 people. Both of these murderous attacks were the work of right-wingers nostalgic for the days of Mussolini's Fascist regime, but left-wing urban guerrillas have been responsible for the majority of terrorist acts, chiefly kidnappings and assassinations aimed at Italy's ruling class.

The proliferation of left-wing terrorists in Italy is partly a product of the tradition of violence in modern Italian society, from the heroic example of the armed struggle of the partisans against the Fascists and occupying German Army in 1943-45 to the outright criminality of the Mafia and similar organisations – of the 80 or so kidnappings a year in Italy in the 1970s, over 90 per cent were non-political. But the terrorist upsurge had more to do with the discredit into which the Italian political system had fallen through years of scandal, corruption and governmental inertia since World War II.

The central problem of Italian politics was the position of the Communist Party, the second largest party in Italy after the ruling Christian Democrats, polling about 30 per cent of the votes in elections. During the 1970s the Communist Party moved more and more towards the centre, developing its theory of Eurocommunism distanced from the Soviet Union, but it remained totally excluded from power. Inevitably, left-wing militants became disillusioned with the communist leadership's faith in the democratic road to government and its abandonment of much revolutionary doctrine. It was from among such militants, opposed to the Communist Party as much as to the Christian Democrat establishment and the shadowy Fascist elements in the ruling bureaucracy, that the leftist terror organisations grew.

The first groups to grow out of the radical agitation of the late 1960s, which was as intense in Italy as anywhere in Europe, were unarmed organisations such as Lotta Continua, Avanguardia Operaia and the many anarchist factions that went under the collective name of Autonomia. But as their political aspirations were frustrated, many members of the far left turned to armed struggle. Of the terrorist groups that thus emerged in the 1970s, the most famous was the Brigate Rosse – the Red Brigades.

Their origins are still obscure, though it is generally considered that the founders were Renato Curcio and Margherita Cagol. It is clear that by 1974 the Red Brigades had established contact with international sources of arms and training which made them equipped to begin an armed campaign. Their first major act in that year was the kidnapping of a Genoese magistrate, Sossi, responsible for the arrest and detention of

many militants in the Genoa area. They wished to exchange him for eight prisoners and he was held for 20 days while negotiations took place. Although a district attorney-general finally refused to release the prisoners – an action for which the Red Brigades later killed him – Sossi was freed and was subsequently very respectful to his captors in interviews, saying that he had been well treated.

Curcio was arrested about three weeks after this kidnapping, but was freed from jail in an armed attack led by Cagol in February 1975. Shortly afterwards Cagol was shot by the police, and in January 1976 Curcio was again arrested with four others in Milan. The Brigades then concentrated their efforts on an attempt to prevent Curcio's trial in Turin. They systematically killed magistrates and jurors to such effect that at one stage no-one could be found who was prepared to serve on the jury.

The climax of the Red Brigades' campaign was to come in 1978, a year in which a massive total of 2395 terrorist acts were recorded in Italy. The Red Brigades produced a 'Resolution on Strategic Direction' declaring Italy to be 'the weakest link in the Western democratic chain', and prepared a major coup to unsettle the whole Italian governmental structure – the kidnapping of the president of the Christian Democrat Party, Aldo Moro. As the one Christian Democrat leader whose name was untainted by scandal, Moro was engaged in an audacious initiative to break the deadlock in Italian politics by setting up a coalition government which would rule with official Communist Party support. The Red Brigades were determined to undermine a development which could only solidify Italian democracy in resistance to revolutionary change.

On 16 March 1978 Moro was driven from his apartment in Rome for his habitual morning prayers in a local church. Later in that day he was to inaugurate the new communist-supported coalition government. But the Red Brigades had different ideas. According to members of the Brigades who were subsequently captured and confessed, the kidnap of Moro had been planned for approximately six months. So important was the operation that a special group had been set up, separate from the structure of the Brigades, to carry it out – a fact that was to have major consequences as events developed.

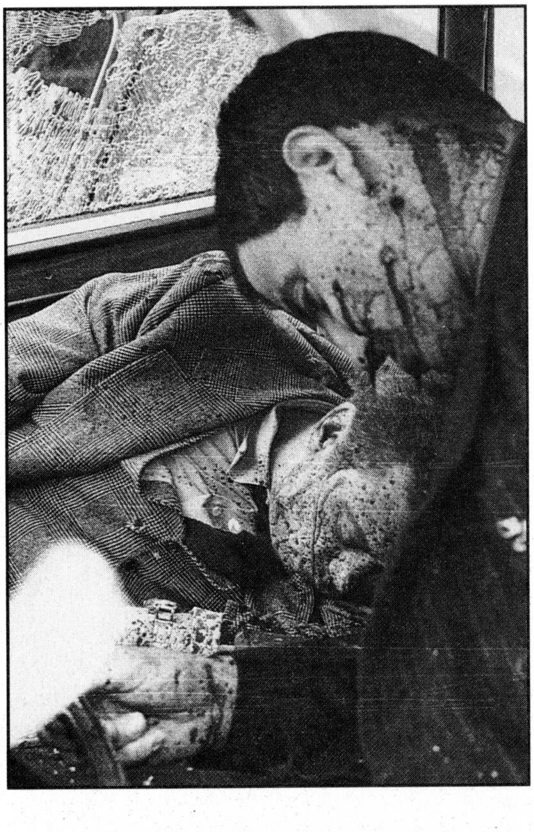

The kidnap group had established as exactly as humanly possible the habits and daily routines of Moro's life. They had observed him in church, watched where he sat in his chauffeur-driven car, observed the movements of his family, and so on. As the planning for the kidnap advanced, the team, composed of 12 people, started to organise the various cars, weapons and hiding places that would be necessary. Moro's life was not in fact especially regular in its routines. There was only one daily recurring event – the journey that Moro, a deeply religious man, always made from his apartment to the Church of Santa Chiara before embarking on his working day. The route took him through a street called Via Fani.

On the morning of 16 March, as usual, Moro was in the back seat of his car with his driver and bodyguard in front. Following was another car with a driver and two more bodyguards. As Moro's car approached the intersection of Via Fani and Via Stresa, a car reversed into Via Fani blocking the way ahead. A Mini Cooper parked by the side of the road prevented Moro's car passing the reversing car, a Fiat 128.

Taking the prisoner

Despite the obvious presence of the car carrying Moro, the Fiat continued to reverse, causing Moro's chauffeur to brake sharply, and the car containing the bodyguards rammed it softly but firmly in the rear. Moro's Fiat 130 was now sandwiched between his bodyguards' Alfa and the reversing Fiat 128. The woman driver of this car and her passenger both leapt out. Moving to cover both sides of Moro's car they produced automatics and riddled Moro's driver and bodyguard with bullets. At the same time four men dressed in the same official-looking clothes and peaked caps moved from where they had been standing on the forecourt of a bar, and started firing on the rear car with sub-machine guns. Two other members of the gang had meanwhile assumed positions in the road to hold back any other traffic which might have interfered.

Moro was bundled into a Fiat 132, which drove off followed by two more cars containing some of the abductors, while others made their escape on foot or on motorcycles. The escape cars drove for a short way and then detoured into a tree-lined private road, where Moro was placed in a trunk which was loaded into the back of a Ford Transit van. This sped him to the place where he was to be imprisoned, a concealed room in a shop near the centre of Rome. Despite the widespread roadblocks and intensive searches that followed the kidnap, the authorities never succeeded in finding him or his abductors.

On the same day as the kidnapping, the new Italian parliament overwhelmingly put into power the government coalition that had been proposed by Moro, bringing the Communist Party into the government process. Almost immediately the government agreed that there would be no negotiations with the Red Brigades.

The first communiqué issued by the Brigades claimed that Moro was being interrogated and was the

Left: The defendants in the Turin trial of Renato Curcio and his associates are led from the courtroom in a former military barracks. Curcio himself had been barred from the courtroom after accusing the presiding judge of corruption. Below: The scene after the abduction of Aldo Moro, as the press and public throng around the trapped cars. Below right: Two of the bodyguards, killed by the terrorists at the time of the kidnapping.

subject of a 'people's trial'. Yet a few days later it was revealed that Moro had been allowed to write letters to his family and to friends in the Christian Democrats. In these letters Moro put forward the idea that his release could be achieved by negotiation, perhaps in exchange for the leaders of the Brigades, including Curcio, at that time being brought to trial in Turin. There was an immediate attempt by the government and the media to discredit these letters with claims that they were obtained under duress, or that Moro had been drugged. (Incidentally, the autopsy carried out after his death revealed no trace of physical torture or drugs.)

As the crisis wore on into its second month, it became clear that Moro was involved in a desperate fight for his life, not only with his captors but also with the leaders of Italy's government. Moro's letters became ever more bitter, especially against his long-time political associates, as they maintained their 'no-negotiations' stance. At times he urged his family to bring about a grass-roots revolt in the Christian Democrats against this policy. As this correspondence went on, the position of the Red Brigades became more and more confused, reflecting a debate taking place inside the organisation, that was also no doubt being affected by Moro's attitude. The autonomous special group set up by the Red Brigades to carry out the Moro kidnapping appears to have followed its own line, independent of any possible control by the rest of the organisation.

In fact the conduct of the Red Brigades throughout the kidnapping shows a confusion of aims. It seems odd that if the kidnapping had been planned for six months, no decisions had been taken about what to do with Moro or what positions to adopt. If the ultimate aim was the release of the prisoners in Turin, the Red Brigades were acting against the experience of the Sossi case. If they believed that Moro would give them information about leading Christian Democrats that they could use, they were both naive and

Plea for life

Above: Aldo Moro in captivity.

Aldo Moro's anguished letters to his Christian Democrat colleagues were a severe embarrassment to them as they pursued their policy of 'no-negotiations'. The following extract is from a letter published on 22 April 1978:

'I believe that you cannot free yourselves from responsibility for the agonising choice that confronts you ... with the easy indifference and cynicism that you have displayed up to now, during these forty days of awful suffering for me. With profound bitterness and shock I have watched you adopt an attitude of rigid rejection....

'I face the solitary fate of the political prisoner condemned to death. If you refuse to intervene, a brutal page will have been written in the history of Italy....'

Right: The discovery of Moro's body in the boot of a Renault 4 in Rome. The car was parked midway between the headquarters of the Christian Democrats and that of the Communist Party, the two parties whose temporary ruling alliance the Red Brigades had hoped to split. Right and below: Red Brigade members believed to be among those responsible for the Moro kidnapping, stand trial. Below right: Intense security accompanied the proceedings against arrested terrorists.

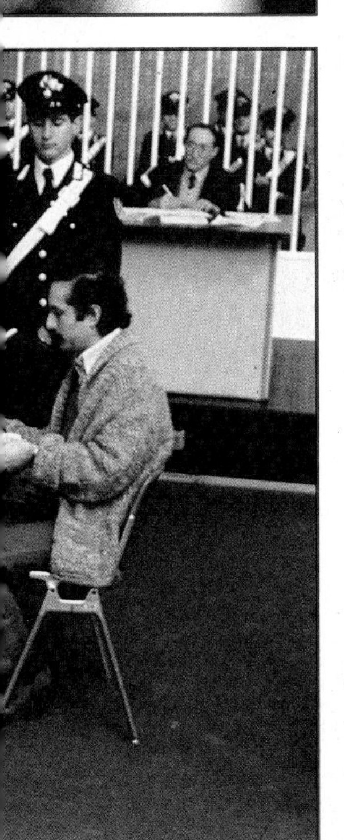

unsuccessful. A phone call made by the Brigades to Moro's family near the end of the drama suggested that their main goal may have been to be accorded some form of political recognition.

Whatever the motives of the Red Brigades, there was undoubtedly a split in the movement over whether to kill Moro or not. His captors first announced that he had been condemned to death after the 'people's trial' on 15 April, but there followed a lengthy delay. It was on 10 May, 54 days after his kidnapping, that Moro's body was found in the back of a Renault 4, parked midway between the headquarters of the Christian Democrats and the Communist Party in Rome – a final ironic punctuation mark to the affair. The hard-liners both in the Red Brigades and in the government had won, and Moro was the sacrificial victim.

A crack-down on terrorism

The results of the Moro killing were hardly favourable to the Red Brigades. His removal from the political scene did aggravate splits within the Christian Democrat Party, and the alliance with the communists did not last – both developments desired by the terrorists – but the alliance was unlikely to have been a success even had Moro lived. The shock of the kidnapping led to a shake-up in Italy's anti-terrorist organisations and the passage of tough legislation which made life more difficult for all militant groups, whether involved in terrorism or not. Rather than encouraging revolutionary attitudes, as urban guerrilla theory suggested, the crack-down discouraged people from getting involved in radical politics. The number of terrorist acts fell sharply from the peak that it had reached in 1978, with 1264 recorded in 1980 – a drop of almost 50 per cent.

By killing Moro the Red Brigades were exposed, even in the eyes of militants, as being at least as ruthless as the political groups they opposed, and they undoubtedly lost support. Leftist groups which continued to express solidarity with other terrorist bodies such as Prima Linea (itself ruthless enough to shoot 10 students at a business college chosen at random in order to discourage others from joining the 'exploiters') distanced themselves from the Red Brigades. It seems clear that if they had let Moro go free after demonstrating that the government would have been prepared to let him die, the Red Brigades could have achieved a major propaganda coup. Why they did not choose this course remains a mystery.

Mike Rossiter

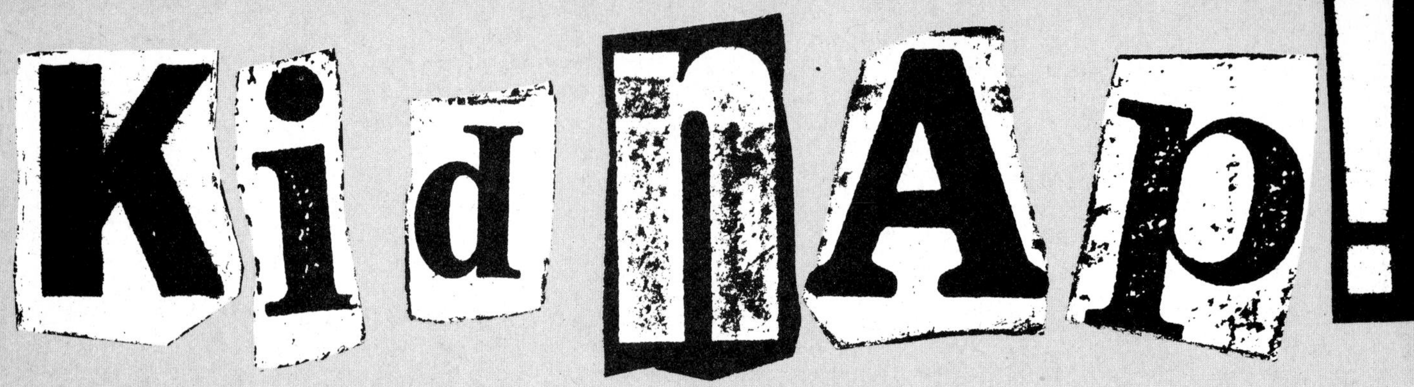

Propaganda, profit and political crime

Together with the hijacking of aircraft, political kidnapping has become one of the most distinctive methods by which modern terrorist groups have brought publicity to their cause. The typical activities of terrorist groups in previous years – assassination, indiscriminate bombings – have, of course, also been employed. But the nature of modern mass communications, and the possibilities of instant publicity, together with the amounts of money that are at the disposal of large corporations, have given the crime of kidnapping a new importance since 1968.

There had been examples of political kidnapping before 1968 – the two British sergeants, Mervyn Paice and Clifford Martin, held and then hanged in July 1947 by the Jewish terrorists of the Irgun were a notorious case. But in general, kidnapping had little place in the guerrilla wars of the 1950s. What changed matters was the growth of urban terrorism, principally in South America but also in Europe during the late 1960s and early 1970s, and the decision by various Palestinian groups that their cause needed publicity.

The hijacking of aircraft and the taking of a mass of hostages is merely an extension of the kidnapping of a single individual; and if that individual is sufficiently famous or powerful, then the publicity and sums of money generated may be large. In general, the taking of a single individual is considered a kidnapping, while the taking of a group of individuals is popularly described as the taking of hostages; but there is an interesting case where the two descriptions merge. In December 1975, terrorists under the notorious 'Carlos' (Ilich Ramirez Sanchez) took over the building in Vienna in which the representatives of the OPEC countries were meeting. The representatives were held hostage for some time, but the incident is normally referred to as the OPEC *kidnap* – presumably on the basis that the hostages were all important figures.

Kidnapping and the taking of hostages have one important element in common, in that they both are attempts to place the onus for the death of those taken prisoner on the state and the security forces rather than on the terrorists themselves. This may be part of a tactic of trying to demonstrate that the state is essentially a repressive force; and it also places great strains on the security apparatus, which has to work out the best way of freeing the victims without appearing to give in to such methods.

Kidnapping can work effectively only where the government involved is genuinely embarrassed by the fact of the kidnap, and will do its utmost to recover the victim unharmed. It would be unlikely that the Israelis would treat the kidnap of one of their officials by Palestinians in the same way that the Argentinians, for example, treated the kidnap of the US ambassador

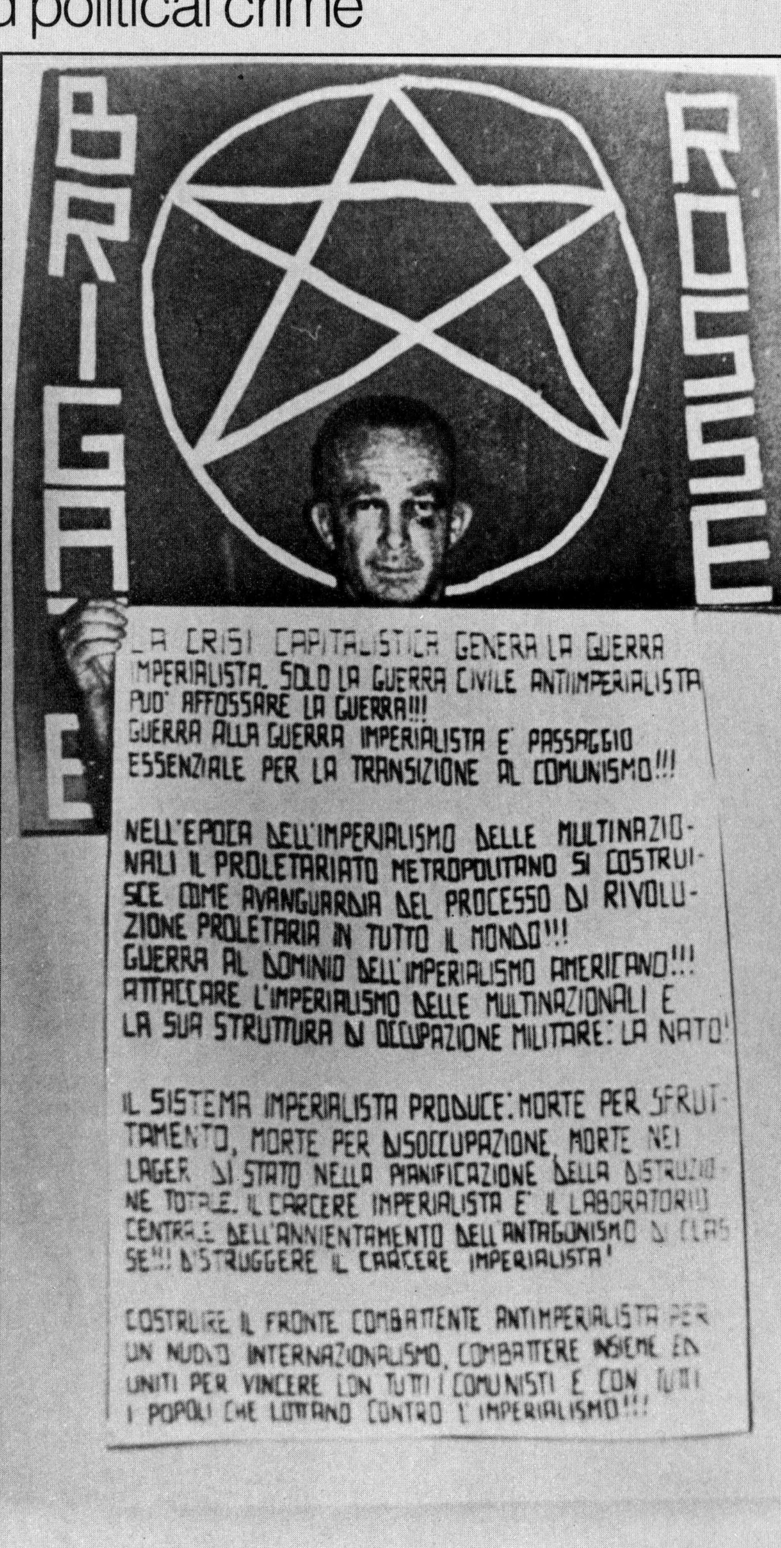

to Argentina in 1969. The Israelis would feel that any of their officials had to risk being a casualty in what they see as a war for survival, and would be unlikely to give in to demands, whereas the Argentinians were acutely conscious that they were responsible for the safety of a major official of their most important ally. For the Palestinian groups of the 1970s to make an effective point, they felt they had to threaten the lives of hundreds of innocent individuals, preferably of many different nationalities (to ensure maximum worldwide concern) caught up in a hijack. But a group operating in West Germany or Italy could expect to create considerable anxiety within the political world by kidnapping one prominent figure.

The aims of the kidnapper

In general, there are five goals for which political kidnappers are aiming. These almost always overlap, in that most of them are involved in any one incident, but they can be described separately. The first of these goals is sheer publicity – to attract world attention to the cause that the terrorists espouse and to show that they are an effective grouping. In this respect, the kidnap of British ambassador Geoffrey Jackson by the Uruguayan Tupamaros in January 1971 was very successful. The Tupamaros brought home to Western Europeans how effectively they could operate and obtained publicity on a wide scale.

Then, there may be the desire to put pressure on foreign interests within a country. The fact that US businessmen have been prime targets for Latin American kidnappers is not unconnected to the fact that radical thought in Latin America generally condemns the economic power wielded by US interests in the continent. And in Turkey, there have been several kidnaps of Nato personnel by left-wing groups who claim that the Western alliance is inimical to their country's interests.

Thirdly, kidnapping may be a means of entering the political arena. The kidnapping of the Quebec labour minister, Pierre Laporte, on 10 October 1970 was a direct attempt by the FLQ to force the hand of the government of Pierre Trudeau during the heated atmosphere following the kidnapping of the British trade commissioner for Quebec earlier that month. Similarly, the Aldo Moro kidnapping in Italy, carried out by the Red Brigades, was in part an attempt to undermine cooperation between communists and Christian Democrats.

These first three aims are rather vague, and were they the only motives behind the crime, then kidnapping would hardly have assumed the importance that it has. The final two sets of motives are, however, usually very concrete, and it is on the fulfilment of these conditions that negotiations hinge, and over which the problems arise. The first of these more concrete aims is the release or better treatment of prisoners – normally, members of terrorist groups captured previously. Most kidnaps include such a demand – from the Tupamaros asking for the release of 150 of their members as a condition for the safe return of Geoffrey Jackson to the Basques of ETA who requested that the death sentence on six of their members be commuted in return for the release of the West German honorary consul whom they had taken in December 1970. Sometimes this aspect of kidnapping has led to interesting strings of incidents. In April 1974, Rose Dugdale stole a valuable art collection which she threatened to destroy unless four convicted IRA men were transferred from British to Irish gaols. She was captured (and the art collection recovered unharmed) but then, two years later, Dugdale's lover, Eddie Gallagher, kidnapped a Dutch industrialist, Tiede Herrema, in an attempt to secure her release (this also failed and Gallagher was gaoled).

The fifth motive concerns money. Few kidnaps, or hijacks for that matter, are not associated with the demand for large sums of money. In some, the money is merely part of the operation, but in others the terrorist group has little further aim. In Argentina during the early 1970s, this was a particularly important element, the climax being reached when the American business executive Victor Samuelson was released in April 1974 by the ERP urban guerrillas after a ransom of over $14 million had been paid. British business executive Charles Lockwood was actually kidnapped twice, by separate Argentinian urban guerrilla groups. The fact that business executives in South America began to take out insurance against the need to pay large ransoms may have

Left: US General Dozier, kidnapped by the Red Brigades in December 1981, here shown beneath the terrorists' banner. The kidnap was in protest against Italian membership of Nato. Below: Political kidnapping in South America could be very effective. These Brazilian political prisoners are being flown to Mexico in exchange for the return of the US Ambassador C. Burke Elbrick, kidnapped by Brazilian terrorists in September 1969.

Above: Irishman Eddie Gallagher (left) is escorted by police from the house where, for 36 days, he had held the Dutch industrialist Tiede Herrema in an attempt to secure the release of Rose Dugdale. After an 18-day siege, Gallagher surrendered to security forces.

contributed to the rapid escalation in the sums of money demanded.

It is the possibility of obtaining large amounts of money that forms the link between kidnapping as a political act and kidnapping as a crime in which profit is the only motive. In Italy, the number of criminal kidnappings has far outweighed the number of politically motivated acts in recent years – as many as 90 per cent of Italian kidnappings in recent times have been purely criminal in motive – and in the late 1970s there were about 80 kidnaps per year. In Northern Ireland the line between what constitutes a political crime and one carried out purely for monetary gain has become blurred. IRA men kidnapped supermarket company head Don Tidey in November 1983 and demanded a ransom of £5 million, while they are widely believed to have stolen the champion racehorse Shergar earlier in the same year, initiating a series of secret negotiations which had little in common with the quest for publicity that marks most political kidnaps.

Money and manifestos

The actual mechanics of political kidnaps tend to follow a rigid pattern. The victims are normally at their most vulnerable when travelling by car; the kidnappers will try to arrange to stop the car, and spirit their target away unharmed or only lightly wounded while behaving with complete ruthlessness towards any security guards – the three guards accompanying Hanns-Martin Schleyer were all killed by the Red Army Fraction members who ambushed them. Then there are the demands – often for a publication of various manifestos (not normally a sticking point in negotiations) – the despatch of photographs of the victim (holding a recent newspaper or some other easily dated article to prove that he is still alive) to the press and television and the major demands – for money and for the release of prisoners.

If the activities of the terrorist groups are stereotyped, so too is the response of the authorities: in spite of the range of possible options, their first impulse is to refuse to meet all the demands of the terrorists, but to enter into negotiations in order to buy time during which they frantically try to locate the hideout where the victim is being held. For if they can locate the hideout, then the whole scenario changes dramatically, and it is they who hold the initiative, and can threaten to storm the terrorists' lair at any moment.

The obvious answer to kidnapping is to refuse point-blank to meet the demands of the kidnappers, in order to impress potential future kidnappers that there is no point in pursuing such a tactic. This hardline approach may be very difficult to maintain, however, especially where the captive is an important representative of a friendly power. A common response is to give in to some of the demands and then to mount a rigorous crackdown on potential terrorists – the first of the major South American kidnaps, that of the US ambassador to Brazil in September 1969, was a success for the guerrillas in that they obtained the release of 15 of their members, but the government then inaugurated a wave of repression that led to the arrest of 4000 left-wingers.

Such extreme procedures are not open to the more liberal societies of Western Europe, and there the response has been more circumspect. Yet in spite of the difficulties, the Western European governments have in general formulated an effective response to the tactic of kidnapping, based upon a refusal to be panicked into over-reaction and carefully implementing measures that have squeezed the life out of terrorism. When the West Germans, for example, had to deal with the kidnapping of politician Peter Lorenz in 1975 by terrorists who demanded the release of five members of the Baader-Meinhof gang, the government capitulated and set the prisoners free. But all the while, it was building up its intelligence network on Baader-Meinhof, recruiting skilled squads to deal with specific outrages. When Hanns-Martin Schleyer was kidnapped in September 1977, an incident linked to the hijacking of an airliner to Mogadishu, the government took a firmer line. The airliner was eventually stormed, and although Schleyer was shot by his captors, the episode in effect broke Baader-Meinhof. A graduated response, in which the civil freedoms of the mass of the population were respected, has proved its worth.

Despite the government successes of the late 1970s, political kidnapping will always be a difficult terror tactic to combat in modern society. Although the most rigorous precautions can be taken to ensure the safety of the individual – special cars, bodyguards, elaborate security at home and in government buildings – the ultimate defence must lie in an effective government response that will deter the terrorists from committing the crime. Since 1980, kidnapping has declined in scale. But who can say that it will not reappear as a terrorist tactic at some time in the near future?

Julian Williams

Below: A Turkish soldier trains his machine gun on terrorists who sit atop the roof of a building where they are holding a 14-year old Turkish schoolgirl hostage. The siege ended in bloodshed when the army shot the two gunmen. The girl, however, was safely rescued.

Key Weapons

THE JAGUAR

The Jaguar is a single-seat attack and tactical-nuclear strike aircraft, built as a collaborative venture by Britain and France. When discussions began on the project in the mid-1960s, the requirements of the Royal Air Force and the Armée de l'Air differed quite considerably. The British were primarily interested in acquiring a new advanced training aircraft to replace the Gnat and Hunter, whereas France needed a strike/attack aircraft to re-equip tactical fighter squadrons operating such elderly types as the Mystère IV, Super Mystère B2 and F-100D. However, as each air force was prepared to accept the other's primary mission as a desirable secondary capability for its new aircraft, sufficient common ground existed to enable a joint requirement to be drawn up. As the programme developed, the RAF changed its ideas about the Jaguar's role. Its initial plan had been to acquire 150 two-seat training aircraft, but in 1970 this was drastically revised and a firm order was placed for 165 single-seat attack aircraft and 35 trainers (two additional trainers were later ordered for the Empire Test Pilots' School). The Jaguar therefore entered RAF service in the strike/attack role and the less costly British Aerospace Hawk T Mk 1 was developed to meet the advanced trainer requirement.

The terms of Anglo-French collaboration on the Jaguar were set out in a memorandum of understanding which was signed by representatives of the two governments in May 1965. This agreement also covered development of the AFVG (Anglo-French variable geometry) advanced strike fighter, a project which was cancelled when France withdrew two years later. The Jaguar avoided this pitfall of international collaboration, but in the event many of the financial savings which were expected from the sharing of research and development costs and the economies of a longer production run failed to materialise. Nonetheless in technical terms Anglo-French cooperation was a success, producing a warplane capable of carrying a heavy warload over a tactical radius of some 800km (500 miles) and operating at low level to evade enemy air defences.

The Jaguar's airframe was produced by the Breguet company in France and by the British Aircraft Corporation (BAC – later absorbed by British Aerospace). The two companies cooperated within the joint organisation SEPECAT (Société Européenne de Production de l'Avion Ecole de Combat et Appui Tactique). The basic configuration followed that of the Breguet Br 121 design study, but numerous engineering changes were incorporated by BAC. Production was split between the two companies, with BAC building the wings, rear fuselage and tail, and Breguet the forward and centre fuselage. Final assembly lines were set up at both Toulouse in France and Preston in Britain. The aircraft's Adour turbofan engines were similarly produced in collaboration between Rolls-Royce and Turboméca, but the avionics fitted to French and British Jaguars were entirely different.

The basic single-seat Jaguar is a small aircraft, with an overall length of 16.83m (55ft 2in) and a wingspan of 8.69m (28ft 6in). Its airframe is constructed mostly of high-strength light alloy, with some titanium components used in the engine bay. The shoulder-mounted wing incorporates full-span, double-slotted flaps and leading-edge slats, which give excellent low-speed handling characteristics during the landing approach. Roll control is achieved through wing-mounted spoilers, rather than the conventional ailerons, and the tailplane is an all-moving unit. The twin Adour turbofans each develop 3645kg (8040lb) of thrust with reheat, and internal fuel capacity is 4200 litres (924 gallons). The twin-wheel main landing gear and single-wheel nose unit are fitted with low-pressure tyres to allow the aircraft to operate from rough airstrips. Armament comprises two built-in cannon, which are 30mm DEFA in the French versions or 30mm Aden in the British. Up to 4535kg (10,000lb) of ordnance can be carried on the fuselage stores station and four underwing hardpoints, and an overwing mounting for Sidewinder or Magic air-to-air missiles for self-defence has been developed for the export Jaguar International.

Previous page: An RAF Jaguar outside its hardened shelter on a German airfield. Above: An underside view of an RAF Jaguar revealing one of its 30mm cannon ports. Opposite page top: A Jaguar releases a 454kg (1000lb) retard bomb on a low level pass at 450 knots. Opposite page centre: A Jaguar in flight, armed with Matra R550 Magic air-to-air missiles mounted on special overwing pylons.

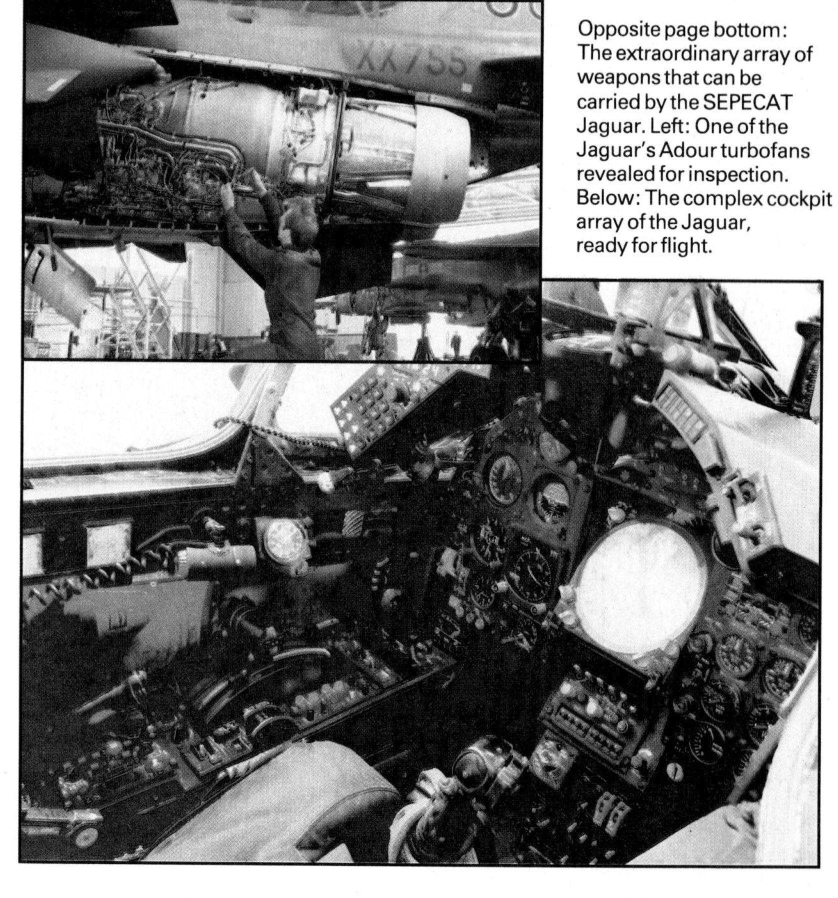

Opposite page bottom: The extraordinary array of weapons that can be carried by the SEPECAT Jaguar. Left: One of the Jaguar's Adour turbofans revealed for inspection. Below: The complex cockpit array of the Jaguar, ready for flight.

Much of the Jaguar's capability as an attack aircraft derives from its avionics systems. Those of the British Jaguar GR Mk 1 are highly advanced, comprising an integrated navigation/attack system which is capable of finding and attacking fixed targets in all weathers. The heart of the system, which is known by the acronym NAVWASS (navigation and weapons aiming sub-system), is a digital computer which receives data on the aircraft's position from an inertial navigation set and conveys it to the pilot on a moving map cockpit display and a HUD (head-up display). The HUD, which has the appearance of a gunsight, is mounted behind the windscreen in the pilot's line-of-sight and displays all essential navigation, flight instrument and weapons aiming data. The inertial navigation set can be pre-programmed with various targets and 'waypoints' along the route. It will then direct the aircraft to its target, often following an evasive routing to avoid enemy defences, without the need for any external references. However, its accuracy can be checked by the pilot referring to a prominent landmark along the route and any drift from the pre-programmed track can thereby be identified and corrected. Once the target is reached, the computer is fed with accurate range information using the nose-mounted laser rangefinder. Thereafter the computer can execute a fully-automatic attack or it can instruct the pilot when to release his weapons. The Jaguar can also detect targets laser-designated by an airborne or ground-based forward air controller. This system enables the Jaguar to find and attack a fixed target with considerable precision whatever the weather, although as the aircraft does not have an attack radar it is not able to detect mobile targets in conditions of poor visibility.

Apart from differences in the avionics, the single-seat Jaguar A of the Armée de l'Air and Jaguar GR Mk 1 of the RAF are broadly similar. The two-seat Jaguar E and Jaguar T Mk 2 conversion trainers have a fuselage lengthened by just under one metre (3 ft) to accommodate the second cockpit and one of the built-in cannon has been deleted. A fifth variant, the Jaguar M, was intended for service with the Aéronavale aboard the French aircraft carriers *Clemenceau* and *Foch*. However, this version was abandoned in favour of the Super Etendard after a single prototype had been tested. In Britain the Jaguar has been

SEPECAT Jaguar

Type Single-seat strike/attack aircraft
Dimensions Span 8.69m (28ft 6in); length 16.83m (55ft 2in); height 4.89m (16ft)
Weight Empty 7000kg (15,430lb); maximum take-off 15,500kg (34,000lb)
Powerplant Two 3645kg (8040lb) thrust Rolls-Royce/Turboméca Ardour 804 turbofans with reheat

Performance Maximum speed at high altitude Mach 1.6 or 1698km/h (1055mph)
Range Combat radius with internal fuel approx 800km (500 miles)
Armament Two 30mm Aden or DEFA cannon with 150 rounds of ammunition per gun; up to 4535kg (10,000lb) of ordnance including tactical nuclear weapons, Martel and AS 30L ASM, anti-airfield, cluster, laser-guided and 'iron' bombs; unguided rockets; two AIM-9 Sidewinder or Matra 550 Magic AAMs on overwing pylons

experimentally fitted with a 'fly by wire' control system, with electronically-signalled commands to the control surfaces replacing the conventional mechanical linkages. Some work has also been done on designing a new, large-area wing for the Jaguar, making use of carbon-fibre composites rather than metal alloy construction.

Britain has taken the lead in promoting the Jaguar International for export. This is because since 1967 Breguet has been controlled by the Dassault company, which has preferred to promote its own products such as the Mirage F1 and Mirage 2000 in competition with the Jaguar. British export successes include orders from India (116 aircraft), Oman (24 aircraft), Ecuador (12 aircraft) and Nigeria (18 aircraft). One option available to overseas customers is a maritime strike version of the Jaguar, fitted with a Thomson-CSF Agave radar.

The Armée de l'Air procured a total of 200 Jaguars, comprising 160 single-seat Jaguar As and 40 Jaguar E trainers. Jaguars first entered service with Escadron 1/7 'Provence' at Saint-Dizier in mid-1973 and currently equip three Escadres de Chasse (EC 3 at Nancy, EC 7 at Saint-Dizier and EC 11 at Toul). Their component squadrons undertake a variety of missions, including tactical-nuclear strike, electronic warfare, ground attack and operational conversion. EC 3/11 'Corse' is responsible for the support of French overseas 'fire brigade' operations and has seen action against Polisario guerrillas in the Western Sahara and also in Chad.

The first RAF squadron to operate the Jaguar was No. 54 Squadron, which received its first aircraft at Lossiemouth in March 1974. There are currently eight front-line Jaguar squadrons in RAF service, plus an operational conversion unit. Nos. 14, 17, 20 and 31 Squadrons operate in the strike/

Left, from top to bottom: Two Jaguars bank over the French coast; a two-seater Jaguar in flight; an RAF Jaguar taxies over rough ground at Boscombe Down; the advanced fly-by-wire Jaguar takes off with the new wing strakes clearly visible.

attack role in RAF Germany. Nos. 6 and 54 Squadrons carry out similar missions with RAF Strike Command in the United Kingdom. Two squadrons (No. 41 Squadron in Britain and No. 2 Squadron in Germany) specialise in tactical reconnaissance and their Jaguars are fitted with an under-fuselage pod containing cameras and infra-red linescan equipment. The units in RAF Germany have recently been supplied with improved electronic counter-measures equipment and laser-guided bombs to improve their operational capabilities. However, all these squadrons are re-equipping with Tornados, which will leave the three UK-based squadrons and No. 226 Operational Conversion Unit as the only operators of the Jaguar within the RAF.

Above: Two Jaguars from RAF Bruggen. The Jaguar in the background is armed with laser-guided bombs on inboard pylons, ECM pod on the port outer pylon and a chaff dispenser on the starboard outer pylon, while the foreground Jaguar is equipped with more conventional armaments comprising eight 454kg (1000lb) bombs. Main picture and below: Sea trials of the French Jaguar M (naval version) aboard the aircraft carrier *Clemenceau*.

Above: Two S version Jaguar International aircraft from the Sultan of Oman's Air Force on patrol over rugged Omani terrain. They are armed with Sidewinder air-to-air missiles on the outboard underwing pylons.

Right: Two Jaguar International aircraft supplied to the Indian Air Force, comprising a single seat S and a two-seat trainer B version. Below: Similar in camouflage scheme to the RAF version, a Jaguar of the Ecuadorian Air Force skims over the jungle highlands on a routine patrol mission.

Revolutionaries in uniform

From military coup to democracy in Portugal

In April 1974 a military coup in Portugal, on the western seaboard of Europe, set in motion events that were to threaten the integrity of the Nato alliance and tip the strategic balance in southern Africa in favour of the communist bloc. It also gave a striking example of how the military can involve itself in politics in a manner far removed from the conventional image of authoritarian colonels imposing order by force.

Portugal was – and is – one of the poorest countries in Europe. From 1932 to 1968 it had experienced the conservative authoritarian rule of Prime Minister Antonio de Oliveira Salazar, under a military president who symbolised the armed forces' support for the regime but did not get involved in political decision-making. In 1968 Salazar was replaced by Marcello Caetano who sought to liberalise the state in small ways, in keeping with the slow but real modernisation of the country's economy. As usual with such attempts to reform a long-established regime, Caetano's measures offended conservatives and failed to satisfy advocates of change.

Both Portugal and its neighbour Spain were being watched by Nato leaders with interest. Portugal was a founder-member of the alliance (although it had been neutral for most of World War II), whereas Spain was not yet a member since, despite its close links with the United States, Franco's regime was not considered acceptable as an ally by European Nato states. To integrate Spain into Nato after Franco's anticipated demise would much strengthen Nato's position in the Mediterranean, and eyes were fixed on the succession in Madrid. Portugal was not considered likely to pose such problems, but it was if anything strategically more vital. This was partly because of its contribution to the defence of the North Atlantic, through its fine deep-water harbours on the mainland and through the Azores – islands in the mid-Atlantic that were an integral part of the Portuguese republic – where there was a major US base. But Portugal's main strategic importance lay in its continuing involvement in Africa.

Since the early 1960s Portugal had been fighting a series of debilitating wars against guerrilla forces in Angola, Mozambique and Guinea. At first embarrassed by Salazar's apparently archaic determination to maintain his country's empire when other Western countries were decolonising, the Nato powers had in time come to see Portugal's resistance to the Marxist liberation movements as vital to Western strategic interests. Angola, in particular, was rich in raw materials and a valuable prize. But despite growing military aid from Nato sources, Portugal was finding the wars an ever-increasing drain on its economy. High casualty rates and the need for four years' conscription – the longest conscription period in Europe – helped confirm the unpopularity of the wars.

The origins of the 1974 coup lay not in any of Portugal's major problems at home or abroad, however, but in a tactical mistake by the Caetano government. In July 1973 the government decreed

Above: A Portuguese soldier displays the symbols of a peaceful revolution – pink and red carnations. Although many Portuguese troops were initially uncertain of their position during the uprising of 25 April 1974, the majority were quick to join the celebrations after the success of the coup.

that conscript officers – mostly university graduates from privileged families – should have improved promotion prospects. Regular officers were outraged, especially those of the rank of captain or major. They saw themselves as having worked hard through years of service to achieve their position by their own efforts, and were now to find themselves by-passed in the struggle for higher rank. Disgruntled officers, initially from the army but soon from all the services, formed themselves into a clandestine Armed Forces Movement (Movimento das Forças Armadas – MFA) and held meetings at which hundreds of junior officers were present. Wider issues, such as discontent with the conduct of the African wars and disapproval of the government's general handling of affairs, soon superseded the initial issue. Most of the officers concerned lacked any clear political ideas, and the leadership of the movement was quickly dominated by a minority with Marxist leanings, such as Colonel Vasco Gonçalves and Captain Otelo Saraiva de Carvalho. The existence of an active Marxist minority in the officer corps was partly the result of the blatant injustices and backwardness of Portuguese society – similar features have provoked such ideological responses among officers in many Third World countries – but also the consequence of the guerrilla wars. Some of the MFA radicals had met and talked with Marxists from the African liberation movements, and all of them had studied the thought of their guerrilla enemies as a part of counter-insurgency training. It was easy to apply the same analysis to impoverished Portugal as the guerrillas had applied to the colonies.

Searching for a figurehead

On its own the MFA was not strong enough to carry out a coup, however; it needed a senior officer as a figurehead to win over the armed forces as a whole. In February 1974 the man they needed was revealed as General Antonio de Spínola. The flamboyant general had returned from Guinea in 1972 with a reputation as a military hero and had taken up the post of deputy chief of staff. In February 1974 he published *Portugal and the Future*, a book proposing a modest change in the country's colonial policy, whose contents had been approved by Prime Minister Caetano and the chief of staff, General Costa Gomes. But more conservative military leaders, supported by the president Admiral Américo Thomás, were outraged; in March they demanded, and got, Spínola's dismissal.

Almost simultaneously, on 16 March, elements of the MFA launched an ill-planned premature attempt at a coup. Ten armoured vehicles and 200 soldiers advanced on Lisbon from the north, only to be stopped, without bloodshed, by elements of the paramilitary Republican National Guard (GNR) and the Seventh Cavalry. The secret police, the DGS, proceeded with a minor purge of officers that confirmed existing hostility to the regime.

The MFA had established contact with Spínola even before his dismissal; now the general agreed to a watered-down MFA programme, although he did not involve himself in operational planning for a coup. The plan was in fact drawn up by Captain Otelo de Carvalho, and was set in motion at just after midnight on the night of 24/25 April by the broadcasting of a chosen popular song on a commercial radio station. At this signal, a column of armoured vehicles set out from the cavalry training school at Santarem, 65km (40 miles) from Lisbon, reaching the Praça do Comercio in Lisbon – where crucial ministries were located – by 0300 hours. Other units seized the radio and television stations and airports, while the headquarters of the Republican National Guard, who were expected to remain loyal to the regime, was surrounded. Much of the army was uncertain in its response, but by the evening of 25 April Caetano had agreed to hand over to General Spínola, and all thought of resistance collapsed. The streets of Lisbon filled with jubilant crowds as civilians fraternised with soldiers and the red carnation was adopted as the symbol of a peaceful revolution. Only four people were killed, outside the secret police headquarters before the policemen were taken off to occupy the cells vacated by their former prisoners.

The coup was only the beginning, however, of a prolonged political crisis. Spínola became president at the head of a Junta of National Salvation, with a civilian government including the leaders of the Socialist and Communist Parties (Mario Soares and Alvaro Cunhál respectively), both former victims of repression by the previous regime and now returned from exile. The Communist Party revealed itself as by far the best organised political grouping in the country, with strong support in the industrial areas near Lisbon and in the rural south of Portugal. But the dominant political presence after the coup was, logically enough, that of the people who had made it – the radical officers of the MFA. To win Spínola's support they had agreed to a mild liberal democratic programme, but their intentions were far more revolutionary. With most right-wing officers removed in the aftermath of the coup – many joining the deposed Caetano in exile in Brazil – the MFA radicals were able to command the acquiescence of their less politicised colleagues. Only three months after the coup, in July 1974, the MFA was able to install its own prime minister, Vasco Gonçalves, and to establish an Operational Command for the Continent (COPCON) under Otelo de Carvalho. COPCON was given responsibility for internal security and would soon use its power to move the country leftwards.

Spínola fought a desperate rearguard action against the Gonçalves government's colonial policy. With the full approval of the Socialist and Communist Parties, all plans to consult the wishes of the population in the colonies had been abandoned; instead, independence was to be granted as soon as possible under those Marxist liberation movements for which the Portuguese left felt such an affinity. Spínola tried to organise a handover in Angola to the two pro-Western parties instead, but his power at home was crumbling. In a desperate bid to restore his authority, at the end of September Spínola called for a mass

Above: Jubilant troops celebrate with civilians after the bloodless coup that overthrew the Caetano administration. Right: Cheers and handshakes greet Dr Mario Soares as he prepares to address a conference in Lisbon. The Socialist Party that Soares led was one of the main beneficiaries of the coup.

Below: The leaders of the Junta of National Salvation, Spínola (centre), Admiral Azevedo (right) and General Gomez (left). Right: Portuguese civilians pass food to victorious troops aboard a tank. It was an armoured column that made the decisive move in the coup.

demonstration by his civilian supporters, during which he would have ordered the arrest of the leading MFA radicals. But COPCON troops and armed Communist militants manned barricades around Lisbon to prevent the Spínola supporters assembling and, admitting defeat, on 30 September Spínola resigned the presidency, bitterly denouncing Portugal's 'new slavery'.

Spínola was replaced by General Costa Gomes, the chief of staff, and the leftward drift continued. By now, a military coup was turning into a full-scale revolution; workers took over their factories, estates in the south were seized by armed peasants, remaining non-socialist parties and news media came under increasing attack, and in the armed forces themselves discipline deteriorated as soldiers took up the radical ideas and refused to obey orders from conservative officers. Opponents of the revolution struggled to

organise a counter-coup. A Portuguese Liberation Army (ELP) was formed by ex-Salazarists in Spain, while inside Portugal Spínola cultivated contacts with officers still under his influence. Spínola hoped that if he could seize key points, the uncommitted army officers would rally to him. However, the coup attempt was botched. On 10 March 1975 Spínola arrived at Tancos air force base, whose commander was one of his supporters, and ordered an attack on Lisbon. Two Harvard trainers, three helicopter gunships and eight transport helicopters carrying 160 paratroopers took off for the capital. The barracks of the radical-dominated Light Artillery Regiment (RAL-1) was bombed and the airport was seized, but no other units responded. Without support the rebels quickly surrendered, and Spínola fled to Brazil.

In the aftermath of these events the radical officers consolidated their power. The Junta was replaced by a Supreme Revolutionary Council, and the leaders of all the political parties campaigning for election to a constituent assembly – that is, parties from the centre leftwards, since right-wing parties were banned – had to formally accept continued military supervision of the state for at least the following five years. The elections, held on 25 April 1975, gave the Socialist Party by far the largest vote, but the MFA ignored this democratic mandate and maintained Vasco Gonçalves in power. The political parties were now clearly split between the Socialist and centre parties which wanted a Western-style democratic regime and the Communist Party and its allies who supported the MFA's revolutionary stance.

The Nato powers watched the developments in Portugal and its colonies with alarm. As it happened, the United States was peculiarly ill-placed to intervene. The experience of Vietnam and the Watergate scandal had made both foreign intervention in general and covert operations by the CIA in particular highly unpopular. Two years earlier, in Chile, the Americans had played an active role in the overthrow of a left-wing regime, but now such action seemed impossible. Some money was channelled to the Socialist Party, seen as the most likely option to stop the communists, and US officials cultivated contacts with non-radicals in the armed forces, but their main contribution to the situation was negative. Firstly, along with other Nato powers, the US refused to provide the financial aid Portugal desperately needed to weather the economic crisis that political events had brought in their wake; secondly, the US Secretary of State Henry Kissinger actively warned the Soviet Union against any involvement, suggesting that it would be seen as contrary to the spirit of detente. The only area where there were plans for positive action in the case of a definitive left-wing triumph was the Azores. To protect their base at Lajes on the islands, the Americans had held discussions with an Azores liberation movement based in the United States – through emigration there were more Azoreans in America than on the islands – and the US government was prepared to recognise the independence of the Azores if the need arose. All this time, Portugal remained a member of Nato, although it was asked to withdraw from the sensitive nuclear planning group.

By the summer of 1975 the situation in Portugal was approaching civil war. The country was dangerously split between the north, where a population of peasant smallholders fearful of communism and loyal to the Catholic Church took part in violent assaults upon Communist Party offices, and Lisbon and the south, where industrial workers and landless agricultural labourers remained solidly behind the left. Divisions within the armed forces were also acute. For the first time the more moderate majority among the officer corps began to organise against the radical MFA leadership. At the same time, pro-radical organisations developed within the other ranks and mutinies broke out here and there. To add to the chaos, tens of thousands of white refugees were arriving from Angola, fleeing the gathering civil war; most were

Below: Portuguese sailors take to the streets in support of a popular demonstration. It was the fact that the armed forces were becoming increasingly discontented with the debilitating African wars that removed a major prop from the authoritarian regime that had ruled Portugal since the 1930s.

bitter against the left-wing government that had 'sold them out'. On the other side, several thousand left-wing adventurers had arrived, eager to fight for the revolution.

By the end of August the government was manifestly unable to control most of the country, and Vasco Gonçalves was forced to resign. There was no replacement available, however, who could command confidence. As the economy and public order deteriorated, it seemed only a matter of time before the backlash struck. The moderate officers were in close contact with the Socialist Party and also with Spínola's organisation in exile which had established a commando force in Spain. Opinion in the officer corps was generally not favourable to the reinstatement of Spínola, however, preferring a mildly socialist democracy. With this in view, they awaited a pretext for a coup.

On 25 November paratroopers known to be supporters of the radical COPCON chief Otelo de Carvalho seized airbases around Lisbon, at Monsanto, Montijo, Tancos and Monreal. Since all aircraft had been removed from these bases just previously and since other units favourable to Otelo were clearly taken by surprise by the move, it is generally assumed that the paratroopers had been 'set up' by their opponents. Forces loyal to Colonel Ramalho Eanes, a member of the MFA who had emerged as the leader of the non-radical officers, went smoothly into action against the apparent attempted left-wing coup. By the following morning the paratroopers had surrendered. Other radical units were also neutralised, the only deaths occurring when pro-Eanes commandos clashed with a unit of the military police. Otelo and some 80 other left-wing officers were arrested, and COPCON was disbanded. The revolution was over.

Eanes became chief of staff and under his supervision Portugal developed into a democracy, but still with a socialist constitution and an armed forces council keeping an eye on the government. Eanes himself was elected president in 1976 (Otelo was allowed to stand in the elections despite having been arrested earlier), and Socialist leader Mario Soares became the first prime minister under the new constitution. One of Eanes' first acts was to begin a massive reduction in the size of the armed forces, so that the large conscript army that had fought the colonial wars was replaced by a smaller, more professional body. Portugal was gradually reintegrated into Nato: in 1978 it formed its first Nato brigade and in 1980 was readmitted to the nuclear planning group. With Spain joining Nato in 1982, the alliance appeared to have come very successfully through the problematic period.

But the most lasting effects of Portugal's flirtation with Marxist revolution were very damaging to the West's strategic position, for on 11 November 1975, only two weeks before Eanes' effective military intervention, the radicals had completed the handing over of all Portugal's African colonies to Marxist liberation movements. Thanks to the MFA, southern Africa had become a crisis point for the West by the second half of the 1970s.

R.G. Grant

Despite the success of his plan for the coup, Captain Otelo de Carvalho (above) was outmanoeuvred in the race for power. After a failed coup in November 1975, Carvalho was arrested and Colonel Eanes (above left, foreground) soon became president of Portugal with Mario Soares (above left, on Eanes' left) as prime minister.

Below: Armoured patrols move through the rubble-strewn streets of Lisbon. During the uncertainty in the year after the 1974 coup, the possibility of street violence and another armed takeover was always present.

Soldiering on

Nato problems of the 1970s

Above: A multinational unit, including troops from America, Italy, Germany and Holland, mans an observation post during a Nato exercise on Salisbury Plain in 1966. Clearly language barriers affected such exercises but the close cooperation of these units not only improved communication but strengthened the morale of Nato troops.

The 1970s opened with Nato members relatively optimistic about future developments between East and West. The process of relaxing tension between the two blocs, which had come to be known as detente in the 1960s, was continuing and in 1969 US President Richard Nixon proclaimed that the end of confrontation was over and that the era of negotiations was beginning. The president's words seemed to reflect reality, since Nato had become wedded to the concept of detente alongside the commitment to deterrence and defence as a result of the Harmel Report in 1967. In November 1969 the Strategic Arms Limitations Talks (SALT), had begun and it was the prospects for these talks, more than anything else, which led to the measured optimism of 1970.

In the SALT negotiations Nato had to rely upon the United States alone – since the talks were bilateral – to represent the interests of the alliance, and this was achieved by patient and thorough consultation between the United States and her Nato allies throughout the discussions. Whilst the SALT talks continued, however, Nato was itself engaged in further talks with the nations of the communist bloc. Ever since 1966 the Warsaw Pact countries had wanted multilateral talks on European security problems – proposals which the Western states had countered with suggestions for talks concentrated on reducing the conventional forces deployed in Central Europe.

Eventually, the Nato allies and other European states agreed to the convening of a Conference on Security and Cooperation in Europe (CSCE), in 1972 in Helsinki. The Warsaw Pact states in return agreed to attend the Mutual and Balanced Force Reduction Talks (MBFR) which opened in 1973 in Vienna. The latter were direct Nato-Warsaw Pact negotiations.

The early 1970s also saw the general pattern of the easing of strained relations reflected in developments in Europe. The new West German Chancellor Willy Brandt was pursuing a policy known as *Ostpolitik* and Brandt's willingness to negotiate with the communist bloc led to the signing of treaties between the Federal Republic of Germany and the Soviet Union (1970), Poland (1970), and the German Democratic Republic (1972) – all of them designed to normalise relations between these states and West Germany. In addition, negotiations on the Berlin question also came to fruition with the signing of the Quadripartite Agreement on Berlin by the foreign ministers of the United States, Britain, France and the Soviet Union in June 1972. Nato was, therefore, encouraged by diplomatic developments in these years, especially when President Nixon visited Moscow in May 1972 to sign the SALT I agreement.

These promising trends in international politics were somewhat counterbalanced, however, by another series of developments that were to become more important as the decade wore on. Firstly, there was the continued imbalance between the forces of the Warsaw Pact and Nato. The MBFR talks were one way of dealing with the problem, but a major difficulty, and one that has never been satisfactorily resolved, lay in the different nature of the weaponry of the two alliances. Nato weaponry was superior – but there was less of it, and the Western European nations did not have the large stockpiles of old equipment that the Eastern bloc maintained.

Above: A Nato conference in Brussels. Although the alliance functioned well in general during the early 1970s, the problems of coping with advances in technology and the difficulties caused to the military budgets of the various member states by world inflation were a constant aggravation.

A constant background factor that all officials of the alliance were aware of during the early 1970s was the possible adverse repercussions of the Vietnam experience upon US commitment to its European allies. There were some proposals in Congress for a reduction of US forces in Europe, but these never became more than vague possibilities, and President Nixon gave a firm pledge that there would be no running down of US troop levels except as part of the MBFR agreements. Nevertheless, when Nixon himself was forced to resign for his part in the Watergate scandal in 1974, there was continued disquiet at possible future developments.

In 1973, the Yom Kippur War in the Middle East revealed some splits between members of the alliance – notably between those members that gave Israel strong backing (the USA and Holland) and those that were less inclined to put themselves firmly behind one side or the other. The Yom Kippur War had two further major effects. The first was that the debate over tactical methods was intensified as a result of the seeming success of new anti-tank and anti-aircraft missiles. The second effect, however, was even more profound. This was the sudden jump in oil prices that the oil-producing states inaugurated when they both cut production and charged more for their goods. Not only did this make the basic costs of running armed forces in the non-communist world higher; it also acted as the central motor for an inflationary spiral that was to have considerable effects upon the ability of many of the Nato states to maintain defence spending at the levels needed to maintain credible conventional forces.

In 1974, there were further disquieting developments. In April, a coup in Portugal toppled the right-wing regime of Marcello Caetano and brought to power groups of army officers and politicians, many of whom held radical political views. At one stage, there was a member of the Communist Party in the Portuguese government. Eventually, however, the more radical elements were excluded from power, and the establishment of a stable democratic regime eased worries. Then, in July 1974, attention switched to the eastern Mediterranean as the Turkish invasion of Cyprus opened up a breach between Greece and Turkey that threatened the integrity of the alliance's southern flank. As with the situation in Portugal, however, after an anxious period the situation was eventually stabilised without irreparable damage to the fabric of Nato.

The fact that these difficulties resulted in local problems rather than fundamental damage was largely due to the continuingly favourable international climate. In 1975, the leaders of virtually all the European states and the USA and Canada signed the final accords of the CSCE in Helsinki, a set of agreeements that marked a high point in cooperation between the European nations.

In the early 1970s, then, Nato had been fortunate that its problems were enclosed within the cocoon of the thawing superpower relationship; but there were ominous clouds on the horizon. Inflation, the breakdown of detente, and the steady increase in Soviet military strength were to combine to produce a very different atmosphere by the end of the decade.

David Johnson

Fighting for time

Nato tactics in the 1970s

After 1967 Nato put together a new set of responses to possible Warsaw Pact aggression. In that year the doctrine of massive nuclear retaliation for any Pact invasion of the West was eased into a new hybrid policy of flexible response. The idea behind flexible response was that Nato's ground forces had become powerful enough to enforce some delay on the Pact's huge armoured columns. If the Pact launched a conventional offensive, Nato would respond with a conventional defence while trying to negotiate an end to hostilities. At best, Nato's conventional forces might succeed in halting the Pact onslaught and defending their territory. Only if conventional defence failed would Nato escalate the conflict, first by launching tactical nuclear weapons and then, if necessary, by a strategic nuclear onslaught. The basic assumption that a Warsaw Pact invasion would be conventional was not well substantiated since Soviet doctrine appeared to advocate the immediate use of nuclear and chemical weapons in support of an offensive, but the well-publicised Nato flexible response doctrine might itself encourage the Pact to limit its use of such weaponry to avoid escalation. Unfortunately many Nato allied governments did not face up to their responsibility to have adequate numbers of properly equipped troops available to make the policy feasible – perhaps lacking belief in the likelihood of a Pact offensive or the validity of the conventional defence strategy or, more likely, because they did not have the necessary money.

Broadly speaking, any menace to the alliance's flanks – Norway to the north and Greece and Turkey to the south – could possibly be contained and the Nato position not hopelessly compromised just so long as the Central Front held. The Central Front was West Germany's eastern border along which hundreds of thousands of men were massed in highly mobile, fully armoured battle groups in the greatest concentration of fighting power the world has seen. There were formidable numbers of heavily equipped troops on both sides but the numerical balance lay on the Pact side, which had 1.1 million troops compared to Nato's 900,000. At a conservative estimate the Pact had 17,500 main battle tanks (MBTs) readily available to launch against the 7000 which Nato could call on at the start of any battle. Even these figures assumed that the French would instantly join the action and this was by no means a certainty throughout the 1970s. If the battle was at all prolonged, allowing reinforcements to reach both sides, the figures looked even worse for Nato. To maintain any hope the soldiers of the West would need a powerful qualitative advantage to stem their enemy's flood of armour.

It was assumed that from the first a Soviet attack would reach to the full depth of its objective; armed commando teams up to company strength would attack airfields, communications and headquarters in the United Kingdom as well as in Germany and the Benelux countries. At the same time airborne divisions would try to seize a major bridgehead in West Germany to the rear of Nato's embattled main units. While this happened thousands of MBTs accompanied by tens of thousands of armoured fighting vehicles (AFVs) carrying infantry, mortars, anti-aircraft weapons, communications and supplies, together with thousands of self-propelled guns, would penetrate Nato's front on a limited number of axes of advance or spearheads to drive for the Atlantic.

Soviet military doctrine stressed that the power of

Left: A British Chieftain on manoeuvres in Germany. The Chieftain's thick armour and impressive 120mm gun made it well suited to a defensive role. Below: A US soldier operates a Dragon ATGW. Nato has placed a strong emphasis on the deployment of such man-portable weapons as an effective counter to the Pact's reliance on armour. Bottom: British troops deploy at speed from APCs during an exercise in West Germany. Note the GPMG gunner, to the left, who has already positioned himself to cover the advance with automatic fire.

massed attack would be aided by shock and manoeuvrability. Once the first echelon of armour had crashed into the Nato positions, the second echelon following up would turn off the axis of advance to savage Nato formations from the flank or rear while the armoured spearhead continued the main thrust. To Nato soldiers it would seem not only that the Soviet armies had broken through to their rear but that Soviet armoured formations were swarming over the battlefield from every direction. To face this they had to evolve tactics to stem the main attacks and to destroy the armoured columns that poured out along their path.

There was no single solution to the problem accepted by all seven of the Nato nations which had soldiers stationed in West Germany. By the early 1970s they had agreed on a policy of forward defence to try and defend as much of Germany as possible from the horror of becoming a battlefield, but this had disadvantages. It was obvious that the massed armour of the main Warsaw Pact attacks would break into their positions to some extent so that counter-attacks would have to be mounted to drive them back, and a defence in depth would have been a happier military solution to the problem. Nevertheless all the allies recognised that there would be at least two phases to the battle – the initial assault and the attempted counter-attack – and sorted out individual national ways of dealing with the problem.

Every nation with front line responsibilities realised that there should be a powerful forward screen of MBTs and infantry armed with anti-tank weapons to make sure that the Pact's forces bumped into something hard immediately. It was also recognised that this screen had to be mobile to conduct a fighting retreat as it tried grimly to 'write down' the enemy armour and as more defenders came in to thicken up resistance. With luck the Soviet onrush could be slowed down and thrown off balance ready for the *coup de grâce* of the counter-attack.

There were differences in the relative importance given to each phase of this process. The West Germans, who made up the largest Nato contingent, had their own operational doctrine which laid down the vital importance not only of a stubborn forward defence but of concentrating maximum effort on a single *schwerpunkt* (or 'decisive point') – in other words they believed in the counter-attack. The Dutch and Belgians were equipped like the Germans and probably shared their ideas. The Americans accepted no laid-down doctrine but would have sought the same sort of battle as the Germans with the added spice of their national belief in firepower and technical innovation: the introduction of armed helicopters, for instance, might well have proved devastating to Soviet armour of the late 1970s. Attacking the American Army has usually proved a bitter and disagreeable experience to those who try it but it should be said that the Americans had their share of troubles in the 1970s: overstretched at first by the Vitenam commitment, the second half of the decade found them with a desperate shortage of reserves once they had abandoned conscription. The French and the Canadians had no front line responsibilities and the only remaining contingent, the British, excited some suspicion among the other nations by their dispositions.

The British have also never accepted a laid-down operational doctrine and prefer to believe in initiative. However, the fact that many of their forces were positioned well forward with no depth at all indicated that they intended to stand and fight, mounting only local counter-attacks. Besides, this equipment lent itself to the national preference for an unflinching resistance scorning manoeuvre, which has brought them a long roll of famous victories and quite a few catastrophic defeats. It was also obvious that their allocated area on the north German plain made it virtually certain they would be full in the path of the hurricane if it came.

The quality of equipment

The most important factor governing the initial 'encounter battles' would be the quality of tanks and tank crews on both sides. The Soviet Union began the decade equipped with the T62 and ended it with the T64. The T62 was a tough nut to crack and its 115mm gun certainly disconcerted the Israeli armour in 1973. The T64 is an even better machine and, although its sister tank the T72 was impressively dealt with by the Israelis in 1982, it would be a mistake to think that all the Nato countries would be up to the high standards of the Israeli Armoured Corps. In addition the T64 has a powerful 125mm gun which would be effective against the heaviest Nato tanks. The Warsaw Pact tank crews would probably be efficient and well trained – the Russians and Czechs have a long, two year conscription period and the Poles and East Germans do 18 months. The scale of tank equipment in the Pact is also lavish – tank divisions have 330 tanks and even motor rifle divisions have some 140.

Against this the Nato allies could deploy some very effective MBTs of their own. The Germans, Dutch and Belgians had the Leopard I which was widely acknowledged as a splendid tank whose 95mm gun was a proven tank killer. The standard of tank gunnery in the German Army has always been very high indeed and its soldiers serve for 15 months. The Dutch do 14 months, but the Belgian Army has only eight months conscription to inculcate the necessary gunlaying skills that would mean the difference between life and death on the battlefield. The American Army MBTs of the 1970s were the M60 and its updated version the M60A1 which were at least as good as their Soviet counterparts with a superior standard of fire control for their hard-hitting 105mm gun. The French AMX30 MBT is a light, highly manoeuverable machine with a fine 105mm gun.

The British fielded the heavy Chieftain tank which was the opposite of the AMX30 in conception. Slow, thickly-armoured and with a massive 125mm gun, it had a glaring defect in its underpowered engine. British soldiers were and are professionals with a standard of gunnery so high that many are openly confident of accounting for five times their number in an 'encounter battle'. However, as British government parsimony delayed the retrofitting of good engines in the Chieftain throughout the 1970s, the more mobile Soviet formations might have shocked them. It is certain enough that a desperate defence of the British sector of the north German plain would have taken a heavy toll of the Soviet juggernaut but, in the end, sheer numbers (10 or 20 to one on any chosen sector) made a number of break-throughs only too probable.

Tank-hunting parties

Once the Soviet spearheads had broken through they would have been engaged by the Nato formations stationed in depth. In the mid-1970s the Americans had the good sense to station two armoured brigades behind I British Corps so that even if the forward defence of the British was pierced, the Soviet tanks could be kept in play while the surviving British formations fought on to try and choke off the armoured advance. The same sort of tactics would have been repeated along the length of the Central Front with tank-hunting parties of Nato infantry equipped with anti-tank guided weapons (ATGWs) and rocket launchers 'writing down' Pact armour in their forward positions while the tank battle raged behind them.

After four days or so it would be legitimate to hope that some Soviet weaknesses would become apparent. In their rush to press forward the leading troops would not clear obstinate Nato infantry from their positions and, once supplies ran short, the Soviet supply system would call for soft-skinned vehicles to take ammunition and POL (petroleum-oil-lubricants) forward. To avoid a massacre of these unarmed elements the Soviet infantry would be forced to clear corridors through the Nato positions. The Warsaw Pact forces were perhaps a little short of infantry due to their emphasis on MBTs and their infantry AFV, the BMP-1, was found to be fatally vulnerable to anti-armour weapons in the 1973 Arab-Israeli War. As Soviet infantry are trained to press home their attacks in their AFVs and only dismount on the objective, they could look forward to some grevious casualties when tangling with Nato positions.

In a typical action of the 1970s they would find their

Below left: A Lynx helicopter in its anti-tank role armed with eight TOW missiles and the Avimo-Ferranti 530 stabilised sight system. Although helicopter gunships have traditionally been associated with US operations in Vietnam, the British and Nato forces have recognised their value on the battlefield as tank killers. Below: A Puma helicopter transports a 105mm light gun during a Nato exercise. It is hoped that in the eventuality of a war in the European theatre, Nato's ability to deploy artillery flexibly will compensate for the numerical superiority of the Pact forces.

vehicles exploding under ATGWs and recoilless rifle rounds at anything between 3000m (3300 yards) from their objectives and 250m (275yds). In the last 200m (220yds) they would be engaged by shoulder-held rocket launchers and many more would be destroyed before the survivors arrived on the objective to dismount and kill the defenders with a storm of automatic fire. The highly-portable ATGWs of the 1970s with their devastating shaped-charge warheads undoubtedly made Nato infantry a potent threat to all types of armour. The experience of the Yom Kippur War in 1973 even led some military analysts to suggest that the whole balance of defence and attack had been altered by the impact of ATGWs, giving Nato defenders a much better chance against massed Soviet armour. In retrospect, however, it is clear that properly supported by mounted infantry, tanks can overcome the ATGW threat under most circumstances.

Nato's main chance of overcoming the imbalance on the ground lay in their air power. Once again the numerical superiority lay with the Warsaw Pact, deploying some 4000 tactical aircraft as against Nato's 2000. However, the Pact's air strength included a large number of obsolescent machines alongside the latest MiG-23s and MiG-25s. Nato relied largely on the F-4 Phantom and the F-104 Starfighter to overcome the Pact's aircraft and its anti-aircraft defences. The major roles of the Nato air forces would have been to provide close air support and to carry out interdiction missions which would deny the Pact its advantage in speed of reinforcement. The Pact's air power would have been deployed largely in a defensive role to cover the armoured advance and prevent penetration of its own airspace. A decisive victory in the air battle would almost certainly have determined the outcome of the land conflict.

It is impossible to calculate the result of a war that never took place. If the Nato forces had succeeded in keeping some sort of integrity in their front line, the Pact spearheads might have been choked off to the rear, providing the opportunity for a counter-attack. But in general, given the Pact's numerical advantage in armour, it is doubtful if Nato could really have mounted a successful conventional defence of Europe in the 1970s and would have been forced to depend on the deterrent aspects of flexible response, as indicated by the tactical and theatre nuclear forces deployed.

P.J. Banyard

Below right: A USAF Fairchild A-10 close-support/attack aircraft. Designed in the early 1970s to counteract the threat of massed armoured assaults, the A-10 tank killer is highly manoeuvrable at very low levels and has the ability to withstand a high degree of battle damage.

Left: A US Nato contingent armed with M16s (fitted with blank firing attachments) and wearing NBC clothing on exercise in Norway. Exercises in rigorous climatic conditions with the added burden of NBC equipment are essential if troops are to be prepared for the possibility of limited nuclear war.

Thinking the unthinkable

The concept of limited nuclear war

From the very beginning of the atomic age, nuclear weapons have been regarded as essentially instruments of 'mass destruction' and nuclear war identified with the annihilation of cities. Given this perspective there is something paradoxical about the very notion of limited nuclear war. Yet once the Soviet Union acquired nuclear weapons, deterrence became a two-way affair and the prospect of a deadlock loomed. The American desire to use nuclear weapons to cast a protective umbrella over her allies stimulated a search for ways in which this might be done without inevitably calling down a retaliatory holocaust on the United States itself. The strategic debate which attempted to solve the problems presented by this decline in the credibility of 'massive retaliation', during the 1950s, inevitably entailed a search for doctrines of limited war.

Clearly the most radical way of avoiding all-out nuclear war would be to refrain from using nuclear weapons at all; to confine warfare to conventional weapons and to regard the 'firebreak' between conventional and nuclear weapons as the major, perhaps the last and only, stopping point in the process of escalation towards the ultimate catastrophe of mutual destruction. This approach has become a powerful influence on Nato strategy and underlies the continual effort to strengthen its conventional component. Already in the 1950s, however, there were those who suggested that nuclear weapons could be used in limited ways, and that these could strengthen deterrence and reduce the costs of defence. Such theories can be divided into those which concern so-called 'theatre' nuclear weapons and those which relate to the strategic nuclear forces.

American nuclear weapons were first assigned to 'tactical' purposes in the early 1950s when the necessary fissile material became fairly plentiful and weapons could be spared from the primary task of deterrence. In addition to diverting atomic bombs to tactical tasks, the appearance of more compact nuclear weapons made it possible to deploy large, specialised nuclear cannon, followed by early short-range ballistic missiles such as the Corporal and later by nuclear projectiles that could be fired from conventional 155mm and 208mm artillery.

At first these weapons were regarded simply as increasing Nato firepower on the battlefield during a European war which would in no sense be limited and which would therefore proceed in parallel with the strategic bombardment of the Soviet Union, whose capacity to retaliate was as yet small. There was little discussion of the significance of tactical nuclear weapons in the process of a possible escalation. Later, however, as the critique of massive retaliation developed, theorists such as Henry Kissinger suggested that nuclear action might be limited to the battlefield, withholding the strategic weapons as a deterrent against direct Soviet attacks on the United States. Until the Soviet Union mastered the techniques of warhead miniaturisation, Nato would enjoy a unilateral advantage, off-setting the Soviet preponderance in manpower and conventional forces. The US Army set about reorganising itself to fight in smaller, widespread units on a nuclear battlefield.

Unfortunately, the most likely battlefield was the homeland of the United States' European allies and as the new doctrines emerged they aroused great anxiety in Europe, particularly West Germany. A Nato exercise in that country in 1955, significantly named Carte Blanche, resulted in several million theoretical civilian casualties, as did a similar set of manoeuvres in the southern United States, entitled Sagebrush. The prospect of a nuclear war limited to Europe was highly alarming, particularly if the Soviet Union became equipped to join in. This spectre of a European nuclear war in which the superpowers' own territory was not 'nuked' played a major part in urging President de Gaulle towards development of a French nuclear force and withdrawal from the Nato military structure in 1966.

A 'flexible response'

With France out of Nato military planning, the other allies were able to adopt the present doctrine of 'flexible response' in 1967. This compromise envisaged a period of conventional defence before recourse to nuclear weapons. Nevertheless, the use of nuclear weapons remained Nato policy if conventional resistance failed and the new Nato nuclear planning group had to reconcile the European, particularly West German, desire to avoid a large-scale nuclear war in Central Europe, and the American desire to postpone attacks on superpower territory. The outcome was guidelines for 'initial use' of nuclear weapons envisaging a 'militarily meaningful demonstration of resolve'. This would involve a use of nuclear weapons on a limited scale for a real military purpose, not a token gesture, but would hopefully bring hostilities to an end. Beyond that stage, the inter-allied dilemmas became more acute, and so far as they are known the guidelines for 'follow-on use' remain uncertain and ambiguous.

In the 1970s, renewed concern about the credibility of American nuclear action on behalf of allies, as the SALT process clearly registered Soviet achievement of at least nuclear parity with the United States, combined with further technological progress to revive debate over tactical nuclear weapons. The advent of nuclear weapons combining low yields with high accuracy encouraged some to believe that these 'mini-nukes' could solve the problem of civilian casualties and might be used almost as freely as conventional weapons from the very outset of a war. Once again it was thought the West enjoyed a technological advantage which could be exploited to redress the imbalance on the conventional battlefield – particularly of armour – with weapons clearly distinguished from the strategic arsenals. Several types of 'tailored' weapons were proposed: Earth Penetrators to bury nuclear charges deeply before detonation, thus producing obstacles without significant fall-out; Minimum Residual-Radiation weapons to achieve the same results on the surface; and, most famous or notorious of all, the Enhanced Radiation Weapon, or 'neutron bomb', to provide a pulse of radiation some 10 times greater than that produced by a 'normal' nuclear weapon of similar yield, lethal even to tank crews under armour and yet with reduced effects of blast and heat.

Ironically, the neutron bomb proposal, far from alleviating anxieties in Europe, increased them by being interpreted as making nuclear war more likely. Moreover, even from the military point of view, there was reason to doubt the efficacy of the new nuclear

Below: A US Tomahawk cruise missile launch control centre (top) and its transporter-launcher make their way through the countryside on a trial deployment. The Tomahawk carries a thermonuclear warhead with a yield of 200 kilotons and has a delivery accurate to 30m (100 feet).

Right: The Soviet battlefield missile, the Frog-7 which can carry a nuclear warhead. Below: The land-launched US Sergeant tactical nuclear delivery system. Its solid-fuel propellant gives it a maximum battlefield range of 140km (85 miles).

Above: British troops move out from the cover of their APC armed with SMGs (stocks folded) and wearing charcoal-lined NBC suits, rubber gloves and respirators. The possibility of fighting in NBC conditions is recognised by most armies and rigorous training in simulated conditions is a regular task. The NBC suits have a combat life of only 24 hours and the canisters on the respirators must be changed every 12 hours. Thin cotton liner gloves are worn under the rubber gloves.

weapons. The number of weapons needed to deal with a massive tank attack was large – measured in hundreds per division – and new conventional ways of dealing with the problem seemed to be emerging. Moreover, Soviet tactical nuclear forces were now formidable and, if these were less sophisticated in some respects, it was not Soviet but Western European civilians who would suffer if the Soviet Union retaliated with larger and less accurate weapons.

So long as tactical nuclear weapons played a part in Nato strategy there was a case for improving and modernising them, but when the decision was made to begin on the task in 1979, the Europeans preferred to start with the longer-range, so-called Intermediate-Range Nuclear Forces (INFs) which could take the war to Eastern Europe and the western Soviet Union and deny the superpowers the immunity from nuclear exchanges once feared by de Gaulle.

Such INFs could prevent the 'decoupling' of a European war from the balance of deterrence between the superpowers. But if this link was maintained, the United States was confronted with the same prospect of annihilation it had faced before when trying to combine deterrence on behalf of allies with a doctrine of massive retaliation. The only solution was to believe that even 'strategic' attacks on superpowers could be limited.

In the 1970s, the idea of limited strategic attacks that might leave the Soviet Union an incentive to restrain its response, first mooted in the previous decade, attracted renewed attention in the United States. Secretary of Defense James Schlesinger took a particular interest in this and by 1974 was establishing 'limited strategic options': 'what we need is a series of measured responses to aggression which have some relation to the provocation, have prospects of terminating hostilities before general war breaks out, and leave some possibility for restoring deterrence'. A modified version of this doctrine was later more formally adopted by the Carter Administration under a noted Presidential Directive 59 (PD 59), and remains part of American strategy. To facilitate it, greater attention has been paid to improving and protecting American capability for command and control, for 'damage assessment' and for rapidly retargeting strategic forces. The last requirement, joined with that for great accuracy, has become part of the case for preserving land-based missiles, such as the MX, within the American strategic arsenal.

Doctrines of limited strategic nuclear war have aroused anxiety paralleling those related to tactical weapons, since they are another way to make nuclear war 'thinkable'. As characterised by Schlesinger and others, the targets for limited action would probably not be nuclear forces, but other military 'assets': perhaps those related to a war in Europe – thus creating a link to the INF debate; special industrial facilities like oil refineries; or perhaps elements in the Soviet 'power structure', such as political or military headquarters. The Soviet Union, for its part, consistently rejected the idea of limiting strategic nuclear war and has announced that any attack on Soviet territory would meet a full retaliation.

Clearly any such attacks would be fraught with extreme danger of escalation. It is far from clear whether, quite apart from political reactions, the technical apparatus of control could survive any but the most restricted use of nuclear weapons. Yet the doctrine is likely to survive in some form, for as long as nuclear war is possible at all, it is obviously better to have some way to limit it than to proceed immediately to an all-out spasm of mutual destruction. In particular, as long as the United States is required to threaten nuclear action on behalf of its allies, even if only to deter nuclear attacks on them, it will obviously need 'options' that leave the Soviet Union an incentive to stop short of a full-scale attack on the United States. The choice between making nuclear war as terrible as possible, to deter its outbreak, and planning to minimise the damage it if nevertheless does occur, seems to be an inherent part of the world's nuclear dilemma.

Laurence Martin

Key Weapons

THE PT-76 AMPHIBIOUS TANK

Although the Soviet Union had displayed an interest in light amphibious tanks as far back as the 1920s it was not until after 1945 that an important type was developed. Work was instigated on a series of designs that included the PT-76 light amphibious tank which was introduced into service in 1952.

The need to have an amphibious capability necessitated the PT-76 having a large hull which is of all-welded steel construction. Hull armour thickness varies from 5mm (0.2in) to 14mm (.55in) with the maximum protection being provided over the front of the hull where attack is most likely to occur. The armour of the PT-76 is, however, very thin and can be penetrated by an armour-piercing bullet from the American 0.5in M2 HB machine gun in widespread use all over the world.

The driver is seated at the front of the hull in the centre and over his position is a single-piece hatch cover that opens to the right. Forward of this are three periscopes. When afloat the centre periscope is replaced by a much longer one which extends to such a height that the driver can see ahead over the trim vane when it is erected at the front of the hull.

The turret contains the commander (who acts as the gunner) on the left and the loader on the right. The turret is of all-welded steel construction and has a maximum armour thickness of 17mm (.71in). Turret traverse is electric with manual controls being provided for emergency use. Over the top of the turret is a large one-piece hatch cover which opens forward and can be locked vertically if required. In the left side of this hatch cover is the commander's cupola which holds three periscopes and can be traversed by hand through a full 360°. The commander has a TSh-66 sight mounted co-axially to the left of the main armament, while the loader has a forward-facing roof-mounted periscope and a roof-mounted white-light searchlight. Around the upper part of the turret are grab rails, a standard feature on Soviet tanks during World War II as very often the infantry were carried into the attack on tanks. There is also a radio antenna on the left side of the turret, and more recently most vehicles in service with the Warsaw Pact have been fitted with a turret-mounted snorkel to provide fresh air to the crew compartment when the vehicle is afloat.

Main armament of the PT-76 is a 76mm D-56T gun which has a semi-automatic vertical sliding-wedge breech block, hydraulic buffer and a hydro-pneumatic recuperator. It has a maximum rate of fire of eight rounds a minute; elevation is +30° and depression −4°, the latter being very low by Western standards. The first examples of the PT-76 were fitted with a D-56T gun which has a long multi-slotted muzzle brake and no evacuator; these PT-76s were known as the Model 1 in the West. The Model 2 (the most common type) has a double-baffle muzzle brake and a bore evacuator about two-thirds of the way down the barrel. The Model 3 is the Model 2 without the bore evacuator, while the Model 4 has the fully stabilised D-56TM gun and is often called the PT-76B.

A total of 40 rounds of ammunition is carried for the 76mm gun with most of this being stowed ready for quick access. The gun was a development of the weapon originally refined during World War II for the KV-1 heavy tank and T-34/76 medium tank and fires ammunition of the fixed type, whereby the projectile is attached to the cartridge case. Types of ammunition that can be fired include AP-T (armour piercing-tracer) which can penetrate 61mm (2.4in) of armour at 1000m (1090yds) and the API-T (armour piercing incendiary-tracer) which has a similar capability. The HE-Frag (high explosive-fragmentation) round would mainly be used in the fire support role, possessing a maximum range of 12,000m (1310yds). The HEAT (high explosive anti-tank) round has a muzzle velocity of 325mps (1066fps) a second and can penetrate 120mm (4.72in) of armour, but its low velocity makes it ineffective in high winds and for engaging moving targets. The HVAP-T (high velocity armour piercing-tracer) round has a better muzzle velocity of 950mps (3117fps) and will penetrate 92mm (3.62in) of armour at 500m (545yds), although past this range penetration drops off rapidly. Mounted to the right of the 76mm gun is a 7.62mm SGMT machine gun for which 1000 rounds of ammunition are carried and more recently many PT-76s have been fitted with a 12.7mm DShKM anti-aircraft machine gun on the turret roof.

The engine and transmission is to the rear of the turret and separated from the crew compartment by a bulkhead. The engine, a V-6 six-cylinder in-line water-cooled diesel developing 240hp at 1800rpm, is a half of the engine used by the T-54 main battle tank (which has a V-12), therefore assisting in the commonality of spare parts and ease of training. The engine is coupled to a manual transmission with four forward gears and one reverse gear. Steering is by clutch and brake, and suspension is of the well tried torsion-bar type with six distinctive rubber-tyred road

Previous page: A column of PT-76 light amphibious tanks wends its way over a mountain pass during manoeuvres designed to test the reliability of the Soviet Army's combat vehicles. Top: A PT-76 at a Moscow parade features the large one-piece hatch locked forward. Above: A PT-76 in the water. That it is a Model 1 can be seen from the D-56T gun barrel which has a long muzzle brake and no fume evacuator. Racks are fitted on the hull rear for the stowage of additional fuel drums.

Above: A PT-76 negotiates ice flows during a winter warfare exercise. As a Model 2 this PT-76 has a double baffle muzzle-brake and evacuator mid-way along the barrel. Also noteworthy are the flat fuel tanks attached to the hull rear. Above right: PT-76 tanks swim across a river revealing their water-jet propulsion systems.

Right: A PT-76 crosses snow-bound terrain accompanied by Soviet ski troops. Below: Elite Soviet naval infantry leap from their PT-76s in a simulated amphibious assault.

wheels, idler at the front and drive sprocket at the rear. The first and last road wheel stations have a hydraulic shock absorber.

The major feature of the PT-76 is its amphibious capability. Before entering the water the trim vane is erected at the front of the hull – to stop water rushing up the glacis plate and so pushing the vehicle further down into the water – and the two electric bilge pumps are switched on. When afloat the PT-76 is propelled by two water-jets mounted at the rear of the hull, one

Above: Mounted on a PT-76 chassis, a ZSU-23-4 anti-aircraft gun system. Other weapons based on the PT-76 chassis include the Frog-3 surface-to-surface missile (right) and the triple SA-6 surface-to-air missile (far right). Below: A line of PT-76s issues forth from a landing ship, trim vanes fixed.

on either side with the water entry port being located in the hull side above the fifth road wheel. When the driver wishes to go left the left water jet is covered and to go right the right one is covered. One of the drawbacks of this amphibious propulsion system is that the entry ports can easily be blocked by weeds or other debris. Maximum water speed is 10km/h (6mph) and the vehicle can be safely used in amphibious operations at sea as well as crossing inland waterways and lakes. One major problem, however, is actually leaving the water and shallow-angled exit points have to be chosen.

The fuel tank contains 250 litres (55 gallons) of fuel and is located in the right side of the engine compartment, but additional fuel tanks can be fitted over the rear engine decks to increase operational range. The PT-76 is not fitted with an NBC system and when originally built did not have any infra-red night vision equipment, but this has since been provided for the driver.

The PT-76 has formed the basis for a complete family of armoured vehicles, the first to enter service being the BTR-50P amphibious armoured personnel carrier. An improved version of this has been manufactured in Czechoslovakia under the designation of the OT-62. The Frog missile systems (marks 2, 3, 4 and 5) also use a slightly modified PT-76 chassis. Components of the PT-76, varying from just the track and roadwheels to almost the complete chassis, have been used in the ZSU-23-4 self-propelled anti-aircraft gun system, the SA-6 Gainful missile system, GSP heavy amphibious ferry and the PVA amphibious crawler tractor, to name but a few. Many of these vehicles have also been exported on a wide scale.

PT-76

Crew 3
Dimensions Length (gun included) 7.63m (25ft 1in); width 3.16m (10ft 4in); height 2.22m (7ft 2in)
Weight Combat loaded 14,000kg (30,865lb)
Ground pressure 0.48kg/cm^2 (6.83lb/in^2)
Engine V-6 water-cooled six-cylinder engine developing 240bhp at 1800rpm

Performance Maximum road speed 44km/h (27.5mph), 10km/h (6mph) in water; range (road) 260km (162 miles); vertical obstacle 1.1m (3ft 5in); trench 2.8m (9ft 3in); gradient 70 per cent; fording amphibious

Armour 10-15mm
Armament One 76.2mm D-56T gun; one 7.62mm machine gun mounted co-axially with the main armament

Below: A PT-76 of the Indian Army stands guard by the Intercontinental Hotel in Dacca at the conclusion of the war with Pakistan in 1971. The PT-76 proved its usefulness in the many amphibious crossings that were such a characteristic of the campaign in East Pakistan.

Above: The Chinese development of the PT-76 – the Type 63 – which features a new and enlarged turret mounting an 85mm gun. Although larger and heavier, the Type 63 retains the amphibious capabilities of the PT-76. Right: A PT-76 of the Finnish Army travels along a snowy track in support of infantry operations.

especially to the Middle East and Africa.

The scale of issue of the PT-76 within the Soviet Army has varied over time but in the early 1970s, for example, each Soviet motor rifle division and tank division had a total of 19 of these vehicles. The PT-76 is used mainly as a reconnaissance vehicle ahead of the main units but has also been used for crossing water obstacles in the first wave of the attack and for artillery support while a beach-head is being established. By early 1984 it had been replaced in front-line units by specialised reconnaissance versions of the BMP mechanised infantry combat vehicle, although it was still being used by Soviet marines. The PT-76 has been exported to a number of countries including Finland, India, Vietnam and Egypt.

China received a number of PT-76 light amphibious tanks from the Soviet Union and subsequently undertook production of an improved vehicle called the Type 63. This is slightly longer, wider and heavier than the PT-76 and retains its amphibious characteristics. Its most important feature is the new turret which is very similar in appearance to that of the T-54/55 tank, although it is constructed of cast sections welded together and is armed with an 85mm gun.

The PT-76 was used in combat in Vietnam in the 1960s and when first encountered took the Americans and South Vietnamese somewhat by surprise, as they did not expect tanks to be employed by the North Vietnamese, although they were easily destroyed by air strikes and infantry anti-armour weapons. They have also been encountered by the South African Army during their clashes with SWAPO (South West African People's Organisation) in Angola where they were engaged and defeated by AML armoured cars armed with turret-mounted 90mm guns. The Indian Army deployed them in the invasion of East Pakistan (now Bangladesh) in 1971 where their amphibious capabilities proved highly effective. The Chinese version was probably used in the Chinese invasion of Vietnam in 1979. Although the PT-76 light amphibious tank is obsolete by modern standards it will doubtless remain in service for many years in those countries outside the Warsaw Pact, and its low ground pressure and amphibious capability make it a very useful vehicle in many tactical situations.

The Turks move in

Invasion and partition of Cyprus

Above: The Turkish fleet moves into coastal waters off Cyprus. The Turks felt forced to intervene on the island because of the coup that brought extreme supporters of *enosis* (union with Greece) to power. Left: Nicos Sampson the leader of the Greek nationalists who deposed President Makarios on 15 July 1974.

Seldom can the conduct of any successful military operation have met such widespread criticism as Turkey's invasion of Cyprus in 1974. The Turkish commanders showed an evident lack of dash as their army ground on its almost stately progress. In addition, the invasion route chosen was tactically unsound and contributed to the slowness of the operation. The combination of delay and difficult terrain gave the Greek Cypriot defenders an opportunity to embarrass the invaders, even if they had no chance of stopping them. On the other hand, the Turks could point to certain rich dividends gained from their deliberate approach: there was limited bloodshed and the population had time to achieve a *de facto* partition that was politically valuable to the invaders.

On the Greek Cypriot side, the invasion came as a miserable end to a dispiriting and bloody internal conflict. The men who had led the guerrilla war against the British in the 1950s had not intended to establish Cyprus as an independent state. Their ambition had been to achieve the political union of the island with Greece, and they had been frustrated in this by the realities of Turkish, rather than British, power. Cyprus lies within sight of mainland Turkey and, as Greeks and Turks are historical enemies, the Turks would have regarded *enosis* (union of Cyprus with Greece) as a threat to their national security. Besides this, a substantial minority of the population (around one fifth) was of Turkish origin and there was reasonable suspicion that they would have little future under Greek rule.

This suspicion was confirmed after Cyprus achieved independence from Britain in 1960; serious trouble broke out between the Greek and Turkish communities in December 1963 and by April 1964 the two sides had been artificially parted (in separate enclaves scattered all over the island) with a buffer force of United Nations troops to provide security. Apart from the UN forces, the only armed forces officially allowed on the island were the British, who had retained two Sovereign Base Areas (SBAs), and token deployments of 990 soldiers from Greece and 650 soldiers from Turkey. No-one was very satisfied with this uneasy settlement but it was at least tolerable to Turkey whose geographical position made her the dominant regional power. The Greek President of Cyprus, Archbishop Makarios, recognised that *enosis* was politically impossible and steered a tricky middle course.

In early 1974 supporters of *enosis* became increasingly violent in their attacks against the Makarios regime. In defiance of the terms of the Cyprus independence settlement, the Greek Cypriots had raised a military force, the National Guard, which numbered almost 18,000 men and counted 32 ageing T34/85 tanks among its weaponry. The force was officered by Greeks from the mainland and strongly supported *enosis*. To protect himself from these potentially dangerous troops, Makarios had raised a personal police force known as the Tactical Reserve Unit which was recruited from his left-wing supporters. In June 1974 the Archbishop, attempting to strengthen his position, demanded that the Greek

government withdraw the 600 officers who commanded the National Guard. The military regime in Athens responded by giving open encouragement to a coup launched by the National Guard on 15 July.

The coup was a sharp and violent business. The National Guard's Lok commando lost 28 men killed in the storming of the presidential palace alone and there was fierce fighting in Nicosia and Paphos. Makarios himself escaped to the security of a British SBA and from there to London, but his police force was overcome and, by noon on 15 July, Nicos Sampson had been installed as the new head of government. Sampson had played a conspicuous part in the intercommunal fighting of 1964, which made him totally unacceptable to the Turks; the British also were disgusted by his presence because he had played a notorious role in the murder of British servicemen in the 1950s.

The case for intervention

The coup gave the Turks a good case for intervention, but there were a number of military imponderables which might endanger an invasion plan. The Greek Cypriots themselves could hardly muster much resistance to an invasion as the National Guard, together with the lightly armed 990 Greek soldiers stationed near Nicosia airport, were the only local forces available to oppose it. The Turks feared, however, that their action might bring full-scale war between mainland Greece and Turkey. They were also unsure whether the British would remain quiescent within their SBAs. Britain and Turkey were co-guarantors of the island's constitution, so the Turks had some right to expect the British to join them in military action; but the generally-held view on Cyprus and in Turkey was that the British would oppose it. The SBAs contained squadrons of Phantom jets as well as light armoured units and professional infantry. These forces alone could be a decisive factor, while the British could also reinforce these assets.

Faced with these uncertainties it might have seemed better for the Turks to have moved with paralysing speed. The Turkish command, however,

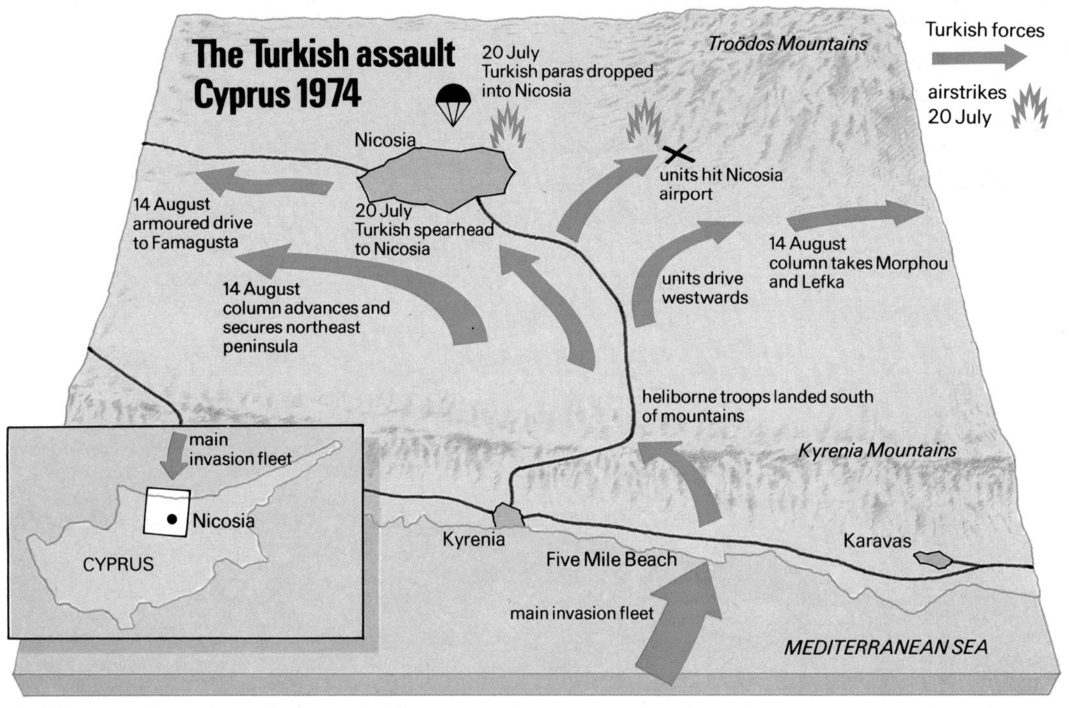

opted for a display of such imposing strength as to deter potential opposition. The quick solution would have entailed landings on either the west or east of the island, followed by a swift advance across the flat central plain to cut Cyprus in half within five or six hours. This strategy was rejected in favour of a more deliberate solution, however, which involved a landing on the north coast and a cumbersome advance through a high mountain range. Although this was militarily the more difficult course, it had real advantages. Foremost was the fact that the largest Turkish enclave on Cyprus extended from Nicosia on the central plain to the port of Kyrenia on the north coast. Throughout this enclave the Turks could expect the population to resist incursions by the National Guard and to welcome the Turkish forces when they arrived. This also meant that they would be presented with a port, Kyrenia, at the very beginning of the operation.

There were also political considerations dictating a landing around Kyrenia. The Turks were very worried about the safety of the Turkish Cypriot population once hostilities began, and felt bound to secure the largest enclave as soon as possible. Unfortunately these Turkish fears were not imaginary and they later uncovered grisly evidence that some Turkish Cypriot civilians had been massacred before the invasion force arrived. By the same token, however, there is much evidence that Turkish soldiers murdered Greek Cypriot civilians as they established themselves in the north of the island. Further bloodshed was probably only prevented by the presence of some 2300 UN soldiers and policemen on Cyprus. Many civilians found safe, if temporary, refuge in the SBAs.

The first, halting stage of the Turkish invasion took place on 20 July. Their air force, which proved highly effective throughout the operation, made telling low-level attacks on the National Guard barracks in Nicosia. The Guard had little in the way of anti-aircraft weaponry. Shortly afterwards, Turkish paratroops were landed in the Nicosia-Kyrenia enclave and a heliborne force was put down just south of the Kyrenia Mountains. Because they intended to use 40,000 men in three divisions, including a tank brigade, the Turks had to bring in the bulk of their forces by sea and, in this area, things did not go quite so smoothly.

Kyrenia turned out to be unsuitable as an invasion port so the invading force and its supplies were put ashore at Five Mile Beach, slightly west of the town. In many parts of the world this would have been a fiendishly tricky operation but the Mediterranean in summer is a comparatively gentle sea and the Turks were lucky enough to enjoy calm weather throughout the invasion. However, the good weather meant fierce heat, with the temperature climbing to over 43°C (110°F) for day after day with the ground tinder-dry. The bombing and artillery exchanges with the National Guard started several major forest fires which did much material damage and also placed some constraints on forward movement through affected areas.

Apart from this the Turkish forces faced few obstacles over the first two days. The few National Guard roadblocks were brushed aside, though Greek resistance had become more coordinated by the time the Turks closed on Nicosia airport. Resistance there was led by the 990 Greek soldiers from the mainland and UN observers described it as nothing short of heroic. It was also effective. Good observation and

Opposite page: Turkish troops advancing south on Cyprus. The Turkish moves were slow and rather deliberate, but this did have the advantage of giving Greek Cypriots the chance to move away from the line of advance.

Below: Ammunition is rushed forward to members of the Greek National Guard holding out in Nicosia, where the most intense fighting of the campaign took place. Below left: Turkish civilians welcome the arrival of the forces from mainland Turkey. The main concern of the invaders in the early days was to protect the Turkish enclaves, especially at Kyrenia, Nicosia and then Famagusta.

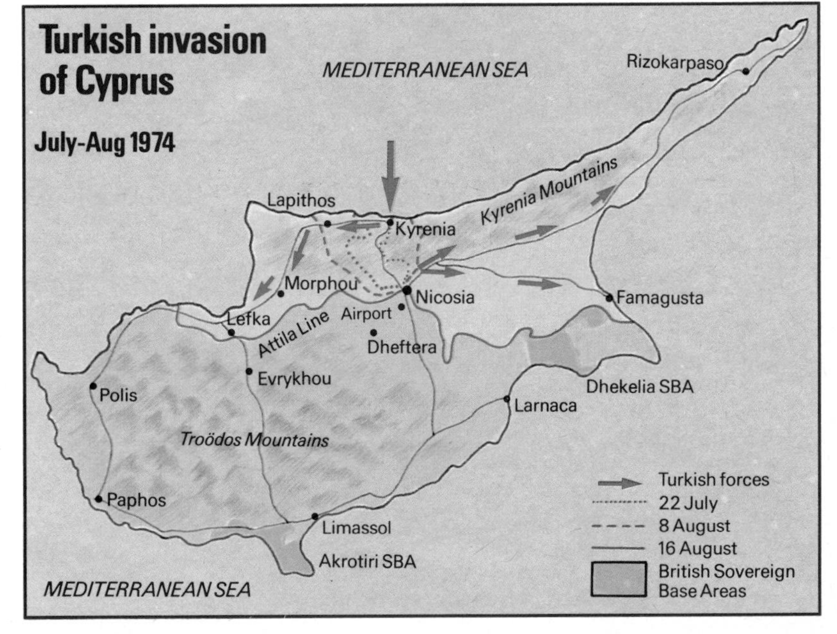

Feigning death

Civilians were massacred by both Greeks and Turks in the course of the 1974 conflict. The following atrocity was uncovered by a *Sunday Times* journalist:

'Having escaped on the Wednesday, before the Turkish tanks arrived, some villagers who lived near the area decided three days later, when the ceasefire was operating, to risk the Turks and go back home to feed their animals.

'What happened to these villagers is based on the evidence of two men, Pedros Yasoumi, a 42-year old shepherd who is recovering in Larnaca hospital from a bullet that went through his elbow, and Athanassis Costea, 16, who had gone back with his father to a separate village to help feed animals.

'Both men were picked up by the Turks near the village of Gaidkouras as they were making their way back on tractors to the safety of the Greek lines. They were taken first to an officer who had made his headquarters in a boat factory on the Famagusta road, and then on to a road junction about four miles away where they sat and waited all afternoon while stragglers from the neighbouring villages were rounded up.

'By 1700 hours about 50 people were gathered at the Prastio junction and the Turks selected 12 and put them on a lorry. The remainder, women and children and the older men, were allowed to go free.

'Then, according to these two men who were two of the 12, they were driven back down the Famagusta road about two miles then 200 yards across an open field to a small deserted building. There three men were told to get out, enter the building and stand with their hands raised. They were shot. One man started to cry out for his children, and according to the shepherd, a Turkish soldier emptied the magazine of a Bren gun into him.

'The lorry then moved on about 400 yards across the field. Three more were ordered out, including Athanassis Costea, and two were killed, Athanassis escaping by feigning death.

'The six men who were left decided that when they were ordered out they would run in different directions in the hope that one or two might survive. Mr Yassoumi claimed that the Turks were so surprised to see them run that they had covered about 100 yards before the soldiers opened fire. Mr Yassoumi was hit in the elbow, fell, feigned death and watched another man who stopped as the Turks came alongside him with the lorry. The man raised his hands and was shot dead.'

communications meant that the Turkish infantry assaults were savagely mauled by the available Greek artillery, which consisted of old British 25-pounders, before being beaten off by withering fire from determined Greek infantry who could not be shifted by repeated bombing from the Turkish Air Force. Turkish troops continued to mount fierce attacks but their approach was inflexible and unchanging. The Greeks held their positions for two days until the UN arranged a local ceasefire and the battle-lines at the airport were frozen in a configuration they still retain.

A general ceasefire ensued on 22 July, leaving the Turkish forces in control of some 1000 square km (400 square miles) of territory. Political changes came thick and fast on the Greek side: on 23 July Nicos Sampson was replaced by the more acceptable Glafkos Clerides and the military government in Athens fell. UN-sponsored negotiations took place in Geneva but Greece rejected Turkish proposals for a federal state. Meanwhile, although the Turkish forces

had not brought their operation to a satisfactory conclusion, with every day that passed their position was becoming stronger. The fall of the military regime in Athens meant that there was no chance of mainland Greece intervening in the struggle and the Greek Cypriots were left to rely on their own inadequate resources. At the same time, Turkish supplies were pouring in an uninterrupted stream across Five Mile Beach. It was clear that the Turks would soon continue their advance.

On 14 August fighting started once more and the Turkish Army creaked forward. The main set-piece in the new offensive was to be an armoured drive on Famagusta, where a Turkish Cypriot community had been besieged by Greek Cypriots for three weeks. The Turkish advance was jovially characterised by a British general who observed it as 'a monument to sloth and incompetence'. He was not alone in this judgement. Every neutral onlooker, from soldiers to journalists, seemed to be critical of the deliberation which attended the Turkish movements but, for once, dash would have been misplaced.

From the first ceasefire line at Lapithos, one column moved westward to Morphou and Lefka while another cleared the peninsula in the northeast of Cyprus. The relaxed pace of the Turkish advance meant there was usually time for Greek Cypriots to evacuate their villages ahead of them. Many took this opportunity, and those who hung on or tried to return were harshly encouraged to leave by the Turks, who thereby created a refugee problem but saved themselves from inheriting a guerrilla or dissident problem. The Turks had by now settled on the aim of creating a separate Turkish state in the north and this goal was well served by the slowness of their advance.

The drive on Famagusta also demonstrated that caution can sometimes save lives. Famagusta was the best port on the island, with a largely Turkish Cypriot population of some 12,000 people living in the old town. The area around however, was predominantly Greek Cypriot with some 35,000 of them living in the modern buildings around the town. Because of its value as a port, the Turks were determined to take the town and because this was obvious, the Greek Cypriots had used the time allowed them to leave. Although the civilians fled there was, at first, no intention that the National Guard should abandon Famagusta and a garrison of 2000 troops with tanks prepared defensive positions.

There was really little question of the Greeks being able to stop any Turkish tank movement. Their T34/85 tanks were completely outclassed. The T34/85 has an old-fashioned 85mm gun which has an effective armour-piercing range of about 1000m (3300 feet) and, with a combat weight of 32 tonnes, it was classed as a tough nut to crack in 1944 but not in 1974. The Turks deployed some 200 M47 and M48 tanks which are comparative monsters of 45 tonnes.

Intelligence or ineptitude?

The effectiveness of the Turkish tank crews who dawdled south on the 14 August to cut the roads between Nicosia and Famagusta was, however, questionable. Observers entertained a strong suspicion that they were not even capable of maintaining radio contact with one another as they weaved around in their slow-motion way which brought them to within 21km (13 miles) of Famagusta that evening. Luckily for all concerned their increasing menace had its effect on the National Guard garrison. The Greek positions had been bombed during the day and sniped at by Turkish Cypriots in the old town. The Greeks had no aircraft and no tank-stopping power, so most of them recognised the inevitable and withdrew during the night. Their only practicable route lay through the SBA at Dhekelia, and the British garrison forced them to surrender their arms before entering. The weapons were restored to them when they left the SBA, but the humiliation was keenly felt.

Those Greek troops who remained in position at Famagusta could do little even to inconvenience the Turks and were forced to withdraw an hour or so before the first Turkish tank entered the town. Astonishingly, this did not occur before the evening of 15 August because the advance was so slow. By this time the Turks held rather more than a third of the island and a ceasefire was arranged along what has become known as the Attila Line. Turkey had achieved the solution she desired by a *de facto* partition of Cyprus and the cautious methods used had avoided undue bloodshed. However, the suspicion must remain that the pace of the Turkish advance was dictated by lack of competence rather than shrewd political judgement.

P.J. Banyard

Left: Turkish troops lead away suspected Greek snipers. The history of violence between the two communities had left a legacy of bitterness that came out in 1974. Above: The Turkish M47 tank was a weapon to which the Greeks had no answer. Above right: Perhaps the most important immediate result of the Turkish invasion of Cyprus was on mainland Greece, where the military junta was totally discredited by the Turkish success, and was replaced by the civilian government of Constantine Karamanlis (left foreground, next to Archbishop Makarios).

Protecting the flanks

Nato's northern and southern wings

Above: Women and children hurry past Turkish troops patrolling the Greco-Turkish border. Despite their theoretical alliance through Nato membership, animosity between Greece and Turkey has been one of the constants of European politics since 1945. Top right: High-ranking Nato chiefs attend an exercise in Turkey in 1975. Above right: Royal Marines disembark at speed from a light-attack craft in Greece. Small units such as this can be used to great effect in disrupting enemy movement.

Iceland, Norway and Denmark, the three countries which between them form what has become known as the northern flank of Nato, were all founder members of the alliance in 1949. Although it was in Central Europe that the crucial problems of the immediate post-World War II period had occurred – the division of Germany, the Berlin blockade, the disputes over Poland and Czechoslovakia – the Scandinavian states could not divorce themselves from such events, nor could they ignore the advances the Soviet Union had made in the eastern Baltic area and Finland during World War II. Initially the Scandinavians considered forming a Scandinavian Defence Union to face the perceived Soviet threat, but they could not agree on the best means of guaranteeing their security. Finland, living in the shadow of the Soviet Union, and Sweden with its traditional neutral sympathies, both chose non-alignment, while Norway, Denmark and Iceland believed their independence could best be preserved by membership of the Nato alliance with its guarantee of American support.

At the other extremity of Europe, in the south, Portugal and Italy joined Nato in 1949, but the two countries generally considered to constitute the southern flank of the alliance, Greece and Turkey – really the southeastern flank – did not join until 1952. Yet their involvement in the confrontation between the West and the Soviet Union went back further: to resist Soviet territorial demands, Turkey had become a close ally of the United States in 1947, and Greece had been the scene of a civil war in which first the British and then the Americans had supported the government in putting down a communist insurgency between 1944 and 1949.

If the states on Nato's northern and southern flanks were motivated to join the alliance by their fear and suspicion of Soviet power, ideology and objectives, the leading Nato powers were glad to accept them as allies because of their important geographical contribution to Nato's strategic position. Both the northern and southern flanks control crucial sea routes used by the Soviet Union. In the north, the Soviet Northern Fleet has to pass through the so-called Greenland-Iceland-UK Gap and along the Norwegian coast to reach the only ice-free section of the Soviet arctic coast around the major naval base of Murmansk. Equally, Denmark controls the freedom of movement of the Soviet Baltic Fleet in and out of the Baltic Sea. In the south, Turkey sits astride the Bosphorus and the Dardanelles – the narrow entry and exit point for the Soviet Black Sea Fleet between the Mediterranean and the Black Sea. The Soviet Union and Nato both regard these choke points for the Soviet Navy as extremely important. Nato would need to reinforce Western Europe, and in particular the northern flank, with large numbers of troops from the United States quickly and early in any conflict, and one of the major threats to the successful accomplishment of this task would be the Soviet Navy. Equally, the Soviet Union would be anxious to establish freedom of movement for its naval forces early in any conflict so as to disrupt Nato strategy. Nevertheless, the strategic advantage might still lie with Nato through its ability to observe movement of Soviet vessels in these restricted sea lanes and in the potential for making Soviet naval activity difficult in time of conflict.

Both the northern and southern flanks have sometimes been considered peripheral to the Central Front where Nato and the Warsaw Pact deploy such huge conventional and nuclear arsenals in an eyeball-to-

eyeball confrontation, and this has sometimes spawned doubts on the flanks as to Nato's determination to defend them. Certainly, the flanks are vulnerable. The northern flank is separated from the Central Front by the Baltic Sea and the southern flank is cut off by the neutral states of Switzerland, Austria and Yugoslavia, as well as by the Adriatic and Aegean Seas. The sheer length of Nato's front line – 8000km (5000 miles) from northern Norway to eastern Turkey – makes it difficult to defend.

On the northern flank, Nato has had to come to terms with member states that are, in terms of military strength, relatively weak members of the alliance. Iceland, small and remote with no armed forces of its own, fulfils a crucial strategic role in the reinforcement plans of Nato as part of the airbridge between the United States and Western Europe. The United States retains an airbase on Iceland at Keflavik and radar stations for surveillance of the North Atlantic. Norway is especially vulnerable, with a population of only a little over four million and a 210km (130 mile) border with the Soviet Union itself. Norway cannot hope to match numerically the forces that the Soviet Union has built up across the border in the Kola Peninsula. Despite this, Norway deploys such standing forces as it can muster in the north of the country and its armed forces are supported by a Home Guard committed to the national concept of 'total defence'. In addition Norway could expect to receive assistance from Nato's ACE (Allied Command Europe) Mobile Force early in any conflict. Denmark also has a small population – some five million – and is faced with the task of defending numerous islands in the approaches to the Baltic Sea, again with relatively small armed forces.

The minimalist approach

Northern Norway, the west coast of Norway, and Denmark would all be important objectives for the Soviet Union in wartime in order to achieve maximum freedom and safety for its navy to operate in the Atlantic. The Svalbard archipelago in the north Barents Sea, a Norwegian possession where Russians and Norwegians both exploit mineral resources, could also in some circumstances become vulnerable to attack. Faced with this threat, Norway and Denmark have adopted a firm but limited stance in their attitude to Nato. Strong neutral, pacifist sentiment exists internally alongside a desire to avoid unnecessary provocation of the Soviet Union. This has led both Norway and Denmark to refuse to allow permanent foreign bases on their territory since 1953, and in 1957 both countries also banned all nuclear weapons from their territories, air space and waters. This minimalist approach reflects the situation in which these states find themselves, and is understood and accepted by other Nato members since it does not detract from their belief that the deterrent effect of the alliance is the best way to preserve their security.

In political terms the northern flank has been remarkably stable. The policies and attitudes of the Scandinavian countries have shown great continuity, and the regional and internal disputes which have plagued the southern flank have been notably absent. However, Iceland has adopted some policies in the past which have distanced it from Nato. In particular the Cod War of 1975-76, a fishing dispute between Nato partners, led Iceland to threaten to withdraw from the alliance, forcing others to make concessions in the interests of Iceland's livelihood. Occasionally, therefore, participation in Nato is called into question in Iceland, although such disputes have always been solved satisfactorily. This is fortunate for Nato, since many observers have predicted an unravelling effect – if one state ever left Nato others might follow and this is something Nato wants to avoid.

The contrast between the stability of the northern flank and the political instability of the southern flank is striking. Both Greece and Turkey have recent experience of military intervention in government – Greece between 1967 and 1974, and Turkey in 1960, 1971 and 1980. On top of this Greece and Turkey have been at loggerheads over Cyprus since its independence in 1960 and more recently they have had major differences over the rights to exploit the mineral resources of the Aegean.

Yet there can be no question of the importance of Greece and Turkey to Nato's strategic position. Until the 1960s, the Mediterranean was a Nato lake, policed by the US Sixth Fleet in the eastern Mediterranean and naval units provided by Britain and the Nato states possessing a Mediterranean coastline. The emergence of the Soviet Black Sea Fleet and its powerful worldwide capability has altered this state of affairs radically. Nato still retains some control of the narrow entrance to the Mediterranean through British possession of Gibraltar and the Nato membership of Portugal and (since 1982) Spain, but Turkey's position at the entrance of the Black Sea is clearly crucial. Greece and Turkey also offer Nato a range of facilities, including ports, airfields and electronic listening posts.

Turkey is able to maintain a very considerable army – the second largest in Nato – and can, therefore, make a far greater contribution to its own defence than can any of the countries on the northern flank. The high plateau of Anatolia also presents an impressive geographical barrier to any Soviet advance. On the other hand the European area of Turkey in eastern Thrace is vulnerable and with control of access to the Black Sea as the prize, its possession could become a vital issue for East and West in wartime. The British Sovereign Bases on Cyprus are available to lend extra weight to the alliance's efforts in the region.

Cyprus has, however, been the most serious divisive issue on the southern flank, bringing Greece and Turkey to the brink of conflict in 1974 when Turkey responded with military force to a Greek-backed coup on the island. The Greeks felt that their Nato allies should have taken firmer action to stop Turkey's invasion of Cyprus and they withdrew from the integrated military structure of the alliance. Turkey, for its part, was subjected to an arms embargo by the US Congress in December 1974 – an ill-considered attempt to pressurise the Turks into withdrawing from Cyprus. In retaliation the Turks suspended the operation of US intelligence-gathering posts on their territory. Under the government of Bulent Ecevit in 1978 Turkey followed a policy of loosening its Nato links and improving relations with the Soviet Union. Defence against Greece was seen as the military priority.

The situation was largely retrieved for Nato in 1980. The military coup of that year in Turkey brought a government eager to re-affirm its Nato links – especially in the light of the Soviet invasion of Afghanistan the previous year – and Greece rejoined the alliance's military structure. The US arms embargo on Turkey had been lifted in 1978, and so as part of the 1980 settlement Turkey allowed the US listening posts to be reactivated under nominal Turkish control. Anomalies and tensions persisted, however. It was agreed that, since Nato's southeastern command was located in Turkey, at Izmir, Greece would have its own Nato command based at Larissa. A significant part of both countries' armed forces remained devoted to their local confrontation, and Greece's adherence to the alliance remained in question.

Although this disunity is a weakness of Nato, the overwhelming strength of the alliance lies in the phrase: 'an attack on one member state is regarded as an attack on all members', and despite the magnetic attraction of the Central Front, the northern and southern flank countries know that it is no different for them. An attack on Norway or Turkey would be a challenge to the whole alliance, and this essential solidarity is the cornerstone of Nato's deterrent posture and its success. There are bound to be differences, but each member state understands that it has an interest in preserving solidarity. **David Johnson**

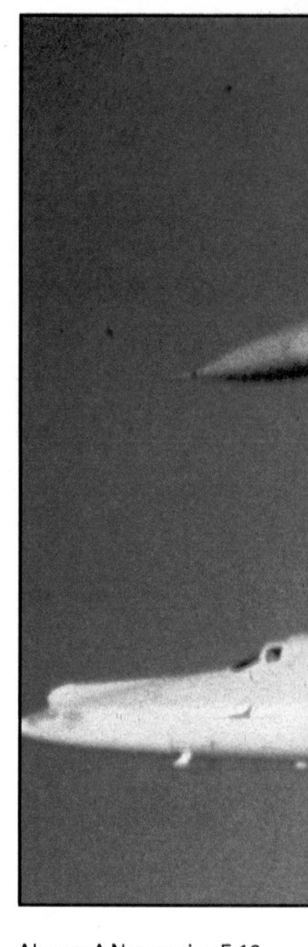

Above: A Norwegian F-16 is scrambled to intercept a Soviet TE-22N Backfire bomber as it penetrates Norwegian airspace. Below: Royal Marines storm ashore in Norway during an exercise. Localised training is aimed at strengthening Nato's northern flank. Right: US troops prepare artillery pieces for airlifting to the Norwegian coast from an aircraft carrier.

278
41

Cold war

The problems of fighting in winter

Despite the sophistication of modern mechanised armies, climatic conditions are still an important factor in determining the conduct of war. It is only urgent requirements which induce modern armies to engage in winter operations – as in December 1979 when the deteriorating situation inside Afghanistan prompted a Soviet mid-winter invasion, though major operations against the guerrillas had to wait until spring. Equally, the Argentinian invasion of the Falklands forced the despatch of a British Task Force in April 1982 with winter fast approaching in the South Atlantic.

The principal problem facing armies engaged in winter operations is, of course, the cold, especially when there are sudden drops in temperature. In 1941 the German Army Group Centre advancing towards Moscow experienced a drop in temperature to −15°C (5°F) with the first winter frost on the night of 12 November, a temperature of −20°C (−4°F) on the following night and temperatures between −30°C (−22°F) and −40°C (−40°F) by December 1941. In November 1950 the US 10th Engineer Combat Battalion, 3rd Infantry Division, landing in Korea, experienced a dramatic fall in temperature from 20°C to −15°C (68°F to 5°F) in the course of just one day's drive north 240km (150 miles) towards the front. Frostbite can occur at only −1°C (30°F) while other cold-weather injuries range from chapped skin, chilblains and 'trench foot' (which arises from a lack of movement in damp conditions) to exposure, where there is a significant lowering of body temperature. Nato arctic-warfare training in Norway has indicated that, if properly clothed and equipped, most men can move comfortably at temperatures of −10°C (14°F), untrained men must be withdrawn to shelter at −20°C (−4°F) and even trained men cannot move effectively at −30°C (−22°F). Paradoxically, real hazard also occurs when temperatures rise to around −5°C (23°F) since the partial thaw will increase the likelihood of damp clothing and resultant cold injuries.

Soldiers returning from the Falklands campaign recalled conditions in which ice pellets removed skin from exposed flesh and sweat froze. Cold effects even the smallest personal details, including defecation: in the words of a veteran sergeant, 'You can manage provided you save 'em up, drop 'em fast and get on with it.' Any prevailing conditions will be exacerbated by height, since air cools with altitude and temperature falls approximately 3°C (5.5°F) for every 300m (1000 feet), while any wind will also lower temperatures. At times during the Falklands campaign windspeed, which averaged 17 knots, rose as high as 60 knots and lowered temperatures to −20°C (−4°F).

Winter conditions can, therefore, result in serious health hazards; in the first winter of their campaign against the Soviet Union the German Army recorded over 100,000 cases of frostbite of which over 14,000 resulted in the amputation of limbs, and between 27 November and 10 December 1950 the US 1st Marine Division in Korea suffered 3083 non-battle casualties, nearly all from frostbite, the situation being made worse by the fact that the Chinese offensive coincided with severe weather. Once the fighting had subsided, the number of cold-weather injuries declined – from 22-29 December 1950, for example, the same division had only 223 non-battle casualties of which 184 were caused by frostbite. In all, US forces in Korea recorded a four per cent rate of cold-weather losses, although this compared favourably with the eight per cent rate sustained by US forces in Italy and northwest Europe during World War II.

Fighting the frost

The major difficulty for the German Army in the Soviet Union when the first frosts occurred in November 1941 was not so much the failure to provide winter equipment as the fact that the logistic system supporting the army had broken down even before the onset of the autumn rains in October. In fact, the first frosts made movement of wheeled vehicles easier but paralysed the railways upon which the system largely depended; winter equipment and clothing could not be brought forward in time. During the Korean War, the problems posed by winter conditions in 1950 were compounded by the haste with which units had been sent from Japan or the United States. The US 17th Regimental Combat Team, 7th Infantry Division, arrived fresh from Japan on 29 October 1950 without gloves, winter clothing or insulated footwear and, indeed, without sufficient food or ammunition.

Above: A 0.3in M1919 Browning machine gun in action in extreme weather conditions. Keeping infantry support weapons operating in sub-zero temperatures is often very difficult: lubricants may freeze while water-cooled weapons are obviously a liability. Below: British troops bivouac on the Falklands.

Above right: Traditional forms of transport may well be most effective in winter. Here, a Norwegian packhorse company passes a column of motor vehicles during Operation Atlas Express held in Norway in 1976. Right: A Centurion tank of the 8th King's Royal Irish Hussars comes to a halt in an icy stream in December 1950 in Korea.

Thereafter petrol and ammunition tended to take priority throughout the UN advance to the Yalu River and subsequent retreat in November.

During the Falklands campaign British forces also suffered from the speed with which the Task Force was assembled. The bulk of the stores of 3rd Commando Brigade had still not been landed when the Argentinians surrendered. Men of 4th Field Regiment, Royal Artillery went two weeks without cookers after the landing at San Carlos on 21 May 1982. While 'yomping' (45 Royal Marine Commando) or 'tabbing' (3rd Battalion, The Parachute Regiment) across East Falkland after the breakout from the San Carlos bridgehead on 27 May, British troops frequently out-distanced supplies of hot food and sleeping bags since priority on the few available helicopters had to be given to moving artillery, ammunition and petrol.

Some arctic training is received by most units in the British Army but the specialists in this form of warfare are 45 Royal Marine Commando. Their training and expertise proved particularly useful during the Falklands campaign, and at least one Marine company took both its arctic and temperate machine guns, thus substantially increasing its firepower. Proper equipment, training and acclimatisation can help towards overcoming the debilitating effects of cold weather operations. During the Russo-Finnish War (September 1939 to March 1940) for example, Finnish troops wore several layers of clothing; insulation against cold derives from still air trapped between the layers – as activity and perspiration increase, layers can be removed without risk. This basic principle remains a key to survival in cold weather. Soviet troops, by contrast, were poorly prepared for the conditions they encountered in Finland but learned enough to cope with the cold far more effectively than the German troops would on the Eastern Front in 1941. In the Korean War, although they suffered cold-injuries, American units such as the 1st Marine Division with training experience in Greenland or the 2nd Infantry Division with training experience in the northwestern mountains of the United States, fared considerably better than untrained units. The US-recruited Filipino contingents felt cold as soon as they landed in Korea in September 1950 when the temperature was still 15°C (59°F), and had to be issued with warmer clothing within two days.

Since the 18th century, the Russian Army had regularly been issued (for winter use) with a pair of boots a size too large. The extra space was to be filled with straw or newspaper, thus preventing frostbite. But in the Korean War ignorance of the effects of the cold led to many American troops wearing leather boots in preference to the heavier 'shoepacs', resulting in far more casualties since wet leather freezes at

Left: The Soviet Army has made assiduous preparations for winter warfare, especially after its experience in the Russo-Finnish War of 1940, when shortcomings in equipment and doctrine were most cruelly exposed by the expert Finnish Army. Here, Soviet infantry have deployed from a BTR-60 APC during a training exercise and are using an AKM assault rifle (foreground) and an RPK light machine gun.

low temperatures. The advantages of training were quickly revealed when one unit had 169 cases of trench foot or frostbite in a two-week period while a neighbouring unit with more careful supervision had only 20 cases at the same time. A cold-weather training programme was immediately instituted throughout the US Eighth Army with cold-injury prevention teams active even at company level and, in the somewhat milder winter of 1951, there were considerably fewer casualties. In the US 2nd Infantry Division, Major-General Young's insistence on daily laundering of socks and regular foot and sock inspection brought total divisional cold casualties down to only 16 for the whole of this second winter, each case being followed by a full investigation to apportion responsibility. The new insulated rubber boot – the thermal or 'Mickey Mouse' boot – issued in the course of 1951 was also a major success, although socks still had to be changed every 12 hours. During the Falklands campaign war correspondents accompanying

Above: Warsaw Pact manoeuvres set against a wintry Central European landscape: Czech Hind helicopter gunships cover the advance of T55s. The implementation of classic armoured warfare in low temperatures requires meticulous training and preparation.

British forces soon appreciated the insistence on keeping at least one pair of socks dry, while waterproof overboots were much coveted.

Apart from its effect on troops, winter weather affects the actual conduct of military operations. At low temperatures, such as those experienced in the Russo-Finnish and Russo-German campaigns, weapons may freeze (as US forces in Korea discovered) unless properly protected. The Finns used a mixture of gasoline and gun oil to prevent rifles freezing, and alcohol and glycerine as anti-freeze in machine-gun cooling systems. The modern Soviet Army has partly solved this problem by using weapons with a minimum number of moving parts and all contemporary armies are now equipped with cold-weather lubricants for their weaponry.

Mobility may also be a problem in low temperatures. Oil will freeze below −20°C (−4°F); the Finns used to drain tank and truck engines every night to prevent freezing and engines were run at least 15 minutes every two hours to prevent damage to batteries. When the German 22nd Panzer Division was ordered to the Don front in November 1942 it had received so little fuel for turning over engines that only one third of its tanks could be started. The lessons of the past, however, have been learnt and most modern armies have winter lubricants for their vehicles. Although it slows tracked vehicles, snow is not usually a major problem for mechanised formations. The modern Soviet Army makes a virtue out of necessity by being prepared to use frozen rivers or lakes as roads or helicopter landing sites, and even has specially-shaped charges for blasting positions in frozen ground.

Winter rain can present as many problems as snow. It was the onset of rain, rather than snow, which slowed the German advance into Russia in 1941; also winter snows are followed by spring thaw. The

Below: Royal Marine Commandos land from a Wessex helicopter in Norway during Nato exercises. In conditions where roads may be blocked, and cross-country travel made very difficult by snow, ice and mud, the importance of the helicopter for deploying troops becomes magnified.

Falklands campaign provides a particularly good example of how wet winter weather can affect operations. The terrain was a mixture of eroded peat, scree and 'stone runs' of boulders covered with slippery moss – there were only 19km (12 miles) of paved road in an area of 12,000 square km (4700 square miles). Although the only month without snow is February, the conditions prevailing during the fighting of May to June 1982 were usually rain, drizzle and mist alternating with windy but sunny days – which at least enabled troops to dry out clothes soaked on the previous day. The ground, however, was constantly waterlogged and fire trenches filled with water. With no natural cover whatsoever, troops had to fashion defences in the form of scrape trenches (shallow pits surrounded by stones). The British Scorpion and Scimitar light tanks performed surprisingly well over the sodden ground but mortars cracked baseplates or buckled bipods after a few rounds as they sank in the peat. The larger 105mm artillery pieces sank after every 20-50 rounds and had to be constantly realigned on targets. Conversely, the peat muffled the effect of Argentine shells. (Snow also blankets artillery rounds; it has been calculated that an 81mm mortar shell hitting deep snow will have a killing range of no more than 100cm.) Another problem in the Falklands was that British arctic ration packs required more water added to the powdered contents than other issue packs. This would have been no problem in the snow conditions for which they were originally designed, but in the Falklands there were few surface water sources and most were contaminated.

Finland, Winter 1940

'At first the Russian soldier did not mind the cold. He had begun his attack on a full stomach and his spirits were high with thoughts of a quick victory. His weapons were big and new, often right from the factory, and the lightweight clothing was only moderately uncomfortable. But things changed as temperatures began to drop to 10°, 20°, 30°, 40° below zero; this was when the real frozen hell of *talvisota*, winter war, began.

'In such cold the Red Army soldier's weapons froze, his food froze, his hands and feet froze. If he greased his weapon too heavily it became useless. If he touched the barrel of his rifle with his bare hand, then pulled it away, he left his own blood. Tank drivers and truckmen discovered that if their engines were not run for a quarter of an hour in every two, their batteries would not work again. Troops needed more food than usual; rations needed to be heavy and hearty rather than hard bread and unsweetened tea if the men were to survive and fight.

'In the deep freeze of *talvisota* human blood froze and plasma was useless. The cold did help the wounded men by stopping the flow of blood, but if they lay too long with torn and bloody flesh exposed the flesh soon blackened and showed signs of the thin greenish fluid that marks gangrene. Finnish medics stuffed their own mouths with syrettes of morphine to thaw them as they went about their tasks of tending casualties. There seemed to be little of this activity on the Russian side because of the meagre, often absent, medical aid force. Most of the Red Army soldiers simply froze to death, like grotesque statues, in whatever position they happened to be at the time they were hit.'

Extract from The Winter War, The Russo-Finnish Conflict 1939-40, *by Eloise Engle and Lauri Paananen.*

Flying blind

Winter also spells problems for aerial operations. Daylight hours are few and visibility may be considerably reduced by rain, drizzle, sleet or snow. To take an early example, the German Sixth Army, trapped around Stalingrad in the winter of 1942, had been promised 500 tonnes of supplies to be air-dropped or delivered every day in order to remain in combat. The weather was so severe, however, with poor visibility and freezing conditions, that such a target was never attained; the daily average dropped or landed from 25 November 1942 to 11 January 1943 being only just over 100 tonnes. Over 550 aircraft were lost from weather, accident or enemy action. In the Falklands, where air cover was vital, appalling weather not only resulted in the loss of a number of helicopters and two Harriers while the Task Force was still at sea, but also the loss of two precious helicopters in attempting to land SAS teams on South Georgia in the face of a 100-knot blizzard on 22 April 1982. Once British forces had landed on East Falkland, flying was further inhibited by freezing mist and low cloud.

Despite rapid technological advances, winter warfare is still in some respects in its infancy. Continual research on the subject has certainly increased the levels at which troops and equipment will perform but while Nato training programmes in Norway help, simulated battle does not truly reflect combat conditions. Winter warfare still remains an extremely hazardous proposition for any army. Technology has yet fully to conquer nature.

Ian Beckett

Key Weapons

US SPY PLANES

The very first use of air power in war was for reconnaissance – in 1794, at the battle of Fleurus, the French Army used a tethered balloon to observe the Austrians. Since then, the use of aircraft for artillery spotting, for strategic reconnaissance and for keeping close visual contact with troops on the ground has been vastly extended. In particular, during the 1950s the USA brought its vast technological resources to bear on the difficulties of obtaining intelligence from the Soviet Union during the Cold War.

By the end of 1952, a partial solution to the problem was seen to be the development of technically advanced reconnaissance aircraft capable of operating at extreme altitude, outside the range of existing anti-aircraft weapons. On 1 July 1953, Bell, Fairchild and Martin were issued with design contracts for just such a machine; after evaluation, the Bell and Martin submissions were chosen for further development.

The Martin proposal was derived from its B-57 airframe, itself a licensed version of the British Canberra bomber. The new model was designated the RB-57D and featured an immense new wing spanning a full 32.3m (106ft). Power was provided by two J57 turbojets and the type offered an operational radius of 3488km (2166 miles) and a ceiling of at least 16,764m (55,000ft).

The RB-57D entered service with the USAF during April 1956. Total production reached 20 aircraft divided by specification into a number of groups. Group A and B aircraft were single-seaters carrying two K-38 and one KC-1 camera with the B machines having provision for in-flight refuelling, a facility not available on the As. The group C aircraft were two-seaters carrying AN/APR-9/-14 receivers together with the Martin Model 320 SAFE (semi-automatic ferret equipment) system for electronic reconnaissance work. The remaining machine, the group D RB-57D-1, was another single-seater, this time equipped with the high resolution AN/APQ-56 SLAR (side-looking radar). Like the Bs, both the group C and D machines had an in-flight refuelling provision.

In Europe, RB-57Ds undertook a number of missions from Rheine-Main in West Germany in the years between 1956 and 1959. Operations in this theatre involved mainly border surveillance, the height at which the aircraft operated allowing them to see deep inside Warsaw Pact territory. By 1959 the RB-57D was suffering major structural problems with wing failures starting to reach dangerous proportions. As a result of this, the majority of the USAF's RB-57Ds were grounded.

Whilst in European service, RB-57s had been periodically overhauled by General Dynamics at Fort Worth in Texas. In the course of this work General Dynamics gained a wealth of experience in the problems associated with such high-altitude aircraft and eventually evolved a proposal for a 'super' RB-57 with an even more impressive performance. This proposal crystallised into the 'Peewee' project and, in 1962, General Dynamics received an order for what was to be the ultimate 'big wing' B-57, the RB-57F. The new aircraft utilised little more than the centre and aft fuselage sections, the tail planes and landing gear of the original airframe. To these were added a re-profiled nose section, a revised and enlarged fin and rudder, TF33 turbofans and an even bigger wing spanning no less than 37.3m (122ft 6in). In addition to the TF33s, two auxiliary J57 turbojets could be hung

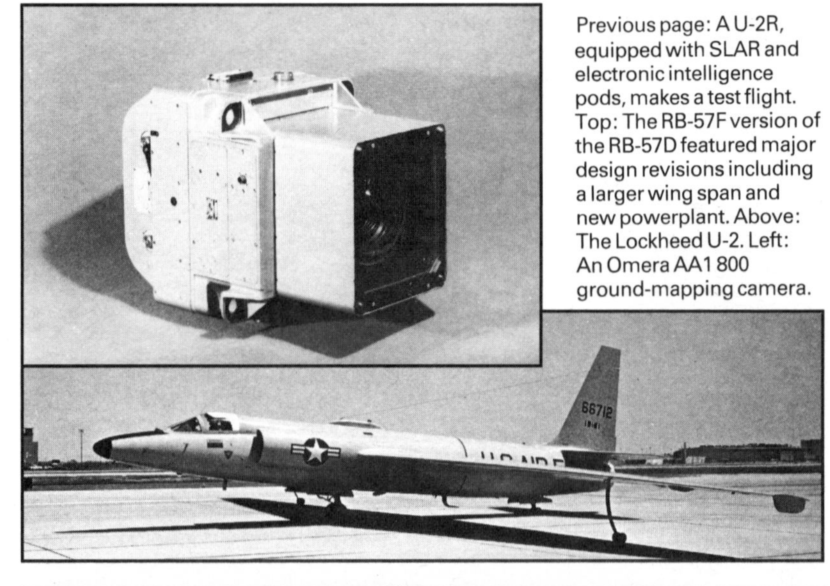

Previous page: A U-2R, equipped with SLAR and electronic intelligence pods, makes a test flight. Top: The RB-57F version of the RB-57D featured major design revisions including a larger wing span and new powerplant. Above: The Lockheed U-2. Left: An Omera AA1 800 ground-mapping camera.

Left and below left: Two views of the U-2. With a service ceiling of 25,900m (85,000ft) the U-2's long-focus camera can record an area some 3540km (2200 miles) by 200km (125 miles), while its electronic intelligence receiver monitors ground transmissions from radio and radar. Top: A TR-1A of the 9th Strategic Reconnaissance Wing. The TR-1 series was developed from the U-2 but had an increased range and higher service ceiling. Above: The TR-1B training version of the TR-1 is provided with a second cockpit for the instructor in place of the usual mission equipment bay.

from the wings to provide additional thrust, a feature which was utilised on all but the longest sorties. The RB-57F made its first flight in June 1963 and proved capable of reaching altitudes in the order of 18,532m (60,800ft).

The RB-57's co-runner in the original competition, the Bell X-16, was cancelled before it ever flew. This was no reflection on its capabilities but was because another type had made its appearance and there seemed little point in producing a third specialised aircraft. The newcomer was the Lockheed U-2. Lockheed was not included in the original competition but the company's designer, Clarence 'Kelly' Johnson, had got wind of the requirement and submitted a private proposal, the Lockheed CL-282. This aeroplane, essentially a modified F-104 Starfighter fuselage combined with a new long-span wing, was firmly rejected by the USAF. Undaunted, Johnson began to canvas his many Pentagon contacts and very soon the CIA began to put its weight behind the Lockheed proposal.

In the end, the CIA got its way and Lockheed was given the go-ahead for Project 'Aquatone', the construction of a high-altitude reconnaissance aircraft specifically for and funded by the CIA. The result of the programme was not the original CL-282 but a modified version of it powered by the same J57 turbojet as that used in the USAF RB-57. Presidential approval for the project was given in November 1954 and the U-2 began to take shape, paid for with $54 million drawn from the CIA's secret funding. Work on the new aircraft was undertaken at Lockheed's Burbank facility, and a prototype was flown on 1 August 1955. The new aircraft revealed its F-104 ancestry and featured a long, narrow drooping wing and a peculiar bicycle undercarriage.

By June 1956 pilot training was complete and 10 U-2s were available for operations. Under the spurious title of WRSP (Weather Reconnaissance Squadron, Provisional) a U-2 unit was based in Germany, and the first U-2 over-flight of the Soviet Union took place on 4 July 1956. The information gained from this mission was considerable and further over-flights were ordered. A total of some 30 U-2 over-flights of Russia had been carried out before the disastrous flight of the U-2 piloted by Francis Gary Powers on 1 May 1960. May Day was chosen for the sortie because it was a major Soviet holiday and it was assumed that the country's defences would therefore not be at peak efficiency. This thinking was faulty and Powers' U-2 was brought down by a near-miss from one of the 14 SA-2 missiles fired at it. The furore resulting from this incident abruptly reduced the CIA's use of the U-2.

The CIA was not unduly distressed by this course of events, however. They had calculated that the U-2 would be operationally viable for no more than two years. In fact, they had been able to use the aeroplane successfully for four years which was regarded as an unexpected bonus.

Despite the continuation of over-flight operations – notably over China – the CIA's use of the type declined after the capture of Powers and the majority of their aircraft were passed to the USAF. The air force U-2s were employed during the Cuban missile

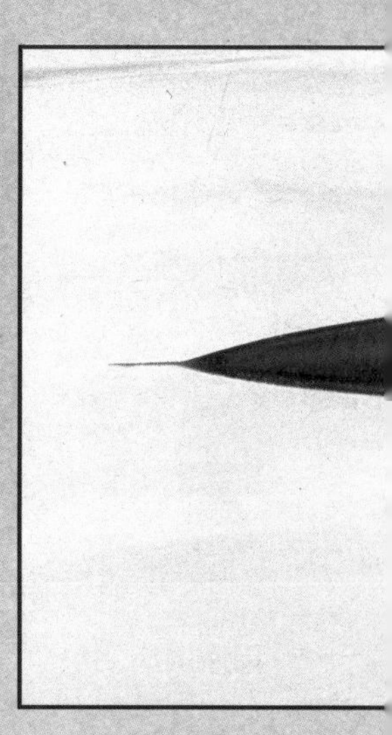

crisis of 1962. On 10 October, President Kennedy approved the first USAF over-flight of the island and from then on until the 28th of the month when the Russians capitulated and began to withdraw their missiles, the air force's U-2s bore the brunt of the continuous surveillance work. The vulnerability of the U-2 was again emphasised during this period when Major Rudolph Anderson's aircraft was destroyed by an SA-2 on 27 October.

Post-1962, both the USAF and the CIA concentrated on less well defended targets in the Far East. In 1964 U-2s were despatched to Bien Hoa in South Vietnam to monitor the Vietnamese-Chinese border area and to provide target photographs for the planning of air attacks against the North. The arrival of surface-to-air missiles in North Vietnam during 1965-66 put an end to such operations and the U-2s maintained stand-off surveillance of the area from then until their withdrawal from Thailand in April 1976. Nationalist Chinese/CIA over-flights of China continued until 1974 but even here the defences were becoming too effective and at least eight U-2s were lost during such operations.

Top: A view of the TR-1 showing its massive 31.39m (103ft) wing span. The TR-1 has a service ceiling of 27,430m (90,000ft) and is equipped with an advanced synthetic aperture radar system, all-weather SLAR and various pieces of advanced electronic surveillance equipment. Above: A TR-1 on show at Mildenhall airbase.

Above: One of the YF-12As which was tested as a Mach 3+ high-altitude interceptor. For tests it was fitted with the Hughes ASG-18 long-range radar and missile armament. Below: The YF-12A's sister aircraft, the SR-71 reconnaissance plane.

The TR-1 was a development of the U-2 and was produced as a high-altitude reconnaissance aircraft for the USAF. By increasing overall size more fuel could be carried, so that the TR-1's range was increased from the 4830km (3000 miles) of the U-2 to 6440km (4000 miles). Based in Europe, TR-1s carry a complex array of electronic surveillance equipment which includes ASARS (advanced synthetic aperture radar system) and SLAR.

Meanwhile, the increasing vulnerability of the U-2 had led Lockheed into the development of a successor, the A-12/SR-71 Blackbird. In the U-2, 'Kelly' Johnson had striven to create optimum altitude performance without bothering unduly about speed. But even as the U-2 entered service it was realised that height alone would not provide indefinite security from interception. The next logical step was to combine speed with altitude, a concept which crystallised in the issuing of a requirement for design proposals during 1958. Lockheed, Convair and the US Navy responded and in the following year, the Lockheed submission was declared the winner. Four years later in 1962, the prototype made its first flight and it soon became clear that this new aeroplane not only possessed a truly remarkable performance but was also an extraordinary example of aeronautical engineering.

As with the U-2, the Blackbird was built with CIA funds and the first 21 examples were 'company' aircraft, bearing the designation A-12. Again like the U-2, the A-12 was a single-seater but there the similarities ended. The A-12 was capable of continuously cruising at close to three times the speed of sound over ranges in excess of 3200km (2000 miles). The creation of such an aircraft posed a multitude of design problems. At speed, the coolest part of the airframe reached a temperature of above 500°C (932°F) and to cope with this the major material used in construction was titanium, a material rarely used before in the aircraft industry and which needed the development of special tools to machine and shape it. The J58 turbojets used to power the type were specially developed and incorporated many of the properties of ramjets when operating at full speed.

Fuel was a major problem, both through the need to provide the required range and to prevent the fuel exploding under the heat stress it would be subjected to. A new low-volatility kerosene was created and a great deal of the airframe was utilised for tankage, some 54,550 litres (12,000 gallons) being carried.

US spy planes

	Span	Height	Powerplant	Max Speed	Ceiling	Range
RB-57D	32.3m (106ft)	20.82m (68ft 4in)	Two J57-P-27 turbojets	1062km/h (660mph)	16,764m (55,000ft)	3488km (2166 miles)
RB-57F	37.33m (122ft 6in)	20.73m (68ft)	Two TF33-P-11A turbofans + Two J57-P-9 turbojets	1059km/h (658mph)	18,532m (60,800ft)	3298km (2048 miles)
U-2	24.38m (80ft)	15.1m (49ft 7in)	One J57-P-13A turbojet	850km/h (528mph)	25,900m (85,000ft)	4830km (3000 miles)
TR-1	31.89m (103ft)	19.2m (63ft)	One J57-P-13 turbojet	797km/h (495mph)	27,430m (90,000ft)	6437km (4000 miles)
SR-71A	16.94m (55ft 7in)	32.74m (107ft 5in)	Two J58-1 turbojets	3380km/h (2100mph)	25,900m (85,000ft)	4800km (2982 miles)

Equally, aerodynamic shaping was critical particularly around the engine nacelles which were the key to the aircraft's ability to sustain such a high speed.

The first the outside world saw of the Blackbird concept was when three YF-12A aircraft were displayed at Edwards air force base in September 1964. These aircraft actually were interceptors and differed from the A-12 in carrying intercept radar, a missile armament and a two-man crew. At much the same time it became clear that a second reconnaissance model existed which carried the designation SR-71A. Like the YF-12A, the SR-71A was a two-seater and differed from the previous models in having a revised nose configuration and an extended rear fuselage. The SR-71 was an air force machine and first entered service in early 1965.

Throughout its operational life, few details of SR-71 activities have emerged. It is known that a detachment of such aircraft has been maintained on Okinawa and that this unit carried out numerous missions in support of the American effort in Vietnam. By 1971 it had completed a comprehensive photographic survey of mainland China. Nearer home, the SR-71 has been active in the Middle East, as evidenced by an Egyptian protest that two such aircraft had violated its airspace during October 1973. Over-flights of Cuba were made in 1978-79 and Blackbirds have been used over Korea, being fired on during 1981. There can be little doubt that these brief revelations are but a fraction of the type's full activities and the SR-71 will almost certainly have been monitoring the situation in the Lebanon and that in the war between Iraq and Iran. And despite the arrival of the satellite as an intelligence-gathering device the spy plane remains the most flexible and cost-effective strategic reconnaissance vehicle available to the West.

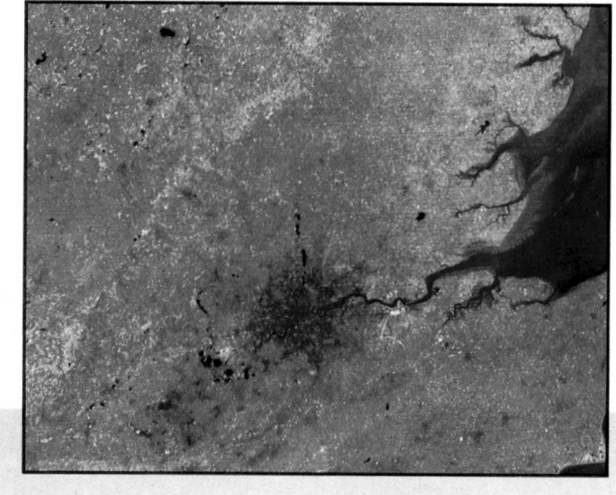

Left: While ground-recording operations flown by the SR-71 are shrouded in secrecy, this aerial photograph of southeast England taken by a NASA Landsat satellite provides an impression of the view afforded by the SR-71's high-altitude performance. Below: With its brake chute streaming behind, an SR-71 comes in to land after a long-range reconnaissance mission.

The phoney peace

South Vietnam, 1973-74

The Vietnam ceasefire agreement of 23 January 1973 was an effective instrument for obtaining a US military withdrawal from the country with a semblance of honour intact. For the rest, however, its complex provisions were treated with complete cynicism by all parties. Officially there was to be a ceasefire-in-place from 28 January, leaving South Vietnam divided into two recognised zones, one under the control of the communists and the other controlled by the government of President Nguyen Van Thieu. There was to be no increase in the numbers of troops or the level of armaments on either side, and the two sides were to negotiate the unification of South Vietnam under a democratically-elected government. An International Commission of Control and Supervision (ICCS) with members from Hungary, Poland, Indonesia and Canada was to supervise the ceasefire.

In fact, no ceasefire ever took place. Through the months leading up to the agreement both sides had struggled to improve their position. The United States had rushed staggering quantities of armaments – valued roughly at $1 billion – into South Vietnam, as well as handing over all US facilities to the Saigon government. The North Vietnamese had fought to consolidate their remaining gains from the 1972 offensive, despite the heavy damage inflicted by the B-52 bomber raids on Hanoi and Haiphong in December. Now, with the ceasefire date fixed, there came a scramble for last-minute advantage. From 26 January, the communists seized hundreds of disputed hamlets, many in key locations on strategic highways, and ran up their flag in the hope of establishing possession of the villages as part of their zone. The Army of the Republic of (South) Vietnam (ARVN) counter-attacked in force, with lavish use of air strikes, helicopter gunships and artillery, both against the newly-seized hamlets and against others flying the South Vietnamese communist banner. On the Cua Viet River, South Vietnamese Marines seized a North Vietnamese base on 28 January – as the 'ceasefire' began – only to be driven out again with heavy casualties. By the end of the first week in February the ARVN had recovered most of the ground lost the previous month, but fierce fighting continued in front of Sa Huynh on the coast of Quang Ngai Province, which the communists had seized as a port to supply their army in the South. Only after the commitment of two Ranger battalions and armoured formations could the ARVN retake Sa Huynh by 20 February.

It was an inauspicious opening to the new phase of the search for peace. Despite the continued fighting, the Americans and the North Vietnamese proceeded to fulfil most of the terms of the agreement which concerned only themselves. There were some sticky moments, but by 29 March the last US military forces and POWs were out of Vietnam and through the summer the US Navy carried out the clearing of mines off the North Vietnamese coast. Only the planned US economic aid for North Vietnamese reconstruction never materialised. The activities of the ICCS, however, in its ceasefire supervision role, degenerated into farce. Formal moves, such as the establishment of Joint Military Commissions of the two sides, remained dead letters. By autumn 1973 all attempts to negotiate a political settlement had effectively been abandoned.

On the ground, the ARVN had the whip hand throughout 1973. In a series of piecemeal advances the government forces nibbled away at communist-held areas, extending their control of population and rice supplies. Quảng Nam and Quang Ngai Provinces were the scene of some of the heaviest fighting as the ARVN extended its hold on the coastal strip. By the end of 1973 it was estimated that Saigon had taken back some 15 per cent of the land held by the communists in South Vietnam at the time of the ceasefire.

Above: A South Vietnamese infantryman in a village recaptured from communist forces shortly after the ceasefire had been proclaimed. He is festooned with some of the equipment that the USA had been pouring into the country over the previous few months: ammunition belts for his platoon's M60 machine gun, an M79 grenade launcher across his knees and M33 grenades attached to his webbing.

The North Vietnamese and Viet Cong forces in the South found themselves largely on the defensive, although they did lay prolonged siege to the South Vietnamese base at Tonle Chan near the Cambodian border. Of course, Hanoi had not renounced its goal of victory in the South, but immediate military advances were ruled out. The 1972 offensive, the intensive US bombing and the mining of North Vietnamese ports had all impaired Hanoi's ability to make war. As so often, the communist leadership perceived that time was on their side. After a period of re-equipment and reinforcement of their troops in the South, accompanied by the construction of a logistic system to match Saigon's American-built counterpart, they would be ready to advance against their enemy, whose foreign support and political stability could only weaken. In late 1973 the communist forces in the South were both out-equipped and outnumbered. In any case, the threat of resumed US military involvement still hung over the communists. US airpower from Guam and Thailand was available at any time, and the administration of Richard M. Nixon certainly contemplated a resumption of the bombing during 1973 as ceasefire violations accumulated.

But in fact US support for Saigon, expressed so forcefully by President Nixon when persuading Thieu to accept the ceasefire agreement, was crumbling fast. The disintegration proceeded on two fronts; opposition to US involvement in Indochina within the US Congress mounted steadily, while presidential authority evaporated in the face of the mounting Watergate crisis from August 1973. Congressional muscle-flexing began with a halt imposed on the continuing US bombing of Cambodia on 15 August 1973 and continued with the War Powers Resolution of the following November which effectively subjected the president's right to make war to prior congressional approval, unless the United States was under direct attack. Congress also cut military aid to South Vietnam, reducing it to $1 billion for 1974 and subsequently to $700 million for 1975.

Power, corruption and lies

This was quite inadequate for South Vietnam's needs. The rapid rise in world oil prices after the Yom Kippur War in October 1973 hit the South Vietnamese armies hard, since their American-style war machine absorbed vast quantities of imported petroleum. The sophisticated weaponry of the ARVN also cost more and more to replace, so that the reduced US aid allocations were soon insufficient even to keep existing equipment running. Spiralling inflation reduced the buying power of ARVN troops' wages to such an extent that theft and corruption became essential to a soldier's survival. The withdrawal of US personnel had brought unemployment and poverty to hundreds of thousands who had made a living in their service, yet most of Saigon's ruling political group and higher officers made fortunes out of black marketeering and other corrupt dealing. One well-known trick was the invention of 'ghost troops' – an officer would claim to have 10,000 men when only 8000 were actually enrolled, pocketing the pay disbursed for the missing 2000. There was little in the behaviour of Saigon's ruling class to raise morale.

From late 1973 the communists moved increasingly onto the offensive. In December Viet Cong guerrillas blew up a 75 million litre (20 million gallon) oil depot near Saigon. By May 1974 the ARVN 18th

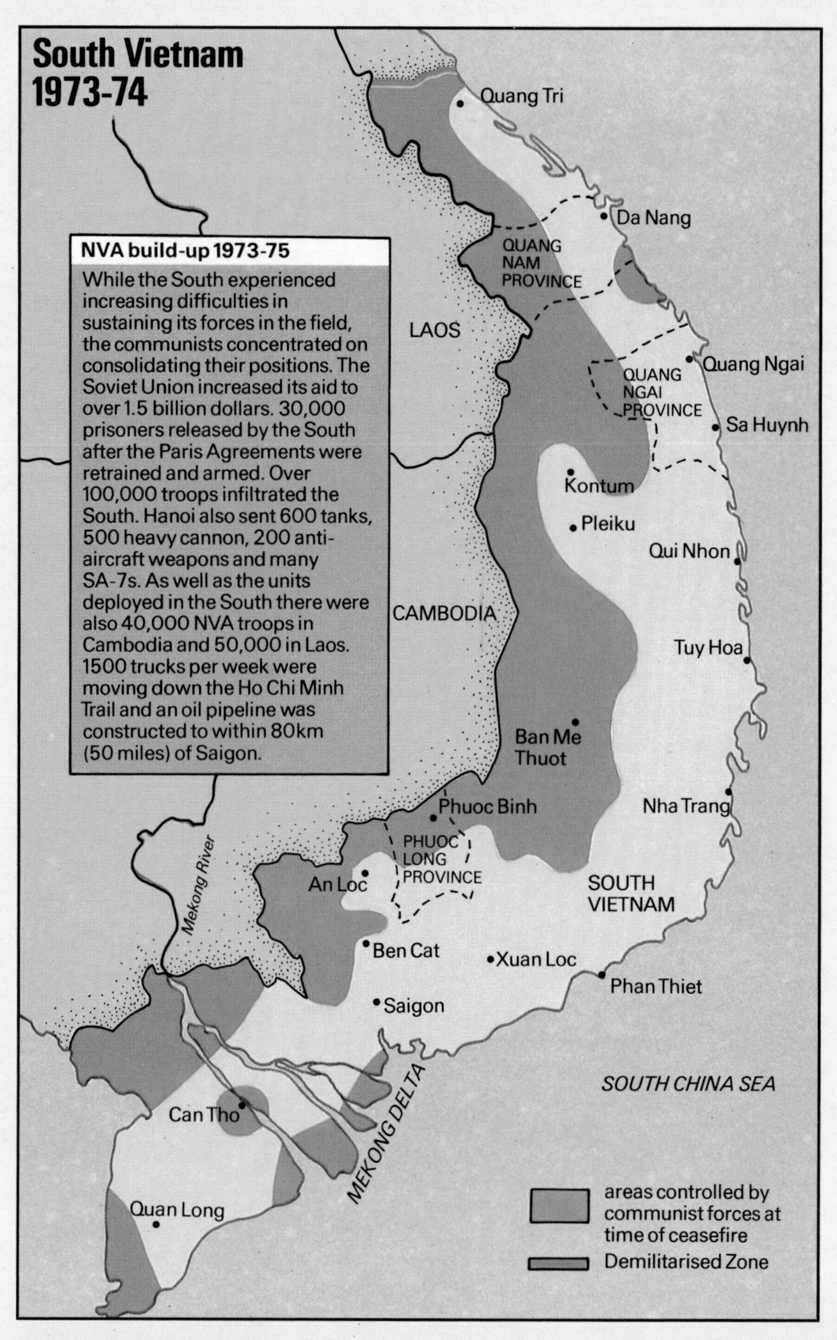

NVA build-up 1973-75

While the South experienced increasing difficulties in sustaining its forces in the field, the communists concentrated on consolidating their positions. The Soviet Union increased its aid to over 1.5 billion dollars. 30,000 prisoners released by the South after the Paris Agreements were retrained and armed. Over 100,000 troops infiltrated the South. Hanoi also sent 600 tanks, 500 heavy cannon, 200 anti-aircraft weapons and many SA-7s. As well as the units deployed in the South there were also 40,000 NVA troops in Cambodia and 50,000 in Laos. 1500 trucks per week were moving down the Ho Chi Minh Trail and an oil pipeline was constructed to within 80km (50 miles) of Saigon.

Top: North Vietnamese Marines march south to reinforce the communist forces in South Vietnam. Above: Members of the International Commission of Control and Supervision, from left: Brigadier-General Wijoge of Indonesia, Major-General McAlpine of Canada, Major-General Szucs of Hungary and Brigadier-General Ryba of Poland. Left: ARVN forces in M113 APCs go into action along Route 1 during a breakdown in the ceasefire.

Division was heavily engaged in the defence of Ben Cat and communist forces were making gains in Quang Nam and Quang Ngai Provinces. Fierce fighting developed around Da Nang in mid-July and on 7 August the nearby district town of Thuong Duc was overrun. Two ARVN elite airborne brigades were committed to restore the situation. ARVN casualties, already heavy at 25,000 dead in 1973, rose to almost 31,000 dead in 1974.

Initially committed to a long-term struggle to undermine President Thieu's regime, the members of the Hanoi politburo were now turning to belief in a far swifter military success. In August 1974 President Nixon had to resign to avoid impeachment over the Watergate affair and the chances of any further US military action dwindled. North Vietnamese engineers had completed a road system in their zone of South Vietnam which had proved its usefulness for the rapid movement of forces during the summer action around Da Nang. The Ho Chi Minh Trail had also been turned into a paved highway – in the absence of US bombers – with an accompanying fuel pipeline. Men and equipment flowed south, while the effectiveness of the ARVN declined daily. Ammunition and fuel for the South Vietnamese forces were strictly rationed. Much of their sophisticated equipment was out of use because of poor maintenance or lack of spare parts. Flying of helicopters and aircraft was strictly limited due to the lack of fuel, and as a result pilots did not receive adequate training. By 1975 the South Vietnamese Air Force had disbanded 11 of its 66 squadrons.

In December 1974 the North Vietnamese politburo took the fateful decision to go for military victory. The order was given for the flow of supplies down the Trail to be put into top gear. By December 1974 the warning signs were clear. In Phuoc Long Province four district capitals fell to the communist forces during the month and on 7 January 1975 the provincial capital, Phuoc Binh, was taken. The communists had effectively seized a whole province without provoking a substantial American reaction. The way was open for a further push which, with unexpected suddenness, would bring the shaky structure of South Vietnam down in ruins.

R.G. Grant

Cambodia's agony

The Khmer Rouge close in on Phnom Penh

By the time of the US withdrawal from South Vietnam in early 1973, the Khmer Rouge guerrilla forces in neighbouring Cambodia were in control of some two-thirds of that country, despite massive US aid to the government of General Lon Nol in the capital, Phnom Penh. Lon Nol had been able to expand his army from under 100,000 to over 200,000 men (at least on paper), but the quality of leadership and the motivation of the troops was poor. The Khmer Rouge forces probably numbered around 60,000 and enjoyed the support of substantial North Vietnamese Army (NVA) formations and NVA supply lines. The heavy US bombing of eastern Cambodia which had begun in March 1969 continued until 15 August 1973 – when pressure from the US Congress forced a halt to the raids – but the expansion of Khmer Rouge control of rural areas and small towns went on apace. By the end of the year the rebels were established within artillery range of Phnom Penh. During January and February 1974 bombardment by communist 105mm artillery left 10,000 people in Phnom Penh homeless. The overcrowded city, its population swollen with a flood of refugees – fleeing the American bombing, the fighting between the two armies and the harsh

Above: Phnom Penh under bombardment in 1975 during the remorseless siege warfare practised by the Khmer Rouge. Below left: Cambodian government troops move across a paddy field. They are armed with US equipment, including M16 rifles, M79 grenade launchers and, unusually, a Browning M1919 air-cooled machine gun.

control of the Khmer Rouge – awaited a final assault.

The communist strategy, however, was to avoid a costly direct attack and apply a slow stranglehold upon their enemy. Khmer Rouge units sealed off all the road routes into the capital, and from then on 92 per cent of the rice, ammunition and fuel required by the government forces and the inhabitants of Phnom Penh had to be brought by convoys of barges up the Mekong River from South Vietnam. As the rainy season drew to a close in December 1974, the river narrowed and convoys became more vulnerable to attack, but just after Christmas it was still possible for a convoy to get through.

However, at 0100 hours on 1 January 1975 an artillery and rocket barrage against Phnom Penh announced the onset of what was to prove the final Khmer Rouge offensive. Its first objective was to complete its blockade by closing the Mekong River lifeline and bombarding Pochentong international airport, the only other possible source of supplies. On the government side, Lon Nol was hoping to hold off the assault until the wet season would once more put an end to campaigning for the year. But that was five months away and without massive US military aid – which the US Congress was reluctant to provide – the regime was unlikely to survive for that length of time.

There were some 60,000 troops of the regular Cambodian Army organised to hold a lengthy, roughly circular perimeter lying up to 25km (15 miles) from the city centre. To the west it took in the airport, 15km (10 miles) from Phnom Penh, whilst to the east the far bank of the mile-wide Mekong was held. The defences were not a continuous line of trenches but a series of strongpoints based on outlying villages astride the main highways radiating out from the capital. The high command planned to hold these positions that were vital for repulsing Khmer Rouge attacks and for keeping the communists' long-range weapons out of effective range of the airport, whilst using their own fire superiority to blast the insurgents out of their emplacements. Such a strategy could be pursued only if the morale of the government forces was sound and the stocks of ammunition high.

Two weapons, and two weapons only, of the whole armoury brought to bear in Indochina, were the key to the battle for Phnom Penh. One was the Chinese Type 63 107mm multiple rocket launcher, firing a 19kg (42lb) rocket to an effective range of 8km (5 miles). The other was the US 105mm M2A1 howitzer, a highly mobile general purpose field piece capable of firing up to four rounds a minute to a range of 13km (8 miles). Twenty of these howitzers had been captured by the Khmer Rouge in previous encounters with government forces and now, together with the Type 63 rocket launcher, they were the weapon used to enforce the blockade of Phnom Penh.

When the offensive began, the Khmer Rouge committed 5000 troops to the banks of the Mekong between Neak Luong, an important ferry-town downstream from Phnom Penh, and the Vietnamese

Above: A Khmer Rouge patrol moves through the wilderness of a defoliated forest. US air raids on Cambodia were continued until August 1973, when pressure from Congress finally forced a halt.

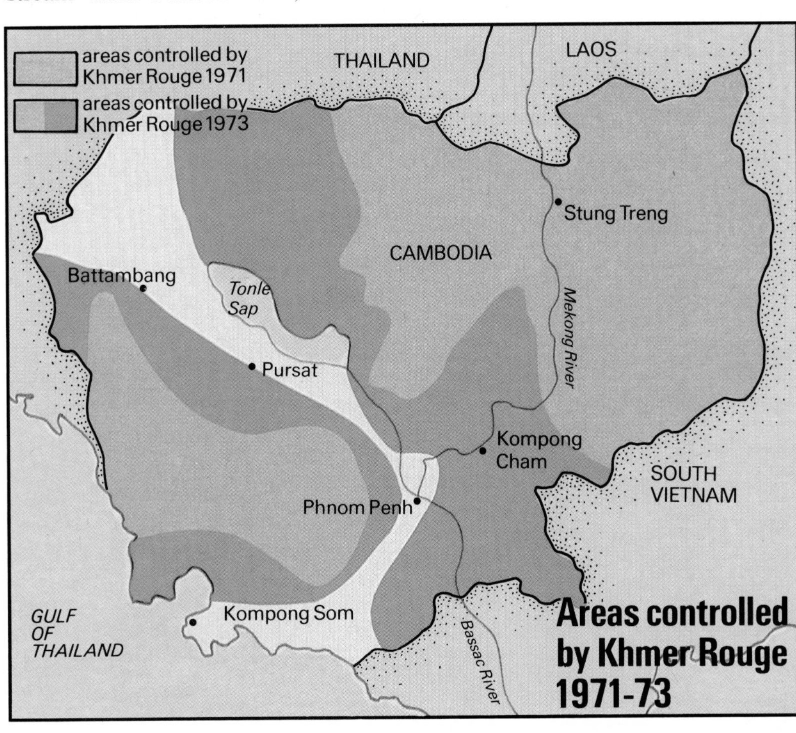

border. At narrow points they placed machine-gun posts, Type 63 rocket launchers and mortars. Throughout January the river was completely blocked.

Around Phnom Penh the critical battlefield was a rough quarter-circle based on the city centre with its circumference covering Prek Pneou on the Toule Sap River, 11km (7 miles) north of the city astride Route 5, and the village of Tuol Leap held by the Cambodian 3rd Division lying a dozen miles due west. All other attacks on the perimeter were to be diversions aiming to dislocate government responses to incursions in the north and west. Occupation of the Mekong's east bank was integral to this strategy as continuous daily rocketing of the city would add to people's war-weariness. Possession of the east bank would also bring Chrui Changwar, the city's naval base, under fire.

On 3/4 January both Tuol Leap and Prek Pneou came under heavy attack as the Khmer Rouge established rocket positions 8km (5 miles) north of Pochentong airport and, in a coordinated movement, encircled the Cambodian 7th Division's headquarters at Prek Pneou. The rocket batteries, though capable of hitting the more westerly civilian airport terminal, were unable at this stage to fire on the vital military complex at the airport lying a little to the east. For the moment the rocket attacks were periodic and brief for fear of counter-battery fire.

On 14 January, in response to the closing of the Mekong supply route, the US began an airlift for the relief of Phnom Penh. A DC-8 shuttle from Saigon brought in rice, while fuel and ammunition were flown in from Thailand. In order to avoid direct involvement, the Pentagon contracted a firm called Bird Air to run the airlift, but many of the aircraft were loaned by the USAF and about half the pilots were USAF reservists. At this stage the Khmer Rouge could not hope to close the airport entirely but only to cause maximum disruption and if possible hit US aircrews – because of its potential political impact, the latter could have led to the ending of flights.

At the very end of January a convoy got through along the Mekong, bringing two weeks' supply of essential goods, but it was the last ever to reach Phnom Penh. By the time the empty barges went back down the river, the Khmer Rouge had introduced a system of floats and mines that could be detonated from the shore; several of the barges were sunk by this

The Khmer Rouge

The Khmer (Cambodian) communist movement – like the communist movements in Vietnam and Laos – had its origins in the formation of the Indochina Communist Party in 1930. In 1941 the party began a low-level underground war against the French authorities, and later against the Japanese, but in Cambodia at least the war was not very successful. Nevertheless, many of the anti-French Khmer Issarak (Free Khmer) guerrillas joined the struggle during the 1940s.

The party dissolved into its national components in 1951, and three years later, with the ending of French rule, Cambodia became an independent state under a neutralist government. Under instructions from Hanoi, most of the Cambodian communists – some 2000 – withdrew to North Vietnam, where they remained, growing more and more isolated from Cambodian politics, until 1970.

A few hundred Khmer communists, however, regarding the North Vietnamese as betrayers of the Cambodian revolution, disobeyed Hanoi and remained underground in Cambodia. During the late 1950s and 1960s, while Hanoi cooperated with the neutralist regime of Prince Norodom Sihanouk, they lived in the hills and jungles of northeastern Cambodia and in the Cardamom mountains of the southwest. Other Khmer communists were to be found amongst the intellectuals of Phnom Penh; typical of these was Saloth Sar (later known as Pol Pot). Saloth Sar went to Paris in 1949 to study electronics but, distracted by his revolutionary activities, he failed his examinations. He returned to Phnom Penh, taught for a while in a private school, and then built a career as a left-wing journalist. Meanwhile, he had secretly become a member of the communist movement, and by 1962 he had risen to the position of deputy general secretary. In 1963 Sihanouk invited him, along with some 30 other left-wingers, to join the government, but Saloth Sar turned down the offer and went underground.

Other communists – including Khieu Samphan, who later commanded the Khmer Rouge army – did participate in government in the mid-1960s, but in 1967 a peasant uprising frightened Sihanouk into a crack-down on the communists, whom he dubbed *'les Khmers rouges'*. Khieu Samphan, and many like him, fled to the hills, and the movement was joined by hundreds of peasants from Battambang Province. Until 1970, however, the Khmer Rouge had minimal impact.

After Sihanouk's overthrow by General Lon Nol in March 1970, however, Khmer Rouge fortunes began to improve. Sihanouk, in exile, announced a new National United Front with his former Khmer Rouge enemies, and urged the peasantry to rise and liberate Cambodia from Lon Nol's military government. In April, representatives of the National United Front, the Pathet Lao and the North Vietnamese met in China to organise a collective struggle against the US and its client governments in Indochina. Hanoi began to supply and support the Khmer communists down the Ho Chi Minh Trail, reinforcing them with regular NVA troops.

Chinese-equipped Khmer Rouge prepare an ambush.

The NVA, sensible of traditional Khmer hostility to Vietnam, issued standing orders to their forces to respect Khmer autonomy in the hope of winning them over into a permanent alliance with Hanoi; but the bulk of the Khmer Rouge – particularly the faction led by Pol Pot – intended all along to exploit both Sihanouk and the North Vietnamese for their own ends. They gradually eliminated pro-Vietnamese Khmer and Sihanoukists from the ranks of the revolutionary forces, and they imposed their own political organisation on the peasantry in areas under their control, transforming a traditional society by brutal means. Whole villages were uprooted and relocated, and Buddhist monks were drafted into the army or forced to work in the rice paddies.

After the fall of Phnom Penh in April 1975, the policy of political transformation by relocation was applied to the capital: the whole population was forced to leave. Sihanouk returned to Cambodia as a figurehead, but after a year, Khieu Samphan replaced him as head of state with Pol Pot as his prime minister.

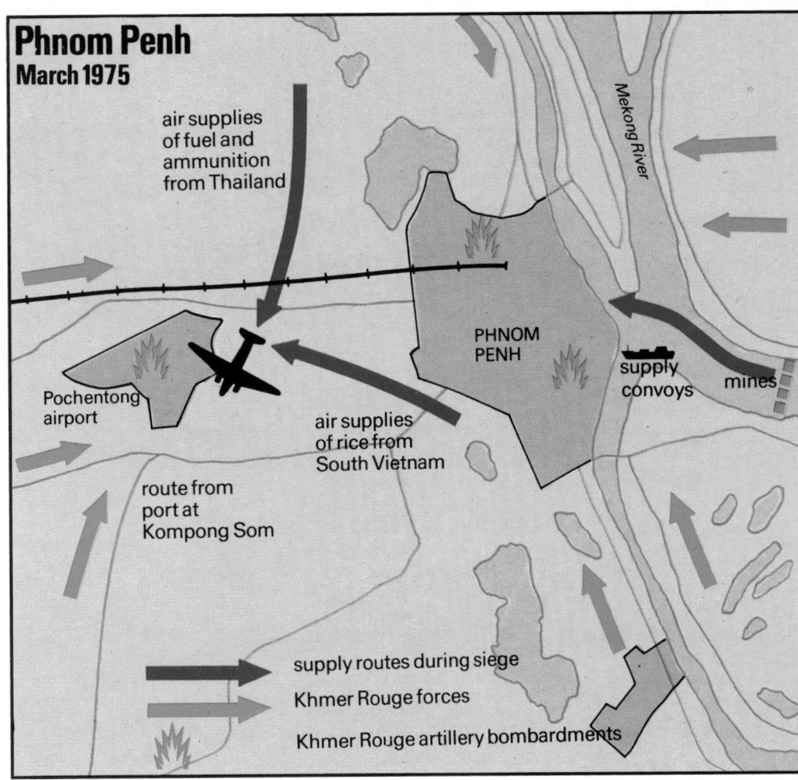

means as they sailed down to South Vietnam. The government's navy made a number of disorganised attempts to clear the river in the following months, but with no success. By the end of March 25 per cent of the Cambodian Navy's ships and possibly as many as 70 per cent of its crew members had been lost.

With the river finally closed, attention focused on the airport. By the end of February the supply situation was becoming acute, with only four weeks' supply of food in store. US flights were 10 times as expensive as river convoys, and although the number of flights was raised to 20 a day on 21 February and 42 a day one week later, they could not hope to compensate for the Mekong's closure. The capital, its population quadrupled by refugees, needed over 700 tonnes of rice a day to feed itself; the airlift could manage only 440 tonnes a day. The daily shortfall was supposedly made up by drawing on reserves gathered locally – a mere 1200 tonnes – or those supplied from Battambang Province before its capture by the Khmer Rouge. However, many people starved. In February the official daily ration was cut to 540 tonnes, of which only a third went to the refugees. Food prices soared. In the first week of March the cost of a 50kg (110lb) bag of rice doubled, Chinese traders shut their market stalls and Save The Children were feeding over 2000 children a day. Medical supplies were scarce. By 9 March Khet Melea, the city's largest hospital, had a stock of 14 pints of blood with which to treat 20-30 civilians a day. Military casualties fared no better with 20 pints between 1000 patients. The capital's 150 doctors were unable to give full treatment to the 250 fresh casualties they were handling each week.

On 6 March howitzer shells forced the closure of the airport to civilian flights and a temporary suspension of the military airlift. But still the Khmer Rouge were unable to achieve the total military closure of the airport. This they could do only if the rocket batteries were moved a mile and the howitzers half a mile nearer. The only way for the government to resolve the situation would have been for its troops to push these positions back out of effective range. However, by March, after four attempts, it seemed incapable of doing so. Over the last two months the perimeter had been pushed in along a wide arc from the east bank of the Mekong to an area southeast of the city. There was an almost daily see-saw as insurgents infiltrated government positions at night, and the army, although increasingly reluctant to fight, counter-attacked during the day. Despite suffering an estimated 20,000 casualties since 1 January, the Khmer Rouge was able to bring up replacements and maintain the initiative.

Meanwhile, the need for further military aid to Cambodia was being discussed by the US government. On 25 February President Gerald Ford told the House of Representatives that if the extra $222 million he had asked for was withheld or delayed, the Cambodian regime would be forced to surrender in a few weeks. Three days later the Senate voted to

Above left: A tanker burns in the Mekong, near Neak Luong, after a Khmer Rouge attack. It was the slow and remorseless application of pressure upon the supply lines of the capital that finally brought down the government of Lon Nol, and the crucial question in this respect was whether the Mekong could be closed to shipping. Below: Last-ditch defence in the streets as government troops desperately try to hold off the Khmer Rouge.

The Mayaguez incident

After the disasters for American policy in Indochina that had occurred in April 1975 – the fall of Saigon and Phnom Penh to communist forces while the US stood impotently aside – the US government was eager for any opportunity to reassert America's military strength and its prestige among its allies. Such an opportunity presented itself on 12 May 1975 when an American cargo ship, the *Mayaguez*, with its crew of 39 seamen, was seized by Cambodia's newly-installed communist authorities.

The ship was on its way from Hong Kong through the Gulf of Thailand to Ban Sattahip, a port in Thailand. It was about 65km (40 miles) off the Cambodian mainland, near the rocky island of Poulo Wai, when it was fired on by a Cambodian gunboat and boarded, only having time to transmit a brief distress message. It seems that the seizure was carried out by edgy local officials, suspicious of any American vessel, but the Khmer Rouge government took up the issue defiantly, accusing the US of violating Cambodian territorial waters and of spying.

President Gerald Ford determined upon a display of American power. Denouncing the Cambodian action as 'piracy', he decided on the afternoon of 13 May, after consultation with the National Security Council, to recover the ship and its crew by force. A battalion of Marines was rapidly flown from Okinawa to the US base at U Tapao in Thailand, close to the Cambodian border. The aircraft carrier USS *Coral Sea*, with its escort of destroyers, was ordered to head at full speed for the Gulf of Thailand. Meanwhile US Lockheed Orion search aircraft had located the *Mayaguez* at anchor off the island of Koh Tang, guarded by Cambodian patrol boats. American strike aircraft established a continuous watch over the vessel, sinking a number of Cambodian boats.

Unfortunately, US intelligence had been unable to establish the whereabouts of the *Mayaguez* crew members (in fact they were being held on the island of Kas Rong). Intelligence had also failed to report that the island of Koh Tang, which the Marines had decided to assault, was defended by some 200 well-armed Khmer Rouge troops. Before dawn on 15 May eight US Air Force CH-53 helicopters set off from U Tapao with their cargo of Marines. As the first helicopter landed on Koh Tang it came under smallarms, mortar and rocket fire; after the Marines had dismounted the CH-53 managed to take off but then crashed into the sea. The second helicopter was forced to return to base, heavily damaged, without having landed, and the third and fourth were both brought down on the beach by enemy fire, one bursting into flames and killing the 13 men on board. The other helicopters eventually landed their Marines, but conditions on the island were difficult, with some reasonably intense fighting.

Meanwhile, a boarding party of Marines who had been heli-lifted onto the destroyer USS *Holt*, seized the *Mayaguez*, which was empty and undefended. A-7 Corsairs from the USS *Coral Sea* carried out strikes against mainland targets at Ream and Kompong Som. In fact, that morning the Khmer Rouge government had declared its readiness to release the *Mayaguez* crew, and as the fighting and bombing went on, a Thai fishing vessel flying white flags sailed up to the destroyer USS *Wilson* with the missing crew members aboard, more or less unharmed.

Although the object of the operation was now achieved, it was still necessary to extract the Marines from Koh Tang. Gunships and strike aircraft pounded the island and reinforcements were landed, allowing a successful heliborne evacuation to be accomplished by nightfall.

Despite the loss of 18 American lives, and the evidence of Khmer Rouge preparedness to release the *Mayaguez* crew before the assault began, the operation was immensely popular in the United States. It assuaged the sense of failure in Indochina and reaffirmed American readiness to take armed action in defence of its interests, at least at a low level.

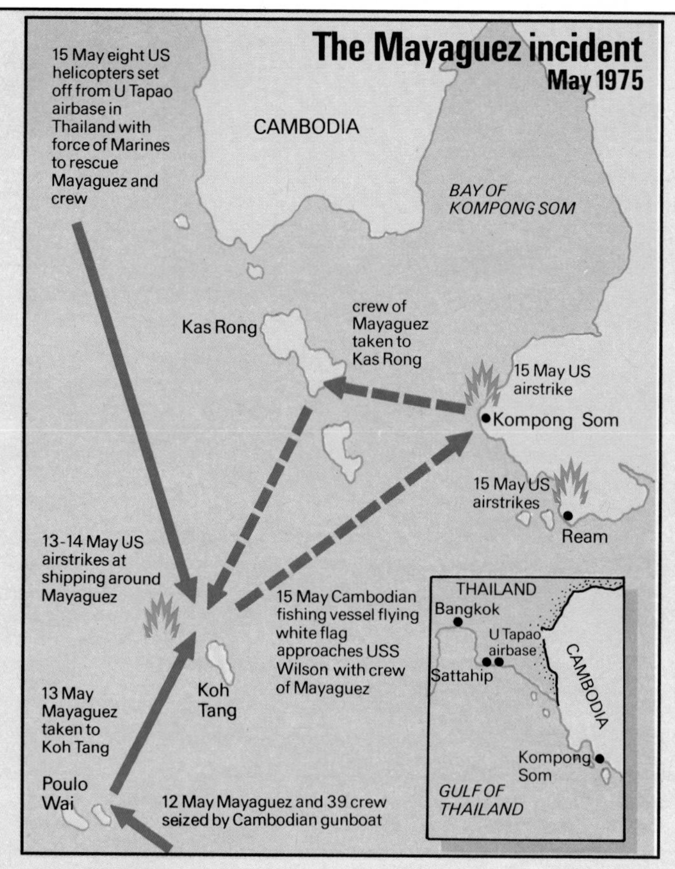

Left: The *Mayaguez*, having been captured by a boarding party of Marines, is towed away by the destroyer USS *Holt* after the attack on Koh Tang island.

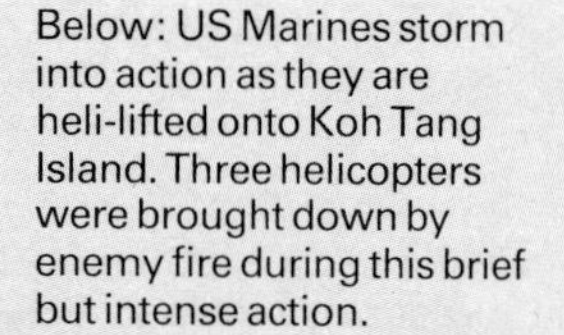

Below: US Marines storm into action as they are heli-lifted onto Koh Tang Island. Three helicopters were brought down by enemy fire during this brief but intense action.

suspend all emergency aid on a temporary basis. Senator Mike Mansfield, Democratic Party leader of the Senate, expressed the prevailing mood: 'More money means more ammunition, more ammunition means more killing. Some day this matter will have to be resolved by the Cambodians their own way. I think the sooner the better.' On 28 March, with the matter still unresolved, Congress adjourned for Easter. By the time it reconvened, military events in Cambodia would have made any further discussion superfluous.

The second week of March saw government forces make their fifth and final attempt to relieve pressure on the airport. The attack, to begin on 7 March, was planned as a large multi-battalion operation supported by US M113 armoured personnel carriers used as light tanks. Plans called for the use of four brigades operating a pincer movement against insurgent positions south of Tuol Leap. Two were to advance on the village directly from the southeast as the others attacked Khmer Rouge positions northeast of Route 4. The advance which had to be replanned and restarted several times over the following week, was quickly disrupted by insurgent counter-attacks elsewhere. On the night of 7 March the Khmer Rouge launched a diversionary attack on Cambodian 7th Division positions around Prek Pneou. Heavy fighting took place 300m (330 yards) west of the marketplace. Though the attempted encirclement failed, it proved sufficient to disrupt the government offensive in the west, two battalions being withdrawn to shore up the Prek Pneou position on 9 March.

The overall impression was of the Cambodian High Command, run ragged by well-timed Khmer Rouge pressure, grabbing a unit here and a unit there, and stuffing them into the perimeter gaps. Brigades were broken in half with one part sent to one sector and the other elsewhere. The government offensive on Tuol Leap did have some limited success (on 15 March the village was recaptured) but the spearhead battalion was soon surrounded and cut off. Attempts to relieve the position were soon bogged down despite the use of T-28 aircraft in support, and by 24 March the loss of six positions around the village forced a general retreat a mile south.

Below: Victims of the continuing bombardment of Phnom Penh. Chinese Type 63 107mm rocket launchers and some 20 captured US M2A1 105mm howitzers were the main weapons that the Khmer Rouge employed in these attacks.

The soldiers' strike

The increasing success of the insurgent blockade was seriously weakening the ability of the Cambodian Army to respond to incursions. The morale of the troops was also at breaking point. On 19 March the 7th Division's 7th Brigade based along Route 5 went on strike, refusing to advance unless paid and supplied with their traditional prerogative, as combat soldiers, of free rice. Nor was the government able to replace the 5000 casualties it had suffered since January. Many perimeter units were down to 50 per cent strength, a few had suffered 75 per cent losses – yet students in the capital remained unconscripted. Prime Minister Long Boret explained that they were not drafted as the government did not want to interrupt their studies. Such reserves as units did receive were of poor quality. A junior officer remarked, 'I get men who are ill or still recovering from wounds. I get people who have had so little training they are almost useless. They are just going to get themselves killed.'

As attacks against the perimeter continued, the bombardment and blockade of the airport worsened. By 18 March up to 60 rockets a day were hitting the civilian and military compounds. Three days later four groundcrew were killed and the airlift briefly suspended. The following day, damage to a US air transport caused further delay. On 28 March a DC-8 flying in rice from Saigon and a C-130 with ammunition from Thailand were hit, causing the third suspension of the daily flights. The airlift did continue, however, and the government, while acknowledging acute food shortages, announced that stocks of ammunition were sufficient to last six weeks.

Time, however, was running out. On 1 April Lon Nol left Cambodia and Cambodian troops were ordered not to fire more than 30 rounds a day and

Right: Weary but triumphant, Khmer Rouge troops enter Phnom Penh on 17 April 1975. Ragged though their uniforms may be, they are well armed with Chinese versions of the Kalashnikov assault rifle, an RPG-7 rocket launcher, and a captured American M79 grenade launcher.

Below: Some of the 316 Marines who were lifted into Phnom Penh on 12 April by 36 helicopters to protect the evacuation of the final US personnel from the city. The operation, codenamed 'Eagle Pull' lasted only four hours, and concluded American involvement in the affairs of this unhappy country.

mortar batteries no more than 50. A new front opened up on the southern perimeter and the ferry town of Neak Luong fell to the communists. On the night of 9/10 April 200 insurgents broke through two government brigades on the outskirts of Phnom Penh and advanced to within 3km (2 miles) of the airport. Air and ground attacks on 11 April failed to dislodge them. After a US airman was killed, the Pentagon ordered the cessation of further direct airlifts, though airdrops by parachute were ordered. With howitzers protected by mines within 6km (4 miles) of the airport, its final closure could only be a matter of time. On 12 April the US embassy was evacuated by Marine helicopter.

On 14 April, after sustained attacks, the western perimeter crumbled and the airport closed as Khmer Rouge units moved into the adjacent Pochentong village. By 0400 hours a battle had developed within 460m (500 yards) of the military terminal. Four hours later government troops deserted their positions and the airport fell. Though the airdrops continued for two more days, the battle for Phnom Penh was over.

At 0600 hours on 17 April, as Khmer Rouge troops marched down the once-fashionable Monivong Boulevard and along the quays of the Toule Sap to be greeted by a sea of white surrender flags, Brigadier-General Mey Sichan (Chief of Operations of the Cambodian Armed Forces) broadcast the final surrender over Radio Phnom Penh. Later Khieu Samphan, commander-in-chief of the insurgents, announced: 'At 9.30 am on the morning of 17 April Phnom Penh was completely liberated by the Cambodian People's Army of National Liberation. The war was won by those who gave up everything – their lives, their possessions, their families to fight in the front lines.' The Khmer Rouge's single-minded concentration on the Mekong and Phnom Penh for 107 days had produced results beyond their initial expectations. Their victory was not, however, destined to bring peace or an end to the sufferings of the Cambodian people.

Ian Westwell

Victory for the Pathet Lao

The communist takeover in Laos

In July 1962, after lengthy discussions at the Geneva Conference on Laos, four years of fighting between rightists led by General Phoumi Nosavan and Pathet Lao communists headed by Prince Souphanouvong was brought to a temporary end. A neutralist coalition government was set up under Souphanouvong's half-brother, Prince Souvanna Phouma, with both communist and rightist participation. This government was, however, short-lived. In 1963 the Pathet Lao ministers withdrew and a new phase of the civil war began as the Royal Laotian government forces confronted the Pathet Lao.

The United States was deeply concerned about the situation in Laos. In 1964 William H. Sullivan was appointed US ambassador to Laos, bringing a considerable experience of the Laotian political situation to bear. US military supplies to the government forces were stepped up, while the CIA mounted extensive covert operations, most notably organising the Meo hill tribesmen into an anti-communist army. The Pathet Lao, for their part, numbered an estimated 35,000 fighting men, supported by units of the North Vietnamese Army (NVA) and supplied chiefly from North Vietnam.

In 1965 the lingering rightist threat to Souvanna Phouma's neutralist government was eliminated when General Phoumi Nosavan fled into exile in Thailand after an abortive coup; Ambassador Sullivan then devoted himself to the maintenance of the government against the threat posed by the communists. The Pathet Lao now controlled northeastern Laos and the eastern areas of the country along the Vietnamese border, and the conflict developed a seasonal pattern. Each dry season, lasting from about November to April, the Pathet Lao launched a westward offensive from their strongholds in the east across the Bolovens Plateau in the south, the central 'panhandle', and the Plain of Jars in the north. During each wet season, Royal Lao forces and irregular units of Meo and Kha hill tribesmen combined, with air support, to launch counter-offensives and recapture positions lost in the preceding dry season.

The great strategic prize to be won in Laos was the Ho Chi Minh Trail along the Laotian border with Vietnam, the vital artery for the passage of North Vietnamese reinforcements and supplies to the communist forces in South Vietnam. The North Vietnamese were determined to keep the border areas under Pathet Lao control in order to protect the Trail, but the NVA, who had at times as many as 100,000 troops in Laos, were for a long time reluctant to over-extend themselves by advancing into the Mekong Valley to overthrow Souvanna Phouma's government. The Pathet Lao were not strong enough to do this on their own, and the result was stalemate.

Above: The CIA base and airstrip at Bouam Long in Laos. The CIA were present in Laos as early as 1960, and their covert operations were extended after 1963, when renewed fighting broke out between government forces and the communist Pathet Lao.

The US government, for its part, was anxious to deny the North Vietnamese the use of the Trail, and in 1965 B-52s began to bomb the border areas. Sullivan managed to persuade the small group of Western correspondents in Vientiane not to report information about United States ground and air operations in Laos to their newspapers, and the bombing was kept secret from the American public until 1969. Forward Air Controllers were sent to Laos in 1966 to guide the B-52s to their targets, and inevitably, given his reliance on the United States, Souvanna Phouma was obliged to acquiesce. After the bombing halt over North Vietnam in 1968 more B-52s became available and operations in Laos were further intensified. But the Ho Chi Minh Trail remained open, and the bombing contributed largely to the Laotian refugee problem.

The United States also attempted to modernise and expand the 70,000-strong Royal Laotian Army in the

Below: A Douglas C-47 transport belonging to the CIA airline, Air America. CIA transports were used to supply arms and ammunition to Royal Lao and Meo guerrilla forces.

hope that it would eventually be able to crush the Pathet Lao. Yet the army never succeeded in winning over the people in the countryside. Its commanders were content at best with periodic offensives from their strongholds, and the army was rife with corruption – including local accommodations with Pathet Lao units, and even arms sales to the enemy. The irregular forces of hill tribesmen supplied and supported by the CIA rose to a peak of perhaps 40,000 in 1970. Major-General Vang Pao's Meo irregulars bore the brunt of the bitter see-saw campaigns in the Plain of Jars, and by maintaining their stronghold at Long Cheng they denied the Pathet Lao access to the political and administrative centre in Vientiane and the royal capital, Luang Prabang. Thailand also supported the United States' effort by allowing Laotian pilots to train on its territory and by sending troops and artillery into Laos.

When Sullivan left Laos in March 1969 to take up a position in the State Department, the situation was still stalemated. A joint Pathet Lao-NVA offensive in 1969 was defeated in September. Souvanna Phouma was clearly worried by increasing NVA involvement in Laos, and early in February 1970 he announced that he would take no action against supply activity on the Ho Chi Minh Trail if the NVA in turn withdrew combat troops from inside Laos. In the same month, the Pathet Lao launched a major new offensive across the Plain of Jars. They advanced as far as the Meo stronghold at Long Cheng and laid siege to it, driving out the USAF personnel and beginning an exodus of civilian Meo. Vang Pao's men managed to hold Long Cheng itself, but the decline of the Meo forces had begun.

The neutralist Sihanouk regime in Cambodia, which had for some time permitted the North Vietnamese to use Cambodian ports to supply communist forces in South Vietnam, fell in March of that year. Sihanouk's successor Lon Nol closed the ports and launched an offensive against the North Vietnamese. As a result, the NVA began to consolidate its position in Laos in order to secure the alternative supply route of the Trail and expand the traffic along it. In southern Laos, as the NVA advanced, the Royal Laotian Army lost two provincial capitals, Attopeu and Saravane.

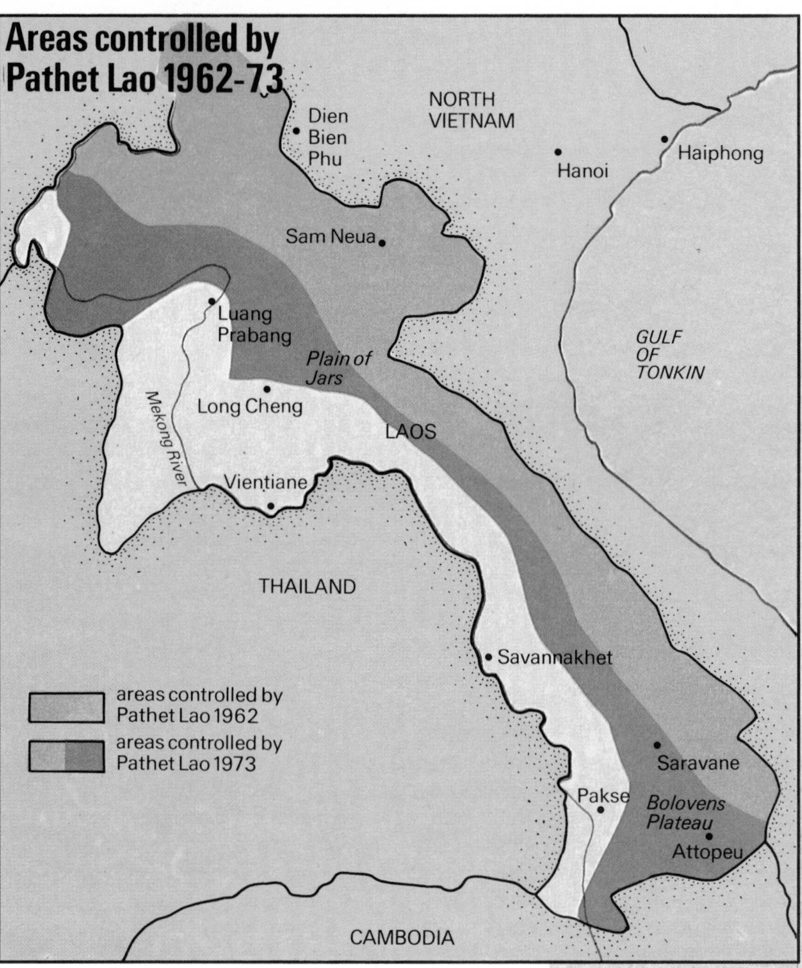

Although these towns had been cut off from government forces in the Mekong Valley for some years, they had been recognised by the communists as government enclaves since the 1962 ceasefire. Attopeu fell on 30 April followed by Saravane on 9 June. The involvement of NVA troops in these actions was regarded as a significant indication that Hanoi intended to abrogate the 1962 agreement completely and become involved more directly in the communist struggle inside Laos.

Left: A column of Meo hill tribesmen collect supplies at a rendezvous with a CIA Sikorsky H-34 helicopter. They are armed with US weapons, including the M1 rifle.

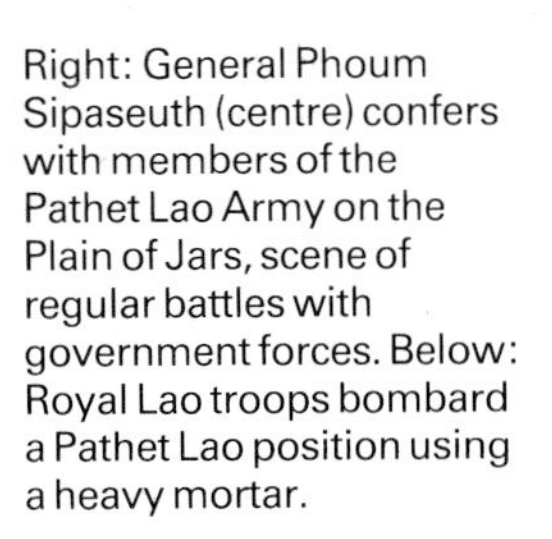

Right: General Phoum Sipaseuth (centre) confers with members of the Pathet Lao Army on the Plain of Jars, scene of regular battles with government forces. Below: Royal Lao troops bombard a Pathet Lao position using a heavy mortar.

Despite US air attacks on the Ho Chi Minh Trail, and incursions by Meo tribesmen, Hanoi's plan to expand the Trail was put into effect. Traffic along the Trail increased and there was a build-up of NVA forces in Laos during late 1970. US military commanders in South Vietnam concluded that the build-up presaged a new offensive in Vietnam, and in February 1971 Operation Lam Son 719 was launched into Laos by the South Vietnamese Army, aiming to cut the Ho Chi Minh Trail, destroy Pathet Lao arms and supply caches and crush NVA opposition, thus disrupting any intended North Vietnamese offensive into South Vietnam. In fact, many of the units were badly mauled by the NVA. The operation was called off and by 25 March the evacuation of ARVN troops was complete.

Retaliatory attacks

After Lam Son 719 traffic began to flow down the Ho Chi Minh Trail again almost immediately, and elsewhere in Laos the Pathet Lao and their allies had remained on the offensive. During February, they besieged the Meo forces at Long Cheng. And even before the incursion, on 2 February, communist forces had taken the town of Muong Soui, west of the Plain of Jars. North Vietnamese sources in Vientiane had been quoted as saying that any South Vietnamese attempt to cut the Ho Chi Minh Trail in Laos would provoke a retaliatory attack on the Laotian royal capital at Luang Prabang, northwest of the Plain. During Lam Son 719, pressure on Luang Prabang did indeed increase: NVA forces advanced down the Hou River Valley and took the Royal Lao garrison at Pak Hou. Pathet Lao guerrillas arrived at Pak Suong where King Savang Vatthana, the Laotian head of state, had a farm; by 20 March the communists were close enough to the royal capital to launch a rocket attack.

The following month, Royal Laotian Army and Meo forces began their counter-offensive. The Meo general, Vang Pao, drove the Pathet Lao out of the hills to the north of their main base at Long Cheng and then pushed on into the Plain of Jars. The United States, however, had decided to halve the number of sorties flown in Laos from July onwards, and so Vang Pao was forced to continue his offensive with reduced air cover. When regular NVA units counter-attacked in December, they were able to drive the Meo tribesmen off the Plain of Jars and take the town of Sam Thong. They began to advance on Long Cheng again. The Meo reverse turned into a rout and by late December the evacuation of Long Cheng had begun.

Meanwhile the communists had also been making gains in the south of Laos. On 16 May 1971 they captured the town of Paksong on the Bolovens Plateau, and they continued to advance westwards towards the provincial capital of Pakse in the Mekong Valley. By late June the communists were approaching the outskirts of the city, and when NVA tanks appeared, Royal Lao soldiers threw down their rifles and ran away. The situation was only saved by a counter-attack carried out by a special commando unit under Colonel Soutchay Vongsavanh and by a Royal Lao Air Force air strike using T-28 aircraft.

By the beginning of 1972, with the defeat of the Meo complete, the military initiative was gradually passing over to the communists, who were receiving increasing support from the NVA. Government forces were hanging on in the west lowlands; virtually everywhere else the Pathet Lao were in control of the countryside. The first few months of 1972 saw a new build-up of NVA troops in preparation for the Easter offensive in South Vietnam, which was contained by South Vietnamese ground forces and US air power. In Laos, clashes continued, with particularly heavy fighting on the Plain of Jars. NVA forces on the Bolovens Plateau pushed towards Pakse again, and Saravane changed hands several times.

The peace negotiations between the United States and North Vietnam in Paris were now well advanced, and Hanoi was under American pressure to order the Pathet Lao to cease hostilities. Souvanna Phouma held talks with Pathet Lao leaders and in late February 1973, less than a month after the ceasefire in South Vietnam, Souvanna Phouma and the Pathet Lao also reached a ceasefire agreement. Laos became involved in the general withdrawal of US military from Indochina. The bombing of the Ho Chi Minh Trail ended, advisers were withdrawn and military aid to the Royal Lao forces declined.

Despite the ceasefire, however, clashes soon resumed between the government and the Pathet Lao, and in 1974 the Pathet Lao made significant gains. In 1975, as Cambodia and South Vietnam fell to communist forces, the Pathet Lao staged their final assault on government strongholds in western Laos. On 16 May they at last seized the southern town of Pakse, and four days later Savannakhet fell. In June the Pathet Lao entered Vientiane itself. After a period of consolidation, Souvanna Phouma's coalition government was formally abolished on 3 December 1975, and his half-brother Prince Souphanouvong, leader of the Pathet Lao, became president of the People's Democratic Republic of Laos. **Michael Dockrill**

Above left: A group of Meo hill tribesmen watch as a CIA agent demonstrates an American-supplied Soviet PSSh-41 sub-machine gun. Top: Prince Souphanouvong, leader of the Pathet Lao, leaves the temple of Wat Mai in his birthplace, the Laotian royal capital of Luang Prabang, after paying homage to the Golden Buddha. Souphanouvong, who became head of the Political Council set up in 1974 to advise Souvanna Phouma's coalition government, had returned to Luang Prabang after 10 years of fighting royalist forces. On 3 December 1975, after renewed fighting, he became president of Laos. Above: Prince Souvanna Phouma, Souphanouvong's half-brother and head of the neutralist coalition until the communist takeover at the end of 1975.

Key Weapons

SOVIET NUCLEAR MISSILES

Above: An SS-3 Shyster IRBM on show in Moscow in May 1980. Developed in the early 1950s it first appeared in 1957 and remained the standard Soviet IRBM until the arrival of the SS-4 Sandal in 1961 which could carry more fuel and had a considerably extended range.

The history of the Soviet Union's nuclear missile programme can be traced back to 1947 and the establishment of the Korolev design bureau. This organisation, backed-up by German rocket research data, has been the backbone of Soviet work in this field and the production of launch vehicles for the country's space programme.

The bureau's first task was the development of a series of ballistic bombardment missiles based on the German V-2 rocket. This early work resulted in two missiles, known in the West as the Scunner and the SS-2 Sibling, which both appeared in the early 1950s. Scunner was little more than a V-2 built in Russia and is best regarded as a concept proving vehicle. The single-stage liquid-fuelled SS-2 was again based on the V-2 but incorporated a degree of local modification and improvement. Sibling appeared in at least two versions.

The 1957 May Day parade in Moscow revealed the next development in the Soviet programme: the SS-3 Shyster, which many authorities believe to be Russia's first truly operational land-based nuclear missile. With a launch weight of around 26,000kg (57,330lb), the 21m (68ft 10in) long SS-3 still showed its German ancestry in the use of exhaust vanes and fin-mounted rudders for directional control. Guidance is believed to have been via a radio link and it has been credited with a range of 800-1200km (497-745 miles) carrying a conventional or nuclear warhead.

With the deployment of Shyster, Russia's first generation of nuclear missiles was complete and the way open for a new family of infinitely more capable weapons. The first of this second generation was the SS-4 Sandal which was deployed operationally in 1960 and remained in limited service in the early 1980s. Like the SS-3, Sandal was a single-stage liquid-fuelled weapon with a launch weight of 27,000kg (59,525lb) and a length of 21m (68ft 10in). Fired from either a silo or a fixed surface pad, the missile could carry a 1.2-megaton warhead over a range of 2200km (1367 miles), guidance being provided by an inertial system. As many as 2000 Sandals were operational in the mid-1960s but by 1977 this number had fallen to around 500, by which time it had been replaced by the SS-20.

The SS-4 was rapidly followed into production by the SS-5 Skean which became operational in 1961. Basically a refined SS-4, Skean featured storable liquid propellants, allowing a much quicker firing time to be achieved at its silo or surface launch sites. Again a single-stage weapon, SS-5 had a length of 23m (75ft 5in) and was capable of delivering a 1.2-megaton warhead over a range of 2200km (1367 miles). At the height of its deployment in the mid-1960s as many as 3500 Skeans were available, but with the advent of the SS-20, this number dropped dramatically and the type is no longer operational.

The SS-2–SS-5 range of weapons were all what are known as either MRBMs or IRBMs (medium-range or intermediate-range ballistic missiles) and as such lacked the range to hit targets in the USA from friendly soil. This was naturally seen as a major shortcoming in the Soviet arsenal and much effort was put into producing a true ICBM (inter-continental ballistic missile).

The first success in this direction was the SS-6 Sapwood. Fired from the Tyuratam test site in August 1957, the SS-6 was officially described as a 'multi-stage ballistic rocket' but it seems likely that more use was made of the type in the role of space vehicle launcher than as an ICBM. Russia's first major oper-

Previous page: The formidable SS-9 Scarp first entered service in 1965 and was by far the largest missile in the Soviet armoury to date. With a maximum range of some 11,000km (6835 miles), the SS-9 is 34.5m (113ft 6in) in length and carries a single very high yield warhead of 20 or 25 megatons.

Right: A pair of SS-8 Sasin ICBMs rolls through Moscow's Red Square in 1965. The SS-8, which has since been phased out, was armed with a 5-megaton warhead and was capable of ranges of up to 11,000km (6835 miles).

Above: A side view revealing the massive dimensions of the SS-9 Scarp ICBM.

ational ICBMs, the SS-7 Saddler and the SS-8 Sasin, both entered service during 1964. These two weapons were produced as complementary systems in the same way as the SS-4 and SS-5. Saddler is reported to have been a 35m (114ft 11in) long, two-stage liquid-fuelled missile capable of delivering a 5-megaton warhead over a distance of 11,000km (6835 miles). Sasin was a similar liquid-fuelled multi-stage weapon but with a length of 25m (82ft 1in) and storable propellants. Like the bigger SS-7, Sasin carried a 5-megaton warhead. Both weapons are now out of service, having been de-activated under the terms of the SALT II treaty.

Impressive as these weapons were, Russia's next ICBM, the SS-9 Scarp, dwarfed them. With a launch weight of 200,000kg (440,920lb), this three-stage liquid-fuelled missile utilised inertial guidance. Scarp entered service in 1965 and has subsequently appeared in four distinct models. The first of these, the SS-9 Mod 1, was the initial production model capable of carrying a 25-megaton warhead over a range of 11,000km (6835 miles). The Mod 2 was equipped with a smaller warhead (20-megaton yield) while the Mod 3 was used to deploy a fourth stage FOBS (fractional orbital bombardment system). Designed to place a nuclear payload in orbit until needed, the FOBS SS-9 Mod 3 was first tested in 1966 and has been since used as the launch vehicle for Soviet 'killer' satellites.

The final version of Scarp was the Mod 4 which was

Below: The three-stage SS-10 Scrag was developed alongside the SS-9 but was not displayed in Moscow until May 1965. Despite its designation as an ICBM the SS-10 used very low temperature propellants which ensured that it could not be stored at operational readiness for any length of time.

Above: In contrast to earlier Soviet ICBMs the SS-11 Sego – first of a new generation of ICBMs which appeared in the latter half of the 1960s – was armed with a warhead of less than 1 megaton.

Below: The SS-N-5 was carried in Golf- and Hotel-class submarines and launched from vertical tubes extending from the keel to the top of the vessel's conning-tower.

the first Russian missile to be equipped with MIRVs (multiple independently-targeted re-entry vehicles), that is separate warheads which can attack different targets after launch from a single 'bus' or carrier. Three 3.5-megaton MIRVs formed the payload of this last version and with the possible exception of a small number of Mod 3s, no member of the family remains in service.

The massive SS-9 was succeeded by a new generation of seven lightweight ICBMs encompassing the SS-11 of 1966 to the SS-19 of 1974. The first of these, the SS-11 Sego measures 20m (65ft 7in) and has a launch weight of 45,000kg (99,205lb). A two-stage liquid-fuelled weapon, Sego has so far been developed in three versions. The first of these, the SS-11 Mod 1, carries a 950-kiloton warhead over a range of 8800km (5470 miles) and entered service in 1966.

The Mod 2 was an improved Mod 1 which never entered service, while the Mod 3 is equipped with three 250-kiloton re-entry vehicles. Latest estimates put the number of SS-11s in service at 550, mostly of the Mod 3 variant.

The SS-11 was followed by the SS-13 Savage (the SS-12 being a short-range battlefield weapon used by the Soviet Army) which entered service in 1969. A 20m (65ft 7in) long, three-stage solid-fuelled weapon, SS-13 is believed to be a product of the Nadradze bureau and carries a 600-kiloton warhead over a distance of 8000km (4970 miles). Some 60 weapons are currently believed to be in service.

Closely linked to the Savage is the SS-14 Scapegoat two-stage solid-fuelled missile which was deployed in limited numbers along the Sino-Soviet border. The 10.4m (34ft) long weapon utilises the second and third stages of the earlier SS-13 to carry a nuclear warhead over a range of 7246km (4500 miles). Savage was backed by the SS-15 Scrooge, another multi-stage solid-fuelled weapon which was first identified during 1965. Credited with the capability of carrying a 1-megaton warhead over a range of 4831km (3000 miles), Scrooge was at first believed to be an experimental weapon but is now known to have been deployed alongside the SS-14. Both missiles have been seen as interim types developed to meet rising Sino-Soviet tension and both are no longer in service.

Mainstream Soviet development continued with the SS-16 which appeared between 1972 and 1974. Designated the RS-14 in the Russian nomenclature, the SS-16 was a 20.5m (67ft 3in) long three-stage solid-fuelled, inertially-guided weapon which carried a 650-kiloton warhead over a distance of 8750km (5435 miles). For whatever reasons, the SS-16 was only produced and deployed in limited numbers and is no longer in service.

More successful was the SS-17 (Soviet designation RS-16) which became operational in 1975 as a partial replacement for the SS-11. Like Sego, the SS-17 is a two-stage liquid-fuelled weapon with a launch weight of around 65,000kg (143,000lb). Three versions of the missile (Mod 1 to 3) have so far been identified, differing in the type of warhead carried. The Mod 1 is armed with four 750-kiloton MIRVs which it can deliver over a range of 10,000km (6215 miles) whilst the Mod 2 carries a single 6-megaton device. The Mod 3 reverts to the four 750-kiloton MIRVs combined with a more accurate guidance system. Estimates put the number of these 24m (78ft 9in) long missiles in service at 20 Mod 2s and 130 Mod 1s and 3s.

Although sequentially later than the SS-17, the SS-19 (Soviet designation RS-18) actually entered service earlier as an SS-11 replacement. The 22.5m (73ft 9in) long SS-19 is a two-stage liquid-fuelled weapon with a launch weight of 78,000kg (171,960lb) and has been identified in three versions. The initial production model, known in the West as the Mod 1, is armed with six 500-kiloton MIRVs which it can deliver over a range of 9600km (5965 miles). The Mod 2, which appeared in 1978, carries a single 10-megaton warhead and employs an improved guidance system. The latest version, the Mod 3, seems to be the Mod 1 combined with the latter guidance package. Current estimates put the number of SS-19s in service at 180 Mod 1s, 40 Mod 2s and 110 Mod 3s.

Backing up these lightweight ICBMs is the SS-18 (Soviet designation RS-20) which was first deployed in 1974. The SS-18 is a 35m (114ft 11in) long two-stage liquid-fuelled weapon with a launch weight of 225,000kg (496,030lb) and has been identified in four versions. The initial model, the Mod 1, is armed with a single 27-megaton warhead which it can deliver over a range of 12,000km (7455 miles). The Mod 2, which was first deployed during 1976, substitutes eight 900-kiloton or ten 500-kiloton MIRVs for the original payload, while the Mod 3 reverted to a single 20-kiloton warhead combined with increased range – 16,000km (9940 miles) – and accuracy. The Mod 4 appeared in 1979 and is armed with ten 500-kiloton MIRVs and as many as four defence-suppression decoys. The accuracy of the weapon again seems to have been improved, US sources crediting it with the capability of impacting within

Below: The Yankee-class submarine is armed with 16 missile tubes for the SS-N-16 Sawfly which came into service in 1968; altogether three versions of this missile have entered service with the Soviet Navy. Bottom: SS-N-6 missiles are transported through Moscow as part of a display of Soviet military might.

Above: A Golf II missile-submarine of the Soviet Navy is photographed in the North Atlantic en route to Cuba. SS-N-5 Serb missiles – contained in three vertical launch tubes – form the offensive armament for this class of vessel.

260m (285yds) of a given target after a flight of 11,000km (6835 miles). Current estimates put the numbers of this devastating weapon at 26 Mod 1s and 3s, 162 Mod 2s and 120 Mod 4s.

The Soviet Union's best known nuclear missile is the mobile SS-20 system which was first deployed in 1977. Believed to be a further product of the Nadradze bureau, the SS-20 is a 16m (52ft 6in) long, two-stage solid-fuelled missile with a launch weight of 25,000kg (55,115lb). Using elements from the earlier SS-16, the weapon has three identified warhead configurations, namely a single 650-kiloton device, three 150-kiloton MIRVs or three 50-kiloton re-entry vehicles. Its range, dependent on warhead, is between 5000km (3105 miles) and 7000km (4350 miles).

To complement this land-based arsenal, the Soviet Union has also produced a range of submarine-launched strategic weapons beginning with the SS-N-4 Sark which was first test launched during 1955. The rough equivalent of the American Polaris A-2, the 15m (49ft 2in) long Sark was a two-stage solid-fuelled weapon with a range of 600km (373 miles) which armed a number of Golf and Hotel classes of submarine but is no longer in service.

Sark was replaced in 1963 by the SS-N-5 Serb missile which was again deployed aboard Golf and Hotel vessels. Armed with a megaton-range warhead, Serb was a 10m (32ft 9in) long two-stage solid-fuelled missile with an estimated range of 1200km (745 miles). By 1975 some 24 submarines were armed with the type but by the end of the decade Serb had been replaced. The next Soviet submarine-launched strategic missile to appear was the SS-N-6 Sawfly which entered service in 1968 aboard Yankee-class vessels. Three versions of this 13m (42ft 8in) long liquid-fuelled weapon have been identified, starting with the Mod 1 which carried a single nuclear payload over a range of 2400km (1243 miles). This was followed in 1972 by the Mod 2 which had an increased range. The latest version, the Mod 3, has a payload of three MIRVs and some 416 examples of this model are believed to remain in service.

Sawfly was followed in 1973 by the SS-N-8 which was again a two-stage liquid-fuelled weapon. Like its predecessor, the 13m (42ft 8in) long SS-N-8 has been developed in three versions, namely the Mod 1 with a 1.2-megaton warhead, the Mod 2 with three nuclear armed re-entry vehicles and the Mod 3 with three MIRVs. Current estimates put the number of SS-N-8s in service at 280 carried aboard 22 Delta-class submarines.

Russia's next operational weapon in this class was the SS-N-18 (Soviet designation RSM-50) which became operational in 1979, again aboard Delta-class boats. With a length of 14m (45ft 10in), the SS-N-18 has a number of warhead options comprising three 200-kiloton MIRVs, six MIRVs of unknown yield or a single 450-kiloton device. Range is quoted as being between 6500km (4040 miles) and 8000km (4972 miles) dependent on the type of warhead fitted, and current estimates quote 13 Deltas as being armed with this weapon. The SS-N-20 entered service during the early 1980s following trials begun in January 1980. Very little is known about the type other than that it uses solid propellants, has a range of about 8000km (4972 miles) with as many as 10 MIRVs and that 20 missiles are carried aboard the Typhoon-class submarines.

Below: The Delta III class is armed with 16 tubes for SS-N-18 missiles which makes it a highly potent weapons platform. The SS-N-18 is typical of the more advanced missile systems in that it can be armed with warheads of differing size in order to suit specific requirements.

The conquerors

North Vietnam's long road to victory

On 10 March 1975, General Van Tien Dung sent in a wave of attacks against the city of Ban Me Thuot in the Central Highlands of South Vietnam, and opened the last act of the Vietnam War. Within a matter of weeks, North Vietnamese tanks were racing towards Saigon, US officials were being hastily evacuated, and the goal that the communist politburo in Hanoi had set itself – the reunification of Vietnam under its control – had been achieved.

What is, perhaps, most impressive about this achievement is the way that the North Vietnamese had managed to keep their war effort going for over a decade, often under intense pressure, until in the end they had outlasted the strength of the USA and eclipsed the US-aided forces of the South. From March 1965 until President Johnson announced a halt in November 1968, for example, the most powerful military nation in the world had dropped an average of 800 tonnes of bombs every day on North Vietnam. By the end of 1968, an estimated 52,000 civilians had been killed by the bombing. The outskirts of the two largest cities had suffered heavy damage, and the remaining cities in the North had been largely destroyed. Hardly any part of North Vietnam had been spared. The country's small industrial base had been decimated; millions of peasants had been forced to live in underground shelters; power plants, roads and railways had been destroyed wholesale. Nor was 1968 the end of the bombing – the US continued to mount occasional raids, and in 1972 full scale bombing was resumed. And yet, despite the bombardment, the North Vietnamese were able to sustain their military effort, bring about American withdrawal, and defeat the South Vietnamese government forces.

The key to understanding how they were able to do this lies in the nature of North Vietnamese society and military organisation, and in the continuity with which the political leadership of the North placed the reunification of Vietnam under Hanoi as its first priority. Most of the political and military leaders of North Vietnam had been fighting for a unified Vietnam under communist rule at least since 1945, when the National Liberation Army under Vo Nguyen Giap brought large parts of the North under Viet Minh control in the wake of Japanese defeat. Then, from 1946 onwards, the Viet Minh were engaged in a struggle to defeat the French – a struggle they had won by 1954.

The revolutionaries themselves were part of an intellectual elite that combined fiercely nationalist anti-colonialism with an orthodox Marxist-Leninist ideology stressing the revolutionary role of the urban 'proletariat' or working class. It is notable that this ideology was distinct from Mao Tse-tung's ideas about the importance of the peasantry. Paying lip-service to orthodoxy, Party ideologists spoke of a

Above: By 1975, the NVA was able to field large, well-equipped armoured units. The T54 pictured here, one of the first to enter Saigon, carries a 12.7mm DShK heavy machine gun.

Right: Ho Chi Minh, the symbol of Vietnamese nationalism, who had worked for an independent communist Vietnam from his student days in Paris in the early 1920s to his death in 1969.

united front of worker and peasant; the reality however was different. In 1945 there were fewer industrial workers in the whole of Vietnam than there were in one medium-sized Chinese city. The 1945 revolution was made not in the towns and cities, but in the villages of the northern border provinces among the peasants.

In the countryside, the Viet Minh faced an uphill struggle to revolutionise the peasantry and organise them to take up the battle for independence and national unification. Over most of rural Vietnam, the peasants were parochial and traditionally-minded. Though many of them resented French and Japanese rule, and the depredations of their landlords, they accepted a hierarchical pattern of authority in the villages; few of them were likely to understand or agree with Marxism. Ho Chi Minh settled for the 'culture movement' as a solution – a programme of popular 'education' in which communist policy was only partially revealed. The Viet Minh were able to harness the traditionalism of the peasantry, winning them over by emphasising the links between the nationalist movement and the Vietnamese past, as well as by providing practical help and promising for the future more food, land and hospitals.

Peasants and propaganda

After 1945, peasant associations were set up to involve more peasants in the war against the French. In Viet Minh areas, villages were administered locally by elected 'people's councils' that were supposed to be dominated by the poorer peasants although, in fact, in the early 1950s 'middle' peasants accounted for half the membership of the councils, and many of them included rich peasants, small capitalists and even landlords. Not until after the defeat of the French in 1954 did the Party go beyond propagandising and mobilising the peasants, and begin a radical redistribution of power and resources in the countryside.

Collectivisation of the land went ahead during the middle and late 1950s, and the people's councils were abolished for a period because of the predominance of 'ugly elements' – landlords and representatives of the traditional village hierarchies. The councils were re-established in 1959, with safeguards against them being dominated by representatives of the old society; but in many areas the real power remained in the hands of administrators and party cadres.

At the same time, the Party was trying to transform the cities. An industrialisation drive began in 1955; during the next ten years well over half a million peasants were moved from their villages and given work in industry, transport or construction.

During the war with the French, the numbers of Viet Minh troops had increased from a few thousand to some 200,000 regulars and well over a million guerrillas and local militia. In this period, General Giap developed the military philosophy that shaped the war in Vietnam thereafter: he advocated the total involvement of the population, including women, in the local militia; constant attack on all fronts using every type of formation; and the use of guerrilla forces able to infiltrate and strike the enemy behind his lines, as well as regular troops.

In the 1950s and 1960s many Chinese communists became fanatical advocates of guerrilla warfare, denouncing regular armies as the 'capitalist military line'. This did not happen in Vietnam. Giap, like most of the North Vietnamese politburo, regarded the

technique of guerrilla warfare as a means rather than as an end in itself, and he always intended that the army would eventually adopt more conventional tactics, becoming a 'regular and contemporary army' when the time was right.

Against superior forces – until 1954 the French, and then later the South Vietnamese with ever increasing US aid – these tactics implied a 'long war strategy'. North Vietnamese determination to reunify Vietnam under Hanoi meant that they were willing to pay the price of a long war of attrition – and they included this attitude in their training of infiltrators. Two North Vietnamese infiltrators who defected after reaching South Vietnam said that the political officers attached to their unit had told them, 'if our generation could not finish the war, our children and our grandchildren would continue it.' By the early 1960s, however, North Vietnamese military leaders were expecting South Vietnam to collapse in 1965 or 1966. What they had not anticipated was the scale of the US build up, which succeeded in keeping South Vietnam in being.

US bombing of the North began modestly in 1964. Despite the bombing, the North Vietnamese war effort – at that stage the continual infiltration of the South and support for the local guerrillas there – was to be maintained at all costs. Even before the start in March 1965 of full-scale daily bombing, the first order for non-essential personnel to leave the cities was issued. The transformation of North Vietnamese society to suit the new conditions had begun.

Over the next two years, the American bombing spread further north and hit a wider range of targets. North Vietnam's newly-formed industrial base was badly hit, and a process of decentralisation of the factories was begun – the slogan adopted was 'the mother factory gives birth to many child factories.' A factory vulnerable to air attack would be dispersed in several small villages; by the time that the bombing of North Vietnam reached its peak in 1968, there were virtually no factories with more than a hundred workers anywhere in the country.

Outside Hanoi and Haiphong, there were hardly any urban centres left at all. But in the capital, life continued. To cope with the regular air-raids, some three million concrete cylinders had been constructed, each having room for one person, every few metres along the pavement. This amounted to three shelters for every person in Hanoi – the idea was that

American bombing forced the North Vietnamese to decentralise their industrial base and to militarise society. Above left: A small foundry evacuated to the mountains northwest of Hanoi.

there would be one near home, one on the way to work and one near the workplace, available for everyone.

The whole population was mobilised to deal with the threat. Women formed 70 per cent of the workforce in both industry and agriculture. Many women were members of the local militia and were able to use rifles, grenades and anti-aircraft guns. The regular army maintained some fifty anti-aircraft gun and missile regiments. Two million civilians, including gangs of youths, formed road repair gangs so that men and material could be transported around the country and the war effort could be continued. Party cadres worked to involve everyone in the war – even in those areas that escaped bombing – by such devices as organising search parties to capture downed American airmen before they could be rescued by helicopter. Equally important were the efforts of the cadres in the villages to counter the effects of US propaganda and 'gifts' dropped by air: they would convince the peasants that cloth or food dropped by the Americans was poisoned, and persuade them to make large bonfires of the gifts.

In the villages, although the independent party cadres continued to operate under the direction of the central party, there was a greater measure of local autonomy from central government. The provincial governments were given more power, and in the north a semi-autonomous zone was created for the hill tribes. The emphasis in the villages was on self-sufficiency and local decision-making, and on local defence. Unlike the cities, where the main policy had been evacuation, the villages were expected to hold their ground, and in areas of heavy bombing this meant going *under* the ground. One striking example is the underground 'city' of Vinh Linh just north of the Demilitarized Zone – a network of tunnels and living spaces extending over hundreds of kilometres and accommodating some 70,000 people who cultivated the land and repaired supply routes during the night and sheltered from the bombs by day.

Above: Despite the American bombing of transport in general, and bridges in particular, North Vietnam was able to maintain the flow of supplies over improvised bridges, thrown up almost as soon as the Americans could destroy them. Above right: Women of a North Vietnamese militia unit crew a DShK heavy machine gun.

By 1968, the size of the North Vietnamese Army (NVA) had been substantially increased to half a million men, of whom 100,000 or more were in South Vietnam. Each unit was accompanied by a political cell from the Party whose task was to indoctrinate and direct the soldiers. A further quarter of a million troops formed a regional militia force, covering the five North Vietnamese military zones. And the paramilitary local militia, functioning as a reserve army and local defence force, numbered some three million men and women.

As the US bombing campaign reached its climax, the Politburo in Hanoi authorised a change of strategy. The result was the 1968 Tet offensive. Giap combined a series of simultaneous attacks using regular forces with guerrilla activity behind the lines. The communist forces were repulsed with heavy losses, but the ability of the North Vietnamese to mount such a massive offensive after three years of heavy bombing demonstrated the success with which North Vietnamese society was equipped to cope with the onslaught.

After the end of the Rolling Thunder bombing campaign in November 1968, North Vietnam began a period of de-escalation and reconstruction that was continued by Le Duan after the death of Ho Chi Minh on 3 September 1969. Villages were rebuilt above ground; evacuees moved back into the cities; schools and hospitals were constructed. Le Duan advocated an improvement in living standards, and in addition to the reconstruction, some economic changes were introduced after 1970 – including material incentives and limited free markets. As agriculture gradually recovered, railways and roads were rebuilt, and many of the dispersed factories were re-united. Industrial production climbed slowly back towards pre-bombing levels.

During the period of reconstruction the war continued. The USAF mounted air raids over Hanoi and Haiphong in November 1970, and the NVA

Above: North Vietnamese salvage metal from a US Navy F-8, operating from the USS *America* off the coast of Vietnam. Below: A North Vietnamese column of captured American M113 armoured personnel carriers. The troops are armed with AK series assault rifles and captured American M79 grenade launchers.

continued to infiltrate men and equipment down the Ho Chi Minh Trail to support the Viet Cong. After the 1971 monsoon, some 120,000 NVA troops and 8000 lorries loaded with supplies were moved into South Vietnam. Giap's new offensive began on 30 March 1972, with simultaneous assaults across the Demilitarized Zone, in the Central Highlands and in the south. It was supported by heavy Soviet artillery and by several hundred tanks – the first time that the NVA had deployed tanks in strength on South Vietnamese soil. The fighting went on for months until the communist forces were repulsed with heavy losses.

In spite of this defeat, however, the communists had demonstrated their ability to escalate the fighting to the level that they felt able to sustain. From the guerrilla raids of the mid-1960s to the tank attacks of 1972 was an important step, and showed just how the development of the NVA was progressing. Still, the US bombing during 1972, and especially the December B-52 raids on Hanoi and Haiphong, hit the North hard, and the North Vietnamese leadership now waited to recuperate its strength before pushing on to another offensive. It had established firm control of wide areas of the South in the 1972 offensive, and patiently built up its forces in the following year. Withstanding some determined attempts by President Thieu's South Vietnamese government to push their forces back, the Hanoi politburo began to move reinforcements down the Ho Chi Minh Trail again.

By 1974 the NVA's transition from a predominantly guerrilla force to a conventional army with heavy tank and artillery support, which Giap had long envisaged, was complete. Out of a total of 19 divisions, 12 were already in the South: the NVA's forces amounted to 225,000 regular troops and 40,000 guerrillas. The ARVN, on paper, could field 13 regular divisions numbering 180,000 men together with Regional and Popular Forces totalling over 480,000 – but it suffered from low morale and a high desertion rate. The irregular forces were comparatively ineffective, and nearly half the regular army was deployed in the far north protecting the approaches to Da Nang, thus leaving much of South Vietnam vulnerable. The NVA had some 600 armoured vehicles and in addition North Vietnamese infantry had heavy artillery support typified by the 130mm gun. And the North Vietnamese forces had sufficient supplies in place for a year's hard fighting.

The main advantage possessed by the South Vietnamese was air power – they had 1507 aircraft, nearly five times as many as the North Vietnamese Air Force. But this air superiority was partly neutralised by communist anti-aircraft capability: in addition to fixed SA-2 installations protecting forward bases in the South, the NVA deployed the shoulder-launched, heat-seeking SA-7 missile very widely. As 1974 drew to a close, therefore, the NVA was an effective, powerful, conventional army, ready to pounce on its weaker foe. The fall of the provincial capital of Phuoc Binh early in January to communist forces – the first time that a provincial capital had fallen in three years – was the curtain raiser as South Vietnam's tragedy moved to its climax. **Barry Smith**

Last act

The communist offensive of 1975

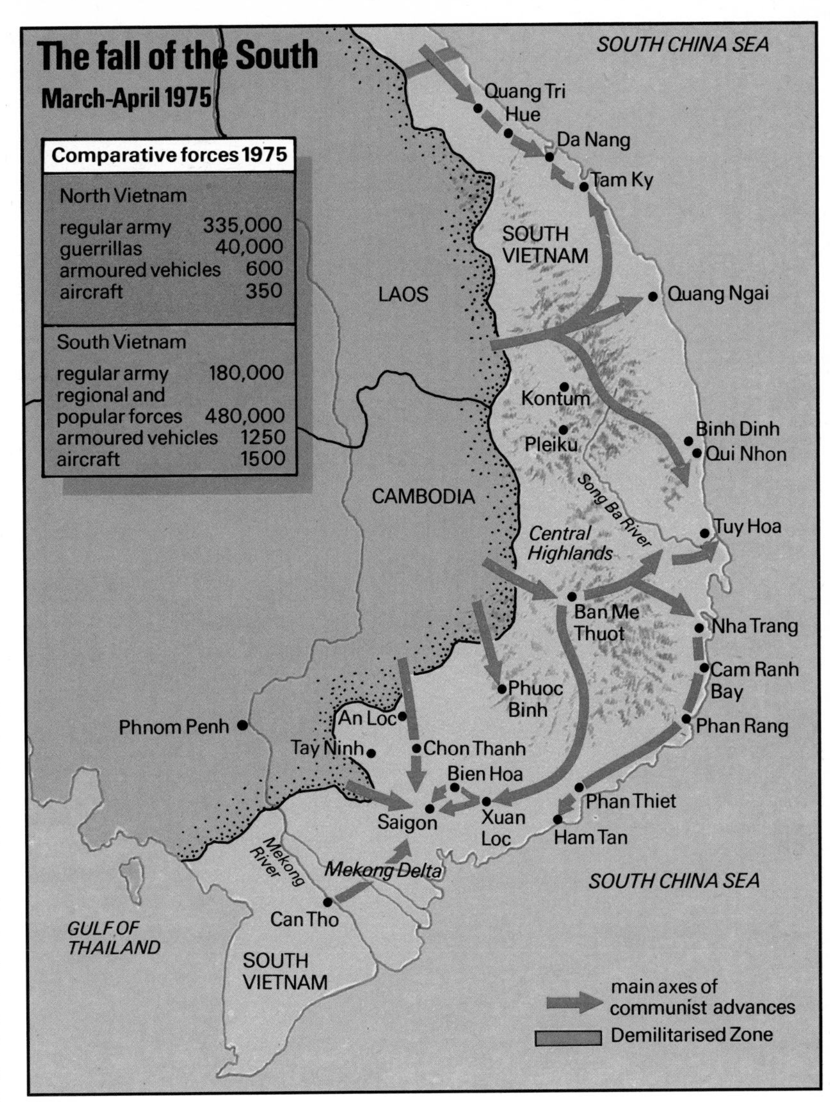

The decision by the North Vietnamese communist leadership to attack the provincial capital of Phuoc Binh in Phuoc Long Province in South Vietnam was taken late in 1974. For some time, hostilities between the NVA forces in the South and the ARVN had been growing in intensity, and the Hanoi politburo saw such an attack as a useful way of getting information. First of all, a large-scale assault would show whether the USA was willing to recommit its forces to Vietnam in order to prevent a serious reverse for the ARVN. The resignation of President Nixon in 1974, the cutting of aid to the South by Congress and the overwhelming American popular distaste for any return to Vietnam indicated that US intervention was unlikely; but the cautious NVA leaders would be able to make sure by this new attack. Then again, the attack on Phuoc Binh would give some indication of the state of effectiveness of the ARVN. The effects of the halving of US aid, the increase in international oil prices, the rising desertion rate and the question marks over the quality of the high command could be gauged by the response to the attack. The NVA forces themselves would not be taking on too much, for most of the province of Phuoc Long was already in their hands.

On 12 December, therefore, the outlying positions around Phuoc Binh came under fire, and the 5500 strong garrison of the city itself was under siege by the 26th. Subjected to pulverising artillery, rocket and armoured attack, Phuoc Binh and most of its garrison were overrun on 6 January – the first time a provincial capital had fallen in three years and the first occasion in two decades when a whole province had been lost. With the Thieu regime making only a token effort to prevent the fall of Phuoc Binh and the Americans confining themselves to formal diplomatic protests to the North Vietnamese on the 11th, the significance of events was not lost upon any section of Vietnamese society. Rumours of crippling ammunition shortages, the lack of artillery and air support, allegations of continuing corruption, incompetence and cowardice within the officer corps, and the sense of being betrayed by the Americans sapped the self-confidence of the military, while defeat in the field and Thieu's inability to ensure American support shook the president's authority with a civilian population whose loyalty and allegiance had never been more than conditional.

The communists now moved to consolidate and develop their success as the pace of the war quickened appreciably throughout Indochina. On New Year's Day the Khmer Rouge had opened an offensive that within a matter of hours brought it undisputed control of the Mekong below Phnom Penh and the roads between the capitals of Cambodia and South Vietnam. Probably driven by a desire to secure a favourable decision before the North Vietnamese might try to do so for them, the Khmer Rouge pressed on to drive President Lon Nol from the country on 1 April and achieve the fall of Phnom Penh itself on the 17th. It was clear that time was running out for beleaguered South Vietnam.

Still reluctant to commit itself to seeking victory in 1975, though it realised for the first time that victory that year was a possibility, the North Vietnamese High Command decided to inaugurate an offensive in the Central Highlands and sanctioned a series of probing armoured attacks in Quang Tri (in the north) and Thua Thieu provinces as the prelude to an attack on Ban Me Thuot, the capital of Dar Lac and a city straddling one of the two major roads between the Highlands and the coast. At the same time Hanoi ordered the 316th Infantry Division south in readiness for operations in the Highlands, and it despatched

General Van Tien Dung to take charge of operations in the South. Dung was second only to Giap in the NVA hierarchy, and his taking over command from Pham Hung and General Tran Van Tra (both then in the North for consultations) reflected Hanoi's determination to exercise the closest possible control over operations in the South. Dung left Hanoi on 5 February, and on the 25th issued his final orders for the Ban Me Thuot operation. After a number of sabotage attacks aimed at cutting the roads into the city, Dung planned to attack Ban Me Thuot on 10 March with three divisions.

The communist timetable had allowed seven to ten days for the taking of Ban Me Thuot, but in the event the city was overrun in little more than a day. Given the failure of an immediate counter-attack, Thieu on the 14th ordered the local corps commander, Major-General Pham Van Phu, to retake the city using regular units drawn from Saigon's main bases in the Highlands, Pleiku and Kontum. Both Kontum and Pleiku were considerably to the north of Ban Me Thuot, however, and in any case the withdrawal of units from these key areas to fight further south involved a certain amount of risk. At the same time, Thieu ordered his northern corps commander, Lieutenant-General Ngo Quang Truong (who was having to deal with the probing attacks through Quang Tri Province), to send the elite 1st Airborne Division further south, to act as a strategic reserve. Implicit in these decisions was a judgement that the ARVN would be unable to hold the Central Highlands, that the country would be broken in two, and that the only possible strategy was to trade space in the northern provinces and Central Highlands in order to buy time to regroup the ARVN to protect Saigon and the Delta, while making every effort to obtain US assistance.

In trying to cede territory in order to buy time, however, Thieu may well have precipitated the disaster he was seeking so desperately to avoid. For in both the Central Highlands and the north, what should have been an orderly series of manoeuvres rapidly turned into panic-stricken flight. Regrouping or retreating in the face of an enemy attack is a difficult procedure for expert troops; for the ARVN, low in morale and without the heavy air support it had been trained to expect, it was an impossible task.

In the Central Highlands, chaos engulfed Dar Lac and Khanh Hao provinces as the shattered remnants of the 23rd Infantry Division tried to fight its way from Ban Me Thuot to the illusory safety of Nha Trang.

Above: the flight from Bien Hoa. Civilians pour south before the NVA forces pushing remorselessly down to Saigon. Top right: A US official punches a Vietnamese fighting to get on one of the last planes to leave Nha Trang on 1 April 1975, hours before the arrival of communist troops. Right centre: The village of Tran Bang, 35km (20 miles) north of Saigon, 25 April 1975. A communist soldier inspects the body of a villager killed by the shelling that forced the ARVN to pull back. Right below: The arrival of the communists in Hue, after the flight of the ARVN forces.

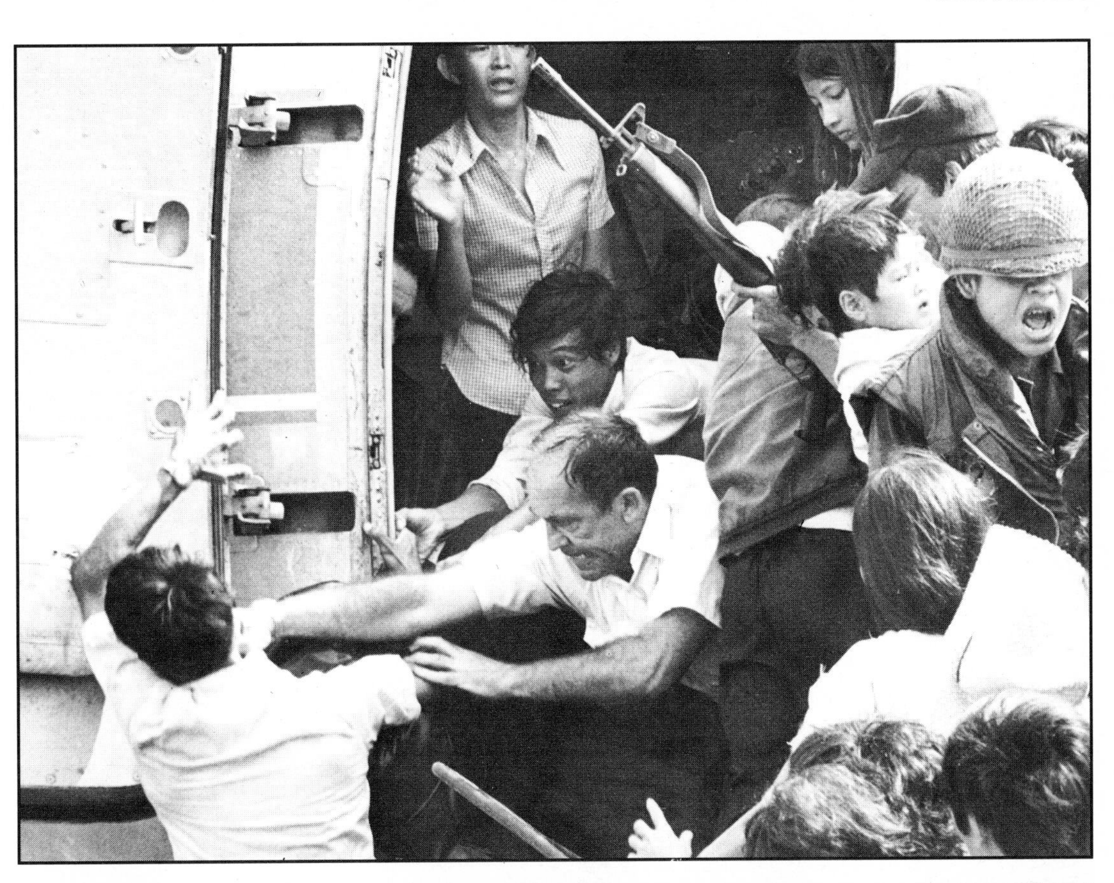

Major-General Pham Van Phu found he was unable to move forces from Pleiku either by air or by the direct route to Binh Dinh, and so chose to abandon Pleiku, the area administration, and the regional and local militias in an attempt to withdraw his regular units through the difficult Song Ba Valley to Tuy Hoa. With 'few orders given and even fewer obeyed' as many senior commanders sought to ensure their personal safety by early escape, the withdrawal from Pleiku was a shambles. No denial programme was put into effect with the result that hundreds of guns and vehicles, thousands of tonnes of stores, and no fewer than 64 fully-serviced aircraft were left to the enemy when Pleiku was abandoned on the night of 15/16 March. Panic inevitably infected those left to the mercy of the communists, and the fleeing regular forces, slowed and impeded by thousands of refugees, were cut to pieces in the Song Ba Valley by the NVA 320th Infantry Division. By the time that these and the forces withdrawn from Ban Me Thuot scrambled back to the coast they had ceased to exist as recognisable military units.

In the north an even greater disaster was unfolding. There the irresolution that gripped Truong's forces stood in contrast to the civilian population's fearful certainty of the fate that awaited it at communist hands. Memories of communist atrocities in Hue during the 1968 Tet offensive spurred a civilian flight south from Quang Tri Province that began almost two weeks before the deserted provincial capital was occupied by communist forces on 19 March. At that point Hanoi decided to develop its offensive in the north while Thieu, in a broadcast intended to rally his nation on the 20th, outlined the seriousness of the situation by admitting the loss of the Highlands. The effect of these two developments was calamitous for Truong's I Corps. Troops used for years to fighting for small hamlets in remote country areas with no thought of retreat suddenly found the basis of past certainty swept aside, and as ARVN morale and discipline wavered its soldiers looked for two things – a line of escape and the safety of their families.

Forced to keep women and children with them because of the vagaries of the supply system, troops who had previously drawn comfort and inspiration from the closeness of their people now put their families' safety before obedience to orders, too often issued by absentee officers. Even before Hue was invested its largely local garrison had melted away, while by the time the city fell on the 26th communist forces to the south had brushed aside feeble opposition in reaching the coast in Quang Tin and Quang Ngai provinces. By taking Tam Ky and Quang Ngai City on 24 March the communists completed the encirclement of some 150,000 troops and perhaps one million civilian refugees in an ever-contracting enclave around Da Nang. Amid fearful scenes of murder, rape and pillage as order and discipline disintegrated, some 20,000 troops and 35,000 civilians were evacuated by sea before the city fell to the communists

Right: Some of the final scenes in Saigon, as ARVN forces pull back into the city. All those associated with the Saigon regime hoped to be able to join in the evacuation of US personnel, but most were to be disappointed.

Below: NVA troops rush across the airstrip at Tan Son Nhut, Saigon's main airport. Below right: Carrying the flags that they will fly from the roof, NVA soldiers enter the presidential palace in Saigon.

over Easter weekend. With Qui Nhon and Nha Trang falling on 1 April and Cam Ranh Bay two days later, the three weeks that followed the fall of Ban Me Thuot saw the communists overrun half of South Vietnam, destroy six of the country's 13 field divisions, and inflict on the ARVN a series of irreversible defeats that shattered morale and Thieu's remaining prestige.

The defeats, particularly the loss of Da Nang and the manner of its being lost, encouraged unprecedented defiance of Thieu. On 2 April the hitherto-docile Senate demanded a change of leadership, a call supported the following day by Nguyen Van Binh, Archbishop of Saigon. With Thieu responding with the arrest of various members of the opposition, defeat encouraged fragmentation rather than unity.

The 'Ho Chi Minh campaign'

Just as the fall of Phuoc Binh had alerted Hanoi to the possibilities that beckoned in the Highlands, so the fall of Ban Me Thuot and Pleiku convinced the politburo that final victory was at last within its grasp. On 24 March Hanoi ordered Dung to recast his plans to ensure the capture of Saigon before the monsoon broke in May, in the so-called 'Ho Chi Minh campaign'. Three fresh NVA divisions crossed the Demilitarized Zone into South Vietnam in the last week of March, a further 58,000 men moving from the North the following month. Between September 1974 and the end of the war Hanoi moved an estimated 250,000 troops into the South, and during the last weeks of the war openly airlifted troops and supplies into Hue, Da Nang and Kontum.

The Ho Chi Minh campaign opened on 7 April when Saigon was shelled, ARVN troops evacuated Chon Tranh and Dung committed the NVA IV Corps to the attack along Route 1. At Xuan Loc the advancing North Vietnamese encountered the 18th Infantry Division, one of the few formations whose commander chose to go into captivity with his men after the war was over rather than into exile without his men while it was still being fought. The 18th Division denied the communists control of Xuan Loc until the 21st, the day that Thieu finally relinquished the presidency, but it ruined itself in the process and was unable to impose real loss and delay upon the communists. With the choice of when and where to mount his attacks and with some 120,000 troops converging on Saigon from Can Tho, the Parrot's Beak, Chon Thanh, Bien Hoa and Xuan Loc, Dung was able to peel away the capital's defences as if they were the skins of an onion.

Washington now washed its hands of Indochina: the Senate refused to provide further military aid to South Vietnam and President Gerald Ford declared on 23 April that the war was over as far as the United States was concerned. The communists brought the Bien Hoa and Long Binh airbases under artillery and rocket attack long before they overran Phan Rang on 16 April, Phan Thiet on the 20th and Ham Tan on the 23rd. On 27 April, the occupation of Nhon Trach enabled the communists to bring Saigon's last air base, Tan Son Nhut, under long-range artillery fire, while the ARVN garrisons at Vung Tau and Tay Ninh were closely invested. On the 28th, Tan Son Nhut itself was bombed by US-built aircraft captured at Pleiku. The victorious NVA was about to enter the capital of South Vietnam in triumph; but there still remained some harrowing last scenes in Saigon itself.

Brian Markworthy

The death of hope

Confusion and chaos as Saigon falls

By April 1975 the Saigon regime was doomed. The thousands of foreigners and the hundreds of thousands of Vietnamese connected with the Saigon government or its foreign backers were faced with urgent decisions – whether to leave, and if so when and how. Under the leadership of Ambassador Graham Martin, a man deeply committed to South Vietnam – his adopted son had been killed early in the Vietnam War – American policy was to avoid a premature evacuation which would have destroyed the last vestiges of confidence in the Saigon government. The Americans still hoped that South Vietnam could mount sufficient military resistance to the communists to secure some form of negotiated settlement rather than unconditional surrender. On 3 April the US initiated Operation Babylift, in which 3000 orphans, mostly of mixed blood, were airlifted out of Saigon, while tens of thousands of the more prosperous Vietnamese arranged their own departure on commercial flights. But no general evacuation took place.

The political situation in Saigon became critical under the pressure of the military defeat, but President Nguyen Van Thieu could stay as long as he had American support. By 19 April, however, it was clear that no further US military aid would be forthcoming, and the American policymakers decided that negotiations for a rapid end to the fighting were essential. Thieu was an insuperable block to a settlement, and on 20 April Ambassador Martin made it clear to Thieu that he must go. In a bitter and emotional television broadcast the following day, Thieu handed over to his vice-president, Tran Van Huong, before being driven to the airport by US officials. The resignation was futile: the new president was no more acceptable to the communists than Thieu, and in any case North Vietnam had already decided to pursue total victory.

By now a small-scale evacuation was underway from Tan Son Nhut, but only about 500 people a day were being shifted out. On 23 April policy changed, and the number rose to some 5000. The airport was soon besieged by thousands of desperate individuals struggling for a place on the flights. US Air Force C-130s and C-141s shuttled back and forth from Guam, where camps opened up for the refugees. Vietnamese with influential foreign friends tried to beg their way onto a plane, others resorted to bribery. Meanwhile, many Vietnamese stuck loyally to their posts in ministries and embassies, assured that their fidelity would be rewarded with asylum when the crunch came.

But many tens of thousands were to be bitterly disappointed. Ambassador Martin persevered with his policy of limiting the scale of the evacuation in the continuing hope that the North Vietnamese would negotiate. On 28 April, at American insistence, General Duong Van Minh (known as 'Big' Minh), took control of South Vietnam. Minh was a neutralist opponent of Thieu whom the communists had suggested they would find acceptable, but the prospect of negotiations was a mirage. The NVA's 130mm artillery was now within range of the centre of Saigon and, perhaps more important, of Tan Son Nhut. Almost immediately after 'Big' Minh's first speech, in which he called for the immediate departure of American personnel, North Vietnamese pilots in captured A-37s bombed the airport. Before dawn the following day communist bombardment had made further fixed-wing evacuation impossible. At last the Americans gave the order for final evacuation by helicopter, as Minh called on his troops to stop fighting.

At noon on 29 April the remaining Americans – numbering some one and a half thousand – rushed to pre-arranged landing zones on Saigon rooftops, as 60 CH-53 helicopters stationed with a Seventh Fleet task force in the South China Sea prepared to carry out Operation Frequent Wind. From the early afternoon they flew back and forth between the fleet and Saigon, lifting off the Americans and those Vietnamese fortunate enough to win a place.

The last to leave

Kenneth Moorefield was one of the US ambassador's aides who remained in Saigon and helped the Marines who were running the helicopter evacuation from the roof of the US embassy. Later he recalled his experience:

'I remember looking down at the courtyard and counting the people left – a little over four hundred, just a few more chopper loads. Not all were Vietnamese. There were a few Koreans and some others – Filipinos, I think – in the group.'

There was a short period in which no helicopters landed. Moorefield went down into the embassy: 'Major Kean had just received a message from the fleet through his tactical net. There were a few of us standing there, and the major said to us, very dramatically, that the message was from the White House: "I've just received an order from the President. Only embassy staffers are to be evacuated from this point on. Don't panic!" He was very dramatic about it. "Don't panic!," he said, as if any of us had the mind or the strength to panic at this point. And I remember turning to Jay Blowers and saying sardonically, "Don't panic! Only Americans will be evacuated from here on. We're not evacuating anyone else!"

'I then went back to the roof and made another eyeball estimate of the bodies in the courtyard: just over four hundred. I knew now that none of them would ever get out.'

Evacuation and devastation

The final scenes at the US embassy provided some of the most unforgettable images of this television war. Marines, who had been flown in with the first helicopters to arrive, confronted a seething crowd of Vietnamese struggling to break into the embassy compound. Rifle butts were wielded to hold the crowd back as the lucky few were permitted to push their way in. Almost all promises had been forgotten. Loyal officials, embassy staff, police officers and even CIA informants and Viet Cong deserters were left behind. Incredibly, the CIA failed to destroy their records, so the communists were to inherit exact details on all who had betrayed them. Many Vietnamese who went to other evacuation posts in Saigon were never picked up. Other Vietnamese found their own transport. South Vietnamese helicopters were flown out to the Seventh Fleet and either deliberately crashed in the sea or landed on flight decks from which the machines were quickly and unceremoniously tipped overboard. Perhaps 70,000 people who had no access to such high technology took to the sea in small craft, desperately hoping to be picked up by US warships. Many were; but many others were drowned or died of the hardship endured.

The American helicopter airlift continued until early on the morning of 30 April, by which time some 7000 people had been heli-lifted out. When the order was given for the last flight, the Marines retreated upwards through the embassy, throwing tear gas grenades to hold off pursuing South Vietnamese frantic for their last chance of evacuation. Then, in the merciless description of North Vietnamese commander General Van Tien Dung, 'after 30 years of military intervention and adventures in Vietnam . . . the US ambassador had to crawl onto the roof of the embassy building to escape.'

It was 0753 hours on the 30th when the last Marines departed. The city was given over to the looting of American homes, offices and warehouses. Soldiers discarded their uniforms in a frantic search for anonymity. Then, with hardly a shot fired, the communist forces moved into Saigon. At 1100 hours a North Vietnamese tank crashed through the gates of the presidential palace (and soon repeated the event for television cameras which had missed it the first time). General Minh broadcast unconditional surrender, and the Vietnam War was over. **R.G. Grant**

Left above: Scenes of chaos as desperate Vietnamese try to break into the American embassy compound on 29 April. Left below: A South Vietnamese helicopter is pushed into the sea from the USS *Blue Ridge* on 29 April, to make room for more aircraft to land. Altogether 15 helicopters from the South Vietnamese forces landed on the *Blue Ridge* on the 29th. Below: Captured for posterity by press and TV cameras, NVA tanks smash their way into the presidential palace in Saigon.

Counting the cost

The balance sheet of the Vietnam War

Protracted interventionary wars such as that fought by the US in Vietnam are wars of balance sheets. The nation's continuing expenditure on intervention must constantly be weighed against achievements to date, losses incurred and the projected final outcome of the conflict. Such factors are regulated by the current political expediency of the level of intervention and the sensitive area of public acceptance of rising levels of cost and casualties. As Sir Robert Thompson, chief of the British Advisory Mission to Vietnam from 1961 to 1965, has pointed out . . . 'if one side has costs which are indefinitely acceptable to it, and imposes on you costs which are not indefinitely acceptable to you, it does not matter what happens in the battles.'

The balancing of cost against achievement, however, was not an easy matter in Indochina. Whereas the current American and UN position in the Korean War could be measured by where the front line lay and the overall balance of forces involved, the war in Indochina was a war without fronts against an enemy that was elusive and at times difficult to identify. The majority of actions during the American involvement were indecisive and fought between small units. In 1968, for example, Viet Cong and North Vietnamese strength in South Vietnam stood at an estimated 250,000 and while 3921 communist ground attacks were recorded, only 126 were in battalion strength. Allied offensive operations such as Cedar Falls and Junction City, which aimed to clear large areas of South Vietnam of Viet Cong activity, failed in the long run since an effective level of troop presence in the areas cleared could not be maintained in their aftermath and the Viet Cong were able to re-infiltrate almost immediately. While the US and allied forces were able to hold out in larger actions such as those of the all-out communist offensive of Tet in 1968, no substantive gains were discernible and the North Vietnamese Army, although severely rebuffed, was far from defeated. During the two weeks of the Tet offensive the US, ARVN and allied forces lost some 4300 men killed and the average US daily artillery expenditure doubled. General Westmoreland immediately requested an additional commitment of a further 200,000 troops on top of the existing 536,000 but faith in the ability of the US Army to win the attritional war was severely shaken; the costs had now risen too high and neither the US public nor the political establishment were prepared to accept them any longer.

By June 1974, the US Department of Defense estimated that the total incremental cost of the US war effort – that is cost over and above what would have normally been spent in peacetime – currently stood at $112,000 million or $145,000 million at 1974 prices. The root cause of this massive financial outlay lay in the American tactical approach and style of warfare which relied heavily on the deployment of massive firepower. During the fiscal year 1969, the most expensive year of US involvement, $21.5 billion were pumped into Vietnam. Of this figure some 80

per cent was spent on US military activities while aid to the South Vietnamese effort accounted for the remainder. Operating a US division cost 20 times as much as a South Vietnamese division and in 1968, the peak year of the US manpower commitment, 40 per cent of the combined US and South Vietnamese military forces were American.

By far the most expensive area of US cost was the prosecution of the air war which in 1969, for example, amounted to some $9.5 billion. During World War II, the US dropped some two million tonnes of bombs in the combined theatres while from 1965 to the end of 1971 more than three times that figure, some 6.3 million tonnes were dropped on Indochina. An indication of the costs involved in the air war can be seen by looking at the figures for one year of the Rolling Thunder campaign. In 1966 148,000 sorties were flown over North Vietnam. With a fighter-bomber sortie costing some $12,000 and a B-52 sortie $45,000 the combined total operational costs for that year amounted to $1247 million. The total tonnage of bombs dropped was 128,000 for the loss of 318 aircraft. Estimated military and economic damage to North Vietnam ran to some $130 million, so that for every one dollar's worth of damage inflicted on the North, the US had to spend 9.6 dollars. During the whole campaign up to the bombing halt of November 1968 some 300,000 sorties were flown, delivering an estimated 860,000 tonnes of bombs. Despite the severity of the damage to the North, the infiltration of men and materials to the South continued and supplies coming to the North from the Soviet Union and China more than compensated for the North's losses.

The balance of foreign aid

Foreign aid was the key to North Vietnam's continued war effort. Verifiable figures for military aid to the North are extremely sketchy but estimates put Soviet aid between 1965 and 1971 at $1660 million and Chinese aid over the same period at $670 million. The North's own defence budget during those years ran to some $3560 million which, combined with foreign assistance, provides a total of some $5890 million. On the other side of the balance sheet, US military aid to South Vietnam, Cambodia and Laos has been estimated at $8540 million for the same period (1965-1971) while the US incremental costs of fighting the war are put at $90,940 million. When these figures are added to South Vietnam's own budget of $3337 million this provides a total of some $102,517 million, more than 17 times the amount available to the North.

In addition to the magnitude of the ever escalating US financial commitment to the war in Vietnam, the American population was also not prepared to accept indefinitely the so-called rising 'body count' or level of casualties sustained. Of the 27 million draft-aged Americans of the Vietnam generation, 2,300,000 served in Vietnam. Between 1961 and 1974 46,370 US servicemen died in battle while some 300,000 were wounded. This amounted to an average loss rate of 1.8 per cent of the US force each year or a one in 55 chance of being killed while serving in Vietnam. ARVN losses were considerably higher; 2.5 per cent of its force was lost annually amounting to a total of some 184,000 South Vietnamese soldiers killed between 1961 and the January 1973 ceasefire. Casualty figures for the North Vietnamese and Viet Cong are far from reliable, one of the main problems being the identification of military as opposed to civilian deaths

Above: Manhandling used shells in the US Seventh Fleet. The Navy provided constant support for the troops ashore. Above left: Bombing up B-52s at Anderson air base on Guam. The bombing campaign was the single most expensive aspect of the war.

Enormous amounts of money were spent on the war, but the financial cost pales before the human tragedy that overtook the individuals involved. Left: Refugees flee the battle zone. Right: A young GI breaks down in May 1967. 16 of his comrades had just been killed when his unit was caught up in fighting in the Central Highlands.

in the case of the Viet Cong, but estimates have put losses at over 900,000 for the period 1961 to 1974.

The real cost of the Vietnam War in human terms, however, fell on the civilian populations of the war-torn countries. Geographically, of the 44 provinces of South Vietnam, the 10 hardest hit by the fighting lay in three areas: the seven northernmost provinces south of the Demilitarized Zone, the area around the Parrot's Beak on the border with Cambodia and the Delta area just south of Saigon. Most of rural South Vietnam was considered by the US as a 'free-fire zone' and this resulted in a massive displacement of the population as inhabitants fled their villages in the face of US shelling and bombing. It has been estimated that two-thirds of the South Vietnamese population of 18 million was displaced during the war as the land suffered the impact of some 10 million tonnes of bombs and shells and 55,000 tonnes of defoliating agents. Munitions and defoliants severely damaged 32 per cent of the total land area of South Vietnam while three per cent was totally devastated.

Estimates of civilian casualties during the war differ radically and high casualty counts were one of the main weapons of the anti-war campaign in the US. In 1967, Martin Luther King, for example, claimed there had been a million civilian deaths and that at least 20 civilians had died for every Viet Cong killed. Edward Kennedy's Senate committee on refugees estimated 430,000 South Vietnamese civilian deaths between 1965 and 1974, and over one million wounded, while later estimates put the figure at 250,000 dead and some 900,000 wounded. Even the lowest estimate provides a rate of under five civilian deaths to every US soldier killed in South Vietnam alone.

The total cost of the American involvement in Vietnam is inestimable. While the cost of military assistance to the countries of Indochina runs into hundreds of billions of dollars, the US continues to pay for its intervention in the inevitable wartime economic inflation, lost production and the continuing expenditure of loan repayment and veteran benefits. Some commentators have also pointed to the so-called 'opportunity costs' of the war, that is to say while the US poured billions of dollars into the Vietnam theatre, the Soviet Union was able to continue to invest in strategic systems which have had a significant effect on the world's balance of power. The bulk of the human cost, however, has been paid by Indochina – a land shattered by war, and where communist victories in 1975 were only the prelude to further harrowing developments. **Jonathan Reed**

Large areas of South Vietnam were completely devastated during the war. Above: The old imperial capital of Hue lies in ruins after the fighting there in 1968.

Below: C-123s of the 12th Air Commando Squadron spray defoliation chemicals along a canal in South Vietnam in 1967.

Key Weapons

WESTERN MICVs

There is an important though sometimes blurred distinction between the APC (armoured personnel carrier) and the MICV (mechanised infantry combat vehicle) or IFV (infantry combat vehicle). The main role of the APC is to transport infantry from one part of the battlefield to another where they then dismount and fight as ordinary infantry. The MICV, however, is designed to operate with the forward armoured units as part of a combined arms team that includes tanks, self-propelled artillery, engineers and helicopters. The tactical requirements of the MICV are demanding: it has to have reasonable armour protection, have a good power-to-weight ratio in order to keep up with the tanks across rough terrain, be provided with a turret-mounted armament, have some provision for the infantry to use their smallarms from within the vehicle, have an NBC (nuclear, biological, chemical) warfare system and a full suite of passive night vision equipment for the driver, commander and gunner. Some countries also insist that the MICV must have an anti-tank capability as well, for example, the US Bradley IFV, and the West German Marder.

The first country to operationally deploy an MICV was not, however, in the West but in the East. The Soviet Union first displayed the BMP-1 MICV in 1967 and the introduction of this vehicle into service within the Soviet Army acted as an important spur to the West to accelerate the development of a similar vehicle.

When the West German Army was reformed during the 1950s requirements for new vehicles were formulated. The need for an APC was so urgent that a modification of an existing vehicle was chosen and this was rushed into service in 1958 as the Schützenpanzer 12-3. By 1960, however, the West German Army had a clearer idea of what it wanted and in that year it awarded contracts for prototypes of a MICV to be built, followed by pre-production vehicles, which were delivered in 1967-68. Following troop trials this vehicle was accepted for service as the Marder with the first production batch being completed in 1970.

The Marder has an excellent power-to-weight ratio, and armour protection over the frontal arc is sufficient to withstand penetration from 20mm projectiles. The two-man turret is fitted with an externally-mounted 20mm cannon with a co-axial 7.62mm machine gun. Many Marders have a Milan (*missile d'infanterie léger anti-char*) ATGW (anti-tank guided weapon) launcher mounted on the right side of the turret which gives it a useful anti-tank capability. Mounted over the troop compartment at the rear is a remote-controlled 7.62mm machine gun, while within the hull sides two firing ports a side have been built. The six infantrymen enter and leave the vehicle via a power-operated ramp in the hull rear.

Previous page: The US Bradley MICV thunders across desert terrain at speed. Above: The West German Marder is an expensive though highly effective MICV and it allows troops to use hull-mounted firing ports or to fight from the deck hatches (top). Below: Besides a 20mm cannon and two machine guns this Marder mounts a Milan anti-tank guided missile on the turret.

The French AMX VCI IFV, which entered service with the French Army in 1957-58, was one of the first postwar vehicles to have firing ports for the infantry and the option of a fully enclosed weapon station. It is now being replaced in the French Army by the AMX-10P which is fully amphibious and fitted with a two-man power-operated turret armed with a 20mm cannon and a co-axial 7.62mm machine gun. The rear troop compartment does not have any provision to aim and fire weapons from within the vehicle apart from two firing ports in the power-operated ramp in the hull rear. There are many variants of the AMX-10P including an anti-tank vehicle with four HOT (high-subsonic optically-tracked tube-launched) ATGWs, command vehicle, mortar towing vehicle, ambulance and various artillery and observation vehicles. For the export market the AMX-10 PAC 90 has been developed which is the basic AMX-10P fitted with a two-man GIAT TS-90 turret armed with a long-barrelled 90mm gun. This vehicle, already in service with the Indonesian Marines, is designed to provide fire support for other AMX-10P vehicles.

The United States Army saw the need for an MICV in the early 1960s and the first vehicle to meet this requirement was the XM701 which used parts of the M110 and M107 self-propelled guns and was fitted with a turret-mounted 20mm cannon, but this did not progress beyond the prototype stage. Based on the M113 APC the FMC Corporation built the XM765 which had firing ports in the rear troop compartment and a new weapons station. This was not selected for service, however, although further development some years later by FMC as a private venture resulted in the AIFV (armoured infantry fighting vehicle) which was selected by the Netherlands in 1975. The AIFV was later ordered by the Philippines and in 1979 Belgium ordered 514 vehicles to be built in the country under licence. For many countries who cannot afford the highly complex Bradley IFV, the AIFV is an ideal compromise. Over the earlier M113 the AIFV offers improved armour protection, greater firepower (25mm cannon against a 12.7mm machine gun) and better cross-country mobility owing to improved suspension.

Above: French Army troop carriers – the AMX VCI (top), the AMX 10P with troops, weapons and equipment (above left) and an AMX 10P swimming a water obstacle armed with a 20mm cannon (above). Below: The US AIFV (with TOW launcher) in Dutch Army service. Below left: Troops fire from an AIFV.

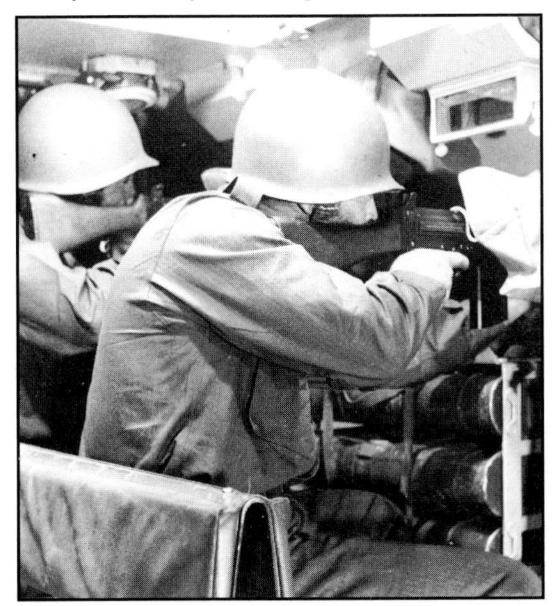

Late in 1972 FMC were awarded a contract to design and build prototypes of a new MICV under the designation of the XM723, with all 12 prototypes to be completed by 1975. At that time prototypes of a new ARSV (armoured reconnaissance scout vehicle) had been built but a decision was taken to cancel this project and build a vehicle to meet both standard MICV and scout requirements. At the same time it was decided that both vehicles would have a new two-man turret (commander and gunner), be armed with a 25mm cannon and have a twin launcher for the Hughes TOW (tube-launched optically-tracked wire-guided) ATGW to give the vehicle a long range anti-tank capability. The infantry fighting vehicle was designated the M2 while the scout or cavalry fighting vehicle, became the M3. In 1977 it was decided to use the same chassis for what is now known as the MLRS (multiple launch rocket system). In 1980 the United States Army ordered 100 M2/M3 vehicles and all of these were completed by July 1982, and subsequently were produced at the rate of 50 vehicles per month. The M2/M3 was named the Bradley and became operational in 1983 in the United States and the following year in West Germany. The United States Army has a requirement for nearly 7000 Bradley MICVs but these will not replace the M113 on a one-for-one basis as in many battlefield roles – such as command post, mortar carrier, logistic support and ambulance – the older M113 is more than adequate.

The M2 has a three-man crew – commander, gunner and driver – and it can carry up to seven infantrymen in the rear compartment. The hull is constructed of welded aluminium with spaced laminate armour added to the hull front, sides and rear for extra protection. All the vehicles are fully amphibious and rely on their tracks for propulsion.

The 25mm Hughes dual-feed Chain Gun is mounted in a power-operated turret which has a stabilisation system that allows the cannon to be aimed and fired whilst the vehicle is moving across country at speed. A total of 300 rounds of ammunition are carried for

Top left: A side view of an M2 Bradley revealing its turret-mounted 7.62mm machine gun and 25mm Hughes Chain Gun. Above: Advancing up a river bed an M2 demonstrates its water-crossing ability. The M2 also has a full amphibious capability; it is able to float and propulsion is provided by the action of its tracks.

Above: The 'cavalry' version of the Bradley, the M3, whose main function is to act as a battlefield reconnaissance vehicle. As with the infantry M2, the M3 has a twin TOW launcher mounted on the left side of the turret. Above right and right: The British MCV-80, which was designed to supplement and extend the capabilities of the FV432 APC. Despite a number of developmental problems the MCV-80's 30mm main armament and good armour protection make it a potent battlefield weapon.

immediate use with a further 600 rounds kept in reserve. Three types of 25mm ammunition are currently available: APDS-T (armour-piercing discarding-sabot – tracer), HEI-T (high-explosive incendiary – tracer) and a training round. Under development is an APFSDS (armour-piercing fin-stabilised discarding-sabot) round with greatly improved penetration. Mounted co-axially with the 25mm cannon is a 7.62mm machine gun, while mounted on the left side of the turret is a twin launcher for the Hughes TOW ATGW, with a further five TOW missiles stowed in the hull rear. A bank of four electrically-operated smoke dischargers is mounted either side of the turret and latest production vehicles have an engine smoke generation system along similar lines to that fitted in Soviet tanks. The M3 cavalry fighting vehicle is almost identical to the M2 but has no firing ports; it has a three-man crew and carries only two infantrymen who can dismount from the vehicle to carry out reconnaissance on foot. The M3 has a greatly increased ammunition carrying capacity compared with the M2 as it is envisaged that on occasions it will have to fight to obtain information.

The United Kingdom's MICV is called the MCV-80 with the first 250 being ordered in 1984. The MCV-80 has a three-man crew – commander, gunner and driver – and can carry seven fully-equipped infantrymen. An unusual feature of the MCV-80 when compared to other MICVs is that there is no provision for the infantrymen to fight from within the vehicle as this is not a British Army requirement. The MCV-80 is fitted with a two-man power-operated turret armed with a Rarden 30mm cannon (as fitted to the Scimitar and Fox reconnaissance vehicles) and a co-axial 7.62mm machine gun. It has no anti-tank capability, however, as the British believe that this role is best left to dedicated vehicles such as the Striker. The MCV-80 has a full range of passive night vision equipment and an NBC system, but no amphibious capability. To give it the latter the vehicle would have to be lighter and armour protection would therefore have been lessened.

The standard APC of the Italian Army is the American M113A1 which has been manufactured under licence in Italy by OTO-Melara. Further development of the M113A1 resulted in the AIFV (armoured infantry fighting vehicle) which has applique armour added to the hull front, sides and rear, new fuel tanks on either side of the power-operated ramp at the hull rear (thereby increasing space in the troop compartment as well as reducing the fire risk), sloping upper sides to the troop compartment with vision blocks and firing ports underneath, and armament comprising 12.7mm and 7.62mm machine guns.

OTO-Melara is currently developing the VCC-80 infantry fighting vehicle to meet the requirements of the Italian Army. This will have a low profile and be fitted with a power-operated turret armed with a 25mm cannon and a 7.62mm co-axial machine gun. At one time it was proposed to fit Milan ATGWs to the side of the turret but it is now expected that a dedicated anti-tank version will be developed instead.

For the export market the company have recently developed the OTO C13 which has firing ports in the rear troop compartment and a variety of weapon stations ranging from a simple 12.7mm machine gun up to a turret-mounted 20mm cannon or even a 90mm gun. Its main advantage over the M113 is its much lower profile and improved armour protection.

MOWAG of Switzerland built some of the first prototypes of the Marder MICV for the West German Army in the early 1960s and since then MOWAG has undertaken a continuous programme of private venture research and development which has culminated in the MOWAG Improved Tornado MICV. This can be fitted with a wide range of armament installations including a new Oerlikon-Bührle two-man power-operated turret armed with a 25mm cannon, 7.62mm machine gun and twin launcher for TOW ATGWs. At present the Swiss Army operates M113A1 series APCs but has a requirement for a new MICV which could be met by the Improved Tornado MICV.

While the major powers are now developing or employing mechanised infantry combat vehicles there are wide differences between many of the vehicles in terms of armour protection, mobility and firepower. In some cases this is because the role of the MICV/IFV on the battlefield is seen differently by the various armies employing them but in other cases the vehicle has had to be developed within clearly defined cost constraints which has meant that many features have been left off.

As the 1973 Middle East war proved, tanks cannot survive on the modern battlefield without the support of other arms, including infantry in mechanised infantry combat vehicles. There are, however, a number of observers who believe that the MICV will not survive on the battlefield alongside the tank unless it has a similar degree of protection. This would mean MICVs weighing at least 40 tonnes but this would make the vehicles even more expensive which in turn would make them unacceptable to most armies.

Below: The Swiss MOWAG Tornado MICV, a well-armed fighting vehicle broadly similar to the West German Marder. Centre and bottom: Two views of the Italian OTO C13, armed with a turret-mounted 0.5in Browning machine gun. Built for the export market the OTO C13 is a rugged and flexible fighting vehicle offering superior performance over conventional APCs.

Rebels and revolutionaries

White Rhodesia and black nationalism

Above: A black soldier of the Rhodesian Army on patrol in the bush, armed with a 7.62mm GPMG. Throughout the 14 years between Ian Smith's Unilateral Declaration of Independence on 11 November 1965, and the final ceasefire of 28 December 1979, the white minority regime was able to field large numbers of black troops. Until the final months of the war, these were all volunteers, largely from the Kalanga tribal group.

On 11 November 1965 Ian Smith, the prime minister of the self-governing British colony of Rhodesia (formerly Southern Rhodesia), delivered a statement that was to have profound domestic and international repercussions. In an historic broadcast, Smith announced that the Rhodesian government had decided to seize independence. This Unilateral Declaration of Independence (UDI) marked the beginning of Rhodesia's 14-year rebellion against Britain. It also led to a long and bloody internal conflict that resulted in over 20,000 deaths.

The rebellion, and the ensuing conflict, reflected the emergence in Rhodesia of two contrasting and mutually exclusive forms of nationalism. At the time of UDI Rhodesia was a country of some four and a quarter million people, of whom the vast majority – over four million – were black Africans. African leaders who claimed to represent this majority had been pressing Britain to grant Rhodesia independence by transferring political power to them; these leaders had chosen the name of Zimbabwe for the new state they wished to create. However, while the African nationalists aspired to establish Zimbabwe, other Rhodesians, and in particular the country's white community, wished to keep the name Rhodesia and the regime associated with that name. Britain could not ignore the Zimbabweans, but neither could it overlook white Rhodesian nationalism. Although the majority of the territory's 220,000 whites had been born in Britain (in 1956, only one third of the white population had been born in Rhodesia), they were established settlers, who controlled Rhodesia both economically and politically.

Indeed, from its very foundation Rhodesia had been dominated by white settlers. Unlike most of Britain's colonies it had been colonised in the true sense of the word. Whites had begun to settle there in the 1890s, when Cecil Rhodes extended British authority and gave his own name to an area then occupied by the Shona and Ndebele peoples; by 1931 the whites had allocated to themselves 198,000 square km (76,000 square miles) of Southern Rhodesia's total expanse of 390,000 square km (150,000 square miles). Britain governed the territory in name only. Between 1890 and 1923 Southern Rhodesia was administered by Rhodes's British South Africa Company. In 1923 it was granted internal self-government, and although Britain retained certain reserve powers, in practice political power was wielded by white settlers. The whites proceeded to build up what by African standards was an advanced and prosperous country, though blacks, who had helped to create this wealth, remained comparatively disadvantaged in social and economic terms. Blacks also found political advancement difficult, because the franchise, though non-racial in principle,

Below: Harold Wilson and Ian Smith meet for talks on the future of Rhodesia in 1965. Resistance to British pressure for constitutional change from the white Rhodesian minority led directly to UDI. Bottom: Smith became a symbolic target for worldwide opposition to white domination in Rhodesia. Here, demonstrators express their opinion in London during the Lancaster House conference, 1979.

was subject to educational and income qualifications that few blacks were able to meet.

For many years this colonial regime went unchallenged. Blacks had risen against the colonists in the 1890s, but the risings were abortive and for the next 50 years they accepted white rule passively. After World War II, however, black attitudes began to change. In 1953 Southern Rhodesia was federated with the adjoining British territories of Northern Rhodesia and Nyasaland to form the Central African Federation. After initially welcoming this move, Rhodesia's small black elite turned against the Federation, as did the elites in Northern Rhodesia and Nyasaland.

The first black political organisation in Southern Rhodesia, the African National Congress, set up in the 1950s by Joshua Nkomo, had only limited aims, but it was accused by the government of fomenting black unrest and was banned in February 1959. Its successor, the National Democratic Party (NDP) was more militant. Established in January 1960 by Nkomo, the Reverend Ndabaningi Sithole, Herbert Chitepo and Robert Mugabe, it demanded not just a redress of grievances but independence under a one-man-one-vote system. With the collapse of the Federation imminent, the NDP hoped that Britain would impose majority rule upon the Southern Rhodesian government. This hope was dashed. At the Anglo-Rhodesian conference of 1961 Britain agreed to a constitution which, although providing for greater African representation, in effect would delay majority rule for several decades. The NDP denounced the agreement and resorted to violence in an attempt to disrupt the registration of black voters; it was banned in December 1961.

Almost immediately the African nationalists formed a new party called the Zimbabwe African People's Union (ZAPU). After sporadic violence ZAPU too was banned, although it soon reconstituted itself. The Zimbabwean cause was weakened, however, in August 1963 when Sithole broke away to form the Zimbabwe African National Union (ZANU). Despite the fact that both ZAPU and ZANU shared a common objective – African majority rule – their rivalry exploded into violence. In 1964 the government outlawed both parties and detained every prominent African nationalist leader, including Mugabe, Sithole and Nkomo.

The white reaction

These measures were symptomatic of a growing determination on the part of the whites to suppress Zimbabwean nationalism. Most of the whites were convinced that majority rule would threaten their privileges and safety, and bring chaos to Rhodesia. Events in newly independent African states, notably the ex-Belgian Congo, served to confirm these fears. As the African nationalists became increasingly militant, a white reaction developed. In December 1962 the electorate voted into office the Rhodesian Front (RF), a newly-created party dedicated to keeping power in 'civilised' hands – even if this meant defying the British government.

Before very long the Rhodesian and British governments were set on a collision course. In late 1963 Britain had dismantled the Central African Federation and within a year had granted independence to Northern Rhodesia (Zambia) and Nyasaland (Malawi), in both cases under black governments. Britain also sought to decolonise Southern Rhodesia, but while the RF government wanted independence on the basis of the 1961 constitution, Britain insisted on certain modifications that would have improved the position of the Africans. As negotiations dragged on, the Rhodesians became more and more suspicious of Britain's intentions, especially after Harold Wilson became British prime minister in October 1964 – Wilson had earlier declared his total opposition to white minority rule in Rhodesia. Talks between Wilson and Rhodesian prime minister Smith got nowhere and on 11 November 1965 the RF finally broke with Britain so that, in Smith's words, 'justice, civilisation and Christianity' might be preserved in Rhodesia.

Britain was determined to reverse UDI, but could

find no effective means of restoring its authority. One option that might have proved decisive was for Britain to crush the rebellion by force; indeed the nationalists hoped that Britain would do just that. The British government, however, declined to pursue this option, partly because of manpower, logistical and economic constraints, and partly for political reasons: the Wilson government had only a slender parliamentary majority and it feared the consequences of ordering British troops to fight their 'kith and kin' in Rhodesia. Instead, the British government imposed economic sanctions against Rhodesia, initially on a selective basis. Sanctions, Wilson argued, would cripple Rhodesia economically, produce political opposition to the Smith regime and thereby force the latter to sue for peace 'in weeks rather than months'.

In theory, there were strong grounds for assuming that sanctions would produce such a result. Rhodesia was dependent upon the import of all its oil and upon the export of a few items like chrome, meat and tobacco for its economic survival; moreover, it relied to a considerable extent upon trade with Britain. It soon became obvious, however, that sanctions were not having the desired effect, despite the fact that Britain had placed embargos on the export of oil to Rhodesia and upon 95 per cent of Rhodesia's exports to Britain. Portugal (which governed the neighbouring territory of Mozambique) and South Africa were sympathetic to the Smith regime and refused to support sanctions; others, including some Eastern bloc and African states, condemned Rhodesia officially while secretly trading with her.

Britain decided to fall back on a policy that combined coercion with diplomacy. Despite earlier statements to the effect that he would never negotiate with Smith, Wilson attempted to negotiate a settlement. The British terms, presented aboard HMS *Tiger* in December 1966, called not for immediate majority rule but for 'unimpeded progress towards majority rule'. All the same, the talks broke down; the United Nations (UN) then made Britain's selective sanctions mandatory. A second attempt by the Wilson government to settle the dispute, this time aboard HMS *Fearless* in October 1968, was also fruitless. Britain's terms were more lenient than those offered in the *Tiger* talks, but the differences between the two sides remained too wide and Smith rejected the proposals; the UN, on its part, had already voted for comprehensive and mandatory economic sanctions.

The African nationalists, meanwhile, faced with Britain's failure to take decisive action against the Smith regime, had decided to resort to guerrilla war. During the early 1960s small numbers of Africans had been given guerrilla training in various African and Eastern bloc countries; within six months of UDI these insurgents were deployed operationally.

The first serious incursion took place in April 1966, when a group of 14 ZANU guerrillas infiltrated into Rhodesia with orders to attack white farms and sabotage power lines. The guerrillas (referred to by the security forces as 'terrs' or terrorists) managed to kill a white farmer and his wife but the entire group was killed or captured; the same fate befell other groups which infiltrated later that year. Larger groups that entered Rhodesia during 1967 and 1968 fared no better. In August 1967 a combined force of 90 insurgents belonging to ZAPU and the African National Congress of South Africa (ANCSA) crossed into Rhodesia near the Victoria Falls. Its presence was reported by local blacks and most of the infiltrators were wiped out. A second joint force, totalling 123 guerrillas, was located and decimated in March-April 1968, as was a third, 91 strong, that entered Rhodesia in the following July. By the end of 1968 more than 160 insurgents had been killed for the loss of only 12 members of the security forces.

By that time it was clear that the nationalists' strategy had failed. ZANU and ZAPU had thrown many of their available guerrillas into the struggle but the political and military impact inside Rhodesia had been negligible. Demoralised by these defeats the nationalists began to indulge in fratricidal strife. Personal, ideological and tribal divisions had been exacerbated by the reverses and the nationalists turned their rhetoric, and sometimes their guns, against each other.

Immigration and segregation

Despite international pressure and guerrilla incursions, Rhodesia flourished. The economy boomed, exports soared and white immigrants arrived in increasing numbers. The government strengthened racial segregation, declared Rhodesia a republic and in 1969 introduced a new constitution that offered the Africans not majority rule but 'racial parity' in the distant future. Having defied Britain, the UN and the guerrillas, the RF was swept back into power in the 1970 general election.

Nevertheless, the Rhodesians lacked international recognition, and they remained interested in talking to the British. When Britain's new Conservative government offered to re-open negotiations, the Rhodesians grasped the opportunity. In November 1971 settlement terms were agreed. Britain eased the conditions presented aboard *Tiger* and *Fearless*, while the Rhodesians, for their part, agreed to modify the 1969 constitution so that Africans could eventually achieve majority rule, rather than just parity. However, the agreement was never implemented. One of the conditions laid down by the British government was that the terms of any settlement had to be acceptable to Rhodesians as a whole, that is to blacks as well as whites. Accordingly Britain sent out a commission to test African opinion. This was regarded by both governments as a mere formality. To their surprise, however, opposition to the deal was galvanised by the African National Council (ANC), a new organisation led by Abel Muzorewa, a bishop

Below: The complexities of southern African economic life are illustrated by the incident below, in which a train carrying Zambian copper through Rhodesia to South Africa has been blown up by guerrillas of Joshua Nkomo's ZIPRA, themselves based in Zambia. The effect of economic sanctions against the Smith regime was blunted by the mutual interdependence of the economies of both white and black states in the region.

who had hitherto shown no political aspirations. Muzorewa was so successful in his campaign that the Pearce Commission, after sounding out African opinion, reported in May 1972 that the majority of Africans rejected the settlement terms. Reluctantly, the British and Rhodesian governments broke off their talks.

ZANU, meanwhile, remained convinced that the Africans' salvation lay in guerrilla conflict, and was planning a fresh offensive against the Smith regime. This time, however, ZANU would be better prepared. Recognising that the incursions of 1968-69 had been disastrous, it had set up an eight-member war council, the Dare re Chimurenga. This body concentrated on organising a Maoist-style protracted struggle designed to wear down the government's human and economic resources. Chinese instructors were imported into ZANU's camps in Tanzania to train recruits of the Zimbabwe African National Liberation Army (ZANLA). ZANU also gained new infiltration routes; it persuaded the Mozambican nationalist movement, Frente de Libertação de Moçambique (FRELIMO) to allow ZANLA guerrillas to operate out of FRELIMO-dominated areas along the Mozambique-Rhodesia border. It was in northeast Rhodesia, where administration was weak and where the white authorities were unpopular with the local Shona population, that ZANU made its major effort. Having built up local support and established arms caches, ZANU finally launched its offensive in December 1972.

Eliminating the insurgents

The offensive, heralded by attacks on isolated white farms in the Centenary district, took the Rhodesians by surprise. However, once they had identified the threat the Rhodesians soon developed countermeasures. An intensive counter-insurgency campaign was mounted, including extensive efforts to separate the insurgents from the population. Some of these measures, notably collective fines and forced relocation in protected villages, caused bitter resentment, but in the short term at least the counterinsurgency policies worked. By mid-1974 the campaign in the northeast, codenamed Hurricane, had begun to turn in the government's favour. The insurgents were gradually eliminated and ZANLA started abducting schoolchildren in order to make good its losses. According to the government over 500 guerrillas had been killed by the end of the year for the loss of only 58 members of the security forces.

At this juncture the Rhodesians were compelled to restrain their counter-insurgency effort as a result of pressure from an unexpected quarter – South Africa. During the first eight years of UDI the South Africans, while remaining officially neutral in the Anglo-Rhodesian dispute, had helped Rhodesia to evade sanctions and had supported her war effort with perhaps as many as 2000 paramilitary policemen. However, after the Portuguese decision to quit Africa in the wake of the Lisbon coup of April 1974, South Africa abandoned its policy of benevolent neutrality. Mozambique was about to come under a black Marxist regime, thus exposing Rhodesia's 1300km (800-mile) eastern border to guerrilla infiltration. In the circumstances South Africa calculated that the Smith regime had become militarily untenable; South African interests would best be served by a quick and peaceful transfer of power from the RF to a moderate and stable black regime.

Zambia too was eager for a peaceful settlement. Zambia's support for the Zimbabwean cause had cost her dearly, particularly after the border with Rhodesia had been closed in 1973. In concert with the South Africans, therefore, the Zambians sought to promote a settlement. While South African premier Balthazar Johannes Vorster used economic leverage to make Smith release detained nationalist leaders – including Nkomo and Mugabe – Zambia's Kenneth Kaunda and Tanzania's Julius Nyerere persuaded the various nationalist factions – ZANU, ZAPU and the ANC – to form a united front under the chairmanship of Abel Muzorewa. A ceasefire was declared in December 1974 (although it was subsequently broken by both sides), South Africa withdrew its forces, and in August 1975 representatives of the RF and the nationalists met at Victoria Falls.

The conference was inconclusive. Smith remained obdurate, and the nationalists seemed unable to sink their differences. Indeed, by the end of the year the nationalists appeared to be in some disarray. ZANU was short of funds and divided by a leadership struggle between Sithole and Mugabe. Among ZANLA guerrillas in the bush, morale sagged and casualties soared. ZAPU fared better, especially when Zambia expelled ZANLA and gave full backing to ZAPU and its military wing, the Zimbabwe People's Revolutionary Army (ZIPRA). However, ZIPRA had not begun military operations in earnest and its leader, Nkomo, entered into bilateral negotiations with Smith in December 1975.

The Rhodesian government's respite was short-lived. By early 1976 guerrilla activity had extended along the entire length of the eastern border forcing the government to set up new operations in east and southeast Rhodesia. The Rhodesians were also compelled to extend national service, call up more white reservists and enlist more Africans and foreigners.

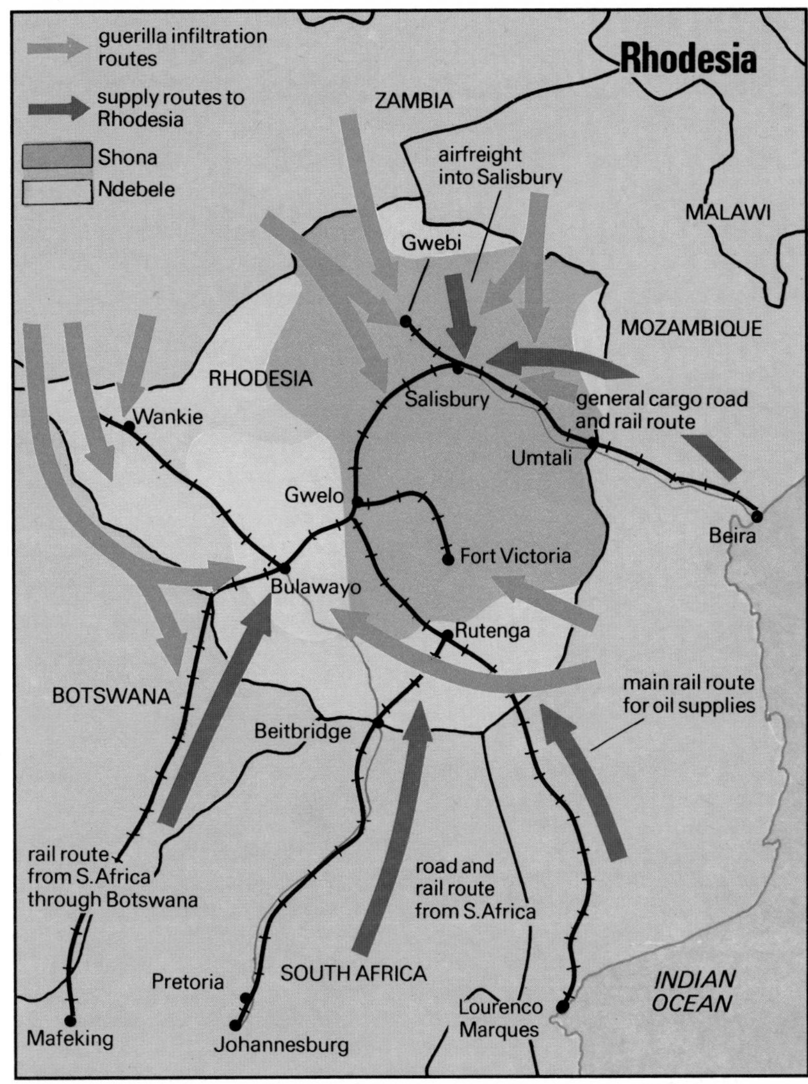

Left top: The guerrillas were able to compel the Rhodesian security forces to assign large numbers of men to the static defence of vulnerable points. Left bottom: In order to deprive the guerrillas of active support, attempts were made to concentrate the black rural population into protected villages. Here, a white farmer has set fire to the huts of his resettled farm labourers in order to prevent their use by guerrillas. Right: Troops of the Rhodesian African Rifles display a variety of rifle-grenades mounted on their 7.62mm FN FAL rifles. Despite their superior equipment and training, the security forces found it more and more difficult to contain the nationalist guerrillas.

Allies and rivals

Born in June 1917, Joshua Nkomo was educated at a Methodist mission school and at university in South Africa. He rose to prominence in the 1950s as secretary-general of the largest black organisation in the country, the Rhodesian African Railway Workers' Union, and from 1952 to 1957 he was president of the African National Congress (ANC). By the 1960s he was already regarded as the father of Zimbabwean nationalism. An expansive, subtle man, he was a typical product of the old African trade union movement, whose willingness to seek constitutional concessions from the white minority regime was to gradually lose him influence within the black nationalist movement throughout the 1960s and 1970s, without gaining anything in return.

Robert Mugabe, on the other hand, though born only seven years later than Nkomo, in February 1924, belongs to a totally different political generation – one which rejected the style and policies of Nkomo. Educated by Jesuits at a Catholic mission school, and at the all-black Fort Hare University in South Africa from 1949-51, where he was a contemporary of Nelson Mandela and Oliver Tambo, both subsequent leaders of the South African ANC, Mugabe moved rapidly to the left in the 1950s under the influence of the Marxist ideas he came into contact with at Fort Hare, and of two years spent as a teacher in Kwame Nkrumah's post-independence Ghana, from 1958-60.

By the time Mugabe entered politics in 1960, it was natural that he should join Nkomo's National Democratic Party (renamed ZAPU in 1961). Nkomo's confidence that Zimbabwean independence would come without the need for radical action infuriated the younger ZAPU activists, however, and when they broke away in 1963 to form the more militant ZANU, Mugabe went too.

While both Mugabe and Nkomo were detained from 1964-74, detention for Mugabe was a process of preparation for power. A cool, self-disciplined intellectual, and an extremely able organiser, Mugabe not only held education classes for his fellow ZANU detainees, but also studied himself for three correspondence degrees, while at the same time retaining close links with the ZANU organisation in Zambia and Mozambique. From detention he organised the internal coup which placed him at the head of ZANU, and after his release in 1974 was able to rapidly impose his leadership upon the ZANLA guerrillas operating from Mozambique.

Nkomo, on the other hand, not only continued to talk to Ian Smith, both while in detention and later, but seemed to rely excessively upon the wide international backing which he received, neglecting the patient development of political support within Rhodesia. While Mugabe's ZANLA forces were increasingly active in eastern Rhodesia, Nkomo's ZIPRA were mostly held back in the safety of Zambia.

In the event, the military strength of ZANLA on the ground, and the fact that it had become identified with the country's largest tribal group, the Shona, ensured an overwhelming victory for Mugabe in the April 1980 election.

Above: Joshua Nkomo and Robert Mugabe in Geneva, 1976.

Moreoever, the Smith government also came under increasing pressures from other governments. After the Smith-Nkomo talks broke down in March 1976 the leaders of the so-called frontline states – Zambia, Tanzania, Mozambique and Botswana – declared their full support for the guerrilla cause; in the same month Mozambique closed its borders to Rhodesian traffic, thus making the RF regime even more dependent on South Africa. The South Africans themselves used this increased economic leverage to apply more pressure. Pretoria did not want the guerrillas to win, but neither did it want an escalation of the conflict – the South Africans still favoured a negotiated settlement. Indeed, after a spectacular Rhodesian raid into Mozambique in August 1976, Vorster pulled out his remaining military personnel (pilots and others who had stayed in Rhodesia secretly) and held back supplies of oil and arms. The following month he went further, threatening to stop all aid unless Smith agreed to new settlement proposals advanced by US Secretary of State Henry Kissinger; the US, fearing that the USSR would exploit continuing conflict, had persuaded Vorster to force the plan on Smith. Under duress, Smith publicly accepted the principle of majority rule and agreed to the US plan – majority rule within two years, though qualified by extensive political and economic safeguards for the whites. To the nationalists, however, these proposals did not go far enough. At the subsequent Geneva conference the nationalist leaders – Muzorewa, Sithole, Nkomo and Mugabe, who by this time had deposed Sithole as leader of ZANU/ZANLA – argued for better terms, while Smith stuck rigidly to the original US deal. The conference broke up in January 1977, with no agreement in sight and with the nationalists more divided than ever.

In the aftermath of the conference the Rhodesian conflict escalated dramatically. Nkomo and Mugabe, who had come together in a loose coalition called the Patriotic Front (PF), resolved to intensify their military campaigns and avoid clashes between their respective forces. ZIPRA, consisting mostly of people from the Ndebele tribal group, lavishly equipped by the Soviet bloc and trained mainly in Zambia and Angola, built up its forces and infiltrated several hundred of its men into western Rhodesia. ZANLA, based on the Shona tribes, trained mainly in Tanzania and Mozambique and equipped with Chinese and Eastern bloc weapons, extended its operations – involving a much larger force of perhaps 3000 guerrillas – inland from the east. The war consequently spread across the entire country and the government had to set up new operational areas in central Rhodesia, in the Salisbury (Harare) region, and along Lake Kariba. It was also compelled to call up older reservists and to recruit still more foreigners and Africans. Dusk-to-dawn curfews were introduced in many of the Tribal Trust Lands, the protected village system was extended, and a more extensive *cordon sanitaire* was set up along the borders with Mozambi-

Below: Ian Smith casts a watchful eye over the swearing-in of Bishop Abel Muzorewa as prime minister of Zimbabwe-Rhodesia in 1979.

Above: Black troops of the Rhodesian African Rifles sweep the bush for guerrillas in southeast Rhodesia, near the border with Mozambique. ZANLA, the armed wing of Robert Mugabe's ZANU, was able to operate with increasing effectiveness from bases in Mozambique, particularly after Frelimo came to power there in 1975.

que and Botswana. Cross-border raids on guerrilla camps increased.

Nevertheless, the security situation continued to deteriorate. The guerrillas, particularly ZANLA, attacked farms, PVs (protected villages), bridges, rail and road traffic, schools, mission stations and other installations; they also established control over substantial numbers of Africans. From the government's point of view, the results were catastrophic. Local administration and services in country areas began to collapse, particularly in Mashonaland, the economy deteriorated and white emigration increased. Guerrilla casualties were huge, but the losses were made good by further recruitment and by abductions.

An 'internal settlement'

In an effort to end the war, while at the same time safeguarding white interests, Smith entered into negotiations with black leaders who shared his dislike of the PF: Muzorewa, who possessed no guerrilla army, Sithole, who had lost control of ZANU to Mugabe, and Chief Jeremiah Chirau, a pro-government senator. This initiative resulted in what became known as the 'internal settlement', an agreement signed in March 1978 which provided for a transitional multi-racial Executive Council headed by Smith, Muzorewa, Sithole and Chirau; one-man-one-vote elections were to follow within a year. This scheme was approved by the whites and in April 1979, amidst unprecedented security arrangements, the elections went ahead. Muzorewa's United African National Council (UANC) emerged the clear victor, winning 50 of the 72 seats allocated to the blacks (28 seats were reserved for whites). In June 1979 Muzorewa was sworn in as Rhodesia's first black prime minister. The country was renamed Zimbabwe-Rhodesia.

Peace, however, remained elusive. The PF denounced the internal settlement as a sell-out to the RF and intensified its insurgency. The security forces retaliated by carrying out cross-border raids on guerrilla camps in Mozambique, Zambia, Botswana and even Angola; they also attacked economic targets in the host states in an attempt to raise the cost of harbouring guerrillas. ZANU and ZAPU losses were massive, but the security forces were now facing an enemy over 10,000 strong and growing stronger every week; not even South African help, which resumed again after the internal settlement, could stem this tide. To make matters worse the US government refused to lift sanctions and the new British government, though sympathetic to the Muzorewa regime, hesitated to back a settlement that had excluded the PF. Instead, Britain agreed at the August 1979 Commonwealth conference to promote discussions involving the Muzorewa government and the PF.

In the event, Britain's new Conservative government was successful. The Muzorewa regime, recognising that it would not get better terms than those offered by a Conservative administration, agreed to talk. So too did the PF, which had problems of its own with casualties, morale and internal dissension, and the frontline states, whose economies were now in tatters. Thus when negotiations opened at Lancaster House in September 1979, there was a chance of success. Britain proposed a ceasefire, disengagement, elections (on a one-man-one-vote basis) monitored by Commonwealth observers and supervised by Britain, to be followed by independence under a new constitution that would reduce white control over the security forces, police, civil service and judiciary and abolish the white veto in parliament. Muzorewa was to step down and as an interim measure a British governor would replace him.

Muzorewa soon agreed to the terms. So too, eventually, did the PF, though only after pressure from the frontline states and a threat from the British foreign secretary, Lord Carrington, to the effect that he would recognise the Muzorewa government if the PF remained recalcitrant. By 21 December 1979 the agreement had been signed by all the parties. In the meantime Britain had lifted sanctions and despatched Lord Soames to assume the position of governor. His arrival in Salisbury, on 12 December 1979, marked the official end of Rhodesia's rebellion. Two weeks later, on 28 December, the ceasefire came into effect and the Rhodesian conflict was deemed to be over.

Francis Toase

War in the bush

Rhodesian methods of counter-insurgency

Counter-insurgency has rarely been a purely military problem for a government and its security forces, and the experience in Rhodesia between 1966 and 1979 was no exception. The war has always to be seen in the context of the wider political and diplomatic activity. Thus, some Rhodesian operations were undertaken to put direct pressure upon the guerrillas or their African hosts for political ends. In October 1976, for example, Rhodesia frustrated guerrilla attempts to launch an offensive coinciding with the Geneva conference by themselves striking deep into Mozambique, while there were a series of raids on economic targets in Mozambique and Zambia in the autumn of 1979 to compel the presidents of these states to adopt a more compliant attitude in the forthcoming negotiations in London.

The fact that the guerrillas sought refuge across international frontiers was in itself a political complication. The Rhodesians had begun operating up to 100km (60 miles) inside Mozambique in cooperation with the Portuguese as early as 1969 and mounted the first large-scale cross-border raid into independent Mozambique in August 1976. The first large-scale incursion into Zambia occurred in October 1978 in response to the shooting down of a Viscount airliner by ZIPRA guerrilla forces operating inside Zambia. There were also raids into Botswana and a spectacular air raid by four of Rhodesia's Canberra bombers on Angolan targets in February 1979. Rhodesia's neighbours were to a great extent dependent upon the Rhodesian railway network for their economic survival and this gave the Rhodesians some leverage. On the other hand, Rhodesia was equally dependent upon South African assistance. South African police were sent into Rhodesia in 1967 but were withdrawn in 1975. The pilots and technicians who remained were similarly withdrawn in August 1976 since the South African prime minister, Johannes Vorster, feared that any escalation of the war would jeopardise his relations with the black African states. Although Vorster's successor, Pieter Botha, subsequently recommitted South African troops to guard vital areas such as the Beit Bridge, it was essentially South African pressure that forced Ian Smith to concede majority rule.

At the time when insurgency began, such complications were not readily apparent and the insurgency itself was limited. The first white man was killed by a so-called ZANU 'Crocodile Commando' in July 1964 but the first systematic attempt to infiltrate guerrillas into Rhodesia did not occur until April 1966. Over the course of the next two years a variety of guerrilla columns were comfortably eliminated by the security forces. However, this early success had repercussions that complicated counter-insurgency techniques later on, since it was regarded primarily as a police action under the control of the British South Africa Police (BSAP). Where the army had been required to offer assistance, temporary brigade areas were established under a Joint Operations Centre

(JOC) containing army, police and civilian representatives. When insurgency became more serious from December 1972 there was a tendency to persist with previous practices, although in September 1976 a War Council was established and a Combined Operations Headquarters (Comops) set up in March 1977. In theory, the creation of Comops should have led to the development of a well-coordinated strategy for the prosecution of the war. In reality, the command system failed at a number of levels through friction between the army and the BSAP as the police were displaced in positions of responsibility on JOCs by the military. Comops lacked effective control over civil affairs and became so entangled in the day-to-day conduct of the war that it neglected long-term planning. Its commander, Lieutenant-General Peter Walls, assumed direct command of all offensive and special forces, leaving the army commander, Lieutenant-General John Hickman, with responsibility only for black troops and white territorials.

Uncoordinated intelligence

Rivalry between police and army was also apparent in the attempted coordination of intelligence. Prior to 1972 it was firmly a responsibility of the BSAP Special Branch as was common in former British territories. The escalation of the conflict, however, all but overwhelmed traditional reliance on informers; the army formed its own Military Intelligence Department in 1973 and an Intelligence Corps in 1975. But the army agencies were regarded with suspicion by the BSAP just as rivalry also emerged between the Special Branch and the intelligence-gathering unit formed in November 1973 by Major Ron Reid-Daly (this unit was renamed the Selous Scouts in March 1974). There was also tension between the army and the Selous Scouts which ultimately resulted in the sacking of Hickman and the court-martial of Reid-Daly in early 1979.

This lack of coordination was a major drawback since the security forces would always be numerically stretched in Rhodesia given the prevailing assumption that the effective limit of manpower was the white male population, an asset which dwindled as white emigration outpaced immigration. At the beginning of the war there were few troops available, the armed forces amounting to only 4600 regulars in 1968 and the frontline BSAP to only 6400 men. Since 1957 white males had been liable to a short period of national service in the territorial Rhodesia Regiment followed by a reserve commitment. By 1966 the initial term of service had risen to 245 days but in December 1972 national service for all whites, Asians and coloureds (those of mixed race) between the ages of 18 and 25 was increased to a full 12 months. As the war progressed so the national service net was widened, embracing those aged 25 to 50 in 1977 and those aged between 50 and 59 in January 1979. The latter were referred to as 'Mashford's Militia' after a Salisbury funeral parlour.

In fact, the majority of the security forces were always black and, until 1979, they were also all volunteers drawn both by the rewards of military service and by traditional family bonds to the administration (as in the case of the Kalanga tribal group who provided many of the 70 per cent of the army and the 75 per cent of the BSAP who were black). Indeed, there was no shortage of black recruits and the Rhodesian African Rifles (RAR) was expanded from one to four battalions during the war. After the internal settlement of March 1978, however, pressure for black conscription arose and it was announced in the following October that it would commence in January 1979. Educated blacks between the ages of 18 and 25 were liable to service and this was then extended to all between the ages of 16 and 60 in August 1979. There is little evidence of any widespread disciplinary problems among black regulars or police but conscription was certainly resented and the measures were never fully implemented.

In addition to these forces raised from within Rhodesia, there were between 1000 and 2000 foreigners serving with the Rhodesian forces, while the South African presence between 1967 and 1975 amounted to perhaps 3000 men at most. In practice, the requirements of the economy precluded full

Rhodesia relied heavily upon its total command of the air in its operations against the nationalist guerrillas, both in the Rhodesian bush and in raids against guerrilla bases in Mozambique and Zambia. Left: An SA 319B Alouette III helicopter lands a patrol in the bush during a 'search and destroy' mission. Below: Attempts were made to deprive the guerrillas of active support by concentrating the black rural population into protected villages, borrowed from the earlier experience of the British in Malaya and the Americans in Vietnam. Manned by members of the poorly trained and indisciplined Guard Force, many PVs proved to be a failure, and some 70 were abandoned in September 1978.

Below: A group of women being searched for weapons by members of the Guard Force as they return to their PV. There was little effort to win hearts and minds.

Raid on New Chimoio

By the closing stages of the war, the Rhodesian forces had refined their techniques for attacking guerrilla bases to near perfection. On 27 September 1979 an assault was launched against ZANLA's formidable New Chimoio base in Mozambique, a system of trenches and bunkers covering 64 square km (25 square miles), housing some 6000 guerrillas. Rhodesian Light Infantry 'stop-groups' were parachuted in to the east of the base and a task force of 200 Selous Scouts mounted in Unimog trucks drove into the guerrilla positions from the west, coordinating their assault with bombing strikes by the Rhodesian Air Force. To deal with trenches, the Selous Scouts employed classic flanking techniques, stationing a small contingent to engage the defenders in frontal fire while the rest of the unit worked around the flanks and took out the position with grenades and smallarms fire.

Fighting raged for three days. Guerrilla resistance centred on a high hill in the middle of the camp which the Rhodesians nicknamed Monte Cassino. The effect of attacks by Hunters – facing curtains of flack from anti-aircraft emplacements – and Canberras was devasting, however, despite the untypical renunciation of the use of napalm to avoid the possible incineration of Rhodesian forces. The RLI stop-groups took a heavy toll of fleeing ZANLA men. By the time the Selous Scouts had fought to the top of Monte Cassino, the scene was, in the words of Reid-Daly, 'reminiscent of scenes from the trenches of the western front in World War I.'

mobilisation and usually only about 25,000 men could be put in the field at any one time. The absolute maximum proved to be the 60,000 men deployed briefly during the run-up to the internal elections of April 1979.

The lack of manpower was one of a number of constraints that had repercussions on both strategy and tactics. It was felt vital, for example, for Rhodesia to counter insurgents in frontier areas and to prevent infiltration into the interior; hence the frequent external raids. The Rhodesian Army was well suited to this aspect of counter-insurgency, having trained for it since the 1950s and having first-hand experience of British operations in Malaya where, for example, Walls had commanded the Rhodesian squadron of the Malayan Scouts (later Special Air Service). There was also more recent experience upon which to draw, and the Rhodesians made a careful study of Israeli techniques. Yet the lack of coordination in command and control could only result in an incoherent strategy. Comops adopted mobile counter-offensives in 1977, following the earlier tendency simply to react defensively to guerrilla infiltrations, but this became, in effect, merely a method of inflicting high kill ratios. No real attempt could be made to hold any cleared areas until the Security Forces Auxiliaries (SFAs) became available after the internal settlement and it was not until as late as 1979 that an area defence system evolved, based on holding 'Vital Asset Ground', roughly the white areas of the interior.

Above: Adapting an old solution to a new problem, Grey's Scouts patrol the bush on the ideal form of transport. While basically a reconnaissance unit, Grey's Scouts could also operate as mounted infantry in counter-insurgency operations.

The 'Fire Force' concept

Large numbers of men were required in static positions guarding important installations, railways and farms and a number of units such as the Guard Force (1976) and the Defence Regiment (1978) did little else. Another reflection of strained resources was the development of the 'Fire Force' concept to offset lack of men through a concentration of firepower and mobility. If guerrillas were located, a Cessna Lynx carrying fragmentation bombs or napalm would attack them. Four or five Alouette helicopters, each carrying a 'stick' of four or five men, would then be deployed to drive the guerrillas back onto about 15 paratroopers dropped at low level from a C-47 Dakota transport. Four such Fire Forces were available, two manned by the Rhodesian Light Infantry (RLI) and two by the RAR, the men being rotated regularly. As the war escalated, however, the Fire Forces became more pressed to respond quickly to conflicting demands for their services. By mid-1979 the Fire Forces were said to be accounting for three-quarters of all guerrilla casualties inside Rhodesia (although the Selous Scouts, whose early role of gathering intelligence was becoming a more aggressive hunter-killer employment, also claimed responsibility for 68 per cent of all kills inside Rhodesia). The size of the 'stick' in Fire Force operations was determined by the capacity of the Alouette, although a number of Bell Huey helicopters later became available.

The nature of the war inside Rhodesia led to the development of a number of other specialised units or techniques. The guerrilla penchant for attacking civilian vehicles led to the use of 'Q' cars – heavily armoured decoy vehicles – while the widespread use of mines by the guerrilla forces resulted in the development of a number of specially designed vehicles like the Hyena, Rhino and Pookie which all featured a V-shaped body to deflect blast. The BSAP also had specialist units such as Police Anti-Terrorist Units (PATU) and the black Police Support Units (PSU) known as 'Black Boots', as well as SWAT (Special Weapons and Tactics Teams) for combating urban terrorism, although this rarely proved a significant threat. The Ministry of Internal Affairs also fielded African District Security Assistants (DSAs) from 1976, while the army's Grey's Scouts was a mixed-race horse-mounted unit often used to patrol the border.

Inevitably, the guerrillas adjusted to Rhodesian tactics but the kill ratio was always favourable to the security forces – it never dropped below 6:1 and at times was as high as 14:1 with individual operations attaining a staggering 60:1 ratio in the Rhodesians' favour. The problem was that the Rhodesians could not prevent guerrilla infiltration and by the security forces' own estimates the number of guerrillas operating inside Rhodesia rose steadily from a mere 350 in July 1974 to 12,500 by the end of the war. Another indication of the expansion of guerrilla activity was the growth in JOCs from one to seven.

Attempts to prevent infiltration by erecting a physical barrier were unsuccessful, the *cordon sanitaire* of border minefields covering 864km (537 miles) of frontier with Zambia and Mozambique at a total cost of 2298 million Rhodesian dollars proving only an impediment and not an impassable barrier to guerrillas. Rains frequently uncovered the mines, animals blundered into unfenced areas and there were always too few men to ensure either adequate maintenance or regular patrols. An alternative means of nullifying the effect of infiltration, in the form of controlling the population through resettlement, was

Below: A white farmer in his 'Pookie'. A home-made vehicle with a V-shaped hull and soft, wide tyres, it was designed to give protection against guerrilla land-mines. Although poor on aerodynamics, the 'Pookie' proved to be surprisingly effective.

also unsuccessful. A pilot scheme began in the Zambezi Valley in December 1973 but resettlement began in earnest with the removal of 46,000 Africans from the Chiweshe Tribal Trust Land (TTL) into 21 'protected villages' (PVs) under Operation Overload in July 1974. Some 234 PVs were built or planned by January 1978, with an estimated population of between 350,000 and 750,000. Too frequently, however, the Rhodesians failed to recognise resettlement as a basis for 'winning hearts and minds'. Many PVs lacked facilities while others were not sufficiently protected by the Guard Force or DSAs. Urbanisation struck at tribal values and it was a measure of their unpopularity and failure that the attempt to control the population in some 70 PVs had to be abandoned in September 1978.

In more general terms too, the Rhodesian approach to winning hearts and minds left much to be desired. An early attempt by the 'Sheppard Group' to develop a coherent socio-economic strategy in 1974 failed and psychological warfare was not developed until 1977, although the security forces did have some success in a contest with the guerrillas over the control of traditional spirit mediums among the Shona people. The Rhodesians tended to concentrate on broadening African representation in government rather than improving the lot of the rural African, and punitive measures went hand-in-hand with positive inducements. Thus, rewards for information or full-scale amnesties were balanced by collective fines, strict food control under Operation Turkey from 1977, and constantly amended law enforcement regulations including the extension of the death sentence for a wide range of offences. The preference for control rather than concession was also illustrated by the extension of martial law to cover over 90 per cent of the country by September 1979.

Nevertheless, the Rhodesians continued to recruit large numbers of African servicemen and police. Equally successful was the development of pseudo-forces – the use of members of the security forces or captured insurgents 'turned' by them to infiltrate guerrilla organisations. It was for this function that the Selous Scouts were primarily raised following an early experiment with pseudo-gangs in October 1966 which was revived by the BSAP in January 1973. Employing defectors from the beginning, the Selous Scouts were often required to call in airstrikes close to their own positions to avoid disclosing their true identities. Similarly, they appear to have attacked PVs on occasion to prove their *bona fides* in the course of seeking to sow distrust among the guerrillas, and it was for this reason that their reputation was somewhat mixed among the rest of the security forces.

Consideration was also given to the possibility of arming loyal Africans and a pilot scheme was launched in Msana TTL in early 1978. The internal settlement then offered the opportunity of recruiting blacks loyal to Bishop Muzorewa or the Reverend Sithole, the SFAs being quickly raised to take over responsibility for TTLs. Known in Shona as *Pfumo reVanhu* ('Spear of the People'), the SFAs were really private armies attached to the political parties of Muzorewa and Sithole. Far from being guerrilla defectors as claimed, they were frequently conscripts or unemployed urban blacks given an over-hasty training programme. Under Operation Favour some 10,000 were eventually deployed with direct responsibility for 15 per cent of the country.

The cost of war

By the end of the war rural administration had broken down in many TTLs, large numbers of schools and hospitals had closed and native agriculture was seriously affected by loss of cattle and the spread of diseases previously under control. There were parallel strains for the whites in the form of increased taxes, declining output and social tension. Officially, the war cost the lives of 410 white civilians and 954 members of the security forces. A total of 691 black civilians and 8250 guerrillas were recorded as having died inside Rhodesia, while civilian and guerrilla losses may have exceeded 30,000.

At the end of the conflict the Rhodesians had surrendered no city or major communications route and the guerrillas had not succeeded in establishing any 'liberated zones', although large areas of Rhodesia were being actively contested. Remarkably inefficient in a military sense, the guerrillas were effective at political subversion and whether the security forces could have contained the insurgency indefinitely is a moot point. At the time of the ceasefire an estimated 38,000 guerrillas remained uncommitted outside the country while within Rhodesia, even with the dubious addition of the SFAs, the ratio of security forces to the guerrillas and their adherents reached only 1:1.15. Manpower had always been the problem, as the Rhodesians had for too long attempted to exert control everywhere rather than consolidating in key areas. Militarily, the war was not lost but Rhodesia's resources were stretched dangerously thin, even without the constant interplay of dominating political considerations that ultimately determined the war's outcome. **Ian Beckett**

From Rhodesia to Zimbabwe

The settlement and its aftermath

Both the frontline states which supported the Patriotic Front, and the South African backers of Rhodesia had an interest in reaching a negotiated settlement. The Lancaster House conference (left), held in London during December 1979, led to a compromise settlement which provided for the election of a new government on the basis of one-man-one-vote.

Between 12 December 1979 and 18 April 1980 Rhodesia passed through a transitional period during which Britain, for the first time, assumed direct responsibility for the affairs of that troubled country. In accordance with the terms presented at Lancaster House by British foreign secretary Lord Carrington, Rhodesia reverted to the status of a British colony. Abel Muzorewa stepped down as prime minister and was replaced by a British governor, who arranged a ceasefire between the rival forces and fresh elections leading to formal independence.

The settlement process was fraught with danger from the very outset. When Lord Carrington despatched the governor – Lord Soames – to Rhodesia on 12 December 1979 the Lancaster House conference had not even finished. Final agreement had still to be reached and there was no guarantee that the Patriotic Front (PF) leaders would agree to the British terms or that the Rhodesian authorities would cooperate willingly with their new British overlords. Soames and his team could only hope that Lord Carrington's enterprising but high-risk diplomacy would succeed. Fortunately for the British team these hopes were fulfilled. The Lancaster House negotiations ended in agreement, on 21 December 1979, and the Rhodesian administration cooperated as planned.

Soames moved quickly to normalise the situation in Rhodesia. Sanctions were removed, the borders with Zambia and Mozambique re-opened, political detainees were released, censorship was lifted and the bans on the nationalists were rescinded. Arranging a ceasefire, however, posed formidable problems. The only independent military force at Soames' disposal was the Commonwealth Monitoring Force (CMF), a five-nation peacekeeping force consisting of 159 Australians, 75 New Zealanders, 51 Kenyans, 24 Fijians and some 1100 Britons, under the command of Major-General John Acland. The CMF's task, codenamed Operation Agila, was to supervise the ceasefire and to receive guerrillas at 39 rendezvous points (RVs) and 14 assembly points (APs). The risks facing this tiny force were enormous. Lightly armed and unfamiliar with the terrain, people and languages, CMF troops were detailed to move into areas dominated by the guerrillas, whose response to the settlement terms could not be predicted. The Rhodesian security forces, who were withdrawn to their bases as part of the agreement, warned that the guerrillas would probably 'take out' the CMF units at the first opportunity.

These fears proved unfounded. The guerrillas gradually began to report to the RVs and APs. By 6 January 1980 some 15,000 had turned up, and by mid-January over 22,000 had reported, of whom 16,500 were from Robert Mugabe's Zimbabwe African National Liberation Army (ZANLA) and 5500 from Joshua Nkomo's Zimbabwe People's Revolutionary Army (ZIPRA); by the time the CMF teams left, on 16 March 1980, there were almost 50,000 guerrillas in the APs. The main problem that arose as the guerrillas came forward was that, fearing attacks from the Rhodesian security forces, they dug themselves into the APs with firearms, mortars and rockets. This was rather discomforting for the small groups of CMF personnel who monitored the APs, but by a combination of courage and tact the CMF established a rapport with the guerrillas and kept the situation under control.

New problems soon arose. Having arranged a ceasefire, Soames had then to maintain it, and to ensure that the elections scheduled for late February 1980 could be held free from violence and intimidation. This was a tall order, since it soon became clear that neither ZANLA nor ZIPRA was adhering fully to the terms of the ceasefire. As many as 7000 ZANLA guerrillas had been held back from the APs, with orders to prepare the ground for the forthcoming elections; ZIPRA held back perhaps 500 of its guerrillas too. In addition, the nationalists also had thousands of guerrillas in camps in Zambia and Mozambique. Worse still, ZANLA began to engage in fairly widescale political intimidation, while the recall of the security forces to their bases had led to an upsurge of crime and banditry.

Soames' answer was to redeploy the Rhodesian security forces, together with some 15,000 Security Forces Auxiliaries who were closely associated with Bishop Muzorewa. The governor had little choice in the circumstances, but his decision led to accusations from the PF that Britain was trying to engineer a Muzorewa victory. Soames was also condemned for allowing South Africa to keep some of its men in the Beit Bridge area (along the Rhodesia-South Africa border) but these troops were eventually asked to leave, and did so by 30 January 1980.

Violence and intimidation

As the elections approached, violence and intimidation increased dramatically. To some extent the intimidation was the work of the Auxiliaries, who were busy trying to promote Muzorewa's cause. There was also some evidence of intimidation by the Rhodesian security forces. The bulk of the incidents, though, were perpetrated by ZIPRA and ZANLA personnel, and the latter in particular.

Intimidation was not the only difficulty facing Soames as the elections approached. There was a possibility that ZANLA would resume military operations if the election results were not to their liking, and there were also rumours that elements of the security forces might stage a post-election coup. These spectres faded, however, before the results were declared. Mugabe's allies in Mozambique insisted that ZANU must abide by the settlement, while Rhodesian supremo General Peter Walls, for his part, promised not to overturn the decision of the electorate.

The elections themselves passed quietly. The white community voted first, to elect representatives to fill the 20 parliamentary seats reserved for them. All went to Ian Smith's Rhodesian Front (RF). Rhodesia's Africans then went to the polls, under the watchful gaze of British policemen, to elect their 80 representatives. It was widely predicted that none of the three major parties – Mugabe's ZANU-PF, Nkomo's Patriotic Front-Zimbabwe African People's Union (PF-ZAPU), and Muzorewa's United African National Council (UANC) – would win an overall majority. Contrary to expectations, however, ZANU emerged the clear victor. In a 93 per cent turn-out, ZANU picked up 63 per cent of the votes, including 75 per cent in Mashonaland, as against ZAPU's 24 per cent (82 per cent in Matabeleland) and the UANC's 8 per cent.

The results sent shock waves throughout the white community. During the war Mugabe had often stressed his Marxist credentials and had threatened to seize all 'colonialist' assets and execute the likes of Ian Smith and General Walls; his more conciliatory electoral statements, which emphasised the need for peace and reconciliation, were dismissed by whites as little more than electoral propaganda. Some whites hoped for a military coup, though true to his word, Walls accepted the decision of the electorate. The supporters of Nkomo and Muzorewa were also shell-shocked, and complaints were made about the intimidation of voters. However, Britain's election commission and a Commonwealth observer group both ruled that the result was a fair reflection of the popular will. The British government accepted these opinions and Soames asked Mugabe to form a government. On 18 April 1980 Rhodesia was granted formal independence as the new state of Zimbabwe, with Mugabe as its first prime minister.

Mugabe's early moves seemed to indicate that far from being a Marxist ogre, he was a man of moderation and pragmatism. The new premier called for reconciliation between former enemies and stressed that he favoured gradual change rather than a sudden Marxist upheaval. He appointed a broad-based cabinet, including members of ZAPU and the white community, and he also asked the British to help train the new Zimbabwe National Army (ZNA), which was to be formed by integrating elements of ZANLA, ZIPRA and the security forces. General Walls, whom ZANU had previously pledged to hang, was asked to stay on and supervise the whole process as head of the Zimbabwe joint military high command.

Mugabe's accession to office and initial magnanimity did not, however, bring peace to Zimbabwe. Conflict soon arose, though this was not so much between white and black as between rival African factions. Whites either adapted to African rule or left the country, but old antagonisms between the predominantly Shona ZANU and the predominantly Ndebele/Kalanga ZAPU resurfaced with a vengeance. As the government gradually put into effect a policy of Africanisation, ZAPU became increasingly resentful of ZANU's growing control over the army, police, judiciary, civil service and media. Indeed, within six months of independence clashes between ZANU and ZAPU supporters – including former guerrillas integrated in the new army – had erupted into full-scale fighting; in Bulawayo

The elections, decided upon at Lancaster House, were held against a background of intimidation and uncertainty over post-election stability. The Auxiliaries backing Bishop Abel Muzorewa, (below, addressing an election rally) failed to save his UANC from total defeat, while the activities of Robert Mugabe's ZANLA fighters during the election campaign were a significant factor in the overwhelming victory of ZANU. Following page: A British policeman takes the weight off his feet while supervising the elections in Zimbabwe in April 1980. As well as policemen, Britain sent some 1100 troops to serve alongside contingents from other Commonwealth countries in the Commonwealth Monitoring Force.

more than 55 people were killed and over 400 injured in two days of conflict and the government had to rely, ironically, on former elements of the Rhodesian security forces – the Rhodesian African Rifles – to quell the disturbances. Further clashes occurred in February 1981, and once again the government turned to its former adversaries for help.

A year later, in February 1982, the authorities announced that they had discovered huge caches of arms in Matabeleland. Mugabe accused Nkomo of plotting to overthrow the government, in collusion with the South Africans, and dismissed him from the government, three other ZAPU ministers were also sacked and Nkomo's senior military advisers, Lieutenant-General Lookout Masuku and Dumiso Dabengwa, were arrested. Mugabe even harped back to the war against the Smith-Muzorewa regime and accused Nkomo of having held back his forces so as to prepare for a war against ZANU.

The dismissal of Nkomo, however, led to more conflict. Former members of ZIPRA began to desert from the ZNA in increasing numbers and 'dissidents', allegedly loyal to Nkomo, began to wage a guerrilla war in Matabeleland. As the security situation deteriorated, the Mugabe government sent in the Fifth Brigade, a North Korean-trained unit composed almost entirely of Shona loyal to Mugabe, with orders to crush the revolt. Nkomo alleged that the Fifth Brigade had been sent to destroy ZAPU and wipe out the Matabele in general, and denounced Mugabe's plan to turn Zimbabwe into a one-party state. Mugabe, for his part, alleged that Nkomo was collaborating with the South Africans and vowed that the army would stay in Matabeleland until all dissident activity was eliminated. By March 1984, the government had an estimated 10,000 troops in Matabeleland, and dusk-to-dawn curfews had been enforced in large parts of the territory. Thus the Mugabe government found itself forced to mount a permanent counter-insurgency campaign.

Francis Toase

Sabotage at Thornhill

On achieving independence in April 1980, Zimbabwe inherited a relatively well-equipped air force, highly-experienced in counter-insurgency operations. During the immediate post-independence period, the Zimbabwe Air Force (ZAF) remained largely unaffected by the painful process of integrating former guerrilla fighters into its ranks experienced by the army and security forces. While its efficiency was therefore less affected, it remained an object of suspicion to former guerrillas who had been on the receiving end of its operations during the bush war.

That suspicion surfaced dramatically following the events of 25 July 1982; during the early hours of that day, three unidentified raiders entered the ZAF's Thornhill base, near Gweru, southwest of Harare, and using phosphorus grenades attached to timers, managed to destroy seven Hawker Hunter FGA-9s, one Hawk, and one Cessna 337 reconnaissance aircraft, severely damaging another Hunter and three Hawks. Damage was in excess of £5 million, and represented some 25 per cent of the ZAF's total strength.

The ZAF board of inquiry, set up on the day of the raid, came rapidly to the conclusion that the raiders probably originated in South Africa, and that they had had some inside assistance. As recommendations were being prepared for the arrest and court martial of three officers at the Thornhill base for negligence, the security forces took into custody six white air force officers, including two members of the board of inquiry.

The subsequent trial, which took place against a background of torture allegations against the Zimbabwean authorities, revealed more about the lax state of security at the Thornhill base than about the identity and motives of the actual saboteurs. While it is generally accepted that the raid was the work of South Africa, firm evidence has yet to be produced. What is certain is that the raid, by destroying a large part of the ZAF's operational strength, severely reduced its ability to operate against anti-government insurgents and saboteurs.

The trial itself, by bringing to public attention allegations that the white officers accused of complicity in the raid had been tortured, severely affected the morale of the ZAF's overwhelmingly white officer corps, and led to a wave of resignations and early retirements, which further damaged operational efficiency. The Zimbabwean government responded by finally releasing and deporting the six accused, in an attempt to regain the confidence of white officers within the armed forces, and by appointing a Pakistani officer, Air Marshal Azim Daudpota, as commander of the ZAF.

Key Weapons

SOVIET MACHINE GUNS

When the Soviet Great Patriotic War ended in 1945 the light machine guns of the Red Army were the 7.62mm Degtyarev DP and DPM. The DP dates from as early as 1926; it was a sound and robust weapon with several features that have been carried over to more modern Soviet machine guns. The DP was a very simple weapon: the locking mechanism employed only a few working parts and these, like the rest of the gun, were designed to be manufactured in as few operations as possible, using only simple machines and relatively unskilled labour. Once in the field the DP could be operated for long periods with only a minimum of maintenance or cleaning and it could take the hardest knocks that front-line service could inflict, which made it popular with front-line troops.

The DP, like any weapon, did have its faults. One was that it used the standard Soviet 7.62mm rimmed rifle cartridge. Ammunition had to be fed via a circular flat pan magazine, mounted over the receiver. This magazine, which gave the DP its distinctive appearance, was rather prone to distortion and was easily damaged in action. This fault only became obvious when the DP had been used in action over prolonged periods. Another major flaw lay in the fact that the barrel was fixed and therefore became overheated after prolonged periods of firing. Normally this would have been only a minor problem, but the operating spring was situated very close to the barrel and thus lost its tempering when the heat became excessive; the result was jams and feed problems. The Red Army had to put up with these problems until 1944 when the DPM, a modified version of the DP, was introduced.

Many of the best qualities of the DP were carried over to the DPM, including its robust and simple construction, but an important change was that the operating spring was moved to a new location and housed in a tube projecting from the back of the receiver. A distinguishing feature of the DPM was the introduction of a pistol grip for the trigger.

Neither the DP nor the DPM are retained in front-line use with any of the Warsaw Pact nations but they are still employed by various militias and reserve units. They are also frequently distributed to left-wing guerrillas who come into the Soviet sphere of influence. Few DPs are likely to be found today but the DMP is still around in large numbers.

After 1945 the DPM was used as the basis for another new Soviet machine gun. It evolved from the need for a type of light machine gun which could be used at company level to produce sustained fire over a much longer period than was possible with the DP and DPM. By careful re-working of the basic DPM it proved possible to employ a belt feed and further re-working enabled the barrel to be easily changed in action when it became hot. The ability to fit the 47-round pan magazine was retained but for this the entire belt feed mechanism had to be removed in one simple operation.

This new design was known as the RP-46 and for a while it was the standard company machine gun of the

Previous page: Left-wing troops man a position in the city of Beirut armed with an SG-43 machine gun and an AK assault rifle. Above: A DP machine gun, revealing its distinctive pan magazine and bipod. Below: The DPM is recognised by its pistol grip; this example is a Type 53, the Chinese version of the weapon. Bottom: A unit of Muslim troops parades through the streets of Beirut in 1980 armed with DP series light machine guns.

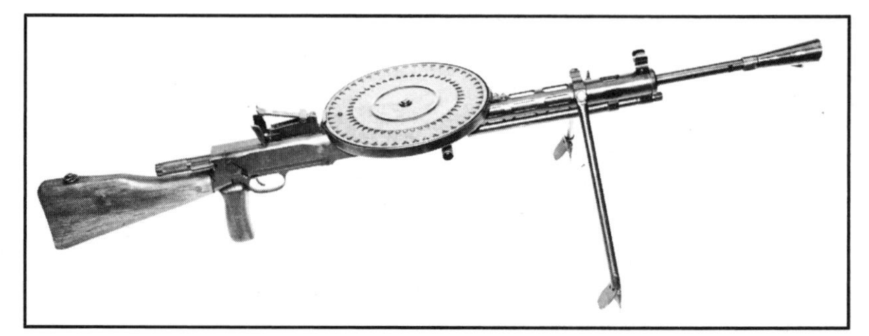

Soviet Army and many other Soviet-influenced armed forces, but its period in service was relatively short. For various reasons it was replaced by later designs but it is still widely used by the Chinese and North Korean Armies. The main reason for the passing of the RP-46 from Soviet use was that it continued to fire the old 7.62 x 54mm rifle cartridge. When the Soviet armed forces adopted the shorter and less powerful 7.62 x 39mm cartridge used by the AK-47 assault rifle, it made sense for a light machine gun to use the same ammunition as the standard service rifle and from this evolved the RPD light machine gun. In some ways the RPD was ahead of its day in design terms but in others it was something of a throwback. Among the better features was the special design of the disintegrating link belt feed: a belt feed can be a nuisance when the weapon is carried (it flaps about and tends to get caught up in clothing or undergrowth), but on the RPD the belt was carried inside a circular drum located under the receiver. This method is now widely employed by modern light machine guns such as the Belgian Minimi, but when the RPD appeared during the early 1950s it was a definite novelty. The RPD did not have a quick-change barrel, however, and to avoid serious barrel over-heating the gunner had to be trained not to exceed 100 rounds a minute. Other problems became evident only when the RPD was in service. For instance, the original model had a cocking handle that moved to and fro as the weapon was fired, and this was soon noted as a feature that had to be removed on later models. The handle snagged easily and, in addition, there was no cover over the handle's slot so dust and dirt soon found their way into the interior. In all there were five different production models of the RPD, not all of them associated with design problems, but it did occasionally make the interchanging of some spare parts between weapons a headache.

As with the DPM, the RPD is no longer a front-line weapon in the Warsaw Pact but it is widely used elsewhere. China and North Korea have both copied the RPD for their own use and many of these, along with ex-Soviet examples, have ended up in guerrilla hands all over the world.

The RPD could trace its ancestry back to the old DP light machine gun as far as the basic operating

Top: The RPD light machine gun with drum magazine. Above: A Syrian soldier stands guard on the outskirts of Beirut armed with an RPD. Left: Holding an RPD a masked Christian Phalangist takes up a rear-guard position on a patrol through the streets of Beirut. Both left and right-wing factions have made extensive use of Soviet weapons during the fighting in Lebanon. Below: A right-side view of the RPD.

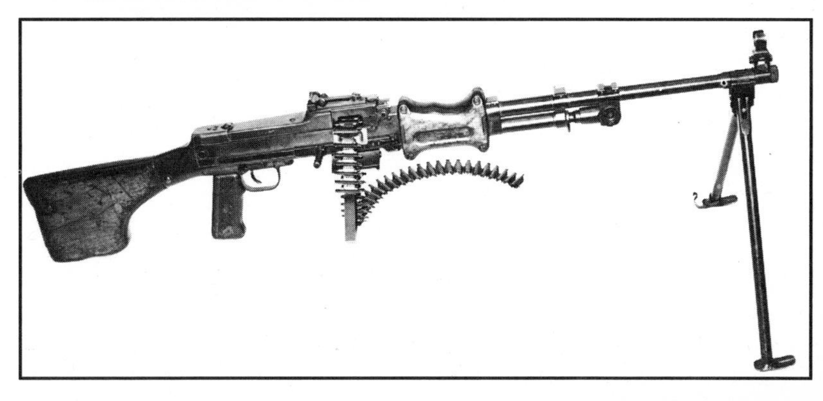

principles were concerned, but by the 1950s the Soviet Army began to favour the more modern and much simpler operating mechanism developed by Kalashnikov, the designer of the AK-47 assault rifle. The basic AK-47 design has proved to be one of the most widely-used and successful smallarms designs ever produced and it made a great deal of sense to adopt the same basic design attributes in a new light machine gun for use at section level. By the early 1960s such a weapon was already being issued to the front line units of the Red Army as the RPK.

The RPK may be regarded as a heavy version of the AK-47 assault rifle and it closely resembles the AK-47 in general appearance. Like the AK-47 it uses a distinctive curved-box magazine mounted under the receiver, but the magazine of the RPK is much larger; there are 30-, 40- and 75-round versions, the 75-round version having a drum magazine. The RPK has a light bipod fitted under the muzzle but otherwise the differences from the AK-47 are few. Thus the RPK has a fixed barrel and care has to be taken not to exceed a fire rate of 80 rounds a minute. In practice this is not a great drawback, since the RPK is used as a section weapon with the rest of the section using AK-47 assault rifles – so the combined firepower from a single section can be quite considerable without relying on the RPK alone. Further limitations are imposed by the use of the 30-round AK-47 magazine in the assault role, leaving the larger 40-round box or 75-round drum magazines for employment in the support role.

Many Soviet smallarms are somewhat rough in appearance due to the lack of care taken in the manufacturing stages – the Soviet philosophy is that if the weapon works it is good enough, and appearances will not help. But with the RPK, standards appear to have changed. The RPK is very well finished and such details as the chamber and bore are chromium-plated, a carry-over from the AK-47. This plating not only makes the weapon easier to clean but also tends to reduce wear and fouling during prolonged use. Another innovation on the RPK is that, whereas all previous Soviet light machine guns were designed, from the DP onwards, to deliver automatic fire only, the RPK has a fire selector mechanism, again a carry-over from the AK-47.

The RPK has an unusually-shaped wooden butt that is designed to allow the firer to hold the weapon well into the shoulder for stability when firing on automatic. This butt gives the RPK a distinctive appearance but there is a version with a folding butt known as the RPKS that is much used by airborne and other specialist formations. A new version of the RPK has recently emerged, the RPK-74, which fires the new Soviet 5.45 x 39mm 'miniature' cartridge as used on the AK-74 assault rifle. In general appearance it is identical to the RPK.

The RPK is now the standard Soviet light machine gun for use at section level but the Soviet armed forces

Above: The RPK is a heavy version of the AK-47 assault rifle, featuring an enlarged magazine (holding 40 rounds), folding bipod and a longer barrel. Below: The RPK in its primary role as an infantry support weapon at section level. Bottom: An Afghan guerrilla prepares to fire his RPK on a convoy of the regular Afghan Army held up in a mountain defile.

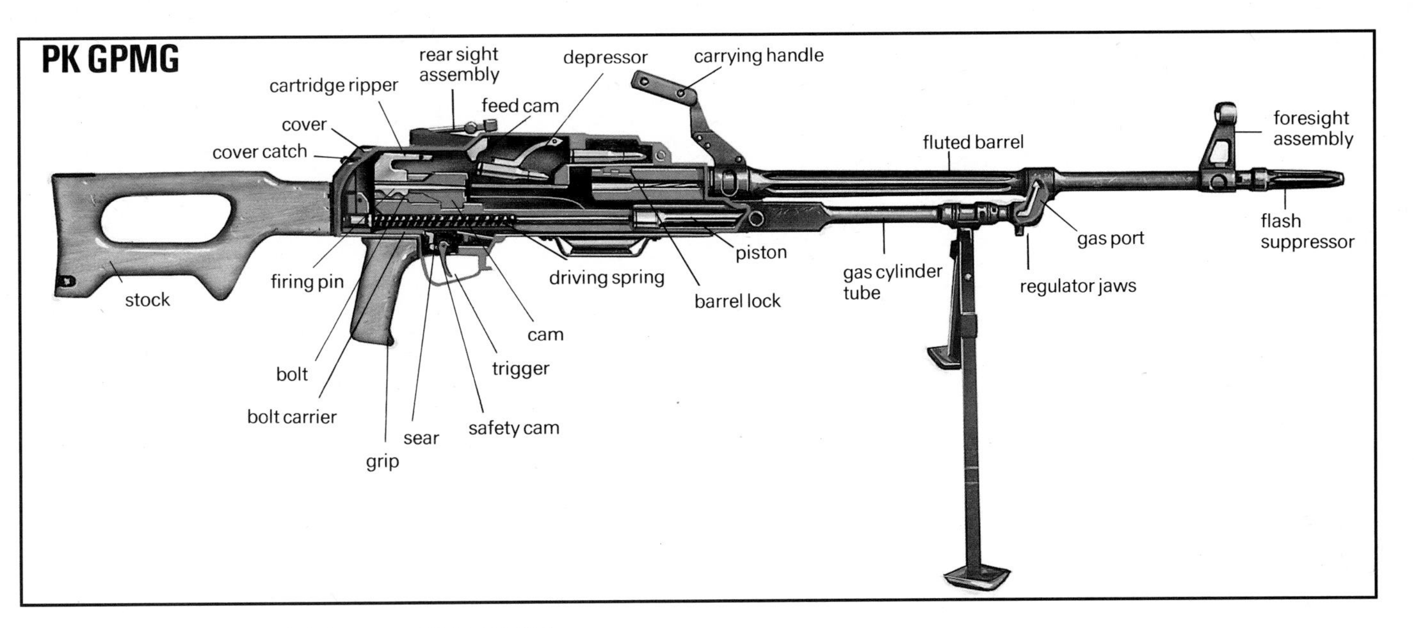

Left: An Afghan guerrilla leader stands by a PKM light machine gun fitted with a box for containing the ammunition belt. He is armed with a West German Heckler and Koch sub-machine gun.

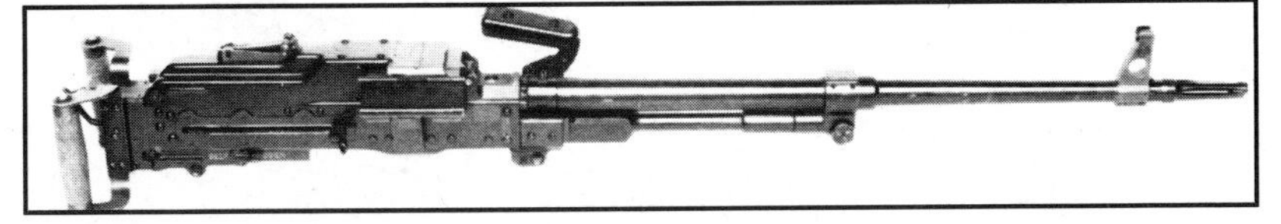

Below: An Afghan guerrilla fires a PKM from the shoulder alongside a downed Soviet helicopter. Inset: A side view of the PKM which shows its distinctive carrying handle and cutaway frame stock. Bottom: The PKB variant is distinguished by twin spade grips and a butterfly trigger.

also use a heavier weapon as a general purpose machine gun at company level and above. This is the 7.62mm PK, a weapon that can be fired from a bipod for the assault role or from a heavy tripod for use in the support role. It fires the old 7.62 x 54mm rimmed rifle cartridge that provides the weapon with a longer potential range than the lighter weapons, but the use of this elderly cartridge must have presented the designers with more difficulties than the use of a rimless one would have entailed. As it turned out the designers did a very good job, for the PK and its derivatives must be rated as being among the best machine gun designs in service anywhere in the world.

The basic PK uses the rotating bolt of the AK-47 and RPK combined with some of the best features of other machine gun designs. It first appeared in 1964 and since then its use has spread to all arms of the Soviet and Warsaw Pact forces. For a machine gun the PK is remarkably light and the weapon has only a few moving parts that are easily removed and replaced for repairs or cleaning. It has a changeable barrel for prolonged firing and ammunition is fed using 100-, 200- or 250-round belts. The ammunition belts are usually fed into the gun from a box carried under the receiver (as on the RPD), but this box is not always needed once the gun is mounted on a tripod or a fixed mount.

The PK is just one of a family of weapons and in its basic form it has a fluted barrel and weighs about 9kg (20lb). When mounted on a tripod for prolonged fire it becomes the PKS, while the PKT is a special version for co-axial mounting on armoured vehicles – this version has a special firing solenoid and a heavier barrel. The PKM is a generally simpler and lighter version of the basic PK and when this model is mounted on a tripod it becomes the PKMS. To complicate matters further, there is a version known as the PKB or PKMB which is a PKM mounted on a tripod with the normal trigger arrangement replaced by twin spade grips and a butterfly trigger.

The PK family of weapons are very simple and effective weapons. The rate of fire is not excessively high, being of the order of 650 to 720 rounds a minute, and so ammunition expenditure need not be over-lavish even during prolonged periods of firing. Recoil forces are relatively low so the weapon can be easily

Left: The SGM, mounted on a heavy two-wheeled carriage fitted with a detachable shield. Despite its cumbersome mounting the SG was a highly effective machine gun capable of accurate sustained fire at extended ranges. The PK series of general purpose machine guns has replaced the SG in front-line Soviet Army service.

handled, even when fired from the bipod. Barrel changing is quick and simple.

The PK family is the result of gradual development from a variety of sources to produce a weapon for a specific purpose. As a general purpose machine gun it is now one of the finest of its type in use anywhere, but there are definite limitations on the performance of a machine gun firing a standard rifle cartridge in the field; for some types of target and application heavier weapons are required. The Soviets have produced many heavy machine guns over the years but the only one that is still likely to be encountered is the Goryunov M-1943, the SG-43. This machine gun was originally designed to be the heavy counterpart to the DP and DPM light machine guns when it was first introduced in 1943, but these days it may be classified as a really heavy machine gun. The SG-43 fires the standard 7.62 x 54mm rifle cartridge and it was designed by Goryunov to replace the venerable M-1910 Maxim machine gun.

The SG-43 carried over several features from the old Maxim, including a wheeled carriage that used a shield to protect the firer. This made the SG-43 weigh in at about 40kg (88lb) which made a hefty load to handle, but the gun itself weighed only 13.6kg (30lb). The SG-43 was belt-fed and air-cooled and had a quick-change barrel device for use during prolonged periods of fire. It was certainly robust and reliable but the overall weight factor led to several changes being introduced. One was to the gun itself which became the SGM, recognisable by the introduction of a fluted barrel. The wheeled carriage was replaced by a lighter tripod which reduced the weight to 27.4kg (60.3lb).

The SG-43 and the SGM are no longer used as front-line weapons by the Warsaw Pact nations but many are still in service with countries around the world, ranging from Egypt to China. The SG-43 or the SGM are virtually standard hand-outs for any nation that comes into the Soviet sphere of influence and although not ideal guerrilla weapons, they are often encountered in use by such formations. Perhaps the greatest use of the SG-43 and SGM is made when the weapons are placed on anti-aircraft mountings, for these machine guns can fire very effective armour-piercing rounds (as can the PK family). Special tank versions known as the SGMT or SGMB are still widely used on some of the older Soviet tank models.

Below: An Afghan guerrilla machine-gun crew awaits the order to fire its SG-43. Lacking the refinements of the SGM, the SG-43 is nonetheless an ideal weapon for the long-range fire-fights encountered in the Afghan conflict.

Soviet machine guns

Model	Calibre/ cartridge	Length	Weight (empty)	Ammunition feed	Rate of fire	Muzzle velocity
DPM	7.62×54mm	127cm (50in)	9.1kg (20.1lb)	47-round pan	600rpm	840mps (2756fps)
RP-46	7.62×54mm	128cm (50.4in)	13kg (28.7lb)	250-round belt	600rpm	840mps (2756fps)
RPD	7.62×39mm	104cm (40.9in)	7.1kg (15.7lb)	100-round belt	700rpm	700mps (2297fps)
RPK	7.62×39mm	104cm (40.9in)	5kg (11lb)	30/40-round box, 75-round drum	660rpm	732mps (2402fps)
PK	7.62×54mm	116cm (45.7in)	9kg (19.8lb)	100/200/250-round belt	650-720rpm	825mps (2707fps)
SG-43	7.62×54mm	112cm (44.1in)	13.6kg (30lb)	250-round belt	650rpm	800mps (2627fps)

No end in sight

Northern Ireland, 1975-78

Over the two and a half years during which he was secretary of state for Northern Ireland, from spring 1974 to autumn 1976, the Labour politician Merlyn Rees reflected what has almost become the regular pattern of British response to the continuing problems of the Province. Secretaries of state begin with political initiatives, and when these fail, they turn to other policy choices in the hope that they might somehow improve local conditions: sometimes security is toughened up, sometimes new public expenditure is introduced.

Rees's chief political initiative was the Constitutional Convention, which began operation in May 1975. Its task was to devise some political arrangement by which representatives of both Unionist and Nationalist traditions could share power. But Loyalist opponents of the plan won an absolute majority of seats in the Convention and were determined to block any meaningful cooperation with the Catholic Nationalists of the Social Democratic and Labour Party. Although there were some private inter-party discussions between Unionists and Nationalists, in the autumn of 1975 the Convention issued a majority report which called for the restoration of devolved government with all the powers – including law and order – enjoyed by the old Stormont parliament. The British government refused to accept the report, but early the following year Rees recalled the Convention and invited it to think again. Agreement on power-sharing still proved impossible and the body was dissolved in March 1976. As the secretary of state observed, its debates and resolutions had made it clear that there was no prospect of agreement between the parties and that no further progress could be made.

Meanwhile, in the mid-1970s the three main trends in security policy emerged which have remained important ever since: criminalisation, Ulsterisation and civilianisation. The first of these developments began when Merlyn Rees announced the end of detention without trial – internment – in July 1975. Although the security forces found the ability to lock up suspected terrorists quite useful, on balance the costs of internment outweighed the benefits, especially in political terms. Arrested terrorists would now be processed through the already-operating Diplock courts.

A second step in the criminalisation process was the abandonment of 'special category status' announced in March 1976. This status had been granted by William Whitelaw in mid-1972 to prisoners who were members of paramilitary organisations. They were allowed particular privileges, including a large degree of autonomy within prison; they were not required to work or wear prison clothes. In effect the status recognised a distinction between 'political' crime associated with the civil disturbances and so-called 'ordinary' crime.

From 1976 the government determined to remove the distinction, partly for practical reasons, since the status made it virtually impossible for the prison

Above: Two soldiers of the Parachute Regiment tend a comrade, wounded while on patrol in Northern Ireland. Between 1969 and 1978, 289 British soldiers, 88 members of the part-time UDR, and 117 officers of the RUC were killed in the Province.

Left: The Belfast control centre of the increasingly professional RUC. Below: Soldiering on during the Republican riots which marked the Queen's Silver Jubilee visit to Northern Ireland in August 1977.

Right: The Queen inspects a UDR Guard of Honour. Below left: The then minister of defence, Roy Mason, gingerly makes friends with an army dog, trained to sniff-out arms and explosives.

authorities to exercise discipline and therefore made the prisons themselves somewhat insecure. There was also a crucially important psychological point to the policy change. By stressing that all criminal activity was alike, and by categorising Republican and Loyalist terrorists with 'ordinary' criminals, the government sought to de-glamorise the paramilitaries. A common criminal, classed with robbers and rapists, is a much less romantic and emotive figure than a nationalist guerrilla or a political freedom fighter. Inevitably, therefore, the criminalisation policy was fiercely opposed by the paramilitary organisations.

'Ulsterisation' indicated the London government's desire for local security forces to take on an increasing share of operations in Northern Ireland. One aspect of this was the development of the locally-recruited Ulster Defence Regiment (UDR), which in mid-1976 had 1500 full-time members and over 6000 part-time. The Regiment provided some relief for the regular forces in routine duties such as patrolling, guarding installations and manning vehicle checkpoints. It was not, however, used on riot control duties.

The expansion of the local police force, the Royal Ulster Constabulary (RUC), reflected a combination of all three trends in policy. Ordinary crime needs to be dealt with by a police force, not an army. It is civilian, not military, and the RUC is a specifically Northern Irish force. The relative size of the main security forces reflects the shifting emphasis of government policy. By July 1976 the number of regular troops had dropped from its 1972 peak of 21,800 to 14,500. By contrast, over the same period the RUC grew from 6300 (regular police and reservists) to over 10,000. The chief constable of the RUC from 1976, Sir Kenneth Newman (later commissioner of the Metropolitan Police in London), was responsible for the introduction of a policy which became known as 'primacy of the police'. Instead of the army taking the leading role in security operations, the police would do this, assisted when necessary by military units. Police patrols, although often accompanied by troops, began to reappear in Nationalist parts of Londonderry and west Belfast.

Newman also did much to press ahead with the progressive professionalisation of the police force. In the latter part of 1976 a unified criminal intelligence system was established. Astonishingly, there had been no systematic collection and analysis of all the available information before this time. Material, particularly relating to car ownership and movements, terrorist suspects and criminal records, was now gathered together centrally and stored on computers.

In September 1976 Roy Mason, a bluff Yorkshire ex-miner, succeeded Merlyn Rees as secretary of state. His previous post had been minister of defence, and it was widely believed that he might favour a tougher security stance with, perhaps, a return to more 'military' methods. Although Mason certainly

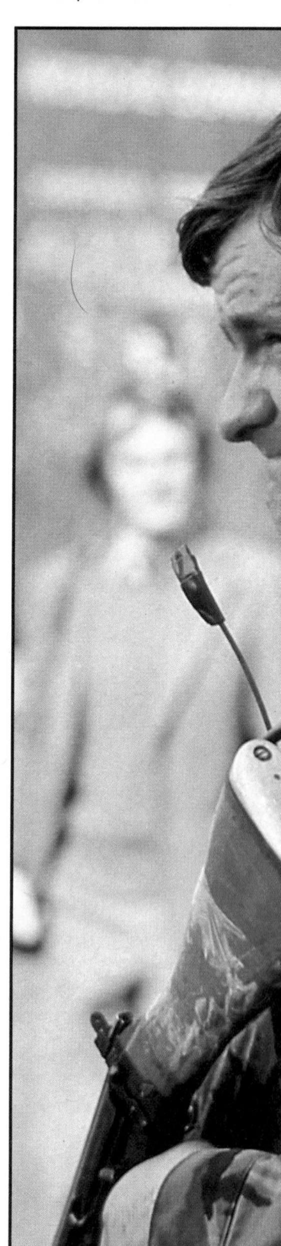

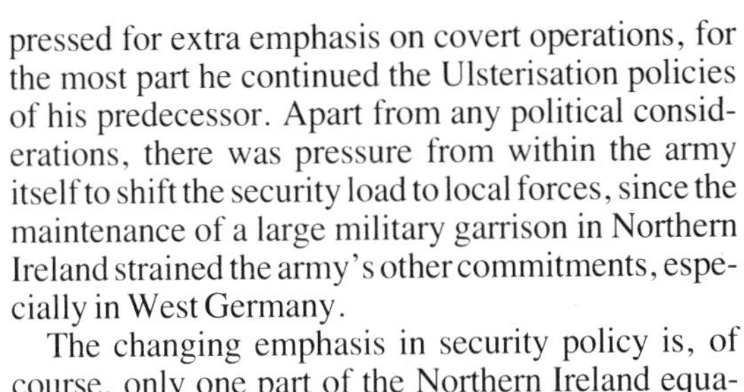

beration Army (INLA), military wing of the Irish Republican Socialist Party, which had broken away from the Officials at the end of 1974. The INLA is also believed to have gained recruits from the Provisionals during their ceasefire in early 1975. The INLA have consistently stood out as the most extreme and violent of the Republican organisations. Reckless and unpredictable, even some Provos describe them as 'wild men'.

The internal Republican violence was provoked, in part at least, by what the Provisionals called a 'truce situation' with regard to the security forces. Between February and August 1975 only four British soldiers were killed as a result of Provisional violence, as compared with 19 over the same period in the previous year. But the number of civilian casualties remained high, principally as a response to sectarian attacks by Protestant groups. Many of these incidents occurred in south Armagh, described by Merlyn Rees as 'bandit country'. At the beginning of September five Protestants were killed when two masked men broke into an Orange Hall and opened fire with a machine gun on those inside. Responsibility for the attack was later claimed by the otherwise unknown Republican Action Force, which was assumed to be a cover for the Provisionals.

pressed for extra emphasis on covert operations, for the most part he continued the Ulsterisation policies of his predecessor. Apart from any political considerations, there was pressure from within the army itself to shift the security load to local forces, since the maintenance of a large military garrison in Northern Ireland strained the army's other commitments, especially in West Germany.

The changing emphasis in security policy is, of course, only one part of the Northern Ireland equation, and it must be viewed in the context of changing terrorist action, both among Republicans and Loyalists. 1975 marked the high point (so far) of Protestant paramilitary activity. In the course of the year 115 deaths were attributed to extreme Loyalist groups. Indeed, 1975 has been the only year in which the number of deaths caused by Loyalists has exceeded that caused by Republicans (102 in 1975). Throughout the long, hot summer there was a series of sectarian assassinations and 'tit-for-tat' attacks. On 31 July a minibus carrying the Miami Showband – a group based in the Irish Republic – was stopped on its way home from an engagement and three members of the band were murdered by Protestant Ulster Volunteer Force (UVF) gunmen. In mid-August two people were killed and 20 injured when a bomb exploded without warning at a Catholic pub in Armagh.

During September further evidence of the Protestant paramilitary resurgence emerged when six men with Ulster Defence Association (UDA) links were charged in a Glasgow court with conspiracy to obtain arms. The UVF, however, were well enough supplied with guns and explosives to mount a concerted series of shootings and bombings throughout the Province on 2 October 1975, in which 11 people died and over 30 were injured. Grim retribution also occurred: four UVF men scored 'own goals' – they were killed when the bomb they were carrying exploded prematurely.

On the Republican side 1975 saw violence break out between the three main paramilitary groups: the Provisional IRA, who were by far the largest, the Official IRA, who theoretically had ceased active operations in May 1972, and the Irish National Li-

Send in the SAS

The semi-independent status of south Armagh Provisionals was emphasised in October when the Crossmaglen Provisional unit exploded a landmine under an army Saracen patrol, killing one soldier and injuring three. On 22 November a secret army observation post in the same area was attacked. Three British soldiers were killed and one seriously injured. This incident effectively marked the end of the Provisionals' 'truce'. While the Provisionals resumed regular attacks on the security forces, the sectarian assassinations continued into the New Year. Again south Armagh saw the worst violence. On 4 January five Catholics were killed in two separate incidents. The next day the Republican Action Force shot dead 10 Protestant workers. The government responded by sending in the Special Air Service (SAS).

During 1976 the SAS scored a number of successes in south Armagh. Although probably fewer than 20 soldiers were initially involved, an immediate effect of their deployment was a sharp reduction of Republican terrorist activity. Over the first 10 months of the year only two members of the security forces, both off-duty part-time members of the UDR, were killed in the area. Both the SAS's expertise in covert operations and the undeniable psychological effect of their reputation exerted a powerful constraint on the Provisionals in south Armagh. But it was not all entirely plain sailing for the SAS. An embarrassing incident occurred in May 1976 when eight members of the regiment were arrested by a Garda (police) patrol 500 metres inside the Irish Republic in County Louth. The men were charged with firearms offences in Dublin. Although it was believed that the soldiers had deliberately crossed the border, the official explanation was that the difficulty arose out of a 'map-reading error'.

The SAS were not the only undercover soldiers operating in Northern Ireland. In May 1977 another operation was revealed when Captain Robert Nairac, a Grenadier Guardsman, was kidnapped from a bar in south Armagh where he had been carrying out intelligence-gathering duties. Nairac had been working in

Right: The crushed wreckage of a child's pram and a bicycle mark the spot where a Provisional IRA getaway car hit Mrs Anne Maguire and her four children. Three of the children died, including a four-week-old girl. The incident brought to the surface a widespread feeling of revulson in Northern Ireland against the rising tide of violence. It led directly to the establishment of the Peace Movement, led by Betty Williams, who had witnessed the tragedy, and Mairead Corrigan, sister of Mrs Maguire (below right).

During the mid-1970s, the nightmare of sectarian murder, particularly in the border areas, grew to horrific proportions. Top: The Miami Showband, three of whose members were murdered when UVF gunmen stopped their minibus as it returned from an engagement on 31 July 1975. Above: In January 1976, Protestant workers, travelling home from work in south Armagh in this minibus, were stopped by gunmen, who ordered the workers out and opened fire, killing 10.

the area for some weeks. The Provisionals admitted capturing him and killed him after a brutal interrogation. A widespread search on both sides of the border failed to find his body.

As the RUC became more professional and efficient, and to meet the threat of successful covert operations, towards the end of 1976 and during 1977 the Provisionals conducted an internal reorganisation. Masterminded by Gerry Adams, they adopted a tight cellular structure. Each cell, or 'active service unit', contained about four people, worked directly with one commander, and the members of a particular cell did not know the identity of other cells. This improved the organisation's security, but a disadvantage was that the arrangement tended to cut the Provisionals off from their wider circle of sympathisers within the Nationalist community. Public support is very important to both Protestant and Catholic paramilitary groups, since it bestows on them a legitimacy which they would not otherwise possess. The leaders of both sets of groups, therefore, were greatly alarmed by one major development in 1976 which threatened to cut away local community support: the emergence of the 'Peace Movement'.

On 10 August 1976 Anne Maguire and her four children were struck by a gunman's getaway car in a Belfast suburb. The driver, a Provisional called Danny Lennon, had been killed in an exchange with troops pursuing him. Two of the children – aged four weeks and eight years – died instantly; a third died the following day. The tragedy occurred during an upsurge of rioting and shootings which marked the fifth anniversary of internment on 9 August, and it prompted Mairead Corrigan, Mrs Maguire's sister, and Betty Williams, a housewife who saw the accident, to start a series of protests against violence.

Although a local journalist, Ciaran McKeown, was involved almost from the very start, the Peace Movement was very largely dominated by women. It promoted a series of dramatic and emotional rallies which brought large numbers of ordinary people from across the sectarian divide together in a call for the violence to stop. On 28 August, for example, over 20,000 people, including deputations from Catholic districts such as Andersonstown and the Falls, marched through the Protestant heartland of the Shankill in Belfast. Similar large demonstrations took place across the Province and elsewhere. The 'Peace People', as they came to be known, excited much international attention. Mrs Williams and Mrs Corrigan were awarded the 1976 Nobel Peace Prize. But the momentum of the early mass meetings was lost when the organisation became formally established and the newly-recruited members found themselves unable to agree on detailed policy objectives.

Within two years the Peace Movement had been reduced to a shadow of its former self, concentrating on small-scale, undramatic efforts at reconciliation. The heady marches of 1977 seem to have been only a temporary 'letting off of steam', expressing widespread, otherwise inarticulate frustration at the continuing violence.

The eclipse of extremism which the Peace People at first seemed to demonstrate was also suggested by the comparative failure of the Loyalist 'constitutional stoppage' in May 1977. The Protestant Workers' strike of 1974 had been an unqualified success in bringing down the power-sharing Executive and the leaders of the 1977 stoppage – mostly the same people as three years before – had high hopes that they could achieve similarly dramatic results. The aim of the strike was to force the authorities to take stronger action against Republican terrorists, but the Protes-

tant community responded largely with indifference and the British government (having learned its lesson from 1974) took quick and decisive action, particularly to prevent intimidation.

After the strike had been called off, Roy Mason took the opportunity to begin talks with the local political parties to see if some agreement on devolved government could be reached. But the politicians proved to be as intransigent as ever and the initiative was abandoned. Thereafter Mason concentrated on making direct rule as acceptable as possible by increasing investment in housing and leisure facilities, and also attempting to stimulate employment.

The high point of Roy Mason's time as Northern Ireland secretary was the Silver Jubilee visit of Queen Elizabeth during August 1977. Unionists saw it as a reaffirmation of the links with Britain, while Nationalists viewed it either with indifference or as an affront. Despite the fact that the IRA managed to evade exceptionally tight security and plant two small bombs in the grounds of the New University of Ulster, one of the places visited by the Queen (neither exploded while she was there), the visit confirmed the government's ability to control and contain terrorism. The Provisionals, nevertheless, were by no means beaten. Just over a week after the Royal visit, in one day no less than 35 incendiary devices were planted at commercial premises in the Belfast area.

Public outrage

The increasing use of fire-bombs reflected the security forces' success in restricting supplies of gelignite. A particular device favoured during the Provisionals' Christmas campaign in 1977 consisted of a small explosive charge attached to a can of petrol. This could then be hung on to the wire grilles which protected many shop and pub windows throughout the Province. When the bomb exploded a ball of fire would blow through the shattered glass. A device like this was set off with very little warning at the La Mon House restaurant near Comber, County Down, in February 1978. Twelve people were burnt to death and 23 injured in the attack, which caused widespread public revulsion. So great was the reaction that the Provisionals temporarily called off this campaign.

Another aspect of the Republican campaign in the spring of 1978 took place in Northern Ireland's prisons. The first people to be denied special category status were convicted in the autumn of 1976. These prisoners refused to wear prison clothes or to work. The authorities insisted that they should submit to ordinary prison discipline and would not allow them to wear their own clothes. The prisoners thus wrapped themselves only in blankets and the protest generally became known as going 'on the blanket'. By the end of 1977 over 100 men were participating in the action. In March 1978, with no sign that the government was prepared to move on the issue, the campaign was stepped up to include what became known as the 'dirty protest'. The prisoners smashed up the furniture in their cells, refused to wash or use any toilet facilities and began to smear the cell walls with their own excreta. So began what became a major theme of the Republican effort as the decade ended: action within the Province's prisons – both 'dirty protest' and later hunger strikes – supported by popular demonstrations in the Catholic community and sustained attempts to enlist international support and sympathy for the cause.

Keith Jeffery

Bandit country

Controlling the borders in Northern Ireland

When British troops deployed in Northern Ireland in 1969, the initial difficulties they encountered were concentrated in the main cities, Belfast and Londonderry. But the border between Northern Ireland and Southern Ireland had been a sensitive area ever since it was established in 1920, and it had been the scene of raids by IRA men from the Irish Republic quite recently in the 1956-62 campaign. The Dublin government had no serious intention of instigating direct military intervention to aid the Catholics in the North, although Irish Army units were moved up to their side of the border, so the British did not need to organise defences against a conventional incursion. What they did need was to prevent the running of arms, ammunition and explosives across the border in support of IRA operations, to counter hit-and-run raids by terrorists based in the Republic, and to assert their authority over areas in which Republican feeling was strong and terrorist activity was soon a constant threat.

There was no doubting the sympathies of much of the predominantly Catholic population of the southern parts of the counties of Down, Armagh and Fermanagh. They had shown strong support for the civil rights movement in 1968-69, and in January 1969 there had been a serious riot in the south Down border town of Newry in which 28 civilians and 10 Royal Ulster Constabulary (RUC) men were injured, and rioters set fire to police vehicles. Following the violence in Londonderry that summer, Newry saw several more days of rioting. When the Provisional IRA began their campaign in 1970, there was no shortage of recruits and passive helpers in the area.

The border itself takes little account of the physical and cultural geography of the region. For example, the area surrounding Crossmaglen, a largely Catholic village in south Armagh only 7km (4 miles) from the border, is cut off from the remainder of the county by a range of hills, and it would perhaps more naturally be part of the Republic – indeed in 1925 it was earmarked for return to the then Irish Free State. Crossmaglen and the area around it has always been an IRA stronghold and in 1970 it was the scene of some of the earliest cross-border operations carried out by the Provisionals.

The artificial nature of the border, in general following no major obstacle such as a river or mountains, contributed greatly to the problems of the security forces in trying to police it. Along the whole 450km (280 miles) of its length, the border is crossed by

Above: A soldier watches carefully from the back of a Saracen armoured personnel carrier while patrolling in the border area. Right: An army patrol moves warily past a Republican monument in Crossmaglen. Note the 'Operation Kremlin' treatment which has been given to the Saracen for service in Northern Ireland including: extra wire-mesh to act as a rocket grenade screen, CS/smoke dischargers, anti-wire posts to protect the commander and thicker armour. To the rear one can see an army observation post. Inset: Blocks of concrete, set into a border road by the army in order to prevent its use by the IRA.

hundreds of minor tracks and roads with no customs checkpoints. It was illegal to cross the border at these points without a special pass, normally issued only to local people with a special reason, such as farmers with land on both sides of the border. But this regulation was almost impossible to enforce and the unapproved crossing points were to prove a major headache for the security forces.

As a result of the length of the border and the nature of the terrain, it was estimated that at least an army brigade would be needed to police it properly. The security forces were, however, unable to afford such a large commitment of troops; in the event, they deployed a battalion of infantry and supporting lancers in armoured cars. Eventually, the border was divided into three sections each policed by a single battalion with support drawn from other units such as the RAF, the Army Air Corps and the Royal Engineers. When the Ulster Defence Regiment (UDR) was formed in April 1970, it provided reinforcements for the British troops in the border area. The first joint UDR-British Army operation, Operation Mulberry, was launched later in the same month. It involved 2000 army troops and 400 UDR members in a full-scale search of parts of Fermanagh, Tyrone and Armagh.

The search for arms caches – to be found in isolated farm buildings, buried milk churns, drains, trees and even, in one case, a badger set – was a major security force activity. Other duties included constant patrolling, establishing a presence in the area, and the setting up of vehicle checkpoints – this being the main way of preventing the infiltration of arms and explosives from the Republic. Initially troops were moved in Pig and Saracen armoured personnel carriers (APCs), and in Landrovers protected with steel

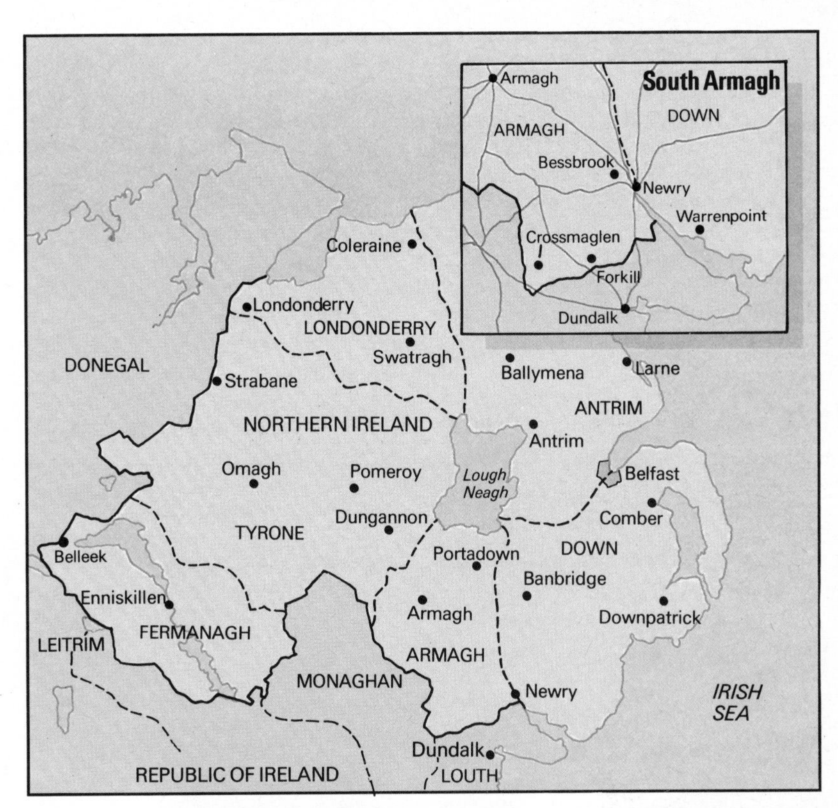

sheeting and asbestos. The Saladin armoured car, with a 76.2mm gun and two 7.62mm machine guns, and the Ferret scout car, armed with a single machine gun, were both widely used on border patrols and to set up checkpoints.

This worked well as long as the army only had to face terrorist gunfire. But when the Provisionals mastered the technique of laying remote-controlled landmines in culverts under roads, ground patrols became extremely hazardous. As only one example of many incidents, on 10 September 1972 three soldiers of the Argyll and Sutherland Highlanders were killed in County Tyrone when 225kg (500lb) of explosives were detonated under their Saracen, throwing the vehicle a distance of some 20m (65 feet) and making a crater 6m (20 feet) deep. Even apart from such losses, the army was finding the deployment of troops by armoured vehicle too slow – by the time troops could arrive at the scene of an incident IRA units were normally able to escape by car to the Republic, where they could not be pursued.

These considerations dictated a greater reliance on helicopters to patrol the border and move troops quickly and safely into action. The small Sioux helicopter was extensively used for reconnaissance, while the larger Scout combined reconnaissance duties with the carrying of small airborne army patrols. Normally loaded with four soldiers, the Scout was especially effective when a vehicle checkpoint needed to be set up in a hurry, landing by the roadside

Right: An army patrol landing from a Scout helicopter, while a Sioux observation helicopter keeps watch overhead. In some border areas, such as south Armagh, the danger of IRA attacks has made helicopters the main form of army transport.

Massacre at Forkill

On 17 July 1975 four British soldiers were killed by a remote-controlled bomb in the Ulster border area, near Forkill, south Armagh. The sole survivor of the blast, Clive Evans, gave the following account of his appalling experience.

"A company of the Green Howards on patrol at the bridge noticed a suspicious device. In fact several things didn't look quite right. They went back to Crossmaglen, reported, and an operation was planned to go in and clear the devices. There was a five gallon oil drum, a milk churn and a white object set back off the road.

We were told there was going to be an operation to deal with the suspect objects and that the date would be given to us. A couple of days before, we were told that the operation was on. I think that it was July 15.

So on 17 July, the ATO, Gus Garside, his No. 2, and the Royal Engineer search adviser, Sammy McCarter, and myself, left Bessbrook at about 9 am by helicopter and flew down to the area where the troops were on the ground and had staked it out. We landed and the helicopter set off back to Bessbrook. We had a quick O ['Orders'] Group with the Officer Commanding.

It was pointed out where we were on the ground and where the devices were. The ATO planned to move forward with his No. 2, the RE search adviser and myself and one rifleman for covering fire. Then the ATO would have gone forward by himself to check on the device.

We went along the inside of a hedgerow. In a field the other side of the hedgerow was the road and a little bit further up the road was where the device was. We went along and then stopped to do a sweep. Without going into detail, we were using a piece of equipment which will detonate any radio-controlled devices in the area. The sweep was carried out, but nothing went bang, so we felt safe to assume that there were no radio-controlled devices in the area.

The line of order setting off again to get onto the road was the OC, Gus Garside, Sammy McCarter, Brown and myself at the rear. We went a further 10 yards until we came to a gap in the hedge and decided to go through it and on to the road.

Now all I remember really is that the OC and Gus Garside went down this bank. We were just coming out on to the road from the hedgerow. Sammy McCarter was at the bottom of the bank inside the hedgerow. Brown was just about to go down on the right and I was about two feet behind him.

Then the explosion occurred. I must have been blown backwards by the blast and I landed face downwards in the field.

The next thing I remember is lying in the field face down with my hands over my head and feeling all the mud dropping on my back, and I could hear stuff falling out of the sky. Then I realised that there had been an explosion.

My ears, God, terrible. It's hard to describe the sound in your ears. And my eyes they just stung like hell. I didn't remember any flash. It's hard to say whether you remember the flash. When I was lying down I can't remember whether I experienced the flash or whether it was when I was lying down that I thought Christ, there has been an explosion. I will never be able to say that I knew there was a flash.

Apart from my ears and my eyes one hand was quite painful. I could open my left eye after a little while and I stood up and I could see a bloody great hole and I could see a body nearly next to me.

I heard someone running towards me and I felt pretty giddy at that point, and sick, and I sat down again. Then I felt someone picking me up and I heard a voice saying 'this one is dead', and I was just dragged off across the field to the corner of the field.

By that time my other eye, the eye I could see out of was stinging again so I closed both of them. In fact someone, one of the soldiers, put a field dressing on the bad eye. I knew it was bleeding, I could feel the blood. But he put the bandage over both eyes so I couldn't see anything.

I just lay there and I could hear people on the radio requesting a helicopter and telling them exactly what had happened and I still just lay there.

I think I realised what had happened when I first stood up and I saw the crater and I saw Brown lying there. I realised then what had happened and I think I realised that there wasn't much chance for them.

My initial reaction was that I didn't think about it at the time. Shortly afterwards when I came-to in hospital I felt it's a waste of life. You know, I mean three of them were good friends of mine. Gus Garside, he was sent out there. I don't think anyone wants to come to Ulster, but he was sent and he came in to do a job of saving life and property by neutralising devices. That's all he had to do. So why kill a man like that? He's got no political motives in what he's doing and all the people in the patrol, none of them were sort of out and out – they didn't have any political views – they were sent there to do a job.

I mean, the week before he had been down to Derrybeg, in Newry. He had done a couple of jobs in Derrybeg, actually. It would have been so easy to not risk his life; to put a charge underneath the suspect car and blow it to pieces and admittedly, a few of the windows of houses in the area would have been damaged. But he didn't do that. He went out and risked his own life to save the property, and neutralised the device in the car. A week later there was a grenade or something.

And then – well that was my reaction. It makes me feel bitter that they lost their lives. I don't know whether it is anger; it is bitterness rather than anger.

My attitude to Northern Ireland and the Northern Ireland people hasn't changed. I have been on a two-year tour. I did a year in Armagh and a year in Bessbrook and had a marvellous time. I have met lots and lots of people and I have got some very good friends in Northern Ireland and I have enjoyed it, believe it or not. I have really enjoyed Northern Ireland; the explosion hasn't really changed my opinion. No, I don't think it has . . . "

and disgorging its patrol in the path of a suspect car. Both Sioux and Scouts were used in conjunction with Wessex helicopters of the RAF. The Wessex can carry 12 fully equipped soldiers, and this capacity was extensively employed. In a typical operation, a reconnaissance helicopter would call up a Wessex to deploy a body of troops at speed in response to an incident. Alternatively, by dropping one search team, moving on to drop a second team elsewhere, and returning to collect the first team later, a single Wessex could enable the army to respond quickly to a whole series of incidents along a given stretch of the border. In the most insecure rural areas, vehicle patrols have been virtually unknown since the early 1970s – troops always move from their bases by helicopter and operate in the field on foot.

From the autumn of 1971 much army effort was devoted to attempts at closing the border decisively by blocking the illegal crossing-points. The Royal Engineers were called in and, with infantry support, they dug holes in a number of roads, filled the holes with concrete, and embedded huge wooden spikes in the concrete: most were ripped out within hours. Clearly, something more decisive was required. The Engineers went in again, blowing large craters in the roads with explosive charges, but IRA units soon developed the technique of driving hijacked vehicles into the craters and then using commandeered earth-moving equipment to fill them up with rubble. The Engineers were harassed with sniper fire and hostile demonstrations by local people as they carried out their work, but they believed they had finally found the answer to their problem when they implanted massive concrete blocks – weighing about a tonne – across the roads. Unfortunately, the IRA blew them up with explosives, and it had to be accepted that the cross-border roads could not be totally closed.

Given the difficulty of sealing the border effectively, the ease with which terrorists were able to operate from the other side of the border and escape afterwards had no purely military solution. If the problem were to be resolved, it would involve a political initiative. When the British and Irish prime ministers, Edward Heath and Jack Lynch, met at the Munich Olympics on 4 September 1972, Heath complained of the IRA's strongholds in the Republic near the border. Events in the Republic itself combined to push Lynch into action against the IRA. Later in September there

Out in Armagh

Patrolling the area around Crossmaglen in south Armagh has consistently been one of the army's most nerve-racking tasks. Here Captain A.F.N. Clarke recalls the first day out in the Armagh countryside for a unit of 3 Para in 1976:

'I check my equipment for the fiftieth time. Map, compass, belt and pouches, codes, personality check-list, stolen car list, ammunition, rifle and lastly my radio operator to see whether he has everything....

'The clatter of the Wessex becomes deafening as it swoops over the top of the police station and round the football pitch to descend onto the helipad. As it touches down we race out and throw our kit in, clambering after it. The shorter the turn-around the better, and within a few seconds we are airborne and moving tactically along at low level, swinging round trees and hills, dropping into little gullies, dodging power lines and telephone wires.

'We are moving down towards Cullaville right on the border with the Republic. The Wessex swings around in a tight turn, drops, flares and touches on the soggy turf. As soon as the wheels touch we are off and running. Guns into fire positions, my section commanders and I showing them the route. There's no time to notice the tight feeling in your stomach, or the nervous playing with the safety catch.

'"O.K. Corporal Menzies, move off."

'I look over to the right and see the third patrol in position on the side of a small hill, to give cover to our two patrols that will be moving. Bill, Corporal Menzies, is moving slowly away towards the road. First objective a vehicle checkpoint on the Crossmaglen-to-Cullaville road.

'"Right lads, let's go."

'Having talked about it in the Mess the night before, we reckon that the chances of getting hit on the first day are pretty small, because the opposition don't know how we are going to operate, and, being far more professional than the cowboys in Belfast, they will not do anything until they are sure of a kill.'

were a series of petrol bomb attacks on Garda (Irish police) stations near the border. In early October, an armed bank robbery in Dublin was attributed to the IRA, and in the following month a series of bombs exploded in the Irish capital. Although the Provisionals denied responsibility, they were widely blamed for these bombings. Lynch took a series of firm measures. The Provisionals' political wing, the Provisional Sinn Fein, was outlawed on 6 October, and in December an amendment to Ireland's Offences Against the State Act was passed making mere police suspicion of membership of the IRA or another illegal organisation sufficient to convict a person in court.

Yet, even with the political will to crack down on the Provisionals, the Dublin government did not possess security forces on a scale to patrol the border effectively. Also, the claim to control the whole of Ireland remained a part of the Republic's constitution, and no Dublin government could afford to be seen to cooperate too closely with the British. The Irish government's measures against the Provisionals were based on fear of terrorism in the South, rather than support for British rule in the North.

Sanctuary in the South

As a result, the Republic remained virtually a safe base for the Provisionals' activities, a sanctuary where they could take refuge after operations in the border area, store weapons and ammunition, manufacture explosives and give their members military training. Attacks against the security forces were even mounted directly from the other side of the border. The RUC station at Belleek, for example, is only 100m (110 yards) inside Northern Ireland, and frequently came under fire from the other side of the river that marks the border. Command wires to land mines were also often run across the border, allowing the terrorists to detonate their devices from a position of almost total safety.

Smouldering warfare was installed as a way of life along the border, and both the British Army and the Provisionals worked at refining their techniques. To cope with bombs controlled by a command wire, for example, the army equipped helicopters with infrared equipment which could spot the wire even if it was well buried and not given away by a trail of newly-dug earth. The Provisionals, however, began using extremely sophisticated radio-control devices to detonate bombs, and the army had to respond by developing and deploying complex sensors and jammers. The Provisionals were both patient and skilful, keeping a careful watch on the operational methods of army units and exploiting the knowledge gained to inflict casualties at carefully chosen moments. They devoted much of their effort to attacks on softer targets than the British Army – off-duty UDR men were especially vulnerable to assassination, and the border area also saw its share of sectarian killings.

By 1976 south Armagh could rank as the most insecure area in all of Northern Ireland. As an example of the operations the Provisionals could carry off in this 'bandit country', in 1976 the RUC station at Crossmaglen, which was being used as a base by 40 Commando, was twice attacked by a 10-barrelled Mark 8 mortar mounted on the back of a truck. It would be fair to say that in Crossmaglen the army existed in a state of siege. The army's efforts to reassert control of south Armagh, however, had considerable success. The deployment of the SAS

from 1976 was the most widely publicised aspect, but the bulk of the work was done by ordinary soldiers, spending two or three days at a time on patrol in the countryside, living rough, and manning secret observation posts at key locations. If terrorist activities could not be stopped, they could at least be limited.

Army operations in the border area benefited, as they did throughout the Province, from the increasing use of computers for intelligence storage and checking. All vehicle checkpoints were linked to a central computer into which they fed a constant flow of apparently trivial information on people's movements, and from which they could call up extensive details on a person or vehicle at a moment's notice. The army's equipment was, of course, constantly updated to give troops the benefit of the latest in technology in all fields. One example among many was the Lynx helicopter, introduced in 1979 as a faster and slightly larger substitute for the Scout, which could provide the latest night and all-weather capability.

Liaison across the border

Another improvement in the security situation came from increasing cooperation with the Irish police. In a typical incident, on 20 September 1979 a Garda patrol discovered a firing point and the beginning of a command wire on their side of the border, informed the Northern Ireland security forces, and gave cover while the explosive device on the northern side of the border was dealt with. In 1980 an Irish border task force was established, and there were several major finds of arms dumps and bomb factories in the Republic in the 1980s.

There can be little question, however, that the Provisionals are capable of operating in the border areas almost indefinitely – as the massacre of 18 British soldiers in two explosions at Warrenpoint on 27 August 1979 tragically confirmed. The extent of local support for the Provisionals has been revealed in democratic elections, as when the imprisoned hunger-striker Bobby Sands was elected member of parliament for Fermanagh and South Tyrone in April 1981. It has been suggested that a solution to the situation might be found through redrawing the border to exclude the solidly Catholic areas from Northern Ireland, but this exercise is unlikely to be attempted. The security forces seem destined to carry on their thankless task in the border areas for the foreseeable future.

Barry Smith

Above: An army patrol in Forkill, south Armagh. Far left: An overturned Saracen on the edge of an IRA bomb crater on a border road. Left: While her husband, a UDR member, works their farm, this Protestant woman stands guard. Below: IRA men in training south of the border.

The secret war

British undercover operations in Ireland

One of the main weaknesses of the security forces in Northern Ireland in 1970 and 1971, as the Provisional IRA began its campaign of terrorist insurgency, was the lack of good intelligence. Frank Kitson, whose book *Low Intensity Operations* was published during 1971 while he was commander of the 39th Infantry Brigade in Belfast, summed up the essence of conducting a campaign of this kind: 'the problem of defeating the enemy consists very largely of finding him,' and he concluded that, 'it is easy to recognise the paramount importance of good information.' The British Army's experience in counter-insurgency overseas during the 1950s and 1960s had also convinced military theorists of the value of seizing the initiative in the psychological and propaganda war. Although Northern Ireland was a part of the United Kingdom and conditions were therefore different from those in Malaya or Borneo, this was no less true of the struggle against the Provisional IRA.

The weakness of military intelligence in Northern Ireland in the early 1970s was partly a result of the unexpected change in IRA tactics; before the outbreak of the troubles the army had only half-a-dozen intelligence personnel in the Province, and these were engaged in routine vetting work. The two distinct government agencies, MI5 and MI6, both had responsibilities in Ireland. MI6, nominally under the Foreign Office, was responsible for intelligence operations overseas and therefore maintained a small presence in the Republic of Ireland. Northern Ireland, however, was covered by MI5 which, with its internal security brief under the Home Office, kept fewer than 10 officers in the Province during the 1960s. The only sizeable intelligence organisation with a network of contacts was the Special Branch of the Royal Ulster Constabulary (RUC), but army intelligence was strictly forbidden to pass on information to them and in any case the Special Branch was understaffed and under-financed – its intelligence network in the Catholic districts was in a state of decay and its files were neglected and outdated. Despite these problems, the army was forced to rely on what little intelligence the RUC could provide, and the fact that the RUC was so distrusted by the Catholic population that it could not function in many Catholic districts was therefore a disaster from an intelligence-gathering point of view.

As support for the Provisionals grew among the Catholics, it became vital for the army to develop its own intelligence networks and two more MI5 men were sent out to help them do this. A high-ranking career diplomat, Oliver Wright, was given the job of intelligence coordinator and the situation gradually began to improve. The first development was improved coordination between the army and the RUC. Army intelligence personnel were seconded to RUC Special Branch and a joint working party began to compile a list of suspected terrorists – though just how defective the list turned out to be became very clear in August 1971. When the security forces moved to intern members of the Provisional IRA that they had 'identified', many of them turned out to have left the country and some were dead.

The month after internment began, army 'psyops' (psychological operations) and information services

Top: Members of the SAS in training. As is common with this regiment, they carry a variety of weapons – in this case an SLR and an M16. The deployment of the SAS in the border areas of Northern Ireland seriously affected the activities of the Provisional IRA, especially after January 1976. IRA reaction to the arrival of the SAS was characterised by a virulent propaganda campaign, including the dissemination of leaflets such as that above.

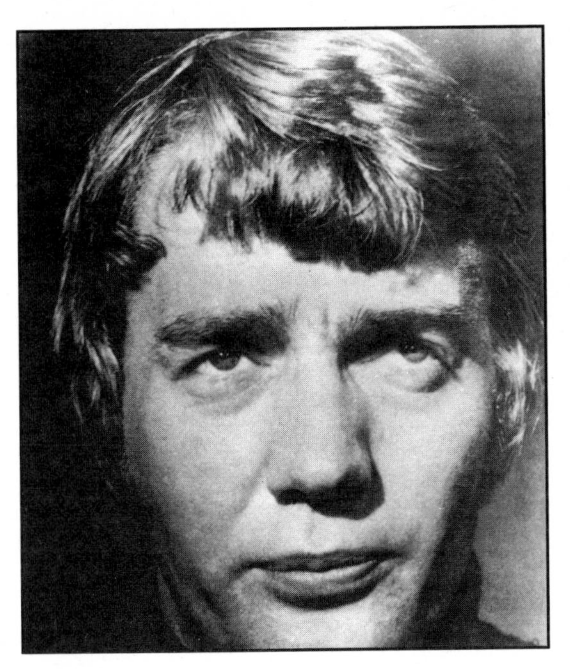

Above left: Kenneth Littlejohn, whose activities and contacts led to serious embarrassment for the British security forces, and particularly for MI6. Precisely what Littlejohn's association with the British secret services consisted of is obscure. He always claimed that he was a trusted agent, with the highest contacts, but British sources have strenuously denied many of his claims – notably that he had been provided with a 'hit list' of IRA leaders who were to be assassinated. Above: Captain Robert Nairac, whose secret activities and ultimate fate are more clearly documented. In May 1977, working undercover, he posed as a Republican Catholic in a bar in south Armagh. The local Provisionals were suspicious, however, and seized him. After a brutal interrogation he was shot. His murderers were later arrested, and confessed. Nairac refused to give them any information during questioning. He was posthumously awarded the George Cross in 1979.

were reorganised – an 'Information Policy Unit' was set up under Colonel Maurice Tugwell at the army headquarters in Lisburn near Belfast. Information Policy's role was to publish anti-IRA propaganda, liaise with the press in order to present events in the Province in a light favourable to the army, and advise the General Officer Commanding Northern Ireland on the public-relations aspects of army operations. The unit has been accused on a number of occasions of deliberately supplying misinformation or 'black propaganda' intended to discredit the IRA, but its role in intelligence *gathering* – Information Policy staff were expected to obtain information from pressmen as well as channelling information to the press – is an aspect of its work that is less often discussed.

In this early period, the bulk of intelligence was obtained by 'overt' means – frequent army and RUC patrols during which troops were able to gain background information, local censuses to build up a register of the population, random vehicle checkpoints and the analysis of captured documents. With the establishment of No-Go areas in Belfast and Londonderry, the supply of intelligence from these areas dried up until after Operation Motorman the following year. During 1972 conflict in the Province worsened and, as it became apparent that internment had failed, the emphasis in intelligence shifted to covert operations.

As early as the last few months of 1969, a small number of SAS men had been sent into Antrim and Down expressly to observe the activities of the Protestant paramilitary groups there, and – although the army long denied their presence – SAS and SAS-trained men were again involved in covert operations in the Province after 1972 when a special team, the Military Reconnaissance Force (MRF), later renamed the Special Duties Team, was established. MRF consisted of some 40 troops armed with Browning pistols and sub-machine guns. One of its tasks was to patrol areas in which the IRA was active; these patrols consisted of two to four armed men in unmarked vehicles.

The most colourful side of MRF intelligence-gathering, however, was its use of 'front' organisations. In the Twinbrook district of west Belfast, MRF ran a dry-cleaning service, the Four Square Laundry, which for several months enabled them to drive a 'laundry van', probably equipped with photographic and listening devices, around Catholic neighbourhoods. The van-driver collected clothes and they were cleaned at the laundry – but not before they had been analysed for traces of explosives or gunpowder. By comparing the sizes of clothes with the sizes of known inhabitants of each house, MRF was able to trap a number of activists, until the Provisionals discovered what was happening. On 2 October 1972 a team of Provisional IRA gunmen attacked the van in Twinbrook, killing the driver.

The Four Square Laundry was not the only front operation run by MRF – other fronts are thought to have included a rather dubious massage parlour, a group of 'lingerie salesmen' who organised 'underwear parties' for the women of Andersonstown, and several door-to-door cosmetics saleswomen who were in fact female members of MRF.

The Littlejohn affair

As the violence in Northern Ireland reached its peak in 1972, other changes in intelligence organisation were introduced. MI6, which had previously been confined to the Republic, began to play a greater part in infiltrating the IRA in the North. Unfortunately, the role of MI6 north of the border was undermined by some adverse publicity, of which the best known involved two brothers called Littlejohn.

Kenneth Littlejohn, who had been dishonourably discharged from the Parachute Regiment in 1959, had a long record of criminal involvement and in the early 1970s he lived in the Irish Republic to avoid arrest. He developed links with the IRA and through a contact of his brother Keith was apparently able to offer his services to Lord Carrington, then defence minister in Edward Heath's government. From February until October 1972 he is generally supposed to have supplied information about the IRA to his MI6 contact, and he later claimed to have been given a hit-list of

Above: The bodies of two Protestants, one aged just 18, killed by the Provisional IRA in November 1974. The Provisionals claimed that the two had been spying for the British Army.

IRA leaders whom MI6 wanted killed – though of course there is nothing to substantiate this claim. The two brothers embarked on a career as *agents provocateurs*, bombing Irish police stations and carrying out bank raids on both sides of the border – raids that had allegedly been 'cleared' by the intelligence services in the knowledge that they would be attributed to the IRA.

Eventually, the Garda (Irish police) decided to put a stop to the activities of the Littlejohns and on 19 October 1972, at the request of the Garda, the Flying Squad arrested Kenneth Littlejohn while he was in London for a meeting with his MI6 controller. Keith was arrested in Torquay on the same day. MI6 disowned the two brothers who were extradited to Dublin six months later and sentenced to a total of 35 years' imprisonment for their part in a Dublin bank-raid.

There were, however, many successful MI6 operations – another of their agents, Leslie Aspin, seems to have been responsible for learning of the Libyan arms shipment aboard the merchant vessel *Claudia* intended for the Provisional IRA; on 28 March 1973, after a tip-off, the Irish authorities seized the boat as it entered their territorial waters. Nevertheless, the publicity resulting from the Littlejohn affair – whatever the truth behind it – led to MI6 personnel being withdrawn from the Republic and the North. MI5 officers were sent to Northern Ireland to replace them.

Naturally enough, this kind of publicity helped the IRA propaganda campaign: during the mid-1970s there was a stream of allegations that undercover members of the security forces were carrying out assassinations and bombings in Northern Ireland and the Republic. Many of these allegations were directed against the SAS – IRA propagandists spoke of 'assassination squads', although British sources have always denied that the security forces operate in this way. Still, the British government was able to use the SAS's fearsome reputation to good effect: the announcement in January 1976 that the SAS were being deployed in the border areas was enough to reduce immediately the scale of IRA operations.

With the 'Ulsterisation' strategy of the Labour government in the late 1970s, the RUC was reorganised to take over some of the responsibility for intelligence formerly held by the army. The RUC's Criminal Investigation Department (CID) was expanded; information obtained by CID interrogators at the interrogation centre in Castlereagh was now to be collated by an RUC Criminal Intelligence Unit. Nevertheless, army intelligence and SAS undercover work continued to play a vital role. As the 'Diplock courts' came into operation, many Provisional IRA activists were convicted and imprisoned.

IRA on the defensive

After Margaret Thatcher's Conservative administration took office in 1979, the major developments in the undercover war were the creation of a new intelligence coordinating committee and the use of 'Supergrasses' – former terrorists who agree to testify against their associates in exchange for immunity from prosecution and a new identity on the UK mainland. The new committee, known as 'The Department', was established under Sir Maurice Oldfield and later it was run by Brooks Richards; it is responsible for coordinating the work done by the RUC Special Branch and the plain-clothes unit of the RUC Special Patrol Group with that undertaken by MI5, MI6, the SAS and army intelligence.

Within a few months of Thatcher taking office, the IRA themselves admitted the importance of undercover work in throwing them back on the defensive – a spokesman said: 'The Brits are very, very good at undercover work. This is what they're into now.' Even though the IRA try to minimise their difficulties, it is estimated that over 80 per cent of their operations are cancelled as the result of the work of British intelligence.

And the work continues. In December 1983 two armed IRA men in a vehicle were stopped by an SAS undercover squad in Tyrone, and both were shot as they tried to escape. In July 1984 another undercover patrol, probably consisting of SAS men, encountered a group of four armed men acting suspiciously outside a factory, also in Tyrone. They challenged the men and opened fire when there was no response. One man, William Price, was killed; the IRA later acknowledged that he was one of their members. The other three were arrested, and they turned out to have a loaded revolver and an automatic pistol. Detonators and cans of petrol were found nearby. **Barry Smith**

Below: A Westland Wessex helicopter picks up an SAS surveillance party which has been escorted back to the helicopter by other soldiers. The surveillance party had just spent days in a 'hide' in the countryside of south Armagh, with sophisticated cameras and monitoring equipment, building up a picture of IRA movements.

Key Weapons

ASW AIRCRAFT

The importance of the nuclear-powered attack and missile-launching submarine to the present balance of power has led to the development of a wide range of counter-systems, including 'hunter-killer' submarines, surface vessels and, most importantly, aircraft. Anti-submarine warfare or ASW aircraft are divided between fixed- and rotary-winged types. Fixed-wing ASW aircraft are either land- or carrier-based and are designed for quick transit from base to patrol area and for long 'on-station' endurance. Helicopter systems are usually shipborne and are an integrated part of the parent vessel's overall ASW capacity.

Electronic sensors are vital to the battle against the submarine and current ASW aircraft are well equipped in this direction. Radar plays an important part in the detection of surfaced targets or the periscopes of submerged vessels. Plotting a submarine underwater is more difficult and is usually handled by the use of sonar or by MAD (magnetic anomaly detectors). Sonar functions in a similar manner to radar but instead of using radio energy in air, it uses sound in water for detection. Sonar installations in ASW aircraft usually take the form of sonobuoys which can be dropped into the water, their information being radioed back to the circling aircraft, or devices which can be winched down from a hovering helicopter – known as dipping sonar. MAD can detect disturbances in the earth's magnetic field caused by the metal hull of a submarine and are usually carried by fixed-wing aircraft in tail booms to minimise the aircraft's effect on the reading. Helicopters fitted with MAD deploy them through a towed array system.

Having found the submarine, the ASW aircraft must have the capability to destroy it. Primary weapons are the homing torpedo and the depth charge. Homing torpedos are usually lightweight weapons which use some aspect of the submarine's operation, such as the noise from its propellers, for guidance. Depth-charges can be either high-explosive or nuclear and are fused to explode at pre-determined depths. They are usually dropped in patterns to maximise the chance of hitting the target vessel.

Chief amongst the current world inventory of fixed-wing ASW types are the American Lockheed P-3 Orion and S-3 Viking, the British BAe Nimrod, the French Breguet Alize and Dassault-Breguet Atlantic, the Japanese Shin Meiwa PS-1, and the Soviet Beriev Be-12 Mail, Ilyushin Il-38 May and Tupolev Tu-142 Bear-F.

Lockheed's P-3 Orion is based on the company's turboprop Electra airliner; it first flew in August 1958 and has so far appeared in three ASW models. The current variant, the P-3C, saw its first flight in September 1968 and is operated by a crew of 10, five of whom constitute a tactical team to operate the aircraft's sensors (including search radar, sonobuoys, MAD and passive receivers to pick up submarine radio/radar transmissions). Besides the 512 aircraft bought by the US Navy, the Orion is operated by Australia, Japan, the Netherlands, New Zealand, Norway and Spain. In addition, Canada operates 18 CP-140 Auroras which are a variant of the P-3C fitted with S-3 Viking electronics.

The S-3A Viking is a turbofan-powered, carrier-based aircraft with a crew of four, including two systems operators. Sensors include search radar, sonobuoys, MAD, passive receivers and forward-looking infra-red. The S-3B has improved sensor/data processing equipment and provision for the Harpoon air-to-surface missile.

BAe's Nimrod is based on the Comet 4 airliner and first flew in May 1967. Crew complement is 12, including a nine-man tactical team, and the RAF operates a total of 34 such aircraft. Sensors include search radar, sonobuoys, MAD and a wing-mounted searchlight. Two versions of the ASW Nimrod have appeared, namely the MR 1 and MR 2. The MR 2 is an up-date of the earlier aircraft incorporating improved and additional sensors and data-processing equipment. Following the Falklands conflict, 16 Nimrod MR 2s have been fitted for in-flight refuelling and have provision for Sidewinder and Harpoon missiles. In this configuration, they are known as MR 2Ps.

The Breguet Alize is a turboprop carrier aircraft with a crew of two and was first flown in August 1951. Some 60 remain in service with the Aéronavale and 24 have been supplied to the Indian Navy. The Dassault-Breguet Atlantic is also turboprop-powered but is a land-based aircraft with a crew of 12. First flown in October 1961, the Atlantic has been in service with the navies of France, West Germany, Holland, Italy

Previous page: Armed with the standard US Navy Mk46 lightweight AS homing torpedo, a Sikorsky SH-60B Seahawk makes a training flight. The Seahawk's ASW equipment also includes search radar, MAD and sonobuoys. Above: A US Navy Lockheed P-3C Orion. Clearly visible behind the wing roots on the aircraft's underside are the rows of sonobuoy dispensers, part of the Orion's sophisticated package of sensors, radar equipment and AS weapons. Below: Two views of the US Navy S-3A Viking. The top picture shows the aircraft with its MAD boom extended as it searches for disturbances in the earth's magnetic field created by the metal hull of a submarine.

and Pakistan. The Atlantic NG, incorporating modernised systems, was flown in May 1981 and was ordered for the French Aéronavale.

The Japanese PS-1 is a turboprop flying-boat with a crew of 10 including a seven-man tactical team which operates search radar, sonobuoys and MAD. The aircraft first flew in October 1967, and a total of 23 PS-1s have been delivered to the Japanese Marine Self-Defence Force.

The Beriev Be-12 can also operate from the water, being a turboprop amphibian which is believed to have entered service with the Soviet Navy during 1965-66. Total production is quoted as being between 100 and 120 aircraft with perhaps 80 currently in service with the Northern and Baltic Fleets. Crew complement is believed to be five and the type's primary sensors are search radar and MAD.

Like the Orion, the Ilyushin Il-38 May is based on an airliner, in this case the turboprop Il-18. Believed to have entered service in 1970, May has a crew of 12 and is equipped with sonobuoys, search radar and MAD. Production is believed to have been approximately 100 aircraft and between 60 and 70 are thought to remain in service with the Soviet Navy. Three Il-38s have been supplied to India and in 1982, a second model (May-B) was identified with extra

Top: One of the 34 BAe Nimrods operated by the RAF. In addition to search equipment, the Nimrod's size enables it to carry a wide range of AS weaponry including mines, torpedoes, depth charges, bombs and nuclear devices. Above left: A French Navy Dassault Breguet Alizé. Above right: An Italian Navy Dassault Breguet Atlantic ASW and reconnaissance aircraft.

Fixed-wing ASW aircraft

Type	Country	Powerplant	Armament	Maximum range	Maximum speed
P-3C Orion	USA	four T56-A-14 turboprops	maximum of 8733kg (19,252lb) of torpedoes/depth charges	7670km (4766 miles)	760km/h (473mph)
S-3A Viking	USA	two TF34-GE-400A turbofans	four Mk54/57 depth charges or four Mk46 torpedoes internally	3700km (2300 miles)	834km/h (518mph)
Nimrod MR 2	UK	four Spey Mk250 turbofans	homing torpedoes/depth charges internally	8340km (5180 miles)	926km/h (575mph)
Alize	France	one Dart R.Da 21 turboprop	one torpedo or three 160kg (353lb) depth charges internally; two 175kg (385lb) depth charges or six 5in rockets externally	2870km (1785 miles)	470km/h (292mph)
Atlantic	France	two Tyne R.Ty 20 Mk21 turboprops	four homing torpedoes or nine acoustic torpedoes or depth charges internally	9000km (5590 miles)	658km/h (409mph)
Be-12	Soviet Union	two AI-20D turboprops	homing torpedoes/depth charges internally; air-to-surface missiles externally	4000km (2485 miles)	610km/h (380mph)
Il-38	Soviet Union	four AI-20M turboprops	homing torpedoes/depth charges internally	7240km (4500 miles)	645km/h (400mph)

The Beriev Be-12 Mail flying-boat (right above) was the primary Soviet ASW aircraft until the introduction in 1970 of the Ilyushin Il-38 May (right below). The Il-38 provides almost twice the range of the Be-12 while its larger size enables it to carry a considerably heavier AS weapon load.

Below: A US Navy ASW helicopter lowers its dipping sonar. The advantage of this system over the sonobuoy is that the highly sophisticated and expensive sonar equipment can be easily retrieved after use and redeployed later.

Left: A US Navy SH-2F Seasprite helicopter drops a sonobuoy. Right top: In full view of a Soviet Foxtrot-class patrol submarine, a Royal Navy HAS Mk2 Sea King helicopter winches up its dipping sonar. This submarine was detected in the North Atlantic en route for Cuba. Right above: The Westland Wasp ASW helicopter which was developed to operate from small platforms on frigates and destroyers.

sensor housings on the lower fuselage.

The Bear-F is a dedicated ASW variant of the long-running Tu-20/142 family. First identified in 1973, Bear-F has a slightly lengthened fuselage and was initially equipped with search radar and sonobuoys as its primary sensors. In September 1980, an example was recorded with a streamlined fairing mounted on top of the fin which may indicate that a MAD installation has been added.

Current ASW helicopters include the US Kaman Seasprite and Sikorsky Seaking and Seahawk, the British Westland Lynx, Sea King and Wasp, the French Aérospatiale SA 321 Super Frelon, the Italian Agusta-Bell AB/204/212 AS series, and the Soviet Kamov Ka-25 Hormone, Ka-32 Helix and Mil Mi-14 Haze.

The Kaman SH-2 Seasprite is a three-seat light ASW helicopter developed from an original utility design during the early 1970s. Sensors carried by the type comprise a search radar, towed MAD and sonobuoys. The Sikorsky SH-3 Sea King four-seater is one of the most widely used ASW helicopters in the world. First flown in March 1959, the SH-3 has been developed in three versions by the parent company (the SH-3A/D/H) and a further three by the British Westland concern (HAS 1/2/5). In addition, Agusta has licence-built the SH-3D for the Italian and other navies and West Germany is currently giving its SAR Sea Kings an ASW capability. The family as a whole uses a wide range of sensors including search radar, dipping sonar, sonobuoys and towed MAD. The Sikorsky SH-60B Seahawk first flew in December 1979 and has been produced for the US Navy as a partial replacement for the Seasprite. Crew complement on the new type is three and the SH-60B is fitted with search radar, sonobuoys, a towed MAD, passive receivers and a ship-to-plane data link.

The British Westland Wasp was a fairly simple

ASW helicopters

Type	Country	Powerplant	Armament	Maximum range	Maximum speed
SH-2F	USA	two T58-GE-8F turboshafts	two homing torpedoes externally	680km (422 miles)	265km/h (165mph)
SH-3D	USA	two T58-GE-10 turboshafts	two Mk46 homing torpedoes externally	1200km (745 miles)	254km/h (158mph)
Sea King HAS 5	USA/UK	two Gnome 1400-1 turboshafts	four homing torpedoes or four depth charges externally	1230km (765 miles)	208km/h (129mph)
SH-60B	USA	two T700-GE-401 turboshafts	two Mk46 torpedoes or two depth charges or two air-to-surface missiles externally	–	269km/h (167mph)
Wasp HAS 1	UK	one Nimbus 503 turboshaft	two Mk44 torpedoes externally	488km (303 miles)	193km/h (120mph)
Lynx HAS 2	UK	two Gem 2 turboshafts	two Mk44/46 torpedoes/four Sea Skua or four AS.12 missiles externally	593km (368 miles)	232km/h (144mph)
SA 321G	France	three Turmo IIICB turboshafts	four homing torpedoes or two ASM.39 missiles externally	1020km (634 miles)	275km/h (171mph)
AB.204 AS	Italy	one T53-L-9 turboshaft	two Mk44 torpedoes externally	426km (264 miles)	222km/h (138mph)
AB.212 AS	Italy	one PT6T-3B turboshaft	two Mk46 torpedoes or two depth charges or two air-surface-missiles externally	420km (262 miles)	260km/h (161mph)
Ka-25	Soviet Union	two GTD-3 turboshafts	nuclear depth charges/torpedoes internally	644km (400 miles)	209km/h (130mph)
Ka-32	Soviet Union	two GTD-3 (?) turboshafts	nuclear depth charges/torpedoes internally	965km (600 miles)	240km/h (150mph)
Mi-14	Soviet Union	two TV3-117 turboshafts	nuclear depth charges/torpedoes internally	483km (300 miles)	240km/h (150mph)

Above: A Royal Navy Westland Lynx operating from HMS *Engadine*. The Lynx is equipped with dipping sonar, search radar and passive receivers and can carry torpedoes, depth charges and air-to-surface missiles. Below: A Soviet Ka-25 which equips the Kresta II-class cruisers of the navy.

ASW helicopter which entered service in late 1963. The Wasp HAS 1 carried no sensors, relying totally on its parent ship for target location. ASW Wasps are or have been flown by the navies of Brazil, Holland, New Zealand and South Africa in addition to that of Britain where it has been superseded by the Lynx.

The Westland Lynx is an Anglo-French project which has been developed as both an army and a naval ASW helicopter. First flown in March 1971, ASW Lynx is in service with the navies of Britain, France, Argentina, Brazil, Denmark, West Germany, the Netherlands, Norway and Nigeria. Sensors fitted to the type include search radar, dipping sonar and passive receivers (Royal Navy only).

The Aérospatiale SA 321 Super Frelon three-engined helicopter first flew in December 1962 and an ASW variant, the SA 321G, entered service with the French Aéronavale during the late 1960s. Some 24 machines were delivered, fitted with search radar and dipping sonar.

The Agusta-Bell AB212 AS is the latest ASW model developed by the Italian company from the Bell UH-1 Huey. The earliest member of the family was the AB204 AS which was based on the UH-1B and was equipped with search radar and dipping sonar. The AB212 AS is based on the later UH-1N airframe and carries search radar, dipping sonar, towed MAD and passive receivers. The two versions have been supplied to the navies of Italy, Spain, Greece, Turkey, Peru and Venezuela.

The Kamov Ka-25 Hormone-A is believed to have entered service with the Soviet Navy during 1965-66. Equipped with search radar, towed MAD and a dipping sonar, Hormone-A has been supplied to India, Syria and Yugoslavia. A replacement for this earlier type was first observed in 1981 and is now firmly identified as the Kamov Ka-32 Helix-A. Following the basic geometry of Hormone but larger, in addition the Helix-A carries sonobuoys.

The Mil Mi-14 Haze-A is an amphibious ASW variant of the Mi-8 Hip-C transport helicopter and it entered service during 1975. With a flight crew of two and 'several' systems operators, the type is equipped with search radar, dipping sonar, sonobuoys and a towed MAD. In service with the Soviet Navy (shore-based), Haze-A has also been supplied to Bulgaria, Cuba, East Germany and Libya.

Blitz on Britain

The IRA campaign on the mainland

Above: With Big Ben wreathed in smoke, firemen struggle to control the flames caused by a Provisional IRA bomb in the Houses of Parliament. This incident, in June 1974, came at the height of the IRA campaign of terrorism on the British mainland, which included the bombing of famous tourist sites, pubs used by off-duty soldiers, and commercial targets in major cities.

The basis for any hope the Provisional IRA possessed of forcing Britain to abandon Northern Ireland was the perception that the British people and the British government were less than 100 per cent committed to the Province. If the Provisionals could make the retention of Ulster within the United Kingdom expensive enough in terms of money and lives, Britain might decide that withdrawal was the preferable option.

By 1973 this strategy, pursued through bombings and shootings in Northern Ireland, was clearly not going to succeed, at least in the short term. Britain had shown its readiness to accept the level of army casualties the Provisionals were capable of inflicting, while the damage inflicted on businesses and the civilian population of Northern Ireland did not directly affect the British public and its leaders. In this situation, the logic of extending terrorist activity to mainland Britain was undeniable.

There had already been one terrorist attack in Britain since the present Irish troubles began, the bomb explosion at the Parachute Regiment barracks in Aldershot on 22 February 1972 which killed a Catholic army chaplain, five cleaners and a gardener. But this was an isolated act by the Official IRA, expressly designed as a revenge for the Bloody Sunday incident in Londonderry the same month. When on 8 March 1973 the Provisionals exploded car bombs near the Old Bailey and Scotland Yard – timed to coincide with a poll on the border issue then taking place in Northern Ireland – it was to be the start of a completely new series of concerted campaigns.

The Provisionals' technique for conducting operations in Britain was based on a small tightly-knit group of relatively experienced personnel, known as an active service unit (ASU). They had no difficulty infiltrating mainland Britain, given the lack of effective controls at entry points from Ireland. Once in the country, they would generally take advantage of the anonymity of large cities: a couple of Irishmen renting a flat in a multi-occupancy building would attract no attention to themselves. They were unlikely to encounter inquisitive neighbours or a prying landlord. To maintain security, contacts with people outside the ASU would ideally be kept to a minimum. The supply and storage of explosives constituted unavoidable high-risk areas; one answer was to import materials from the continent in freight containers – unlikely to be opened by customs – and store them in lock-up garages, but even this was vulnerable to police searches. Known pro-IRA or revolutionary left-wing activists in Britain were extremely vulnerable to police investigation, and if such people became involved in bombings or simply came into contact with a bombing team, the authorities' task of finding the terrorists was greatly simplified, but a tight ASU was impossible to catch except by the chance methods of patrols, searches and tip-offs from members of the public.

During the summer of 1973 Provisional IRA

Above: A bomb, planted in the luggage compartment of this coach carrying British servicemen and their families, killed 12 when it exploded on the M62 on 4 February 1974.

attacks in England became a commonplace. There was a spate of firebomb incidents in prestigious central London stores such as Harrods and Liberty's, as well as several large explosions. On 12 September two bombs killed six people in London, a foretaste of things to come. There was also an outbreak of bombings in Birmingham, one device killing the bomb-disposal expert sent in to defuse it.

But it was not until 1974 that the full horror of a terrorist campaign was brought home to the British public. Bombings of targets including Madam Tussaud's and the Boat Show in January inflicted no injuries, although they caused much material damage. On 4 February, however, a 25kg (50lb) bomb exploded on a coach carrying army personnel from Manchester to Catterick along the M62. Nine soldiers and three civilians were killed. This heralded a series of attempts to hit at army personnel off their guard – a far softer target than the alert and well-defended soldiers in Northern Ireland. The Clare-Deverell barracks in Ripon was bombed in March, for example, and in October a bomb was left in a pub in Guildford frequented by soldiers, killing five people including four army personnel. Prestige targets in London continued to be hit: Westminster Hall in the Houses of Parliament was bombed in June and the Tower of London in July.

Public outrage

Despite the mounting public outrage at these incidents, successive British governments had resisted pressures to introduce special legislation to deal with IRA terrorism in Britain, but the events of November 1974 were to change attitudes substantially. As a prelude, at the beginning of the month another soldiers' pub, this time in Woolwich, was devastated, killing two people. Then, on 14 November, James McDade was blown up by a device he was planting outside Coventry telephone exchange. McDade was a prominent IRA member who was a Birmingham resident, and Irish Republicans in the city were determined to demonstrate publicly their feelings at his death. Such a gesture was totally unacceptable to the authorities and on 20 November all demonstrations in memory of McDade were banned.

Early the following evening, the *Birmingham Evening Mail* received a phone call warning that bombs had been planted in the Rotunda – a major complex in the centre of Birmingham – and in a tax office in nearby New Street. Within less than 10 minutes, bombs exploded in the Mulberry Bush pub at the Rotunda and in the Tavern in the Town on New Street. The carnage in the crowded bars was appalling: the final death toll was 21, with 180 people injured, many seriously. The impact on public opinion in Britain was overwhelming, and there were even some attacks on Irish people in England. A Prevention of Terrorism Act was rushed through parliament in two days, giving the authorities the power to exclude suspected terrorists from mainland Britain, returning them to Ireland North or South, and increased police powers to hold suspects.

There was, however, no immediate let-up in the Provisionals' campaign. The following two months saw a series of bombings in London – including an

Below: Marion (left) and Dolours Price pose for a holiday snapshot in front of 10 Downing Street in the days before the terror campaign they mounted on mainland Britain.

The Balcombe Street siege

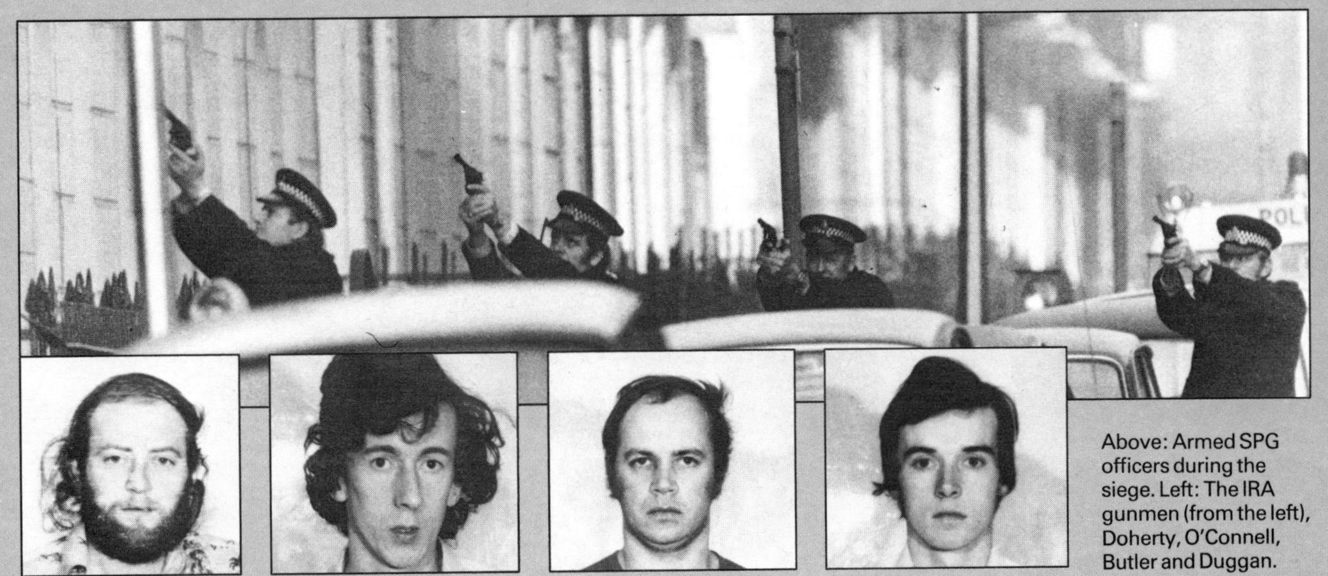

Above: Armed SPG officers during the siege. Left: The IRA gunmen (from the left), Doherty, O'Connell, Butler and Duggan.

Hundreds of plain-clothes police officers, many of them armed, were patrolling the West End of London on the evening of Saturday, 6 December 1975. They were part of an enormous trap laid by the Metropolitan Police, which was convinced that the Provisional IRA active service unit, responsible for the recent campaign of shootings and bombings in the London area, would continue its series of attacks on West End restaurants that weekend.

At about 9.00 pm, police officers patrolling in an unmarked car noted a suspicious blue Ford Cortina in Mount Street, Mayfair. Keeping the vehicle under observation, they saw it approach Scott's Restaurant, which had recently been the target of an IRA bomb attack. Two shots were fired from the Cortina and the police gave chase. Within minutes, other police vehicles, including armed units of the Special Patrol Group (SPG), had joined the pursuit.

After heading north through central London, the Cortina was cornered and abandoned in Park Road, Marylebone and the chase continued on foot. The police exchanged shots with the gunmen, who discharged several bursts of automatic fire. In the confusion, the fleeing men dropped a holdall, which was subsequently found to contain automatic weapons and traces of explosive.

The IRA men finally took refuge in a block of flats in nearby Balcombe Street, occupying the living room of Mr and Mrs Matthews, whom they took hostage. While police rushed to block any possible escape routes, the men now cornered in the small first-floor flat telephoned Scotland Yard, demanding a car to Heathrow airport, and a flight from there to the Republic of Ireland. The reaction of Sir Robert Mark, commissioner of the Metropolitan Police, was immediate and clear: there would be no deals. Having negotiated the installation of a direct landline communications link between themselves and the trapped IRA men, the police cut off the flat's telephone. The siege of Balcombe Street had begun.

The police strategy at this stage was to establish a dialogue with the besieged men, and to impress upon them the utter hopelessness of their position. Electricity supplies to the flat were for the moment maintained, in order that the sheer volume of police firepower surrounding the flat might be projected into the besieged living-room through television news bulletins.

The police were well prepared with firearms to cope with the situation. Between early 1973 and December 1975 some 15 per cent of London policemen had taken a basic four-day weapons training course, while specialist units such as D11 – marksmen who made their operational debut in Balcombe Street – had been organised and given access to equipment on the Home Office list of recommended weapons.

The key element in police strategy, however, was psychological. Throughout the siege senior police officers constantly referred to a team of doctors and psychiatrists. On their recommendation the flat was supplied with fresh water and a portable lavatory, but food was only offered in exchange for the release of Mrs Matthews. Psychological pressure was maintained during the night by shining powerful lights into the sitting-room from the street outside.

The police were unsure exactly how many IRA men were in the Balcombe Street flat. Only three spoke to the police negotiators, Detective Chief Superintendents Jim Neville and Peter Imbert, both of the Bomb Squad, and even with the use of sophisticated listening devices, there was no clear evidence of the presence of the fourth IRA man. The terrorists' rejection of the first police offer of food in exchange for the release of Mrs Matthews was seen as a signal of their determination to resist.

Police attempts to develop contacts with the gunmen received a setback on the Tuesday, when the gunmen threw the landline telephone out of the window. Acting on the advice of Home Office consultant forensic psychiatrist, Dr Peter Scott, the police now decided to reduce the pressure on the besieged men, and dropped the price of food from the release of Mrs Matthews, to simple consideration of her release as a possibility. The gunmen were in no mood to compromise, however, and continued to ignore the container of food which dangled outside the window of the Matthews' flat.

The crucial breakthrough came on the Thursday when the gunmen accepted food supplies for the first time since the siege had begun. The police restricted this food to a cold meal of sandwiches, in order to maintain a degree of pressure.

Suddenly, on Friday, 12 December, it was all over. The final surrender came unexpectedly soon for the police, who had been preparing for a more long-drawn-out siege. Firstly one of the terrorists asked for the return of the landline set, and soon arrangements were being agreed for the release of Mrs Matthews in exchange for a meal. Shortly afterwards, Mrs Matthews and a hooded IRA man appeared on the balcony of the Balcombe Street flat, and after a brief discussion, she was handed over to an armed police officer. Finally, the gunmen themselves left the flat, one by one, their hands behind their heads.

At their subsequent trial, early in 1977, the four men, Martin Joseph O'Connell, aged 25, Edward Butler, aged 28, Harry Duggan, aged 24, and Hugh Doherty, aged 26, were all found guilty of six murders committed between August and November 1975. All four were sentenced to life imprisonment.

attack on the home of the former prime minister, Edward Heath – as well as explosions in Bristol, Bath, Aldershot and Manchester. This was a time when the Provisionals were attempting to negotiate a ceasefire with the security forces in Northern Ireland, however, and a part of any deal had to be an end to operations in England. The British authorities doubted the Provisionals' ability to control their operatives on the mainland, but when an effective truce took hold in Belfast at the end of January 1975, the bombings in England also stopped.

Above: Police and soldiers stand amid the carcasses of horses slaughtered by the IRA bomb attack in Hyde Park, 20 July 1982. Right: Police officers examine the wreckage of the car in which the bomb that exploded outside Harrods, in December 1983, had been planted.

Far right: A police officer watches from Whitehall as a Provisional IRA car-bomb explodes in Great Scotland Yard during the mid-1970s wave of mainland bombings.

Limited security

Taking stock of the situation at this juncture, the British police could claim considerable successes in anti-terrorist operations. There had been numerous arrests – Marion and Dolours Price for the Old Bailey car-bombing, for example, and six men picked up boarding the Heysham-to-Belfast ferry after the Birmingham pub bombings – and the cooperation of the public was assured. But stopping the terrorists altogether was clearly out of the question; the introduction of the sort of security existing in the cities of Northern Ireland, with extensive restrictions on movement in and out of city centres and physical barriers to bomb attacks on likely targets, would have constituted a victory for the IRA's campaign to undermine normal life in Britain.

In August 1975, with the truce in Northern Ireland in tatters, the terrorist campaign in Britain began again. On 29 August a bomb in Kensington Church Street, London, killed a bomb disposal expert. Four days later two people were killed and seven injured by an explosion at the London Hilton hotel. On 10 October a man was killed by a bomb hastily abandoned outside Green Park tube station by bombers who had been interrupted while preparing an attack, and later in the month a device placed under the car of Conservative member of parliament Hugh Fraser killed his neighbour, a renowned medical specialist, who was investigating the device.

Then the target changed to expensive restaurants: on 29 October a diner in a Mayfair restaurant was killed and 17 people were injured in a no-warning attack, and similar explosions followed through to November. Provisional leader Seamus Twomey later explained these bombings as designed to hit 'the sort of person who could bring pressure to bear on the British government'. On 27 November Ross McWhirter, known to the public for his part in creating the *Guinness Book of Records* but also a leading right-wing political figure and outspoken opponent of the IRA, was gunned down at his front door.

This rash of incidents was soon to come to a close, however. On 6 December the ASU responsible for most of the autumn 1975 campaign was trapped by police in a flat in Balcombe Street, Paddington. After a lengthy siege they surrendered and were arrested. The loss of these four men was undoubtedly a severe set-back to the Provisionals' operations in England, although they were able to mount two more waves of bombings in early 1976, one in February sparked off by the death of Frank Stagg (convicted for his part in bombings in 1973) after a prolonged hunger-strike in Wakefield prison, and the other following the collapse of the Northern Ireland Constitutional Convention in March.

The 'Great Britain Brigade'

But by mid-1976 the Provisionals were in some disarray both in Northern Ireland and in Britain. British intelligence work had taken a heavy toll of terrorists. In Britain alone more than 100 people had been convicted of involvement in the bombings. The Provisionals were forced to rethink their strategy and to tighten up their organisation. After a lull during which this reorganisation took place, by the beginning of 1977 the Provisionals' 'Great Britain Brigade' was ready for a show of strength. On 29 January

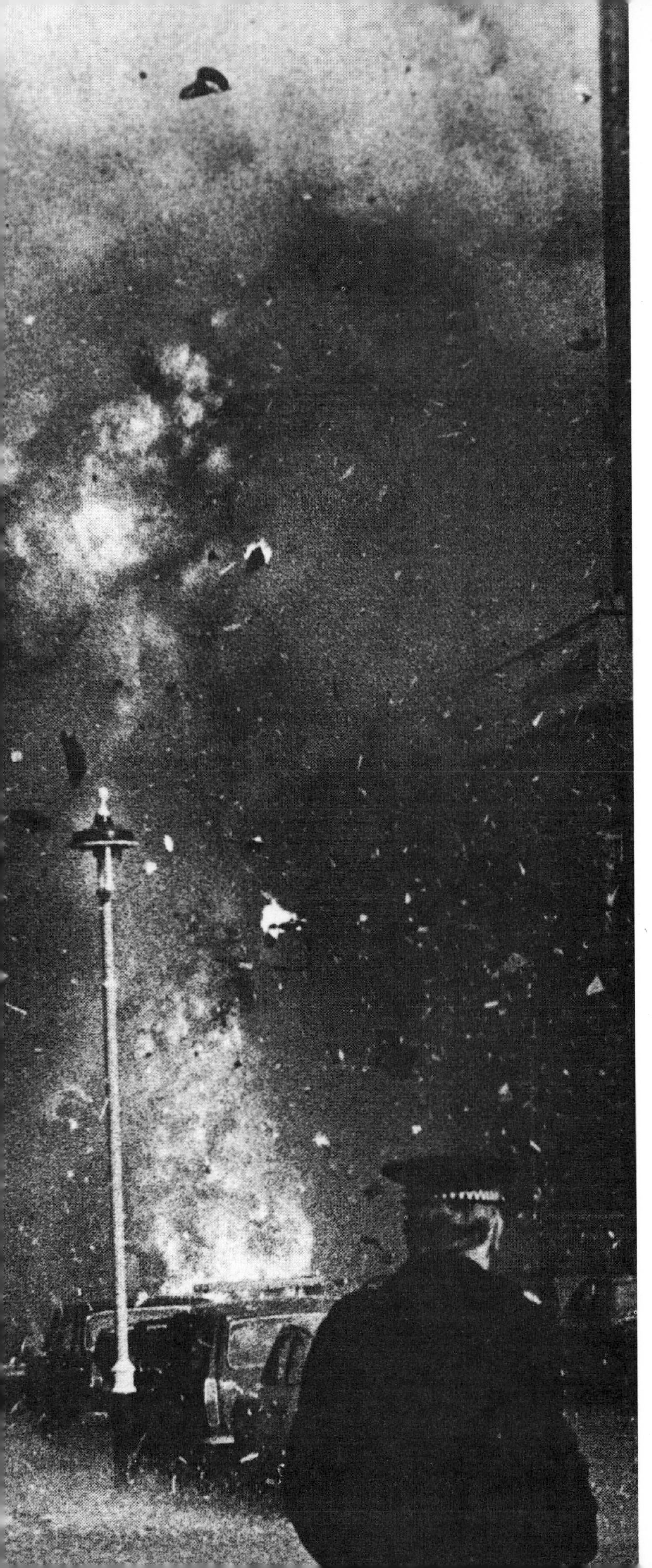

they set off no less than 13 devices in less than an hour in London's Oxford Street area, in some cases using the new-style incendiary bombs which had appeared in Ulster the previous year.

The Provisionals' main difficulty standing in the way of another major campaign was, as one of their spokesmen admitted in mid-1978, the problem of organising adequate supplies of explosives and other essential materials. In any case, their strategic thinking was turning against attacks on shopping centres or leisure facilities in favour of strikes against the army, major industrial installations and leading public figures. In January 1979 a gasometer in Greenwich was blown up and an explosion made a hole in a fuel storage tank on Canvey Island. In March the Provisionals extended their campaign to Europe, assassinating the British ambassador to the Netherlands, Sir Richard Sykes, and later taking the British Army of the Rhine as a target.

It was also in March 1979 that the Provisionals' rival, the Irish National Liberation Army (INLA), first made its mark in Britain by killing the Conservative Party's Northern Ireland spokesman Airey Neave; a 1kg (2lb) bomb strapped to his car exploded as he drove out of the House of Commons' underground car-park.

A failed campaign

Although attacks continued sporadically, through 1980 and the first nine months of 1981 the Provisionals concentrated their propaganda effort on the hunger strikes in Ulster prisons. They believed that bombs in England would tend to undermine their efforts to win public sympathy. The moment the hunger strikes were called off, at the start of October 1981, a wave of bombings struck London. On 10 October two passers-by were killed in a nail-bomb attack on British soldiers outside Chelsea barracks. The following week Lieutenant-General Sir Stuart Pringle lost a leg when his car exploded outside his London home. Further bombings included three in Oxford Street, one of which killed a bomb-disposal expert.

The wave of bombings passed, but the Provisionals' ability to strike with appalling effect remained unblunted as the 1980s wore on. On 20 July 1982 they blew up the Regent's Park bandstand where a detachment of the Green Jackets were giving a concert, and almost simultaneously devastated a troop of Household Cavalry which was riding past Hyde Park on their way to Buckingham Palace. Nine people died as a result of these attacks and many suffered appalling injuries, as did the cavalry horses. In December 1983 a car-bomb in front of Harrods during the pre-Christmas shopping rush killed five people; a Provisional spokesman condemned the unit which had carried out the attack, but it was not certain that the return to indiscriminate attacks on the public lacked official sanction from the terrorist leadership.

Despite their proven ability to operate as terrorists in England, the Provisionals must be forced to regard their campaign on the mainland as essentially a failure. The notion that the British public might be terrorised into support for the movement to pull troops out of Northern Ireland has proved totally false. As in most other countries where urban guerrilla tactics have been used, in England the terror campaign has been able to inflict damage but unable to affect policy in any way useful to the terrorists.

Graham Brewer

Bombs and bomb-disposal

A war of nerves and technology

The army officer shouted: 'Fire!' A second later the car-bomb exploded. What had been a Vauxhall became a tangled, roofless wreck, a fierce fireball erupting at its centre, the sound of the blast pounding and echoing. 'That,' he said, as the flames roared and crackled, 'is what we try to prevent.'

But this time it had all been deliberate. The old car with a blast incendiary inside it was on the testing range at the Army's School of Ammunition in Warwickshire, where the Royal Army Ordnance Corps (RAOC) trains the men who must risk their lives dealing with bombs in Northern Ireland, Britain – and sometimes elsewhere in the world.

It was the mass bombing of cities in World War II that first brought bomb-disposal to the fore. Then, in the postwar period, the British Army found itself having to cope with booby-traps and other terrorist devices in the colonies – particularly during the campaigns in Palestine and in Cyprus. It was during the struggle against Provisional IRA terrorism from 1970 onwards, however, that the greatest advances in bomb-disposal were achieved.

The army's bomb disposal unit in Ulster – 321 Explosive Ordnance Company – has 'neutralised', as they put it, over 3500 bombs in the Province since the start of the troubles in 1969. The actions of the Provisional IRA have provided a severe test for the Ammunition Technical Officers (ATOs) who confront the bomb-disposal task – or explosives ordnance disposal (EOD), as it is known – and their training involves not only instruction in the very latest technical developments but also a severe test of their psychological fitness to cope with tension and function with analytical calmness in the face of any situation at any moment of the day. For the RAOC's bomb-disposal teams the war against the bomber is a constant one – a battle of wills and wits as each side tries to stay ahead of the other, using technology, experience and an understanding of the adversary's mind.

Primitive beginnings

When the Provisionals' bombing campaign began in earnest in 1971, both their devices and the army's response were primitive by later standards. A substantial package of commercial gelignite attached to an alarm clock was originally the terrorists' staple device – an effective enough weapon as long as nothing went wrong with the timing. Many ATOs initially considered it their business to go in and defuse a bomb by hand, often with more heroism than circumspection. The result was the loss of far more of these brave men than the army could afford, especially when the Provisionals began to add anti-handling devices to their bombs – an explosive charge attached to a microswitch sensitive to the slightest movement. Techniques for dealing with bombs from a distance were fairly straightforward and often improvised. The main principle was to disintegrate the charge: suspected car-bombs were blown up, anti-tank rounds were fired against devices, and on some occasions army marksmen were even used to shoot the timing mechanism off the bomb.

By 1972 the Provisionals had started to manufacture their own explosives, since supplies of commercial gelignite were drying up after tighter controls had been imposed. Using such readily available substances as chemical fertilisers and weedkillers – sodium chlorate, for example – sugar and fuel oil, they were able to make large quantities of very powerful explosive. The disadvantage was that many of these mixes were highly unstable, and especially

Below: A charge, planted by a remote-controlled army 'Wheelbarrow', explodes in a car suspected of containing a terrorist bomb. Notice the wire, bottom left, running from the car to where army bomb-disposal experts can detonate the device at a safe distance.

Below right: Flames gut the La Mon Hotel, Comber, County Down, on 17 February 1978. The IRA incendiary bomb was attached to the grille of the dining-room window, launching a huge ball of fire into the hotel, crowded with diners on a Friday night. 12 people were burnt to death. Bottom right: A smaller-scale incendiary device, but equally effective. When planted in department stores, cassette bombs such as this can cause enormous damage.

dangerous in the hands of inexperienced terrorists. The number of 'own goals' was very high – perhaps over 50 terrorists were killed by their own bombs in 1972. This was the heyday of the car-bomb, a very wasteful use of explosives since much of the charge is used up simply in demolishing the vehicle, but with a spectacular impact on the public and the media. It also saw the development of the technique of remote-controlled bombing in rural areas, with command wires often run across the border to make the operative comparatively safe.

But 1972 was also the year when the army made a major technical advance with the introduction of a remote-controlled robot to deal with suspected bombs. Constantly up-dated, these 'Wheelbarrows' have proved invaluable through the years. The original model was a three-wheeled vehicle, but tracked versions have proved more versatile. The Wheelbarrow is electrically-driven by battery-operated motors and commands are generally transmitted through a cable from a control box, although radio-control has been introduced more recently to improve manoeuvrability. A boom rising above the chassis carries a selection of the devices which make the Wheelbarrow useful. One attachment almost always found is a television camera which transmits to a monitor viewed by the operator. Other accessories can include a shotgun – to break through windows or blast suspect packages – various handling devices and grabs, and even a downward-firing nail gun, fired into the floor once a Wheelbarrow enters a doorway, to prevent the door closing behind it. An innovation which has been very successful is the 'pig-stick', an attachment that can disintegrate an explosive charge by firing a 'bullet' of water into it at high speed. The introduction of Eager Beaver remote-controlled armoured forklift trucks made the Wheelbarrow even more manoeuvrable, being used to lift it into positions it could not otherwise reach. There is no question that Wheelbarrows, several of which have been destroyed during operations, have saved the lives of ATOs, although the operators take great care not to take many risks with these valuable devices.

A killer's 'signature'

The army also made great strides in bomb intelligence. A special unit was set up in Northern Ireland in 1974, drawn from both the army and the police, to collate all available information on bombings.

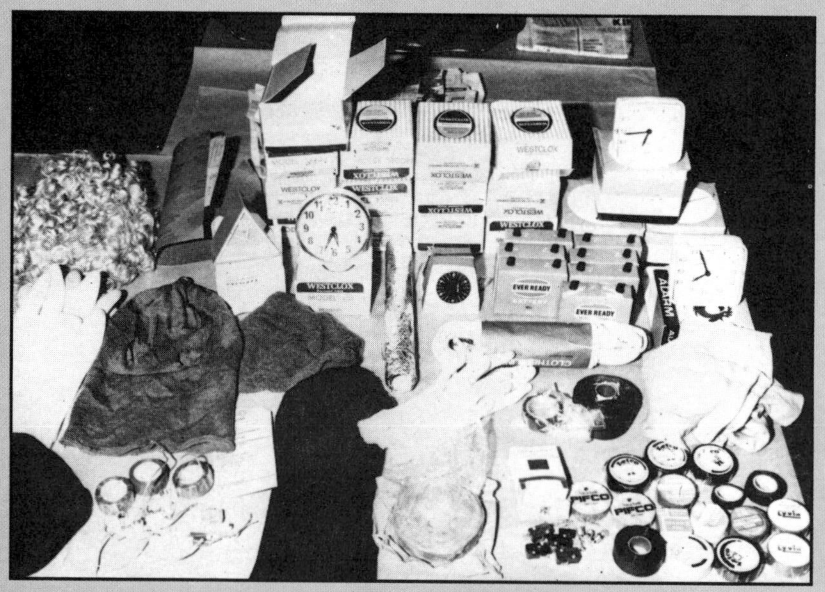

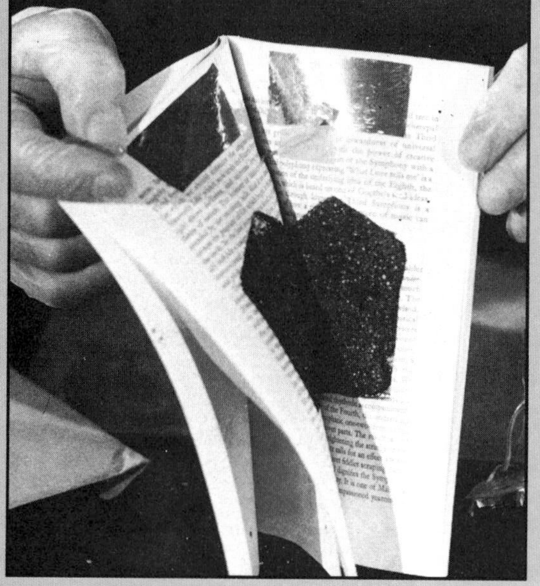

Above: The ingredients of terror – this equipment, seized by police in a raid on a Manchester flat in 1976, could have been bought in any hardware store. Left: Even small devices could be deadly – the explosive concealed in this book could cause severe injury, or even death. Opening the book would separate the metal strips at the top of the page, igniting the explosive. Timed devices, such as that shown far left, were more unreliable, and many bombers were killed while planting them.

Through scrupulous examinations of bombs – whether exploded or unexploded – the experts were soon able to build up such comprehensive dossiers on the bombers that the 'signature' of a given device could be readily identified. The intelligence unit would be able to recognise the individual bombmaker by his personal techniques almost as clearly as by a fingerprint, and they would also recognise varying sources of explosives and detonators. The amount of detail in the picture this built up – later extended to all weaponry – was such that the supply routes and movements of terrorists could be charted with great accuracy.

Electronics and expertise

But the Provisionals also developed their skills and techniques far beyond their original amateurism. They recruited a number of men with unquestionable scientific and technical expertise who, remaining far from the battlefield in the south of Ireland, gave the terrorists the benefit of some of the latest developments in such fields as electronics. They also refined the process of explosives manufacture, employing experienced people including laboratory technicians, so that 'own goals' became a thing of the past. The standard terrorist explosive became a mixture of ammonium nitrate crystals and fuel oil, known to the security forces as 'Annie'. Obtaining the raw materials for this presented no problems. Calcium-carbonate based ammonium nitrate fertiliser could easily be reduced to crystals, which on their own were almost entirely safe. The crystals were taken forward from the manufacturing centres to dumps near the border with Northern Ireland, from where they were shipped to units in the North. Only at a late stage were the crystals mixed with fuel oil to create the explosive charge.

Despite the ease with which quantities of explosive could be produced, the Provisionals also became more restrained in the size of bombs they employed. Whereas in rural areas (where the main target was security force vehicles) and on the British mainland, large explosive charges have continued to be employed, in populated areas of Northern Ireland a preference has developed for smaller devices or incendiary bombs. This was partly to preserve resources and partly to limit civilian casualties, which had proved very damaging to the Provisionals' support in Catholic areas.

Two types of incendiary devices have become typical of the Provisionals. One is the cassette incendiary, comprising a simple audio-cassette packed with incendiary material and linked to a simple time fuse. Such bombs could be placed inside stores – in the pocket of a coat on a rack, for example – to devastating effect. The other form of incendiary device was much larger: the Provisionals discovered that a small explosive charge attached to a one-gallon petrol container would produce a fireball some 5m (15 feet) in diameter. These began to appear in 1977, often being attached to the protective grilles outside windows. The fireball would project into the building, producing rapid incineration.

When using explosives rather than incendiary devices, the Provisionals have generally lost faith in the

Right top: Royal Army Ordnance Corps Ammunition Technical Officers amid the tools of their trade. The remote-controlled tracked 'Wheelbarrow' is fitted with an extendible boom, to which are mounted a TV camera and a five-round automatic shotgun. The other equipment includes a TV monitor, a telescope, and an 84mm Carl Gustav shoulder-fired recoilless gun. Right: A 'Wheelbarrow', in action on the streets of Northern Ireland, blasts open the boot of a suspect car.

use of timing mechanisms, preferring remote-control or booby-trap mechanisms. Command-wire detonation is still used, but radio control has been extensively employed in recent years. The Provisionals have become experts at radio-control techniques. Basing their equipment on model aeroplane transmitters or citizens' band gear, they have introduced pulse coding to avoid accidental interference from other radio users, and tone coding to provide a sophisticated electronic lock against jamming by the security forces. The most effective response the army has been able to mount to radio-controlled bombing has been the deployment of monitoring equipment which can pin-point the source of radio transmissions.

Radio-controlled destruction

Booby-trap bombs have varied from devices responding to slight movement – on the same principle as the anti-handling contraption – to sophisticated light-sensitive mechanisms using photo-electric cells. On one occasion, for example, a soldier who ripped down a pro-IRA poster uncovered a light-sensitive cell cleverly concealed under it, setting off a potentially deadly explosion. On the whole the use of booby-traps in Northern Ireland had declined by the 1980s, since the security forces were too careful and experienced to fall for them. The radio-controlled method was far more deadly and difficult to combat.

The Provisionals have become the terrorist world leaders in bombing techniques, but through countering them the British Army has equally come to lead the world in EOD. The RAOC training programme guarantees a constant supply of men with the highest level of technical knowledge and totally reliable psychological balance – 'neither cowards nor cowboys,' as it has been expressed.

Stuart Birch and Brian Markworthy

The sun sets over HMS *Ark Royal*, a symbol of the global role Britain was leaving behind. Inset left: A Parachute Regiment patrol peers across the Berlin Wall into East Germany. The British Army of the Rhine and the Royal Navy's force of Polaris submarines (inset below), now form the most important elements of Britain's Europe-centred defence policy.

Searching for a role

British defence policy, 1968-75

The period between 1968 and 1975 was one of general uncertainty in British defence policy. Despite the categorical nature of the British government's supplementary statement of 16 January 1968, ordering a withdrawal of forces from east of Suez by 1971, after which they would be 'concentrated in Europe', subsequent trends and decisions suggested that neither the Labour nor the Conservative Party was sure of its defence priorities. The retention of bases in the Mediterranean, at Hong Kong and at the host of staging-posts designed to allow a rapid deployment of reinforcements to Southeast Asia, implied a continued desire for global capability, while the declared commitment to Europe lacked both substance and conviction.

Initially, this was perhaps understandable – the habits of Empire died hard and the rejection of Britain's second application to join the EEC (November 1967) precluded a political concentration on Europe – but it ran counter to developments on the international scene. In August 1968 the Warsaw Pact invasion of Czechoslovakia acted as a timely reminder of Soviet strength and capabilities, focussing attention onto the manpower and equipment deficiencies of the Nato alliance and reinforcing the need for close cooperation to maintain an effective deterrent. So far as Britain was concerned, there is evidence to suggest that the Labour government recognised the importance of Europe – Prime Minister Harold Wilson highlighted the 'need for the greater unity of Europe so that the view of Europe as a whole could be more strongly concentrated on any threat to freedom in Europe' and Secretary of State for Defence Denis Healey advocated the revival of a strong 'Eurogroup' within Nato – and this was reflected among the allies as a body when, in September 1968, they voted to halt any further reduction of Western forces, but it was only a passing phase. In an era of growing detente, epitomised by the start of the Strategic Arms Limitation Talks (SALT) in 1969 and the development of West Germany's policy of *Ostpolitik,* Europe seemed secure enough, particularly beneath the nuclear umbrella provided by the United States. Such an optimistic analysis was preferred by most West European countries, including Britain, as it avoided the need to devote large amounts of money to defence improvements.

Nevertheless, when the Conservatives re-entered office in June 1970, they inherited the framework of a 'Eurocentric' defence policy, in which the traditions of global commitment had been eroded and a regional concentration at least explored. This undoubtedly suited the new prime minister, Edward Heath, whose 'Europeanism' was already well known and was soon to lead to Britain's accession to the EEC (effective from 1 January 1973), although it would be wrong to imagine that he was responsible for a final shift to Europe in defence matters. On the contrary, his term of office (1970-74) saw a significant return to global commitments as the right-wing of his party sought to overturn what it saw as the disastrous consequences of Healey's defence cuts of 1966-68. As early as July 1970 a supplementary statement extended the life of the aircraft-carrier force and spoke of a need for Britain to 'resume, within her resources, a proper share of responsibility for the preservation of peace and stability in the world'; a sentiment which quickly led to the negotiation of a Five-Power Defence Agreement (1971) whereby token British forces would cooperate with those of Australia, New Zealand, Malaysia and Singapore to protect collective interests in Southeast Asia. At the same time, the deployment of a small British contingent (principally drawn from the Special Air Service Regiment) to Oman to aid the Sultan in his counter-insurgency campaign in Dhofar Province, implied a revival of interest in the Gulf area, while a decision to maintain the Simonstown Agreement with South Africa and, more controversially, to sell arms to that state, indicated an intention to project policy towards the South Atlantic. Cuts to the size of the British Army were cancelled – in 1970 the imminent disbandment of the Argyll and Sutherland Highlanders and the amalgamation of the Gloucestershire and Royal Hampshire Regiments were deferred – and there was even talk of reintroducing the fifth boat to the Polaris fleet, despite its cancellation in 1964.

But such a reversal of policy trends could be no more than a temporary affair. Healey had been forced to devise his reforms in a desperate attempt to save money, and this continued to be a major consideration, particularly at a time of increased commitment to Northern Ireland. Simultaneously, the Europeans were demanding a firmer British commitment to regional defence, in line with Heath's declared policy of political and economic integration. These two factors worked together – stronger European links would offer financial savings through 'burden-sharing' of defence tasks and weapons development – and further pressure was exerted by the perceived need to create an effective European voice in the process of East-West relations. The American monopoly of negotiations with the Soviets manifested in the SALT agreement of 1972 and even in the preliminary stages of the more obviously regional Mutual and Balanced Force Reduction (MBFR) talks and the Conference on Security and Co-operation in Europe (CSCE), had led to strains in the Atlantic alliance, producing a widespread feeling that if European views were to be taken into account, the Europeans themselves had to be capable of expressing them as part of, or even separate from, the American negotiating stance. Britain was an essential link in this chain, enjoying a 'special relationship' with the United States which the Europeans needed to exploit if they were to prevent a break-up of Nato. This became even more crucial in October 1973, when American policies towards the Middle East during the Yom Kippur War – policies which included a unilateral nuclear alert in response to Soviet threats to intervene with force to protect Egypt – alienated the European states and threatened to destroy the alliance. It began to look as if the Eurogroup would have to assume responsibility for its own defence and if that was to stand any chance of success, Britain and her Polaris nuclear force, together with her conventional armed services, had to be included.

A commitment to Europe

Heath was therefore under mounting pressure to introduce a more definite European defence commitment, and this was further increased by one of the more obvious results of the Yom Kippur War – the sudden and dramatic rise in oil prices. At first glance, this might be assumed to have acted as a reinforcement to Conservative policies of renewed commitment to the Gulf, but in reality it produced such an economic crisis in the West that already-stretched defence budgets came under intolerable strain, enhancing the attractions of burden-sharing and resource concentration. Britain suffered more than most, having been economically overstretched since the end of World War II, and amid raging inflation and attendant social unrest, Heath's government was defeated at the polls in March 1974. It was replaced by a Labour administration which even after another election in October could command only a small majority in the Commons, leaving it vulnerable to left-wing pressures for reduced defence spending. In December 1974 it was announced that £4.7 billion was to be cut from the defence budget over the next five years and the new secretary of state for defence, Roy Mason, was presented with the problem of how best to achieve this without undermining the essential security of the state.

Mason was probably given the outline requirements of this task at a Cabinet meeting in November 1974, the central theme being a need to reduce the burden of defence spending to levels consistent with those of the other Eurpean members of Nato. There certainly appeared to be a discrepancy – according to 1974 figures, Britain was devoting about 5.5 per cent of her annual gross national product (GNP) to defence, compared to an average in Europe of between 3 and 4 per cent. Admittedly, in terms of hard cash, this did not necessarily mean that Britain was spending more but so far as expenditure priorities were concerned, it was an anomaly. The declared aim of Mason's review was to reduce the figure to 4.5 per cent of GNP, and although he approached the problem sensibly, consulting closely with the chiefs of staff, nothing could prevent the introduction of radical solutions. The results were presented to the Commons in March 1975 and they were dramatic. In order to effect immediate financial savings, manpower levels in the armed forces were to be reduced by 38,000 over the next four years, the 'commando carrier' building programme was cancelled and deadlines for the delivery of a number of new weapons were 'stretched'. Of much more significance, however, was the section of the review which dealt with long-term strategic priorities, for it was firmly laid down that henceforth Britain was to devote her defence resources overwhelmingly to Nato. Other needs were specified – 'to provide insurance in cases where foreign or domestic policy is not able to solve problems by peaceful means' and 'to contribute to foreign policy and help to protect overseas interests' –

Top: A Puma helicopter of No. 230 Squadron RAF lifts in supplies to a British Army outpost in Belize. These outposts, strung along the border with Guatemala, and isolated by thick jungle, depend totally on helicopter support. One of Britain's few remaining military commitments overseas, Belize has a garrison of 1800, including an armoured reconnaissance troop (above), and one parachute battalion (above right).

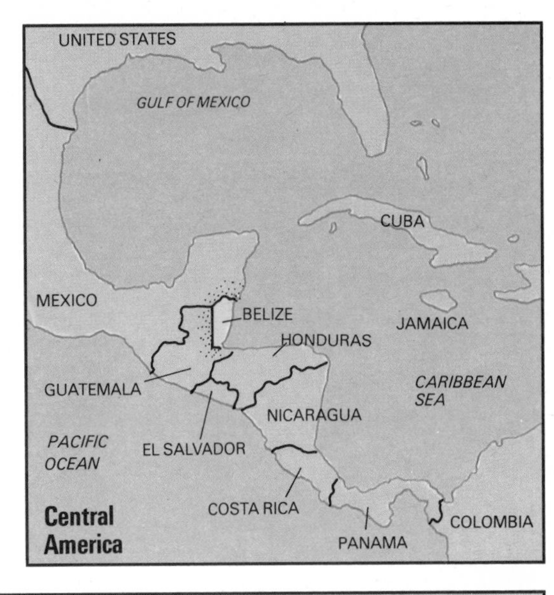

but these were subordinate to the overriding priority of European commitment.

Such a policy review clearly necessitated changes to the existing deployment of the armed services, and these too were laid down in 1975. All British forces, it was announced, were to be withdrawn from Malaysia/Singapore, the Indian Ocean and Malta by 1979; Hong Kong was to be made the responsibility of a self-contained Gurkha Field Force; no warships were to be deployed on a regular basis east of Gibraltar; RAF Transport Command was to be drastically cut; research and development of new weapons was to be curtailed and certain residual commitments overseas, including the Sovereign Base Areas on Cyprus, were to be reviewed. The Polaris force was retained

Belize – an enduring commitment

Belize, or British Honduras as it was known before June 1973, is a largely empty, jungle-covered territory of about 20,500 square km (8000 square miles), situated between Mexico and Guatemala on the east coast of Central America. First settled by British wood-cutters in 1638, it now contains approximately 175,000 people from a bewildering array of ethnic groups, including Caribbean blacks, Spanish-speaking whites, Mayan Indians and even Chinese, held together by a common desire to retain their independence from neighbouring states. They have good reason to feel threatened: since the demise of the Spanish-American empire in the 1820s both Mexico and Guatemala have laid claim to all or part of Belize and the territory has remained distinct only because of British protection.

Guatemalan claims have proved the more pressing, causing a series of crises since the end of World War II which have yet to be fully resolved. In February 1948, as Guatemalan troops massed on the border, Britain had to despatch a naval force, comprising two warships carrying elements of 2nd Battalion, Grenadier Guards, and although this proved sufficient to deter invasion, an infantry company had to remain behind as a permanent garrison. As Belizean nationalism, expressed through the People's United Party (PUP), developed, the external threat re-emerged, particularly when, in 1964, Britain agreed to grant internal independence. Guatemala broke off diplomatic relations with Britain and, despite United States mediation, a negotiated settlement of rival claims remained elusive. In January 1972 Guatemalan forces again moved up to the border, causing the British to send the aircraft carrier HMS *Ark Royal* into the Caribbean and to redeploy 2nd Battalion, Grenadier Guards to Belize. Although neither the United Nations nor the Organization of American States (OAS) accepted Guatemalan claims, it was obvious that the issue was still a very real one.

The PUP now demanded full independence, with no surrender of territory or off-shore mineral rights; the Guatemalans reacted with yet more troop movements. In late 1975 Britain once again responded with reinforcements to the garrison, sending nearly 1000 troops, a frigate and six Harrier 'jump-jets' to Belize. Negotiations with Guatemala continued, but to no avail, necessitating the retention of the new force levels even after Belizean independence in September 1981. Three years later, amid speculation that the British intended to withdraw as part of the Conservative government's policy of defence rationalisation, the garrison still comprised about 1800 men, centred upon a battalion of infantry with armoured reconnaissance, artillery, air defence, engineer, helicopter, naval and Harrier support. Most of the troops have little to do beyond observation and jungle training, but their existence is crucial as a symbol of continued British commitment. If that commitment should cease, with over 20,000 Guatemalan soldiers available, the prospects for long-term territorial security would probably be poor. A negotiated settlement of the problem is the only answer, although this would involve compromises which neither side seems prepared to make.

(although discussions about a replacement had already led to an unpublicised decision to up-date the existing missile system rather than purchase a new one), but in every other respect Britain was restricted to a purely regional defence role, concentrated on Europe. If this was the case, Mason concluded, the target reduction to 4.5 per cent of GNP would be achieved by 1984-85.

But the changes could not end there, for if Britain was to devote her energies to European defence, her armed forces needed to be restructured accordingly. This consideration, together with the desire to make savings wherever possible, led to changes in the British Army of the Rhine (BAOR), where the command level of brigade disappeared and the existing three armoured divisions were reconstituted as four, deploying the same overall total of tanks but enjoying a flexibility more suited to a European battlefield. At the same time, forces in Britain were reorganised into three 'Field Forces', each containing a mix of Regular and Territorial Army units and assigned specific Nato-orientated roles in the event of war. Neither innovation was definitive but the principle of European priority had been irrefutably established.

This was a decision which could (and probably should) have been made 20 years earlier, in the aftermath of the Suez affair, and the delay can have done nothing to ease the pressures upon defence spending. Nevertheless, the 1975 review was a watershed, representing for the first time a general awareness of Britain's decline from global power and a recognition that European defence had to have top priority. The process may have been forced upon reluctant politicians of both parties by means of a wide variety of domestic and foreign pressures, and it could be argued that the 1975 decision to afford priority to Europe was made for the wrong reasons, resulting from financial constraints rather than a careful consideration of security needs. But the fact remains that Britain was now pursuing a viable and relevant defence policy. The problems were by no means over – despite a reduction of spending to 4.75 per cent of GNP by 1979, the financial crisis remained, and despite the concentration on Europe, residual overseas commitments such as Belize and the Falklands continued to demand attention – but a clear set of principles and priorities had at last emerged.

John Pimlott

Above: A product of successful Anglo-French cooperation, the SEPECAT Jaguar all-weather attack aircraft was specifically designed for service in the European theatre.

Below: British accession to the EEC, at this ceremony in Brussels, was an important milestone in the long march back from Empire.

Key Weapons

THE T34 TANK

One of the most famous and successful tanks ever built was the Soviet T34. When it appeared against the Germans for the first time in mid-1941 it caused a sensation, forcing them to re-evaluate their tank and anti-tank tactics and equipment. The T34 was a masterpiece of tank design and was a major influence on further development in this field.

As the result of Soviet experience with tanks in the Spanish Civil War, it had become apparent to Soviet designers that contemporary models could not stand up to the new high-velocity anti-tank weapons that were then entering service in most armies. As a result, work was directed towards producing new types of steels and armour plate and at the same time designers from several artillery design bureaux were working on new tank guns with long barrels and higher muzzle-velocities. In addition, much effort was devoted to the development of tank diesels.

A number of interesting prototypes were produced in the late 1930s, the most promising being the T32, a design submitted by Mikhail Koshkin and Aleksandr Morozov which was able to mount a 76mm main gun. After trials at the Soviet Armoured Forces Proving Ground in Kharkov in July 1939 it was decided to increase the T32's armour and on 19 December the new design was accepted for service, receiving the designation T34. The Kharkov Locomotive Factory was pressed to produce two prototypes and at the same time the Defence Committee issued instructions that industry was to produce 220 examples of this new tank and that in 1941 a production base capable of supplying the army with significant quantities must be established.

When it first appeared, the T34 was noted for its well-shaped hull and turret armour, its powerful 76.2mm gun and its remarkable suspension, running gear and diesel engine. The use of the V-2 diesel engine reduced the fire risk and significantly increased the range of operation of this tank in comparison with those powered by conventional engines. The independent suspension, a development of the Christie system used on the BT tank, permitted high speeds even on rough terrain, while wide tracks enabled the vehicle to traverse mud and snow quite easily.

The T34 was nonetheless a crudely built tank which lacked the refinements of comparable Western vehicles, but its overall design simplicity facilitated mass-production methods and it could be rushed from the factory both quickly and cheaply. Despite the massive disruption of Soviet industry caused by the German invasion, around 40,000 T34s were produced during the war, an extraordinary engineering feat. On the other hand, component parts were often not of a high standard and breakdowns were frequent. A particular area of weakness was the transmission, so much so that some tanks carried their own spare transmissions tied down on the hull deck. In addition crew comfort and safety were minimal: working conditions were extremely cramped and within the turret quick reactions were needed to avoid the lethal recoil of the main gun. During the course of the war a series of design modifications helped improve

Previous page: T34 tanks of the 4th Guards Tank Division prepare to parade through Red Square in 1946. Above: T34 tanks being assembled at a tank plant in the Urals. The tank was first produced at Kharkov, but the German invasion led to production being shifted further east.

Left: The BT series was an ancestor of the T34. The Christie suspension system employed by both types permitted excellent cross-country mobility as demonstrated here by this BT-2.

Right and centre: Two views of a T34. Originally the turret was of rolled plate welded together but the pressures of wartime led to the introduction of a cast turret. Two models of gun were used in the T34: the Model 1939 L-11 and the Model 40 F-34 introduced in mid-1941.

Below: A T34/85 negotiates 'dragon's teeth' anti-tank barriers during the celebrations for the thirtieth anniversary of the Red Army. The Germans were impressed by its ability to move across such obstacles.

Left: Members of the T34 family in action: T34s of the Third Belorussian Front in 1944 (top); T34/85s in the Ukraine (centre); an SU-85 with two T34s behind (below). The SU-85 first entered service in August 1943 and production ended in the summer of 1944.

Top right: A T34/85 captured by the Israelis. The T34/85 has been in operation throughout Africa, Asia and Europe: it has seen action in Angola (above), the Horn of Africa, with the Egyptian Army (right), in Indochina and, most recently, in Lebanon, and had a major impact on the early stages of the Korean conflict.

reliability, although such advances did not benefit the crew who continued to have to operate in an extremely unpleasant environment.

The T34 was originally equipped with the 76.2mm L-11 gun mounted in a welded turret, but in order to accelerate production a new turret that could be quickly cast was developed by Morozov and during 1941 the new F-34 Model 40 tank gun was adopted which had a longer barrel and a higher muzzle velocity. Designers carried out modifications according to the experiences gained from combat. New tracks were employed, as were wheels with internal dampers; a new design of gun mantlet was introduced and additional armour over the hull machine-gun was installed. Different series of tanks varied in detail according to the abilities of the different factories producing them. A new model received a cast hexagonal turret and was first used during the Battle of Stalingrad, later receiving an observation cupola for the commander and a 5-speed gearbox.

During the second half of 1943 a larger turret was designed, in which was mounted an 85mm gun, a modified variant of the Model 1939 anti-aircraft gun. This new model, designated T34/85, was approved for mass production on 15 December 1943. The T34/85 was originally distributed to elite units but when production reached a high rate it became the standard tank in all armoured units.

At the end of World War II the T34, in its various models, was the Soviet Union's most important tank and it remained so until the mid-1950s when the T54 became the Soviet Army's main battle tank. The T34 was used alongside the T54 during the Hungarian intervention of 1956 and even as late as 1968 reserve units crossed the border into Czechoslovakia equipped with T34s. Outside the Soviet Union the T34 has had a long career and remains in front-line service with a number of Third World armies.

The T34 formed the spearhead of the North Korean Army's armoured formations when they swept

through South Korea in the summer of 1950. The 150 T34s deployed by the North Koreans proved to be the major threat to the hard-pressed South Korean and US forces in the early stages of the conflict. The T34's armour protection was immune to the US infantry's 2.36in Bazookas and it was only when the North Korean tank forces were overwhelmed by aerial interdiction and tank counter-assault that the threat of the T34 was contained. Certainly the T34 was a more rugged combat tank than the US M4 Sherman.

In the Middle East the Soviet-supplied Arab armies deployed T34s on a number of occasions. During the 1956 war the T34 was the main battle tank of the Egyptian Army but the superiority of Israeli tactics ensured that the tank had little effect on the course of the conflict. Since the 1960s the Arabs have received more advanced tanks but a number of T34s still remain in reserve.

In Africa the T34 has been used in those disputes in which the Soviet Union and her allies have an interest. Thus T34s have seen action in the Horn of Africa in the conflict between Somalia and Ethiopia, and in Angola South African raiding forces have encountered T34s operated by the Cuban-backed Angolans.

T34s saw action in the wars in Indochina, being used by the communists in Vietnam, Cambodia and Laos. Although no match for the well-armed troops of the US Army the T34 proved itself an effective fighting vehicle when used against poorly-equipped and demoralised troops of the various US-backed governments.

Not only did the T34 have a long life as a conventional tank, but it has subsequently become a highly versatile armoured fighting vehicle. A whole range of tank recovery vehicles have been developed from the T34 by Czechoslovakia, East Germany, Poland and the Soviet Union. In the area of self-propelled weapons the T34 chassis has provided the basis for the Soviet SU-85 and SU-100 SPGs, while in Egypt T34s have been fitted with 100mm anti-tank guns and in Syria a number of T34s have had their turrets removed and 122mm D-30 howitzers installed. The Chinese Army has utilised the T34 as a self-propelled anti-aircraft gun system. Designated as the Type 63 SPAA gun, it consists of a T34 tank minus its turret which has been replaced by a new armoured mounting holding two 37mm AA guns. Possessing an effective rate of fire of 80 rounds per minute it has a vertical range of 8000m (26,250ft). A number of Type 63s have been employed by the Vietnamese armed forces.

T34/85 Medium Tank

Crew 5
Dimensions Length (gun included) 7.5 m (24 ft 7in); width 2.92m (9ft 7in); height 2.39m (7ft 10in)
Weight 32,000kg (70,547lb)
Engine V-2-34 12-cylinder water-cooled diesel developing 500hp at 1800rpm

Performance Maximum road speed 50km/h (31mph); range 300km (186 miles); vertical obstacle 0.79m (2ft 7in); trench 2.49m (8ft 2in); gradient 30 degrees

Armour 18mm-60mm (0.71in-2.36in)
Armament One 85mm M1944 Z15-S53 gun; two 7.62mm DT machine guns

Right: A Czech T34 chassis equipped as a bridgelayer. First publicly displayed in 1960, the bridgelayer has a maximum span of 22m (24yds).

Right: An armoured recovery vehicle based on a T34 chassis being used for construction work in Czechoslovakia. Engineering troops often engage in building work in Warsaw Pact countries.

Below: A Chinese Type 63 self-propelled AA gun, exhibited in the United States. These are also used by the Vietnamese, who have themselves built similar models.

Bitter fruits

The post-independence civil war in Angola

In 1964 the wind of change had blown across most of black Africa, but Angola – the heartland of Portugal's African empire – appeared to be firmly and securely under Portugal's control. In what was then Leopoldville (now Kinshasa), capital of what was then the Congo (now Zaire), were the rundown headquarters of what at the time appeared to be the chief Angolan liberation movement, the Revolutionary Government of Angola in Exile (GRAE). It was run by a rather sinister figure in dark glasses, the 'president', Holden Roberto. His one asset appeared to be not his idle, dangerous, ganja-chewing guards but his close relationship with his brother-in-law General Joseph Mobutu (now Mobutu Sese Seko), at the time commander-in-chief of the Congolese Army and soon to be the country's autocratic ruler.

In early 1961, in the wake of the troubles and killings of Belgians in the Congo, Holden Roberto's followers in the north of Angola had massacred over 300 Portuguese settlers. The reprisals taken by Portugal's colonial army had been swift and ferocious. More than 20,000 of the Bakongo, Holden Roberto's tribe, are rumoured to have been killed.

The Bakongo tribe spread across a great swathe of territory that overlapped colonial boundaries. But their traditional capital, the capital of what had once been an extensive African empire, was the city of M'Banza in the north of Angola that the Portuguese had rechristened São Salvador. Holden Roberto had been born in São Salvador though he had lived most of his life across the river in the Belgian Congo (Zaire). It was he who had formed the first (forbidden) political parties in the Portuguese colony of Angola, and who had in 1962 proclaimed the GRAE with himself, of course, at its head. His advantage was that the Bakongo were a vigorous people who had tasted freedom and power in one part of their territories – Joseph Kasavubu, the Congo's first president, was a Bakongo – and were ready to struggle for it elsewhere. His disadvantage was that he represented only the Bakongo and that the Bakongo were limited to the north of Angola. Only about one in ten of the six million Angolans were Bakongo. It was inevitable that other leaders should spring up elsewhere in that vast country to represent the other tribal or ethnic groups.

Jonas Savimbi defected from the GRAE in 1964. He had been a close associate of Holden Roberto, playing foreign minister to the older man's president. But Savimbi, a burly, smiling bearded figure with plenty of charm, found it hard to play second fiddle to the dour Bakongo leader. He went to the south of Angola, to his own people, the Ovimbundu, who were three times as numerous as the Bakongo in Angola; and two years later he founded the União Nacional para a Independência Total de Angola (UNITA). Ever since then Savimbi has led UNITA from southern Angola, the one leader always to have fought from inside the country. After Savimbi's defection and in view of the lack of any striking successes in northern Angola or on the diplomatic front, it became hard for Holden Roberto to maintain the fiction that he was leading a united government-in-exile. The GRAE gradually faded away, to be replaced by the more militant and military Frente Nacional de Libertação de Angola (FNLA).

The third liberation movement on the Angolan scene was a somewhat more sophisticated group, the Movimento Popular de Libertação de Angola (MPLA). Founded in 1956, the MPLA was much more of an urban movement than the other two, its great strength lying in the capital of the country, the port of Luanda, where half a million people (including 150,000 Portuguese) lived. The MPLA was above all the party of the intellectuals and theorists, and as such (inevitably in the context of the struggle against the Portuguese dictatorship) very much influenced by Marxism. There were many pure blacks in its ranks – its nominal leader was a black poet, Agostinho Neto. But there were many pure Portuguese in the party too, and above all there were many *mestiços*, Angolans of mixed Portuguese-African blood, free therefore from tribal links and loyalties.

Until 1974 the Portuguese hung on. The 55,000 Portuguese conscripts needed in Angola alone were a great drain on the resources of such a small country as Portugal, but even 'Major' Iko Carreira, who commanded the MPLA forces, could only claim that his men had 'created insecurity' in roughly a tenth of

The three leaders who fought for power in post-independence Angola. Top: Jonas Savimbi, whose UNITA forces were based in southern Angola; heavily mauled by Cuban troops, UNITA gambled on South African intervention to redress the balance. Above right: Holden Roberto, leader of the FNLA which operated from bases in Zaire, relying heavily on CIA and mercenary support. Above left: Agostinho Neto, whose MPLA forces had the advantage of support from the withdrawing Portuguese garrison in the lead-up to independence, as well as the subsequent backing of Soviet arms and Cuban troops.

Angola's territory, and that was only in the remote east of the country near the border with Zambia. The FNLA was largely inactive, and UNITA suffered the disadvantage of operating in areas bordered by Rhodesia and Namibia – territories run by Portugal's white allies.

Then, on 25 April 1974, the whole situation suddenly changed. In an almost bloodless revolution the autocratic Portuguese regime was overthrown by the Armed Forces Movement and an anti-fascist Junta of National Salvation took control of Portugal, to the vast enthusiasm of the people. All governor-generals and civil governors overseas were dismissed and the feared political police was disbanded. In Angola over 1200 political prisoners were freed. Was this a prelude to decolonisation? At first it seemed not. In Angola the MPLA rather unexpectedly announced that they were ready to negotiate, but the FNLA and UNITA both declared they would fight on. On 11 May, however, the chief of staff of the Portuguese Army, General Francisco da Costa Gomes, made the startling admission that 'the armed forces have reached the limits of neuro-psychological exhaustion'. In other words, Portugal's conscript army was simply not prepared to fight on; and on 1 July, reluctantly but inevitably, the new president of Portugal, General Antonio de Spínola, formally offered complete independence to the 'overseas provinces' of Angola, Mozambique and Guinea, Portugal's 'inalienable empire' in Africa.

Portuguese abdication

Guinea became an independent state almost without difficulty two months later. In Mozambique an unofficial ceasefire in July was followed by an August truce, an attempted coup by Portuguese settlers in September (that collapsed after three days), a transitional government, and then full independence the following June. It was only in Angola that things went very wrong for the Portuguese: and they inevitably went wrong because it was only in Angola that three liberation movements were struggling for power.

It was agreed that Angola would become independent on 11 November 1975, the 400th anniversary of the founding of Luanda by the Portuguese. In the long 18-month run-up to independence the once-proud colonial masters gradually abandoned all pretence of controlling the situation and all hope of bringing the warring factions together in a transitional government. The Portuguese Army was certainly in 1974 still by far the strongest military force in the country. But it had lost the will to fight, it had swung sharply to the left, and many of its units gave open assistance to the MPLA cadres who now began to surface in Luanda and to impose their own version of *poder popular* – people's power. The longer-established Portuguese, the settlers, artisans, tradesmen and the rich minority of plantation owners, right-wing by both inclination and tradition, tended on the other hand to support anyone who opposed the MPLA. The situation in Luanda was further complicated by the presence nearby of 4000 Katangese gendarmes, relics of the Congolese civil wars. Fleeing Mobutu's bloody persecution, they had taken refuge in the east of Angola, and the Portuguese had used them as black mercenaries in their struggle against the MPLA. But after the revolution of 25 April the authorities had no idea what to do with them; they were interned near Luanda. On the other hand the MPLA knew only too well their fighting qualities; and by one of those swift reversals that often happen in African politics the Katangese gendarmes virtually became the shock troops of the MPLA in its struggle against the FNLA. Besides, the Katangese, largely Balunda tribesmen, hated the Bakongo. On the other hand an internal power struggle in the ranks of the MPLA had led to one of its vice-presidents, Daniel Chipenda, defecting to Holden Roberto's camp with 2000-3000 well-trained fighters of the 'Chipenda Brigade'. 'We do not want civil war,' Chipenda declared in January 1975, 'but if Neto wants this we are prepared to face it.' Already in Luanda there were almost daily clashes between armed groups of FNLA and MPLA supporters, which left 50 dead, then 70 dead, then at the end of April, after the fifth proclaimed ceasefire, nearly 1000 dead. Civil war was now a certainty, and the Russians took a hand: they shipped large consignments of arms to the faction they inevitably supported, the Marxist-orientated MPLA.

Predictably the Americans reacted. President Gerald Ford set aside $32 million to be channelled by Secretary of State Henry Kissinger and the Forty Committee into direct or indirect support for the rival movements, Holden Roberto's FNLA and, in the south, Jonas Savimbi's UNITA. Kissinger was determined, for reasons of worldwide prestige, not to see another 'Western' ex-colony taken over by a pro-Soviet movement. Curiously, other communists – the

Above: Although financed by the CIA, backed by neighbouring Zaire and stiffened with units of white mercenaries, FNLA troops such as these were totally outgunned by the MPLA, which was lavishly supplied with modern arms and equipment by the Soviet Union and its Cuban ally.

Chinese – now also supported the FNLA with arms and advisers (though on a very limited scale), for their own anti-Russian reasons. But what really made Kissinger see red was the most dramatic event of the low-key civil war and one that was almost immediately to transform it into a high-key affair. This was, in July 1975, the totally unexpected arrival off the shores of Angola of a small force of Cuban commandos who, with the back-up of the Soviet fleet, launched a naval assault on the UNITA-held port of Lobito and proceeded to drive UNITA forces out of the nearby vitally important railhead of Benguela.

With just over three months to go till independence Cuban President Fidel Castro proceeded to pour troops – mainly, and sensibly, black Cubans – into the country while the Portuguese, still the official rulers, looked helplessly on. $14 million had already been passed by the Americans to their ally Zairean President Mobutu, on the understanding that he would intervene with his own troops or by supplying arms to his brother-in-law Holden Roberto. Now, in reaction to the Cubans, a CIA Angolan Task Force was set up, operating from the Zairean capital, Kinshasa. The CIA's director, William Colby, told Henry Kissinger that he would need $100 million to be sure of winning the civil war; but this vast sum was not forthcoming. Indeed, in the end the US Congress cracked down and forbade the allocation of any further sums at all. But in any case much of the $32 million already allotted stuck to Mobutu's fingers, and much was wasted, on inefficient World War II rifles, or on such extraordinary expenses as the construction of an ice factory on the Zaire River to supply FNLA troops with frozen fish. Above all, after Vietnam, the Americans could not dream of sending in their own troops or even their own military advisers.

Cuban involvement

The white stronghold of South Africa had, however, been equally alarmed by the appearance of Cuban revolutionary forces on the African continent. In August 1975, South Africa reacted by sending helicopters and troops across the border to protect the hydroelectric works at Ruacaná. Meanwhile fierce fighting had been raging in Luanda where, with Cuban help and Soviet arms, the MPLA had attacked and destroyed the FNLA headquarters in the capital – 300 died and over 1000 were wounded. A month later 500 FNLA troops, besieged since the fall of their headquarters in São Pedro fort, broke through the besiegers to flee north. At once the MPLA consolidated their hold on the capital. In the south UNITA were driven out of their headquarters at Nova Lisboa (Huambo) on the Benguela railway, and moved further inland to Bié. It began to look as if all was over bar the victory celebrations. The Portuguese high commissioner, Admiral Leonel Cardoso, announced that all Portuguese troops would be withdrawn by 11 November. Hundreds of thousands of Portuguese and *mestiços* began to flee the country. The coffee, sisal and cotton crops went unpicked. The diamond industry collapsed. Soviet transport planes flew in tanks, artillery and troop-carriers for the MPLA and their Cuban allies.

But in a sense the MPLA had struck too soon, and by their very success had alarmed their neighbours. In the north Holden Roberto reorganised his forces, and President Mobutu allotted two Zairean battalions and a squadron of Panhard armoured cars to aid the FNLA. In the south, the South Africans decided to give far more committed support to UNITA. The FNLA and UNITA were temporarily reconciled; Daniel Chipenda and the Chipenda Brigade were transferred to the south to join up with Jonas Savimbi's shattered forces. In South African-ruled Namibia Colonel Santos e Castro, the tough Portuguese commander of the black troops who had fought with the Portuguese – the Flechas (arrows) – assembled a striking column, equipped with South African armoured cars and, protected by South African Alouette helicopters, crossed the frontier at the end of October, a fortnight before independence, to link up with the Chipenda Brigade and UNITA forces. By early November the column had recaptured Sá da Bandeira (Lubango) and Moçamedes and was heading for the line of the Benguela railway.

But it was in northern Angola that the drive for the capital seemed to have the greatest chance of success. Some 500 FNLA soldiers supported by two Zairean battalions and 100 fighting Portuguese settlers, drove for the capital which Holden Roberto hoped to enter in triumph on 11 November. On the eve, 10 November, a decisive battle was fought only 40km (25 miles) to the north of Luanda, at Caxito. It proved a disaster for the FNLA. Outgunned in close combat by AK-47s, terrified by the massed volleys of Soviet Katyusha rockets, the FNLA fled from what they had christened Nshila Wa Lufu – the road of death. It was almost the end of the FNLA as an organised fighting force. On the evening of 10 November Admiral Cardoso almost surreptitiously lowered the Portuguese flag, told the press unconvincingly that 'Portugal is departing without a feeling of guilt or shame' and slunk away with the remaining Portuguese troops to board the troopship *Niassa*. Next day the MPLA triumphantly proclaimed independence in Luanda with Agostinho Neto as president of the People's Republic; the FNLA triumphantly proclaimed independence in Ambriz with Holden Roberto as President of the Democratic Republic; and UNITA triumphantly proclaimed independence in its traditional (recaptured) headquarters at Nova Lisboa, proposing more modestly a 'Joint National Council for the Revolution'. In Luanda thousands of MPLA supporters fired their rifles in the air, hitting an incoming Red Cross flight and scaring away a planeload of Portuguese dignitaries who had been arriving to join in the celebrations. But in reality even for the MPLA there was not all that much to celebrate. In the south the South African-backed columns were advancing rapidly and apparently unstoppably; and in the north there was no knowing what new forms of intervention the CIA and President Mobutu might once again dream up.

In swift succession the UNITA/FNLA/Flechas columns in the south recaptured Benguela and Lobito (16 November) and Malanje airport (17 November). They were only 320km (200 miles) from the capital. But the first, fatal cracks had appeared in their unity: Chipenda's men had looted and massacred 'liberated' villages, and fighting had broken out between UNITA and FNLA troops. The South Africans had had a handful of their own supporting troops captured and, fearful of a full-scale battle with the Cubans (which the Cubans too had up to now avoided), demanded massive Western intervention – which failed to materialise. All sides drew breath in December, preparing for the last round.

Below: A burnt-out MPLA T-34/85 marks the passage of the South African column marching on Luanda. Bottom: An FNLA unit, including white mercenaries, advancing on Luanda from the north. Armed with a collection of American World War II-vintage M1 carbines and captured Soviet AK-47 assault rifles, their motley equipment was matched only by the low level of their morale.

Above: Fidel (left) and Raul Castro (far right) welcome Agostinho Neto to Cuba after the MPLA victory in the Angolan civil war. The MPLA remains heavily dependent upon Cuban support, and an estimated 25,000 Cuban troops were in Angola in the mid-1980s.

In the north Holden Roberto held three major towns strung along the Zaire border: Santo Antonio (now Sovo) on the coast, São Salvador, his 'capital', in the centre, and Maquela to the east. In despair at the poor fighting qualities of his Zairean allies, he decided (with CIA approval) to switch tack: the new plan was to hire a thousand British ex-paratroopers in order to turn the tide. Had he had time to organise recruitment, had his recruiting agents been reliable, and had recruits of the right quality been forthcoming, they might indeed have halted the Cuban/MPLA advance. But they came only in small, dispersed packets: first four, then 19, then 96, then – when it was almost too late – 23 plus eight Americans arrived. Furthermore, most of the ex-paratroopers were also ex-criminals. Their leader, a Cypriot – born Costas Georgiou – who called himself 'Colonel Callan', had spent five years in jail for armed robbery in Northern Ireland, and he was typical enough of the mercenary dregs that followed. Nevertheless, militarily, even this tiny handful showed extraordinary courage and ability in attacking the advancing Cuban/MPLA columns head on, driving deliberately into their ambushes and knocking out Soviet tanks with hand-held rocket launchers. As field commander of the FNLA, Callan virtually disbanded the black troops and relied on British and Portuguese mercenaries alone. But the only method of discipline he knew was killing; and when he had 14 of his own British mercenaries executed on 1 February for would-be desertion, morale collapsed. Two days later Callan himself was wounded and captured.

Santo Antonio fell to a surprise MPLA attack on 7 February; Maquela was evacuated two days later. The FNLA's new field commander, Peter McAleese, an ex-SAS sergeant, tried to defend São Salvador against thousands of advancing troops with only 30 mercenaries, lost seven men when one Land Rover was destroyed, and on 15 February evacuated the city itself without a fight.

Meanwhile in the south, Cuban forces now strengthened to 13,000 faced at a distance substantial South African forces, but both still avoided direct clashes except for artillery duels. Nova Lisboa, Savimbi's 'capital', again fell to the MPLA. In that battle, on 9 February, UNITA lost 600 men, and Jonas Savimbi announced wisely that he and his forces would take to the bush.

Holden Roberto, of course, was safe in Kinshasa, but a broken man, all hopes destroyed. The Americans called a halt to their operations, the CIA distributed the remaining $4.8 million in the kitty (all went to Mobutu as neither Holden Roberto nor Jonas Savimbi could be found) and in March the South African government announced that it would be withdrawing the last of its troops from the Ruacaná dam. Savimbi, his guerrilla forces reduced to a mere 100 men in the deep south, bombed from the air and tracked by Cuban/MPLA columns, appeared to be in a hopeless situation.

The civil war was over and President Agostinho Neto ruled the country. The captured mercenaries were put on trial and, amid a blaze of publicity, Callan and three others were executed. It was a triumph for the MPLA, for Castro and for the Russians, and a body-blow not merely to Portuguese pride but to South Africa, Henry Kissinger, the CIA, and in general the West.

Anthony Mockler

White power

South Africa counters black insurgency

For over two decades the white-ruled Republic of South Africa has based its security policies upon the perception of an escalating, communist-inspired military threat, both conventional and insurgent. South African fears of a conventional attack by African and/or Eastern bloc forces first arose in the early 1960s and greatly increased after the advent of Marxist regimes in Angola and Mozambique during the mid-1970s. In practice, however, southern Africa's black states have been neither willing nor able to carry out such an attack and the chief danger to the Republic has come from 'Azanian' insurgent movements.

The origins of this conflict can be traced back to the period between 1948 and 1960, years of growing confrontation between South Africa's government and the country's African nationalists. As the government proceeded to implement its policy of apartheid, strenghthening white supremacy and institutionalising racial segregation, the African nationalists became increasingly militant. The African National Congress (ANC) which had previously sought to gain limited political advances through constitutional action, turned to methods such as civil disobedience in an attempt to make the government abandon apartheid and move towards a non-racial, democratic socialist system. The Pan Africanist Congress (PAC), a rival nationalist movement founded in 1959 by former ANC members, by contrast adopted as its objective a system of government by and for blacks only. However, neither movement deflected the white government from its chosen course. As far as the majority of whites were concerned, African majority rule – of either the ANC or PAC variety – was anathema and the African nationalists were threatening the security of the state. Indeed, the government suppressed African nationalist protests with increasing severity during the 1950s and eventually, in the wake of the shooting of black demonstrators at Sharpeville on 21 March 1960, outlawed both the ANC and the PAC.

The African nationalists then reconsidered their strategy. Concluding that non-violent protest was useless, both the ANC and the PAC formed clandestine military wings with a view to overthrowing the South African state by force. The ANC, in conjunction with the outlawed South African Communist Party (SACP) created Umkhonto we Sizwe (Spear of the Nation), a predominantly but not exclusively black movement. PAC members formed Poqo, whose name – 'only' or 'pure' – indicated that it was an exclusively black African movement. Umkhonto we Sizwe decided to wage a sabotage campaign, so as to disrupt communications, undermine order and demoralise the regime and its supporters; it also sent recruits abroad for guerrilla training so that at a later stage it might initiate an insurgency in selected areas of South Africa. Poqo opted for a terrorist campaign, to be directed against whites and against non-whites – blacks, Asians and Coloureds (persons of mixed race) – who cooperated with the authorities. Umkhonto's campaign began on 16 December 1961, when bomb

Above: Political debate, South African style. The exclusion of blacks from access to political decision-making has left rioting as one of the few possible forms of political expression for the majority of the population.

Left: Nelson Mandela, born 1918 in the Transkei, became one of the most famous leaders of the ANC in South Africa during the 1950s, when he organised campaigns of civil disobedience in protest against apartheid. Leading the ANC into illegality in the early 1960s, Mandela helped organise its military wing, Umkhonto we Sizwe, and was jailed in 1962. He remains the most famous prisoner of the South African regime.

Above: Well-armed police survey the bodies of black demonstrators, victims of the Sharpeville massacre of 21 March 1960. In all, 69 Africans were killed and 178 wounded when police opened fire. The massacre shocked the world, and convinced many of the regime's internal opponents that only armed struggle would bring real change in South Africa.

attacks were carried out against government buildings and installations in several major cities, while Poqo's campaign began soon afterwards in early 1962.

At the time this twin insurgent threat appeared to pose a serious challenge to the South African government. The authorities faced the formidable task of maintaining control over a vast country – 1,221,037 square km (471,445 square miles) in size – containing 16 million people, of whom 11 million were black Africans, half a million were Asians, one and a half million were Coloureds and only three million were whites. The personnel available to perform this task were far from numerous. The South African Defence Force (SADF), an all-white force based upon a small nucleus of regulars – the Permanent Force – and selective national service, could muster some 78,000 men, if the Citizen Force – former national servicemen available for further periods of part-time service – and the Commandos or local militias were included; its standing operational strength, however, was only 11,500. The South African Police (SAP) numbered some 26,000, of whom 13,000 were black. Moreover, international opinion was hostile to the South African government. The government in Pretoria, led by Hendrik Verwoerd, had become an international pariah and the United Nations had thrown its political and moral weight behind the African nationalists.

In the event, however, the ANC and PAC campaigns soon ran into difficulties. For one thing, weapons were hard to come by. Few blacks had official access to arms and the infiltration of arms into the country was impeded by the existence of a *cordon sanitaire* of territories sympathetic to Pretoria – white-settler dominated Rhodesia and Portuguese-ruled Angola and Mozambique. The PAC had to fall back upon the use of pangas, axes, knives and assegais, while the ANC used home-made bombs that were often of poor quality. Secondly, insurgent activities were hampered by the government's apartheid regulations. The African 'homelands' were administered by officials and chiefs in the employ of the government, the movement of blacks in white areas was rigidly controlled by the 'influx' and 'pass' laws, and those blacks who lived in white areas were accommodated in separate townships easily sealed off by the police. And thirdly, blacks did not respond enthusiastically to the insurgent campaigns, either because they did not support the nationalists, or because they feared the consequences of opposing the authorities.

The insurgents' difficulties were compounded by the South African goverment's counter-measures. To some extent, Verwoerd relied upon the army, using troops to guard key installations such as dams, power stations and oil storage depots. The primary role in the counter-insurgency campaign, however, fell to the SAP, and in particular to the Security Police. Under B. J. Vorster, who became minister of justice in August 1961, the Security Police branch was rapidly strengthened and the SAP in general enlarged to 34,000 by 1964; this strength was augmented by the establishment in 1961 of a Reserve Police force, whose civilian volunteers could be called on to perform ordinary police duties, thus releasing regulars for more urgent duties. Under Vorster, the SAP was also given greatly extended powers of arrest and detention, designed to help them uncover plots and gain information from detainees. The SAP also built up its network of informers.

It did not take the police long to produce the intended results. During 1962 and early 1963 Poqo had attacked African chiefs and policemen, murdered a small number of whites and sabotaged various installations, particularly in the western Cape. By May 1963, however, over 2000 Poqo suspects had

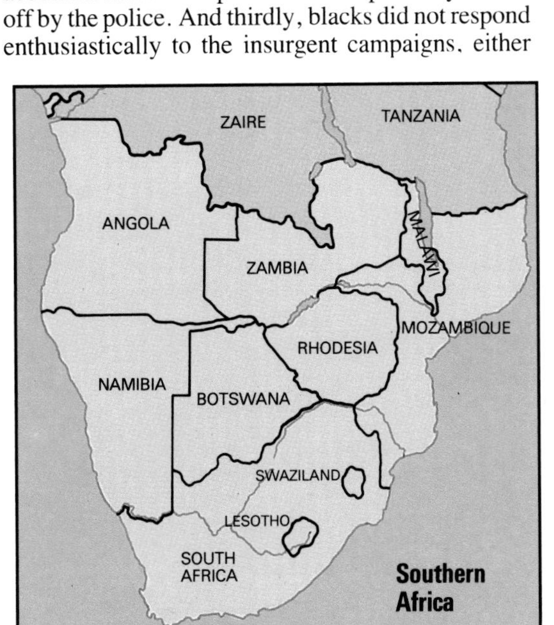

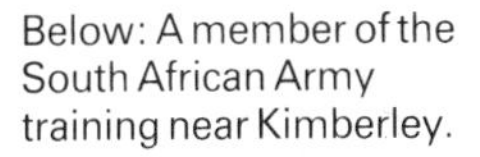
Below: A member of the South African Army training near Kimberley.

been arrested and the movement virtually broken. Umkhonto we Sizwe, which carried out nearly 200 acts of sabotage between December 1961 and May 1963, did not last much longer. Its head, Nelson Mandela, was arrested in August 1962, and in July 1963 most of its other leaders, plus valuable files, fell into police hands when the SAP raided the movement's supposedly secret headquarters at Rivonia, in the Transvaal. The African Resistance Movement (ARM), an insurgent group which was active in early 1964, met a similar fate.

Having crushed the ANC and PAC campaigns, South Africa was able to enjoy a period of immunity from insurgent attack. Over the following decade internal sabotage was virtually non-existent and attempts by the ANC and PAC to infiltrate insurgents into the Republic failed disastrously.

Despite the lack of a serious threat, the South African government made a considerable effort to enhance its defence capabilities. New equipment was manufactured or imported (despite the UN's arms embargo of August 1963) so as to modernise the SADF, conscription was extended to all white youths in 1968, and the period of service liability in the Citizen Force was also extended. These measures were symptomatic of Pretoria's growing fears over developments in nearby territories. South Africa was able to adapt easily to the independence in the late 1960s of Botswana, Lesotho and Swaziland, since all three states remained utterly dependent upon her economically. The Portuguese withdrawal from Angola and Mozambique in 1974-75, however, was a different matter, exposing South Africa's ally, Rhodesia, the buffer territory of Namibia and even South Africa itself, to the risk of guerrilla attack.

The South African government's initial response to these perceived dangers was to launch a diplomatic initiative. From the mid-1960s on, Pretoria had been pursuing a policy known as 'dialogue', designed to open up contacts and improve relations with black African states. As the Portuguese withdrew, the South African government attempted to convert dialogue into a policy of detente with black Africa. Rhodesia was pressurised into negotiating with the Zimbabwean nationalists, and Prime Minister Vorster took a similar pragmatic line towards Mozambique. Vorster made no attempt to interfere in the affairs of that country and proceeded to renew certain economic agreements with Mozambique both before and after independence in June 1975. In Angola, however, the detente policy broke down. South Africa was tempted into armed intervention in the civil war which ended in the victory of a Marxist government that backed SWAPO guerrillas fighting against South African forces operating in Namibia.

Over the following years the South African government was beset by increasing security problems. In 1980 Robert Mugabe came to power as prime minister of independent Zimbabwe, broke off consular relations with South Africa and expressed his full moral and political (though not material) support for the South African liberation movements. Relations with other neighbouring states – Mozambique, Swaziland, Lesotho and Botswana – also became strained as the Azanian nationalists, using these states as conduits, resumed their military campaign against the Republic. Following the Soweto riots of June-November 1976 thousands of young blacks had fled the Republic, many of them to join the PAC, which trained its forces in Libya and China, or the ANC/SACP, which used Tanzania, Angola and Mozambique as its main training grounds. From the late 1970s onwards both movements, but the ANC/SACP in particular, began to infiltrate insurgents into South Africa; Mozambique, and to a lesser extent Botswana, Lesotho and Swaziland, were used as infiltration routes, despite official protestations by these states that they did not support the liberation movements at the military level. Between late 1976 and late 1979 over 50 attacks were reported by the South African authorities. Subsequently, in the early 1980s, guerrilla activity escalated markedly. Attacks were made on targets such as police stations, railway lines, electricity pylons and government buildings and installations. Among the most spectacular attacks were those on the SASOL fuel complex, on 1 June 1980; on the Koeburg nuclear plant, on 19 December 1982; and on the headquarters of the South African Air Force, on 20 May 1983.

This surge of SWAPO and ANC/SACP guerrilla activity did not, however overstretch the military resources of the South African state. Using its substantial economic wealth Pretoria built up a powerful military machine with a standing operational strength of 70,000 and a total mobilisable strength of over 400, 000. Manpower was increased by extending the period of national service from 12 to 24 months, by extending the period of service liability in the Citizen Force and Commandos, and by recruiting Coloureds, Asians and black Africans on a voluntary basis. The South African government did not let the military initiative rest with the insurgents. The Portuguese withdrawal may have shifted the balance of power against white rule, but South Africa remained the regional leviathan, the dominant economic and military power. Under Pieter Botha, who became South African premier in October 1978, Pretoria began to use this preponderant power, especially in the military field, to undermine the willingness of neighbouring states to support the Namibian and Azanian guerrilla movements and the ability of those movements to continue their struggle. This policy had two facets: the launching of cross-border attacks on insurgent bases and the furnishing of military assistance to anti-government dissidents in those states.

Angola, which hosted SWAPO, bore the brunt of the cross-boarder raids. From 1978 on there were at least half a dozen major incursions into southern Angola by SADF units. Raids were also launched against what Pretoria described as ANC/SACP offices and bases in Lesotho, in December 1982, and in Mozambique in January 1981, May 1983 and October 1983. In the first of these raids into Mozambique South African forces used captured Soviet vehicles and simply drove into the Mozambican capital, Maputo, and shelled their designated targets. Perhaps more punishing has been the policy of giving military assistance to rebel groups such as UNITA in Angola and the Resistançia Nacional Moçambicana (ReNaMo), dissident Mozambicans who were waging an insurgency against Samora Machel's Marxist FRELIMO regime. By the early 1980s ReNaMo was active in six out of Mozambique's 10 provinces. Pretoria also encouraged the Lesotho Liberation Army in its fight against the government of Lebua Jonathan and dissident Zimbabweans against the Mugabe regime.

This policy of 'destabilising' states hosting Aza-

The ANC's military campaign developed significantly after the emergence of radical black states in Angola, Zimbabwe and Mozambique, and South Africa experienced serious insurgent attacks for the first time. Concentrating at first on economic targets, such as the SASOL fuel complex (shown left burning after a bomb attack on 1 June 1980), the ANC campaign soon spread to urban targets, such as the headquarters of the South African Air Force in Pretoria bombed on 20 May 1983 (above). South Africa responded by increasing pressure upon its black neighbours, forcing them one by one to cut off support for the ANC. The agreement signed at Nkomati in March 1984, by Prime Minister Pieter Botha of South Africa and President Samora Machel of Mozambique (below) was an example of the success of this policy.

nian and Namibian liberation movements carried grave risks, especially as Angola and Mozambique had treaty relations with the USSR, but by 1984 that policy was beginning to produce results. Reassessing its stance on the Namibian question the MPLA government in Luanda signed the Lusaka Accord, whereby the SADF would withdraw from areas of southern Angola it had been occupying since 1981, in exchange for an Angolan pledge not to allow SWAPO back into that territory. The results on South Africa's other front were even better. In February 1982 Swaziland, fearing that it would become a battleground, secretly signed a non-aggression pact with Pretoria and expelled ANC. Lesotho also took steps to appease the South African government. After the SADF raid in 1982 and subsequent economic pressure, Lesotho persuaded ANC members to leave for Mozambique. Bostwana too, without being attacked, decided to clamp down on the activities of Azanian refugees at the Dikwe camp early in 1983. Finally, the Marxist Machel fell into line. Brought to its knees by ReNaMo insurgency, South African military and economic pressure and its own economic mistakes, the Machel government decided to parley with the South Africans. These talks resulted in the Nkomati agreements of March 1984. Pretoria agreed to cut off its aid to ReNaMo, while Mozambique agreed to bar the ANC/SACP from its territory. The South Africans had managed, at least temporarily, to 'destabilise' the 'destabilisers'.

Francis Toase

Namibia

The struggle for statehood

On 26 August 1966 South African paramilitary forces operating in the vast, sparsely populated, mineral-rich territory of Namibia (then called South West Africa) attacked a camp occupied by guerrillas of the South West Africa People's Organisation (SWAPO). This skirmish, in which two guerrillas were killed and several captured, marked the start of what was to develop into one of the longest conflicts since World War II. Eighteen years later, in mid-1984, South African forces and SWAPO guerrillas were still locked in conflict and, in the meantime, the war had spilt over into the neighbouring state of Angola.

The South African government's involvement in Namibia can be traced back to World War I. In 1915, at the behest of the Allies, Pretoria's forces invaded and seized the then German colony of Süd West Afrika. After the war South West Africa, as it became known, was entrusted to the South African government under a League of Nations 'C class' mandate, which meant that Pretoria could administer the territory as an integral part of South Africa. In 1946 Pretoria asked the League's successor, the United Nations, for permission formally to incorporate South West Africa into South Africa. The UN refused, recommending instead that the territory be placed under the UN's International Trusteeship system pending full independence.

The South African government disregarded this recommendation and proceeded to govern South West Africa under a modified form of its own apartheid (racial segregation) system. The territory's white community (14 per cent of the entire population), which had colonised the southern two-thirds of the country (the 'Police Zone'), was granted representation in the South African parliament, while the territory's 10 non-white ethnic groups were offered a form of limited self-government in their own separate areas or 'homelands', mainly in the north of the country. In 1969 South West Africa was incorporated into South Africa as a *de facto* fifth province. These policies, however, served to antagonise the UN, which by the early 1960s was dominated numerically by Afro-Asian states. In October 1966 the UN General Assembly revoked South Africa's mandate over South West Africa, and in June 1968 the Assembly renamed the territory Namibia and called for its independence. Three years later, in July 1971, the International Court of Justice declared South Africa's presence in Namibia illegal.

In the meantime South Africa's control over Namibia had come under threat from within the territory, mainly from newly formed nationalist groups. The first such movement was the South West African National Union (SWANU), set up in May 1959. SWANU, however, was based on the comparatively minor Herero tribe and never really posed a serious challenge to the authorities. By contrast, SWAPO, a rival organisation established in April 1960, represented a serious threat. SWAPO had begun life in 1957 as the Ovamboland People's Congress and was based on the populous Ovambo tribe, which by the early 1960s numbered some 270,000 people, or 46 per cent of the entire population. Moreover, SWAPO

Top: South African troops in Namibia train for the bush war against SWAPO guerrillas. Above: A mercenary with the South African forces advances through swampy terrain. Right: SWAPO in training. Despite their military inferiority, SWAPO proved effective at mobilising political support.

represented a military as well as political threat to the South African government: whereas SWANU had declined to take up arms, SWAPO decided to use force to oust the South Africans. After fleeing to Tanzania in the early 1960s, Sam Nujoma and other SWAPO leaders began to organise an armed struggle against the South African regime. Namibians were secretly recruited for guerrilla training, and after receiving such training in various African and Eastern bloc states, returned to Namibia via camps in Tanzania and Zambia. The first batch of trained insurgents infiltrated Namibia in late 1965. Equipped with Soviet and Chinese weapons they proceeded to establish base camps in the centre-north of the territory – Ovamboland. One of these camps, located at Ongulumbashe, was discovered by the authorities and attacked on 26 August 1966, a day subsequently honoured by SWAPO as marking the opening of the 'final phase' of its 'liberation struggle'.

At the time, SWAPO's chances of success were somewhat limited. Few trained insurgents were available, SWAPO's fighting strength being numbered in hundreds rather than thousands. Moreover, most of Namibia's vast land area – 824,269 square km (318,252 square miles) – was arid, thus lending itself to South African aerial reconnaissance. Ovamboland was an exception to this rule: parts of it were thickly wooded while other parts were covered in abundant vegetation during the rainy season, the summer months of December to March. But access to Ovamboland was a problem. SWAPO's bases were situated in Zambia and the insurgents would therefore have to infiltrate either through southeastern Angola, which was under Portuguese control, or through the northeastern part of Namibia, where the South Africans had established a number of military bases. And even if the insurgents were to reach Ovamboland they would run considerable risks, since the tribal authorities were by and large loyal to the South Africans.

Undaunted by these considerations SWAPO persevered. During the next eight years a pattern of guerrilla warfare was gradually established. Small groups of insurgents, armed with light weapons of Chinese or Eastern bloc manufacture, infiltrated Namibia to conduct sabotage attacks against installations, kill pro-government blacks and harass the security forces; the usual infiltration route used by the insurgents was the Caprivi Strip, a 402km (250-mile) long panhandle of land located between Angola, Zambia and Botswana. At the same time, SWAPO's in-country adherents sought to politicise the people, mobilise support and establish a viable political structure within Namibia itself.

The task of countering these SWAPO activities fell primarily to the South African Police (SAP), which knew the territory well and had given specialised counter-insurgency training to some of its units. The SAP soon developed a pattern to counter SWAPO's operations. In-country, the SAP monitored SWAPO's political activities, and when it was deemed necessary detained known or suspected SWAPO adherents. Up-country, the SAP attempted to prevent the insurgents from gaining access to Namibia by blocking off the Caprivi Strip. Armed policemen, equipped with two-way radios and armoured vehicles, conducted continuous patrols along the Strip in an effort to track down and kill the insurgents.

These counter-insurgency measures met with some success. The South African government was able to keep the military situation well under control. SWAPO's military wing – the People's Liberation Army of Namibia (PLAN) – issued grandiose propaganda statements but in reality its military impact inside Namibia appears to have been negligible.

This did not mean, however, that the South Africans had things all their own way. PLAN tied down several thousand South Africans, it carried out one or two spectacular attacks and its deployment of landmines in the Caprivi Strip after May 1971 caused real problems to the SAP. More important from SWAPO's point of view was that it made significant advances on the political front. The SAP kept SWAPO off balance by detaining its leaders, but by exploiting internal dissension caused by South African policies SWAPO was able to build up popular support. This was particularly evident after the strike by Ovambo contract workers (who provided over 70 per cent of the labour used in white areas) in December 1971-January 1972. The strike was settled quite quickly but unrest continued, especially in Ovamboland. Border fences were torn down, chiefs and officials were attacked and property was destroyed; moreover, as a result of a SWAPO-inspired boycott, over 97 per cent of the electorate declined to vote in

the Ovamboland homeland's first general election in August 1973. As a result of these developments the South African government rushed in police reinforcements. They introduced a form of martial law in Ovamboland in February 1972, and allowed the tribal authorities to take punitive action against dissidents. Pretoria also increased the strength of the South African Defence Force (SADF) in Namibia, sending in army units to relieve the overstretched SAP. By June 1974 the army had assumed official responsibility for all counter-insurgency operations along the border.

Outside interests

The security situation soon deteriorated further. Following the Lisbon coup of April 1974 the Portuguese decided to quit their colonies, including Angola. This exposed Namibia's 1600km (1000-mile) northern border to guerrilla infiltration, for as the Portuguese withdrew from Angola, SWAPO began to set up bases in the southern part of that country. This development, coupled more generally with the dangers and opportunities presented by the outbreak of civil war in Angola, drew the South Africans into that country. In August 1975 a small number of SADF troops were sent over the border to guard the vital Ruacaná dam, which was being built to provide water and electricity to Namibia. Two months later, encouraged by the United States and by certain black African states, South Africa launched a major incursion, involving perhaps 2000 men, with a view to preventing the Marxist Movimento Popular de Libertação de Angola (MPLA) from defeating its rivals, the Frente Nacional de Libertação de Angola (FNLA) and the União Nacional para a Independência Total de Angola (UNITA). The South Africans achieved spectacular successes against MPLA and Cuban forces, and with the assistance of UNITA (which had previously shared certain bases with SWAPO) they were able to locate and destroy many SWAPO bases in southern Angola. Soon, however, the South Africans found themselves logistically overstretched and politically isolated, and consequently withdrew from Angola between January and March 1976. As they did so, SWAPO re-established itself in southern Angola, with the official blessing of the MPLA government and its Cuban and Soviet backers.

In the wake of the Angolan civil war SWAPO's position improved markedly. Recruits began to flow into the camps in increasing numbers: by mid-1976 SWAPO's strength stood at 2000 and by 1978 it had reached some 10,000. Futhermore, these recruits were given better weapons, provided by the Soviet Union through Angola, and better training, by Soviet, Cuban and other Eastern bloc personnel in Angola. In addition, SWAPO gained increasing moral and political backing from the UN General Assembly, which in December 1976 formally expressed its support for SWAPO's armed struggle. The South African government, by contrast, had to contend with a mandatory arms embargo imposed by the UN in November 1977 and continuous Western pressure to negotiate an internationally acceptable settlement. Thus SWAPO emerged both politically and militarily strengthened and, not surprisingly, it decided to intensify its armed struggle. Operations were extended through Ovamboland, and to a lesser extent to Okavangoland, Kaokoveld and the white farming areas to the south.

The South Africans, however, proved to be for-

Below: Sam Nujoma, leader of SWAPO, with one of his backers, East German leader Erich Honecker, at a meeting in Angola in February 1979. SWAPO relies heavily upon arms and training from Eastern Europe.

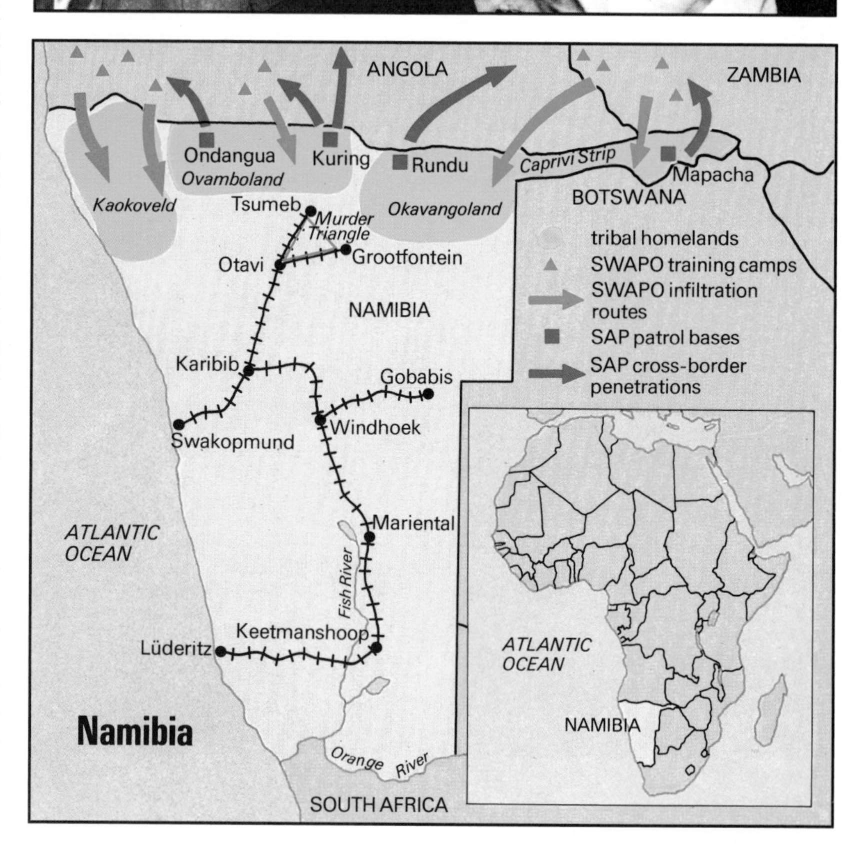

Above: UNITA forces training in southern Angola. Support for UNITA's guerrilla war against the Marxist MPLA regime in Angola is an example of South Africa's liberal interpretation of forward defence. Above right: A mass grave choked with the bodies of Namibians killed in a South African cross-border raid into Angola in 1978. The ability of the South African forces to carry out such attacks robbed SWAPO of any security in its guerrilla bases.

midable foes. Pretoria regarded Namibia as a vital buffer territory and the government was loath to let it fall into the hands of what they considered to be a Marxist terrorist movement. Consequently the South African government responded to SWAPO's intensification of the war by devoting a substantial proportion of its military resources to the counter-insurgency effort in Namibia. Troop levels were raised considerably – perhaps to 30,000 or 40,000 (official figures were never released) – by deploying not only regulars but conscripts, reservists and non-white South Africans; these troops were backed by artillery, light armour, helicopters such as the Puma and Alouette and fixed-wing aircraft such as the Impala, Canberra, Buccaneer and Mirage III: Pretoria also launched an intensive drive to tap local manpower, both white and black. This initiative resulted in the formation of the South West Africa Territory Force (SWATF) in August 1980 and the South West Africa Police (SWAP) in April 1981. By the latter date nearly 30 per cent of all operational forces under South African command in Namibia were Namibians.

This build-up of military strength was accompanied by the introduction of a full-scale counter-insurgency campaign with socio-political as well as military dimensions. At the socio-political level the South African government attempted to undercut support for SWAPO, and deflect international pressure, by jettisoning its apartheid policy in Namibia. The 'homelands' scheme was preserved at the regional level of government, but racial discrimination was gradually phased out and efforts were made to promote a viable political alternative to SWAPO in the form of moderate multi-racial parties such as the Democratic Turnhalle Alliance (DTA) and its successor the Multi-Party Conference (MPC). Alongside this, South Africa initiated a civil action programme, under which SADF personnel provided agricultural, educational, and medical assistance to locals, and an amnesty programme designed to encourage disillusioned SWAPO supporters to defect. Each of these policies produced benefits, but support for SWAPO remained strong, notably in Ovamboland, and the UN continued to insist on an internationally acceptable settlement of the Namibian question.

South Africa's attempts to counter SWAPO militarily centred upon standard counter-insurgency techniques. Troops and policemen were deployed on protection duties, in order to guard against attacks on installations, townships and individuals such as tribal chiefs. White-owned farms in the so-called 'murder triangle' between Grootfontein, Tsumeb and Otavi were linked to the SADF's Military Areas Radio Network (MARNET), a measure similar to Rhodesia's Agric-Alert system. Villagers were resettled in protected villages, though apparently not on an extensive scale outside Caprivi and Okavangoland. Emergency regulations were extended to cover most of the northern districts, giving the security forces the authority to ban meetings and impose curfews as well as wide powers of search, detention and arrest. Intelligence operations were stepped up, and special units such as Koevoet (Crowbar) were authorised to engage in so-called counter-terrorist activities. 'Search and destroy' missions were mounted, using armoured cars, mine-proofed armoured personnel carriers, and also horses and scrambler motorcycles, which provided speed and mobility over rough ground; these missions were often led by San (Bushman) trackers, who were capable of outrunning many species of antelope. Helicopters were also used, though not on a lavish scale. Instead the SADF relied on a system of ground-based 'Mobile Reaction' or 'Quick Reaction' forces, whose role was to track down insurgents after the security forces had learnt through intelligence or patrols of a PLAN presence. As well as operating inside Namibia these forces regularly crossed into Zambia and Angola on 'hot pursuit' missions.

The South Africans also tried hard to prevent the guerrillas from entering Namibia. The SADF attempted to block off the infiltration routes from southern Angola by establishing a *cordon sanitaire,* comprising a one-kilometre deep clearing, fenced and fortified, along the border. However, this 'free-fire zone' or 'no-go area' only impeded, rather than stopped, SWAPO infiltration. The SADF therefore adopted other measures to prevent infiltration: pre-emptive attacks on SWAPO bases and covert intervention in southern Angola.

The first substantial pre-emptive raid was launched in May 1978, after a build-up of SWAPO forces in southern Angola and an upsurge of guerrilla activity in Ovamboland. South African forces burst over the border and attacked three widely separated locations. The results of this attack were disputed, with Pretoria claiming to have killed hundreds of guerrillas and the Angolan government maintaining that the victims of the raids – 1000 casualties – were mostly civilian refugees. Either way, deep-penetration pre-emptive attacks became a standard feature of South African strategy from that time on. In June 1980, for example, the South Africans mounted a three-week operation during which they overran a sprawling forward headquarters, plus a series of sub-camps, bases and staging posts spread out over 130 square km (50 square miles) of southern Angola; according to Pretoria, the SADF killed some 360 guerrillas for the loss of only 17 of their own men. Even more successful was Operation Protea, a 13-day incursion carried out in August/September 1981. During the preceding year SWAPO had replenished its arsenal and regrouped its forces and SAM systems had been installed by East Germany. The South Africans responded with a combined air and land operation described as their biggest such operation since World War II. The SADF claimed that for the loss of only 10 of their own men they neutralised the air defences, killed around 1000 SWAPO, Cuban and Angolan troops and seized between 3000 and 4000 tonnes of military equipment including tanks, APCs, SAMs, AA guns, rocket-launchers and light weapons collectively valued at over £120 million. They also killed four Russians and captured a Soviet NCO. Operation Askari, a further incursion launched in December 1983, also brought spectacular results. The SADF claimed to have captured another cornucopia of Soviet weaponry and to have killed 500 SWAPO, Cuban and Angolan forces for the loss of only 21 of their own troops.

These cross-border raids were augmented by covert intervention in southern Angola. It has been alleged that certain SADF units have operated there on a more or less permanent basis, attacking economic targets and conducting 'search and destroy' sweeps in SWAPO-dominated areas. Apparently the personnel involved, ex-FNLA guerrillas officered by white South Africans (and after April 1980 by ex-Rhodesians), wear unmarked uniforms and use captured Soviet weapons. It has also been alleged that South Africa has intervened in Angola by sponsoring Jonas Savimbi's UNITA, which resorted to guerrilla warfare against the MPLA and its Cuban backers after the Angolan civil war. Apparently the SADF supplied food, arms and training to UNITA and occasionally handed over to Savimbi's men areas of southern Angola cleared of SWAPO, MPLA and Cuban forces by SADF incursions. Partly because of this assistance and partly because of popular support from the Ovimbundu and Chokwe tribes, UNITA proceeded to dominate much of southeastern Angola. For the South Africans themselves, the UNITA connection provided a means of establishing a buffer zone in southeastern Angola, and pressurising the latter into reconsidering its support for SWAPO.

This combination of covert and overt intervention in Angola gave the South Africans a marked advantage in the war against SWAPO – although such a strategy was extremely dangerous, inviting the risk of UN sanctions and the possibility of a sharp riposte from the Soviet Union which had signed a treaty of friendship with Angola in October 1976. However, the South Africans persisted and the results were impressive. By taking the war to southern Angola the South Africans managed to frustrate successive build-ups of men and material by SWAPO and thereby reduce infiltration to manageable proportions. Moreover, as a result of South African pressure the MPLA began to modify its stance on the Namibian question. After sustaining some $8000 million-worth of economic damage between 1975 and 1983, the Angolans decided to parley with Pretoria. These talks resulted in the Lusaka Accords of February 1984, whereby South Africa agreed to disengage its forces from areas of southern Angola it had been occupying since 1981, while the Angolans promised to bar SWAPO from the areas vacated. By that time, according to the South Africans, SWAPO's military activities had been confined largely to Ovamboland, and its losses were running at nearly 1500 men a year, as opposed to SADF losses of between 50 and 60 a year. At the political level, however, the South Africans were making much less progress. SWAPO was estimated by outside observers to have widespread support, especially in Ovamboland. By mid-1984, therefore, the future of Namibia still hung in the balance.

Francis Toase

Below: A South African outpost in the Caprivi Strip. In the early years of the SWAPO insurgency the Caprivi Strip was the centre of guerrilla infiltration from Zambia, but the change of power in Angola made the latter country a far better base for SWAPO operations.

MILITARY HANDGUNS

Modern handguns may be divided into two main categories, the revolver and the automatic, each of which has its own advantages and disadvantages. The central feature of the revolver mechanism is the cylinder – chambered to hold on average six cartridges – which revolves to bring a fresh chamber to the firing position with each operation of the trigger. There are relatively few moving parts, and the revolver is therefore reliable and easy to maintain. In comparison with the automatic, however, it is bulky, which under some circumstances may be a drawback.

The compactness of the automatic, or more accurately the semi-automatic, derives from its method of operation, which has, however, the disadvantage of being more complicated than that of the revolver. Ammunition is held in a magazine, usually in the butt of the pistol, and fed by pressure from a simple spring mechanism to the firing position with each action of the slide. The slide normally operates on the blowback principle, being propelled backwards along the barrel of the pistol, which it houses, by the recoil force of the discharged cartridge. Although there are some automatics which operate by different methods, most feature a variation on this blowback principle.

Since World War II, the tendency has been for the military to adopt the automatic as the standard-issue side-arm, while the greater reliability of the revolver has recommended itself to police forces.

In military service, a pistol is of little use on the modern battlefield where the longer range of assault rifles easily exceeds the 40-50m (45-55yds) effective range of a trained marksman armed with a handgun. It remains useful only for those combat personnel operating in a confined space such as aircrewmen or tank crewmen simply because there is only enough room for a small weapon. A handgun may also be useful in close-quarter combat such as fighting in built-up areas or in trenches, but only when nothing better is available. This being so, the fact that effective handguns were developed in the first 30 years of this century has meant that development since then has been slight.

Of the automatics now in military service, the Colt ·45 M1911/M1911A1 is the most venerable design, dating from the first decade of this century. Still the standard-issue side-arm of the United States armed forces, the M1911A1 is almost the only military pistol to retain the ·45 cartridge, and it is universally regarded as well overdue for replacement, many of the 418,000 still in service having been virtually rebuilt many times since their manufacture. To date there has been at least one unproductive competition in order to find a replacement for the M1911A1, but the results have been inconclusive, many would say for political reasons. It is still planned to replace it with a 9mm Parabellum automatic, to be known as the XM9, but the Colt ·45 seems certain to stay in use for some time.

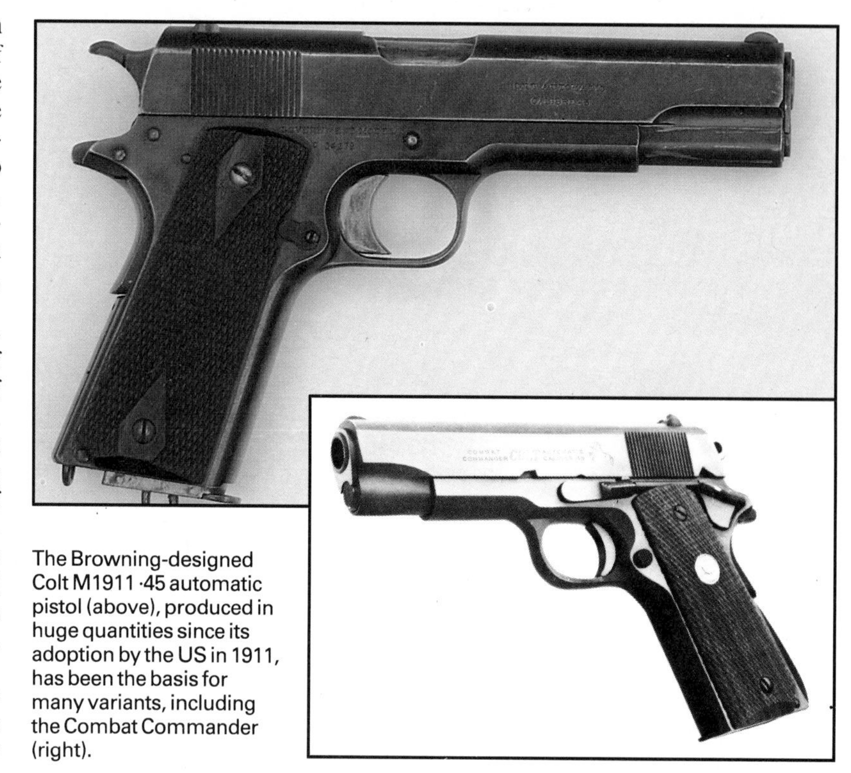

The Browning-designed Colt M1911 ·45 automatic pistol (above), produced in huge quantities since its adoption by the US in 1911, has been the basis for many variants, including the Combat Commander (right).

Previous page: A Sandinista guerrilla in Nicaragua, armed with a Colt ·45 automatic pistol. Though of limited military value to conventional armies, the handgun is an important weapon in the arsenal of many insurgent movements. Often more easily obtainable than heavier weapons, it has the advantage of being easier to conceal for clandestine operations.

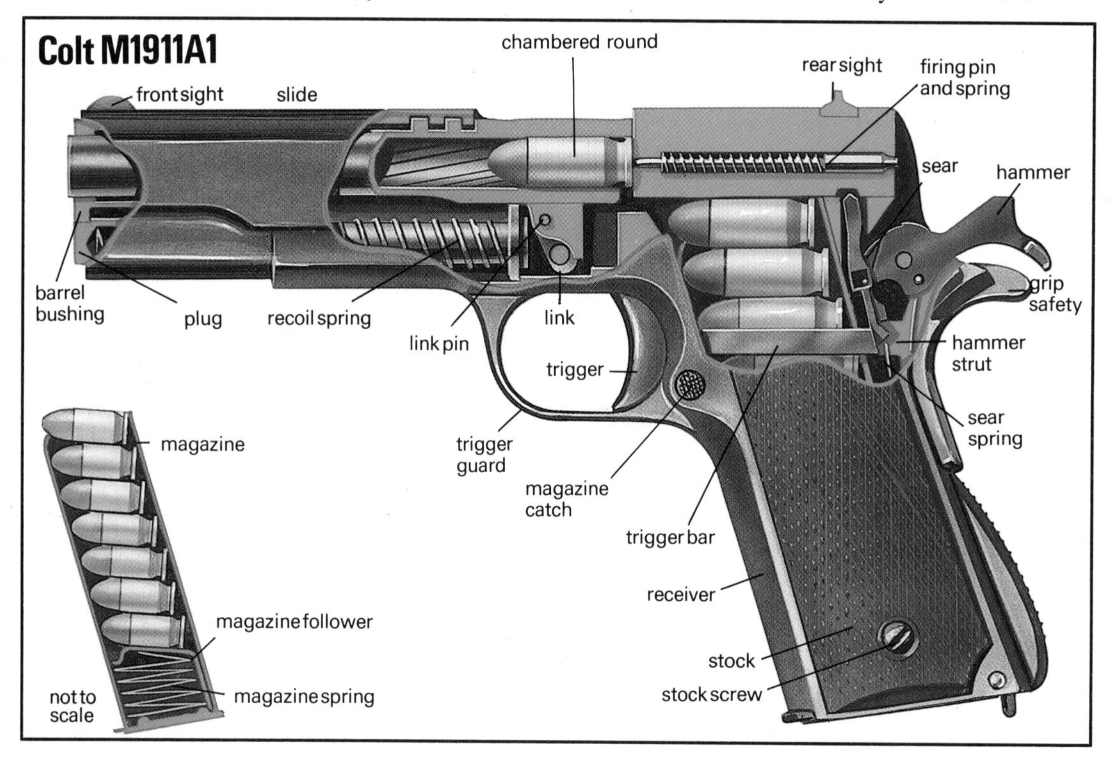

Right: A classic design, the Walther PP, introduced in 1929, has been a major influence on subsequent handgun development on both sides of the Iron Curtain. Far right: The Walther P5, like the PP designed specifically for police work, is a cut-down version of the P1, itself a modern development of the wartime P38.

Above: The 9mm Browning High-Power, standard pistol of the British and many other armies. Right: The Walther P38, World War II handgun of the Wehrmacht. Below: The P38 in use in the 1970s with Rhodesian reservists.

The Colt M1911A1 is not the only veteran design still in production. The Browning 9mm High-Power, patented in 1927, and like the M1911A1 designed by John M. Browning, is produced around the world in many versions, and must outnumber virtually all other pistols in use today. Despite its weight and bulk (the magazine holds 13 rounds), it is still one of the best service pistol designs. It is strong, reliable, and capable of absorbing hard knocks without malfunctioning. Production rights to the Browning design are held by FN of Belgium, who produce several 'special' versions, including a cut-down model.

Another group of pistols whose design originates from the pre-World War II period are those produced by Walther in Germany. The Walther PP was originally designed as a police weapon (Polizei Pistole – hence the initials), and was introduced in 1929 while the PPK (Polizei Pistole Kriminal) was introduced in 1931 for use by plainclothes policemen, being a smaller version of the PP and hence more easily concealed. Both pistols fire the 7·65mm round and are excellent weapons which are still widely used by many police and military forces, including the British Army.

Walther also produce the P1, a modern version of the World War II 9mm P38. The P1 is lighter than the P38, which first introduced many of the features now common in modern automatic pistol designs. The P1 has an external hammer, which may be operated by either single or double-action, several safeties, and a button next to the rear sight, which rises when the magazine is empty. The P1 now uses some light alloys in its construction, a common feature with many modern pistols, which along with the use of plastic components can considerably reduce the weapon's weight. Walther also produce the 9mm P5, which was designed around a West German police specification, and may be regarded as the modern equivalent of the PP. It embodies several features from earlier designs, allied to some new safeties which make the P5 a very easy and safe pistol to use.

Apart from the Browning and Walther designs, many other pistols in use in the 1980s incorporate principles which date back several decades. A typical example is the Swiss SIG range, which is widely regarded as being the finest made today. The basic design principles of the SIG pistols, however, come from a French Petter design, first produced well before World War II. Over the years these pistols have been developed to a remarkable degree, and many

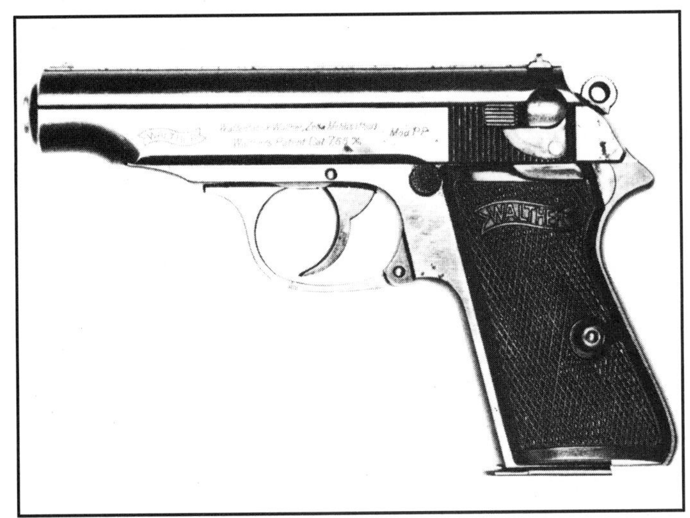

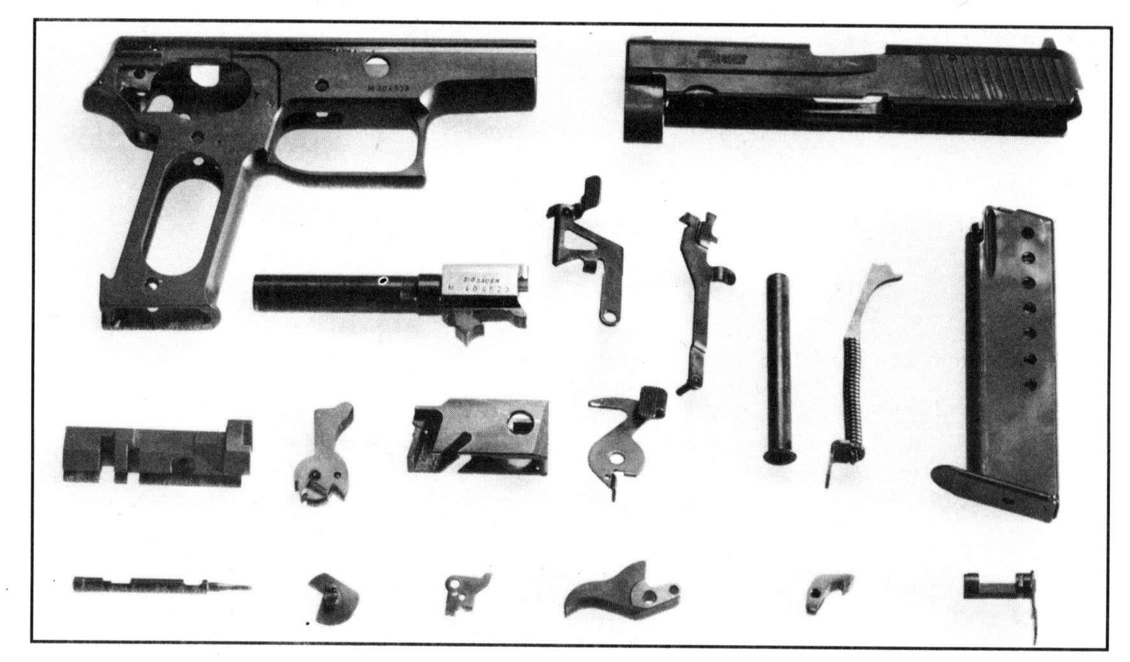

Right: A stripped-down 9mm SIG-Sauer P225 pistol. The complexity of its operation, and the relative difficulty of maintenance, are a drawback of the automatic when compared to the simple, easily maintained revolver.

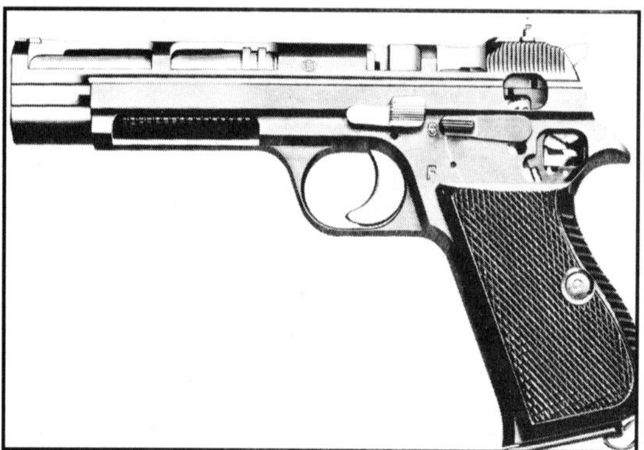

Left: The Swiss SIG 9mm P210, part of a fine family of pistols which operate on the French Petter principle.

Left: The German firm of Heckler & Koch produce a range of pistols, including this P9S, which share a characteristically modern appearance, and are rugged and easy to maintain.

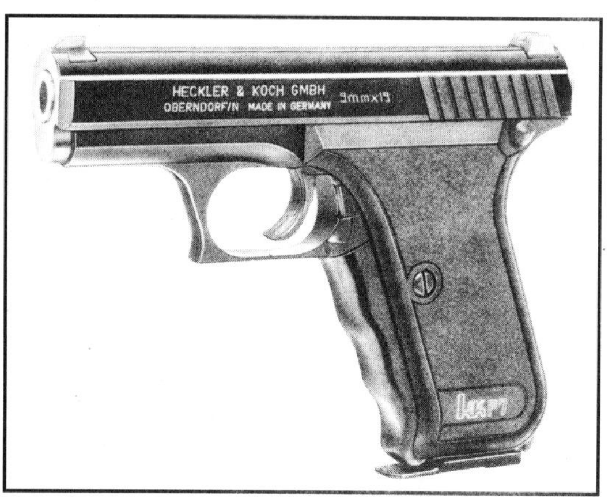

Left: The Heckler & Koch P7, in service with the West German Bundeswehr, is a tough 9mm combat pistol. Right: The much-praised Steyr GB incorporates a chrome barrel with hexagonal twisting.

refinements have been added. In recent years, SIG have joined with the West German Sauer concern to produce even better pistols.

One of these is the P226, which was one of the original entries in the US armed forces' XM9 contest. The P226 is now one of the most sought-after of all modern pistols for its balance, finish, and overall practicality. One of the earlier SIG models, the P220, is in service with the Swiss Army, as well as being produced for export, as is the P210. All of these pistols feature an external hammer, which can be cocked by the thumb if required. If the pistol is cocked, but not fired, it is possible to apply a safety mechanism which allows the hammer to be lowered onto the firing pin without discharging the pistol. This is now a common requirement for modern automatic pistols, which was lacking in many earlier designs.

Another German manufacturer is Heckler & Koch, whose pistols range from the HK4, through the P9S and the VP70M (which might possibly be regarded as a form of machine-pistol), to the advanced P7. The common feature of all Heckler & Koch pistols is their striking appearance, and all designs make use of the same curved, sweeping lines. This actually contributes to their utility, as the smooth outlines prevent snagging on clothing. The Heckler & Koch pistols embody all the demands of modern armed forces, including all the usual safeties, ease of maintenance and cleaning, few moving parts, and robust construc-

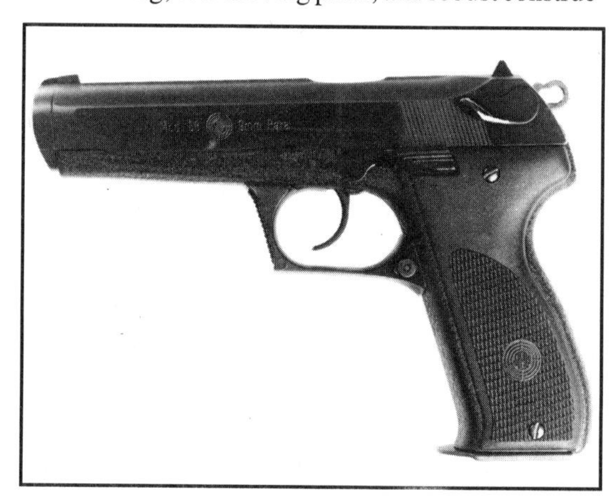

tion. Typical of Heckler & Koch designs is the recent P7, which was originally designed for use as a police weapon, but has now also been adopted by the West German Army (Bundeswehr). It is a very simple and rugged weapon, with few moving parts to jam or break, and it can be stripped down for cleaning in seconds. Like many modern pistols, it employs the 9mm x 19 Parabellum cartridge.

In Austria, Steyr-Daimler-Puch have for many years been producing superlative weapons of all kinds, and their GB 9mm pistol is no exception. It is a superb pistol, although it has yet to find a large-scale market. It is unusual in many ways, the most important being that exhaust gases, bled off from the barrel after firing, are used to delay the rearward progress of the slide, in order to ensure safe locking. This principle was first used in the World War II German Volkspistole, and though rarely used since, is a safe

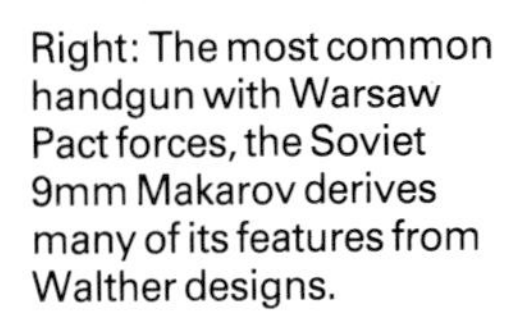
Right: The most common handgun with Warsaw Pact forces, the Soviet 9mm Makarov derives many of its features from Walther designs.

Left: Typical of many modern combat revolver designs is this French Manhurin ·357 Magnum MR73. Right: The Czech 7.62mm CZ 52 was adopted by the Czech Army as an alternative to the Makarov. The Czechs have managed to maintain their own arms industry, despite the almost universal employment of Soviet weapons in the Warsaw Pact.

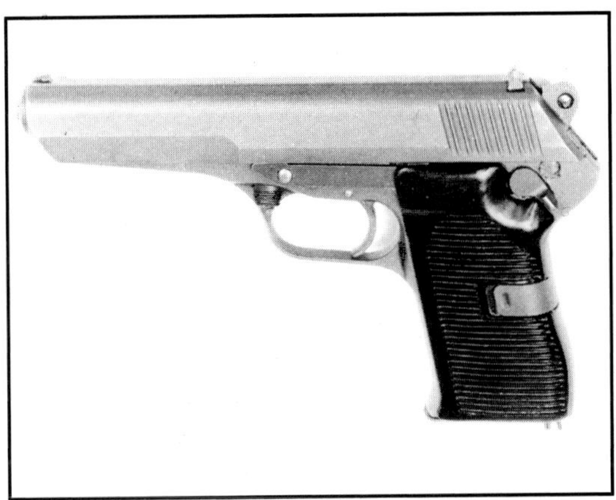

Left: The Manhurin is in use with the Groupe d'Intervention de la Gendarmerie National (GIGN), the French anti-terrorist unit. Right: Another Warsaw Pact variation on the Walther theme is this Polish P64 9mm pistol, in service with the Polish Army.

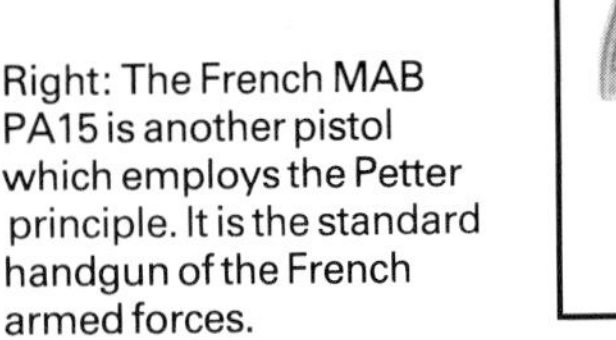
Right: The French MAB PA15 is another pistol which employs the Petter principle. It is the standard handgun of the French armed forces.

and simple locking method. The barrel of the GB is chromed, in order to reduce wear and to ease cleaning, and in place of the normal rifling, a smooth form of hexagonal twisting of the bullet is used. The magazine in the pistol grip can hold 18 rounds, which is useful in combat, yet the GB sits easily in the hand, and can be fired with none of the 'jumpy' recoil normally present in a 9mm pistol.

In Eastern Europe, the Soviet Union has long been unadventurous in pistol design, and currently relies upon the 9mm Makarov for its standard service side-arm. The Makarov is unexciting in overall design and handling, but in common with all Soviet smallarms, it is very sturdy and well able to take the trials of Red Army service life.

In recent years, however, a new Soviet pistol has emerged, in the form of the 5·45mm PSM, which is a small weapon, perhaps intended for use by the security services. The cartridge is very low-powered, however – it would appear to have even less power than a normal ·22 round. The pistol resembles the Walther PP in appearance, and is not yet in service in large numbers.

Not all Warsaw Pact forces use the Makarov. The Czechs favour their own Model 52, calibered in 7·62mm. This is a sound design, though unspectacular, and was adopted by the Egyptian Army as well as by the Czechoslovak Army, but it is no longer in production. Czechoslovakia now produces the 9mm Model 75, but this has yet to find a customer.

The Polish Army employs its own 9mm P64, which may be regarded as an up-dated Walther PP. The P64 is an attractive and compact design, with few frills, and may be fired using single- or double-action.

In France, the Manufacture d'Armes de Bayonne (MAB) continues to produce several pistols based on the Petter principle, which dates back to well before World War II. Nevertheless, all the MAB pistols are strong and serviceable weapons, one of which, the PA15, is now the standard pistol of the French armed forces. Manhurin, another French company, produces several types of revolver, including the ·357 Magnum MR73, which is in many ways typical of such weapons being produced today. It has a six-round cylinder, which swings out sideways for reloading, and it features a single- or double-action trigger mechanism.

In Italy, Beretta maintain their traditional high standard of automatic pistol designs. During World War II, a Beretta pistol was a highly-prized trophy, and modern Berettas are no less sought after. It was a Beretta design, the Model 92, which was deemed to be the best entrant in the abortive XM9 contest, but it is only one in a whole range of excellent weapons. Most of the modern Beretta pistols use either a 13- or a 15-round magazine, and differ in the types of safety fitted, as well as in other small details. Some are chambered to take the 9mm Short cartridge, but the Model 92 and its variants are chambered for the ubiquitous 9mm Parabellum.

Meanwhile, what of the world's largest pistol-producing nation: the United States? The two giants of the industry, Colt and Smith & Wesson, continue to produce an array of revolver designs, many of which seem to differ only in the markings applied. Many small companies find it profitable to manufacture spares for the ever-popular M1911, or to devise all manner of imaginative 'commando' variants. The Ruger company is making considerable inroads into the revolver market with a range which covers several calibres, nearly all of which are manufactured from stainless steel. Ruger pistols are now in service with police forces and paramilitary formations throughout the world, but have few innovatory features, apart from their seemingly indestructible construction.

Only Smith & Wesson offer any novel designs, including a pair of 9mm automatics, known as the Models 459 and 469. These can trace their ancestory back to the Model 39 of 1954, but recently, no doubt spurred on by the impetus of the US Army's XM9 programme, the design has been refined considerably. The Model 459 is now a 14-shot pistol, with an aluminium frame, while the Model 469 is a slightly shorter version, holding only 12 rounds.

Below: The classic Beretta Model 1934 7·55mm automatic. The wartime service pistol of the Italian Army, it was a sought-after souvenir for Allied troops. Below left: A modern design, the Beretta Model 92 is an excellent combat pistol. Below right: The Model 92's 15-round magazine. Bottom: One of the few modern American designs, the Smith & Wesson Model 459, is a 14-shot aluminium-framed pistol.

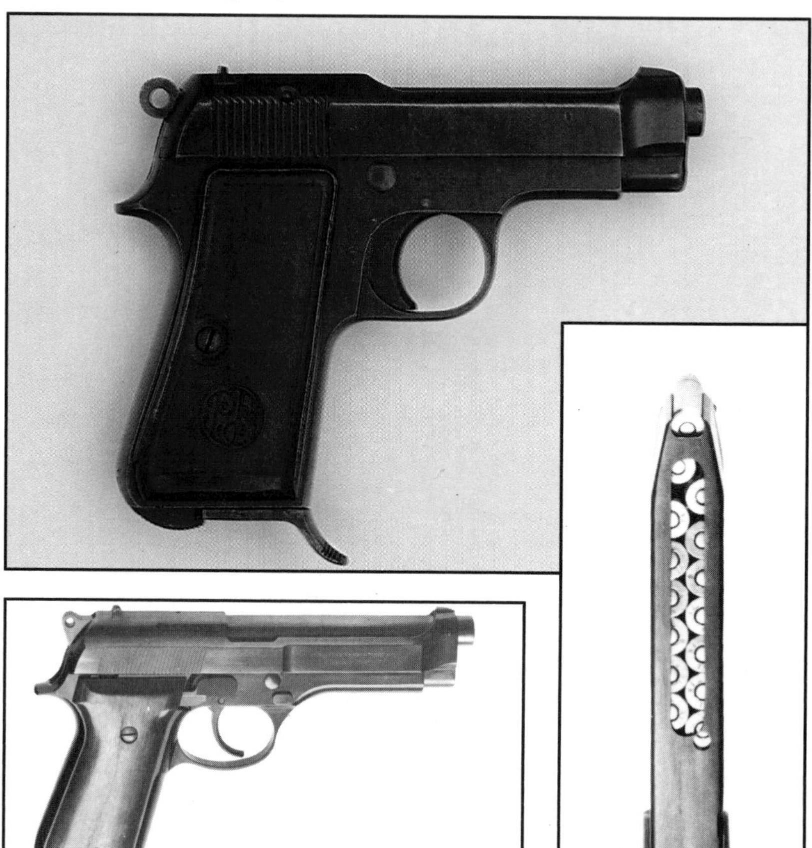

Index

A

B

C

D

E

J

K

L

M

N

O

P

Q

R

S